THE YORK HOUSE BOOKS
1461–1490

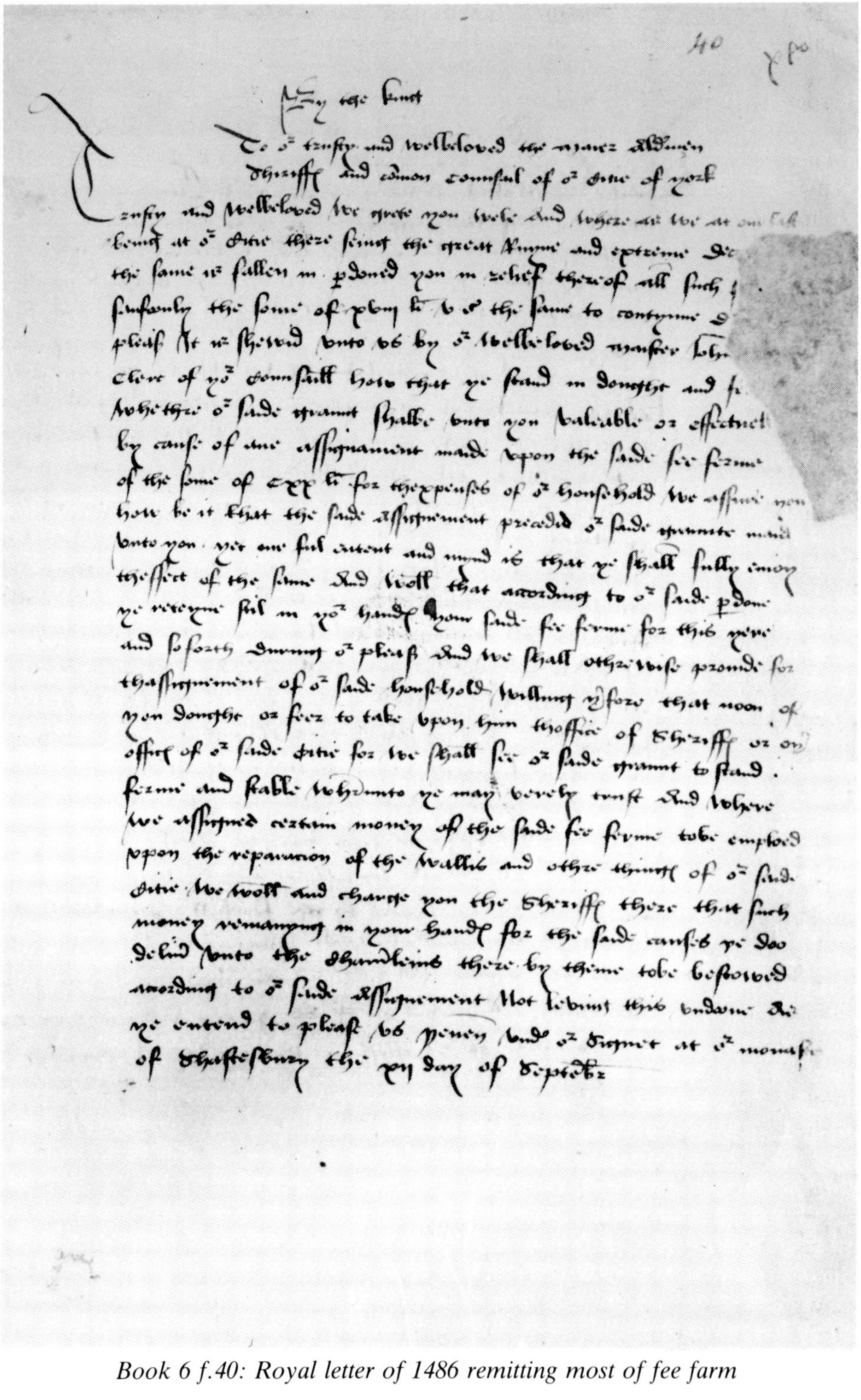
By the kyng

To our trusty and welbeloved the mayre aldermen
shireffs and comon counsail of our Citie of york

Trusty and welbeloved we grete you wele And where as we at oure late
beyng at our Citie there seing the greet ruyne and extreme de
the same is fallen in pardoned you in relief thereof all such f
singulerly the some of xlvij li. v s. the same to contynue d
pleas It is shewed unto us by our welbeloved maister [illegible]
Clerc of your counsaill how that ye stand in doubte and f
whether our saide graunte shalbe unto you valeable or effectuel
by cause of an assignement made upon the saide fee ferme
of the some of xxx li. for thexpenses of our houshold we assure you
how be it that the saide assignement precede our saide graunte made
unto you. yet our ful entent and mynde is that ye shall fully enjoy
theffect of the same And woll that according to our saide pardon
ye reteyne stil in your handes youre saide fee ferme for this yere
and so forth duryng our pleas And we shall otherwise provide for
thassignement of our saide houshold willing therfore that noon of
you doubte or fere to take upon hym thoffice of Shireff or any
office of our saide Citie for we shall see our saide graunt to stand
ferme and stable wherunto ye may verely trust And where
we assigned certain money of the saide fee ferme tobe emploied
upon the reparacion of the walles and other thinges of our saide
Citie We woll and charge you the Shireffs there that such
money remaynyng in your handes for the saide causes ye doo
deliver unto the Chamberlains there by theime tobe bestowed
according to our saide assignement Not levyng this undone as
ye entend to pleas us yeven undre our signet at our monaste
of Shaftesbury the xj day of Septembre

Book 6 f.40: Royal letter of 1486 remitting most of fee farm

THE YORK HOUSE BOOKS
1461–1490

VOLUME II:
HOUSE BOOKS FIVE–SIX

Edited by
LORRAINE C. ATTREED

ALAN SUTTON
for RICHARD III & YORKIST HISTORY TRUST
1991

First published in the United Kingdom in 1991 by
Alan Sutton Publishing Ltd
Phoenix Mill · Far Thrupp · Stroud · Gloucestershire

First published in the United States of America in 1991 by
Alan Sutton Publishing Inc · Wolfeboro Falls · NH 03896–0848

British Library Cataloguing in Publication Data

The York House Books.
  1. York (England), history, 1399–1485
  I. Attreed, Lorraine C. (Lorraine Christine) *1954–*
942.843

  ISBN 0-86299-936-7

Library of Congress Cataloging in Publication Data applied for

Typesetting and origination by
Alan Sutton Publishing Limited.
Printed in Great Britain by the Bath Press, Avon.

CONTENTS

HOUSE BOOK VOLUME 5
1483–1489

HOUSE BOOK VOLUME 5
1483–1489

[f.1]   **Duke of Buckingham's Treason Revealed**
             13 October 1483

Memorandum that the xiijth day of the moneth of Octobir in the ffurst yere of the reing of King Richard the thyrd, John Otyr yoman of the crown broght a lettyr to my lord the mair, aldermen, shireffes and commonalte of thys cite of your York, the tenour of the wich insuyth:

By the king

Trusty and ryght welbelowed we grete you wele, and lete you wite that the duc of Bukingham traiterously is (turnd) turned upon us contrary to the duete of hys ligeance and entendeth the utter distruccion of us, you (all) and all othre oure true (subge) subgiettes that have taken our part whos traiterous entent we with Goddes grace entende briefly to resist and subdue; we desire and pray you in our hertly wise that ye woll send un to us asmany men defensibley arraied on horsbak as ye may godely make to our towne of (la) Leicestre the xxj day of thys present moneth withouten faile as ye tendre our honneour and your owne wele; and we shall so see to you for your reward and charges as ye shall hold you wele content, (gevno) geving ferther credence to our trusty servaunt this berer. Yeven under our signet at our cite of Lincoln the xj daie of Octobre.

To our trusty and right welbeloved the maire, aldermen, shireffes and commonalte of our cite of York

[f.1v]   **Proclamation Against Duke of Buckingham To Be Read**
              16 October 1483

Memorandum that the xvjth day of the moneth of Octobre in the furst yere of the reing of King Richard the thyrd a prive seall was direct to my lord the mair, my maisterz hys bredir, and the sherffes of this cite, the tenour wherof insuyth:

By the king

a prive seall to proclaim the duc of Bukyngham tratour Trusty and welbelowyd we grete you wele, and woll and straytely charge you that in all suche placez within oure cite of York as to you shalbe thought most expedient ye do make open and solempne proclamacions in forme folowing: For asmoche as the king our soverayn lord Richard the therd by the grace of God king of England and of Fraunce and lord of Irland understandeth for certan that the duc of Bukingham traitoursly is turned upon hym contrarie the duetie of hys liegeaunce and entendeth the utter distruccion of our said soverayn lord, the subversion of hys reyume and thutter disheriting of all hys true liege peple, oure said soverayn lord therfore considering the wele and suerte of hys roiall persone, the tranquillite and peas of hys said royume and subgettes, taketh and reputeth the said duc as hys rebell and traitour, and chargeth and commaundeth all hys true subiegettes so to take hym. Also our said soverayn lord chargeth and upon peyne of deth commaundeth that no maner person of what astate, degre or condicion he be, at the commaundment or desire of the said duc or any other in hys name (arre) arreise, assemble or make any maner commocion otherwyse than accordeth with our said soverayn lord lawes and peas, but that they and every of them be redy to attende upon our said soverayn lord or suche as he shall commaunde them for the repressyng and subduyng of the traitours entent and purpos of the said duc; and over thys oure said soverayn lord straitly chargeth and commaundeth that no maner persone whatsoever he be in any wise attempt or presume to robbe, spoill or hurt any of the tenauntz, officers or other persone belonging to the said duc, his rebell and traitour, so that they reise not ne make commocion or assembles of hys subgettes ayenst his [**f.2**] peas; and if the said dukes tenauntes, (officeris) officers or other do then they to be taken as the kinges ennemys and traitours, not ffailling in publisshing thys our commaundement as our singuler trust is in you. Yeven under our prive seale at our cite of Lincolne the xv day of Octobre the first yere of oure reigne.

Wherupon the said xvjth day of Octobre my said lord the mair and my said maisterz hys bredir the aldermen and the sheryffes made proclemacion in diwyrs places of the said cite acordyng to the said commaundment.

Lease of Ouse Bridge Messuage
20 September 1483

dimissio Johanni Sponer [*A hand drawn in the left margin points to this entry.*] Memorandum quod vicesimo die mensis Septembris anno primo regni regis Ricardi tercii dimissio facta fuerat [*sic*] sub sigillo officii maioratus per Johannem Newton maiorem, Johannem Beverley, Thomam Foulleby et Johannem Shaw camerarios, Johanni Sponer servienti maioris ad clavem, de uno mesuagio in quo idem Johannes Sponer inhabitat super pontem Use, habendo et tendendo sibi et assignatis suis a festo Sancti Martini proximo futuro usque ad finem xx annorum extunc proximo sequentium, reddendo inde annuatim maiori et communitati et successoribus suis seu custodibus pontis predicti qui pro tempore erunt viginti solidos ad terminos usuales prout per cartam indendatam inde confectam plenius apparet etc.

[*lease to John Sponer* On 20 September 1483, the mayor and chamberlains leased to macebearer John Sponer a messuage in which he was living upon Ouse bridge, to have and to hold the messuage from the forthcoming feast of Martinmas for a term of twenty years, rendering annually to the mayor and commonalty and their successors 20 s. at the usual terms, as is made fully clear by the indented charter.]

[f.2v]   **Enrollment of Land, Transfer Charter**
           23 October 1483

carta Ricardi (leyd) Ledys de messuagio in Skeldergate Memorandum quod xxiij° die mensis Octobris anno regni regis Ricardi tercii post conquestum Anglie primo, quidam Ricardus Ledys filius et heres Rogeri Ledys nuper de Westwyk generosi venit coram Johanne Newton tunc maiore civitatis Ebor' et ostendit quandam cartam sigillo suo (sigr) signato quam quidem cartam (ut) ⟨fore⟩ factum suum coram prefato maiore cognovit et (peit) petit eandem cartam ut factum suum inter recorda dicte civitatis irrotolari ⟨potest⟩ [*sic*] cuius quidem tenour sequitur in hec verba et est talis:

Sciant presentes et futuri quod ego Ricardus Ledys filius et heres Rogeri Ledys nuper de Westwyke generosi defuncti, dedi, concessi et hac presenta carta mea confirmavi Johanni Nevill, Radulpho Crathorn militibus, Miloni Willesthorp, Willelmo Ryther armigeris, et Ricardo Beilby heredibus et assignatis ipsius Ricardi unum magnum messuagium sive tenementum situatum in Skeldergate in Ebor' cum domibus, edeficiis et (gad) gardino cum suis pertinentiis eidem messuagio sive tenemento pertinentibus nuper in tenura predicti Ricardi Belby. Et quod quidem messuagium et cetera premissa cum suis pertinentiis situantur et (jo) iacent ex oposito messuagii Thome Neleson aldermanni civitatis Ebor' et se extendunt in longitudine a regia strata de Skeldergate predicta ibidem ante usque ad le Oldbale ibidem retro, et in latitudine a tenemento abbatis et conventus monasterii Sancti Germani de Selby ex una parte et tenementum Martini del See militis ex altera parte, habenda et tenenda predicta mesuagium, tenementum, domos, edeficia et gardinum cum pertinentiis suis predicta nuper in tenura predicti Ricardi Belby superius specificati, prefatis Johanni, Radulpho, Miloni, Willelmo et Ricardo Belby heredibus et assignatis ipsius Ricardi de capitalibus dominis feodi illius per servicia inde debita et de jure consueta. Et ego vero predictus Ricardus Ledys et heredes mei omnia predicta messuagium, tenementum, domos, edificia et gardi-num cum suis **[f.3]** pertinentiis nuper in tenura predicti Ricardi Belby superius specificati, prefatis Johanni, Radulpho, Miloni, Willelmo et Ricardo Beilby heredibus et assignatis ipsius Ricardi contra omnes gentes warantizabimus et imperpetuum defendemus. Et ulterius noveritis me prefatum Ricardum Ledys attornasse, deputasse et loco meo constituisse dilectos michi in Christo Gilbertum Salesbury capellanum et Petrum Couke civem Ebor' meos veros et legitimos attornatos et deputos coniunctim et divisim ad intrandum (vie) vice et nomine meo in messuagium, tenementum, domos, edificia et gardinum illum cum suis pertinen-tiis et possessionem et seisinam, inde michi et heredibus meis recontinuandum et alios quoscumque inde amovendum et expellendum posteaque ad deliberandum plenam et paceficam possessionem et seisinam inde pro ⟨me⟩ et nomine meo prefatis Johanni, Radulpho, Miloni, Willelmo et Ricardo Belby secundum vim, formam et effectum presenta carta mee ratum habiturum et gratum quicquid predicti attornati sive deputati mei pro me et nomine meo fecerint seu eorum alter fecerit in premissis. In cuius rei testimonium huic presente carte mee sigillum meum apposui hiis testibus Johanne Newton maiore civitatis predicte, Thoma Neleson, Johanne Tonge aldermannis, Ricardo Hardsang et Willelmo Barker vicecomitibus eiusdem civitatis et aliis. Date xxj° die Octobris anno regni regis Ricardi tercii post conquestum Anglie primo.

[*charter to Richard Ledys concerning a messuage in Skeldergate* On 23 October 1483, Richard Ledys, son and heir of gentleman Roger Ledys formerly of Westwick, came before the mayor, showed a charter made under his seal, and asked that the charter be enrolled among the city records. Its form is as follows:

Know [all men] present and future that I, Richard Ledys, son and heir of Roger Ledys late of Westwick, gentleman now deceased, have given, granted, and by this present charter confirmed to John Nevill and Ralph Crathorn knights, to Miles Willesthorp and William Ryther esquires, and to Richard Beilby and his heirs and assignees, one large messuage or tenement lying in Skeldergate in York, with houses, buildings, and a garden with all its appurtenances pertaining to it, lately in the tenure of Richard Belby. This messuage lies across from the messuage of alderman Thomas Neleson and extends in length from the street of Skeldergate in front to the Old Baile behind, and in width from the tenement of the abbot and convent of the monastery of Saint German of Selby on the one side and a tenement of knight Martin del See on the other. They are to have and to hold this messuage and all its appurtenances of the chief lords of that fee by the services thence owed and accustomed by right, and I, Richard Ledys, will warrant and defend forever that messuage [**f.3**] to John and the others against all people. I depute and appoint in my place Gilbert Salesbury, chaplain, and Peter Couke, citizen of York, to act as attorneys, and to deliver full and peaceful possession and seisin to John, Ralph, Miles, William, and Richard, according to the force and meaning of my present charter. In testimony of which I have affixed my seal and those of witnesses John Newton, mayor of York, aldermen Thomas Neleson and John Tonge, sheriffs Richard Hardsang and William Barker, and others. Given 21 October 1483.]

[f.3v]   Slander of City Cordwainer Denied
**   16 December 1483**

a record for John Key Memorandum that the xvj^th day of the moneth of Decembir in the ffurst yere of the reing of King Richard the thyrd Thomas Wrangwysh alderman, Richard Marston and William White of the xxiiij^ti and of the counsell of the cite of York, (Ro) Johannes Barker taillour, Robert Nyghtyngale, Hugo North, Ricardus Wodburn, Robert Baitman, Stephanus Hoghson, ⟨⟨and⟩⟩ Johannes Ormerord, ⟨William Lewty⟩ and Thomas Nelson smyth come afore my lord the mair in to the counsell chamber of Owsebrygh and testefid ⟨and record that were⟩

where it was nosyd and by ewyll persons wykydly disposid sayd that John Key (taillour) cordwener shold be a theyff and stele (a f) a hors in the yorney now late made with our sovereyn lord the kyng to Saylsbery, all the said personz whos namys beyn above wryttyn, the wich were soghers in the said yorney, that the said John Key was of good disposicion and trewly delt in the said yorney and that the hors that the said John Key had was (o) the hors of one of the servauntes of Cheney the wich is tratour un to the kyng and (we) that the said hors was taykyn upon Chenys grownd for as moch as he that awght the said hors was tratour un to the king.

[f.4] Assize of Wine
27 December 1483

Assisa vini capta in (Tolonde) ⟨le Tollboth⟩ civitatis Ebor' coram Johanne Newton maiore, Ricardo Hardsang et Willelmo Barker vicecomitibus eiusdem civitatis die Sabbati scilicet xxvij° die Decembris anno regni regis Ricardi tercii primo.

Robertus Walker, Thomas Gray, Rogerus Brokhols, Georgius Kyrk, Petrus Cuke, Cristoforus Bentley, Willelmus Paynter plumber, Willelmus Pykard, Johannes Loundesdale, Johannes Stokysley, Thomas Burgh, Thomas Welles goldsmyth, Nicholaus Vicars, Ricardus Symson wyredrawer, Henricus Albayn jurati qui dicunt super sacramentum suum quod dolium vini optimi de Gascwyn' novi apud portum de Hull valet viij libras. Item dicunt quod dolium secundi vini ibidem valet vj libras xiij solidos iiij denarios. Item dicunt quod dolium tercii vini valet viij marcas. Super qua assisa proclamacio facta fuit quod lagena novi vini de Vascon' vendatur pro x denariis et non carius sub pena ⟨qua⟩ (incunb) incumbit.

[Assize of wine held in the Tollbooth in York before mayor John Newton and sheriffs Richard Hardsang and William Barker on Saturday 27 December 1483.

Jurors Robert Walker, Thomas Gray, Roger Brokhols, George Kyrk, Peter Cuke, Christopher Bentley, plumber William Paynter, William Pykard, John Loundesdale, John Stokysley, Thomas Burgh, goldsmith Thomas Welles, Nicholas Vicars, wiredrawer Richard Symson, and Henry Albayn swore that a tun of the best new wine of Gascony in the port of Hull is worth £8, that second-best wine is worth £6 13 s. 4 d. a tun, and that third-best wine is worth eight marks a tun. The assize then proclaimed that a gallon of new wine of Gascony is to be sold for 10 d. and no more under proper penalty.]

[f.4v] Bond to Accept Arbitration
13 January 1484

Johannes Huton potter et Christoforus Edmondson et Agnete uxor eius Memorandum quod xiij° die mensis Januarii anno primo regni regis Ricardi tercii Johannes (Newto') Huton potter ex parte una et Christoforus Emondson et Agnes uxor eius ex parte altera venerunt coram Johanne Newton tunc maiore civitatis Ebor' et obligerunt se et eorum quilibet per se obligavit domino regi stare arbitrio, (ordinacio) ordinacioni et judicio Thome Gray goldsmyth, Thome Fynch junioris, Willelmi Deykyn et Conandi Gossepe de et super omnimodis accionibus, contraversiis, debatis et demandis inter partes predictas habitis, motis sive movendis racione quacumque a principio mundi usque in diem confeccionis presencium sub pena x librarum ⟨dicto⟩ domino regi forisfaciendarum per ipsum ⟨partem⟩ arbitrium ⟨sive iudicium⟩ dictorum arbitratorum (diligenter) ⟨recusantem⟩ sine (minime) minime perimplentem etc., ita quod arbitrium dictorum arbitratorum fiat et reddatur citra festum Annunciationis Beate Marie Virginis proximo futurum etc.

[*John Huton, potter, and Christopher Edmondson and Agnes his wife* On 13 January 1484, potter John Huton on the one side and Christopher Emondson and his wife Agnes on the other side came before the mayor and bound themselves to abide by the arbitration and judgement of goldsmith Thomas Gray, Thomas Fynch junior, William Deykyn and Conand Gossepe over all actions and debates had or moved between them from the beginning of the world to the present day, under penalty of £10. The arbitration is to be made and given by the coming feast of the Annunciation of the Blessed Virgin Mary.]

Lease of City Lands
3 November 1483

dimissio Johanni Gretham Memorandum quod iij^cio die mensis Novembris anno regni regis Ricardi tercii post conquestum Anglie primo, maior et camerarii civitatis Ebor' nomine dicti maioris et communitatis civitatis predicte dimiserunt Johanni Gretame tapiter alias dicto Johanni Gretame vectori unum messagium in quo idem Johannes modo inhabitavit in Jubergate in civitatem predictam ac duo tenementa iacentia ibidem videlicet unum tenementum nuper in tenura Johannis Wynder et alterum tenementum ibidem nuper in tenura Alicie Welden et duo gardina insimul iacentia eidem messuagio annexa, habenda et tenenda omnimoda supradicta prefatis Johanni Gretham et assignatis a festo Sancti Martini in yeme ⟨tunc⟩ proximo sequente (aitum) annuatim et de anno in annum extunc proximo sequentem quam diu idem Johannes vixerit reddendo de eisdem annuatim maiori et communitati civitatis predicte et successoribus suis quadraginta solidos legalis monete Anglie ad festa Pentecostes et Sancti Martini in yeme per equales porciones; proviso semper quod si [*blank*] capellanus aliquod jus seu titulum habeat in in [*sic*] uno gardino dictorum gardinorum quod hoc nullatenus idem Johannes Gretham et assignati prefatis maiori et communitati et successoribus suis pro dictis messuagio, tenementis et prefato altero gardino prefatis integrant firmam xl solidorum ad festa predicta ut patet per indenturam etc., inter maiorem et dictum Johannem sub sigillum officii maioris predicti prout in eodem plenius apparet.

[*lease to John Gretham* On 3 November 1483, the mayor and chamberlains in the name of the whole commonalty leased to weaver John Gretame a messuage in which John was living in Jubbergate, and two tenements there, one in the tenure of John Wynder and the other formerly held by Alice Weldon, plus two gardens annexed to the messuage. He is to have and to hold all of these from the feast of Martinmas for the rest of his life, rendering annually 40 s. at Pentecost and Martinmas, as is more fully stated in the indenture made between the mayor and John.]

[f.5] Record of Feoffment Enrolled
10 January 1484

[R] *carta Ricardi Ledys facta Ricardo Beilby et aliis etc.* Memorandum quod x^{mo} die mensis Januarii anno regni regis Ricardi tercii post conquestum Anglie primo quidam (Richard) Ricardus Ledys filius et heres Rogeri (Ledes) Ledys nuper de Westwyke generosi venit coram Thoma Mynskip (c) generoso tunc clerico (ex) commune civitatis (predicte) ⟨Ebor'⟩ tempore Johannis Newton tunc maiore eiusdem civitatis et ostendit quandam cartam sigillo suo signato quam quidem cartam fore factum suum cognovit coram prefato Thome Mynskip et petiit eundem Thomam eandem cartam ut factum suum inter recorda dicte civitatis irrotolari potest ad cuius instanciam carta predicta irrotolari de recordo prout tenour eius est in forma sequenti:

Sciant presentes et futuri quod ego Ricardus Ledys filius et heres Rogeri Ledys nuper de Westwyk generosi, dedi, concessi et hac presenta carta mea confirmavi Johanni Nevill, Radulpho Crathorn militibus, Miloni Wyllesthorp, Willelmo Ryther armigeris et Ricardo Beilby heredibus et assignatis ipsius Ricardi duo cotagia sive tenementa cum suis pertinentiis in Ebor' situata et iacentia in Skeldergate ibidem inter messuagium Martini See militis ex una parte et mesuagium predicti Ricardi (Bel) Beilby ex altera parte, et que quidem cotagia sive tenementa nuper fuerunt in tenura Ricardi Walson ibidem; habenda et tenenda omnia predicta cotagia sive tenementa cum suis pertinentiis prefatis Johanni, Radulpho, Miloni, Willelmo et Ricardo Beilby heredibus et assignatis ipsius Ricardi Beilby de capitalibus dominis feodi illius per servicia inde debita et de jure consueta. Et ego vero predictus Ricardus (Leidys) Ledys et heredes mei omnia predicta cotagia sive tenementa cum suis pertinentiis prefatis Johanni, Radulpho, Miloni, Willelmo et Ricardo Beilby heredibus et assignatis ipsius Ricardi contra omnes gentes warantizabimus et imperpetuum defendemus. Et ulterius noveritis me prefatum Ricardum Ledys attornasse, deputasse et loco meo constituisse dilectos michi in Christo Petrum Coke et Thomam **[f.5v]** Welles cives civitatis Ebor' (nos) meos veros et legitimos attornatos et deputos coniunctim et divisim ad intrandum vice et nomine meo in predicta cotagia sive tenementa cum suis pertinentiis et possessionem et seisinam inde michi et heredibus (me) meis recontinuandum et alios quoscumque inde amovendum et expellendum posteaque ad deliverandum plenam et paceficam possessionem et seisinam (jude) inde pro me et nomine meo prefatis Johanni, Radulpho, Miloni, Willelmo et Ricardo Beilby secundum vim, formam et effectum presenta carta mee ratum habiturum et gratum quicquid predicti attornati sive deputati mei vice et nomine (mei) meis fecerint seu eorum alter fecerit in premissis. In cuius rei testimonium huic presente carte mee sigillum apposui hiis testibus Johanne Newton maiore civitatis predicte, Thoma Neleson, Johanne Tonge aldermannis, Ricardo Hardsang et Willelmo Barker vicecomitibus eiusdem civitatis et aliis. Data octavo die Januarii anno regni regis Ricardi tercii post conquestum Anglie primo.

[*Richard Ledys's charter made to Richard Beilby and others* On 10 January 1484, Richard Ledys, son and heir of Roger Ledys, deceased of Westwick, came before Thomas Mynskip, gentleman and common clerk of York and showed a charter under his own seal which he asked to be enrolled among the city documents, in the form following:

Know [all men] present and future that I, Richard Ledys, son and heir of gentleman Roger Ledys late of Westwick, have given, granted, and by this present charter confirmed to knights John Nevill and Ralph Crathorn, to esquires Miles Wyllesthorp and William Ryther, and to Richard Beilby and Richard's heirs and assignees two cottages or tenements with their appurtenances lying in Skeldergate between the messuage of Martin See, knight, on the one side and the messuage of Richard Beilby on the other side. These cottages were formerly in the tenure of Richard Walson. They are to have and to hold these cottages of the chief lords of the fee by the services thence owed and accustomed by right, and I will warrant and defend forever the cottages to John and the others against all people. I depute and appoint in my place Peter Coke and Thomas **[f.5v]** Welles, citizens of York, to act as attorneys and to deliver full and peaceful possession and seisin to John and the others according to the strength and effect of the present charter. In testimony of which I affix my seal and those of witnesses John Newton, mayor of York, aldermen Thomas Neleson and John Tonge, sheriffs Richard Hardsang and William Barker, and others. Given 8 January 1484.]

[f.6]   **Representatives Ride to Parliament**
                24 January 1484

Memorandum quod die Sabbati videlicet xxiiij° die mensis Januarii anno regni regis Ricardi tercii post conquestum Anglie primo Milo Meitcalff recordatorus, Ricardus York et Thomas Wrangwysh aldermanni equitabant ad parliamentum domini regis Ricardi tercii.

[On Saturday 24 January 1484, recorder Miles Metcalf and aldermen Richard York and Thomas Wrangwysh rode to the parliament of Richard III.]

Memorandum that a bras pot and a hynglaver lieth for xl d. of Richard Davyes per Roland' [*incomplete*]

[f.6v]   **City Chamberlains Reimburse Predecessors**
              26 May 1494

Memorandum the xxvjth day of May the yere of the regn of Kyng Henr' vijth after the conquest the ixth at the dwellyng place and mansion of Richard Garnet in Skeldergate tofore the right wurshipfull sirs Michaell Whyte maier of the citie of York, Richard York knyght, Nicholas Lancastre, John Harper, John Gilliot, William Whyte and George Kirk aldermen; it [was] agreed and fully determyned betwix Richard Williamson, Richard Garnet and theyr felowes late chamberlayns of the citie opon that one partie and Alayn Staveley, George Essex and theyr felowez and nowe (charb) chamberleyns of this citie opon that other partie, that the said Alayn, George and theyr felowes shal pay and content unto the abovesaid Richard Williamson, Richard Garnert and theyr felowes iiij^Cxviij li. iiij s. viij d. of lawfull money of Yngland due unto theym apon the fote of theyr accomptes and by theym laid down for the common well of this citie in maner and forme ensuyng; that is to say the said some of (iiij^C l) iiij^Cxviij li. iiij s. viij d. to be devyded in thre, and therof the first parte to be paid (as) at (m) the fest of nativitie of Seynt John Baptiste next ensuyng, and at the fest of Seynt Martyn in wynter then next folowyng a secund part, and at the fest of (fe) the nativite of Seynt John Bapt[ist] that shalbe in the yere of our lord a m^lcccclxxxxvj° the iijth part in ful payment and contentacion of the seid some of iiij^Cxviij li. iiij s. viij d., to whiche paymentes and contentacions the said Alayn, George and theyr felowez tofore the said presence hath fully agreed and promysed.

[f.7 blank]

[f.7v]   **Discharge from Franchise, Restoration to Franchise**
              20 and 27 January 1484

Richard Gaskwyn dischargid

[*entry struck through*] (Memorandum that in the ffest of Saint Julian in the ffurst yere of the reing of King Richard the (furst) thyrd, John Newton than beyng mair of the said cite dischargid Richard (Weddyrbere od) Wedyrby odyrwys callid Richard Gaskwyn ⟨of hys ffranchys⟩ by caus he was disabediaunt rebyll and woldnot cum to the said mair when he sent for hym.)

restorid to hys ffraunches Memorandum that the xx^{ti} of Januar' in the yere abovesaid the said Richard was restoryd to hys fraunches by the hole consent of the holl counsell, for the wich he has paid vj s. viij d.

City Merchant Gains Permission to Sue
14 February 1484

Robert Walker Memorandum that the xiiijth day of Februar' in the first yere of the reign of King Richard the third, John Newton then mair of the cite of York gafe licence to Robert Walker of the said cite merchaunt to sue Rogere Esshdale baxter for ⟨all⟩ such mater of variance as ys dependyng bitwix theym, in such courtes and places as the said Robert semeth most behufull.

[f.8 blank]

**[f.8v]   Suit and Arrest
                  19 February 1484**

xix° die Februarii anno primo regni regis Ricardi tercii Perceptum quod capias Willelmum Gerrard yoman et Johannam Ellot uxorem Johannis Ellot ⟨et Elenam Dalemere⟩ (uxo) ad sectam dicti Johannis Ellot.

   [*19 February 1484* Order for the arrest of yeoman William Gerrard and Joan Ellot, wife of John Ellot, and of Ellen Dalemere, at the suit of John Ellot.]

**[f.9]   Arrests and Bonds to Keep the Peace
                  November 1483 X February 1484**

Ad hunc de tempore Johannis Newton maioris

capias Preceptum quod capias Thomam Conyers de E[bor'] generosum ⟨alias dictum Thomam Conyes⟩ ad sectam Roberti Lille capellani ac vicarii de Bisshopthorp etc.

(xxiiij^{ti}) xxvj° die Novembris anno primo regni regis Ricardi tercii Manucapcio Thome Conyer de Ebor' generosi alias dicti Thome Conyes quod ipse dampnum corporale non faciet seu fieri procurabit quovismodo ⟨in Robertum Lille capellanum⟩; Willelmus Robynson inholder, Ricardus Teysdale wever, Hugo Lytster questor, Johannes Skypwyth taillour, quilibet manucaptorum predictorum sub pena x librarum et dictus Thomas sub pena xx librarum domino regi solvendarum.

summa viij s. ij d. (xj° die Decembris anno primo regni regis Ricardi tercii) vacat *quia venit pro eo* [*entry struck through*] (Manucapcio Willelmi Stenson (cape) clerici quod ipse dampnum corporale non faciet nec fieri procurabit quovismodo ⟨Johanne Worsley⟩ seu alicui alio de populo domini regis; Thomas Conzers de Ebor' gentilman, Rogerus Emson de eadem cobler, Robertus Day de eadem lytster, Thomas Riche de eadem hatmaker.)

manucapcio capias Preceptum quod capias Isabellam Bolton viduam nuper de Newall in parochia de Otley ad sectam Johannis Brown de Farnley in parochia de Otley, xviij° die Decembris.

capias Kyrstymes Preceptum quod capias Johannem Ellot de civitate Ebor' yoman ad sectam Elene Dalemer vidue.

ij^{do} die Januarii Robertus (Kendale) Walker merchaunt, Thomas Welles golds-myth, Robertus Holme gentilman et Johannes Haystynges gentilman venerunt coram Johanne Newton maiore civitatis Ebor' et manuceperunt pro Johanne (Johanne) Peghan merchaunt quod ipse Johannes Peghan dampnum vel (d) malum aliquod corporale non faciet nec fieri procurabit quovismodo in Ricardum Dowe-son clericum sub pena cuiuslibet manucaptorum predictorum x librarum et dictus Johannes Peg(h)an sub pena xl librarum.

[f.9v] *penultimo (de) die Januarii* Preceptum quod capias Willelmum Harper (scolaler) filium Willelmi Harper civitatis Ebor' cordwener ad sectam dicti Willelmi patris pro securitate pacis.

septimo die Februarii anno regni regis Ricardi tercii primo Manucapcio Johannis Levetson de Pomitfret in comitatu Ebor' questoris quod ipse dampnum corporale non faciet seu fieri procurabit quovismodo in Ricardum Glover seu alicui ⟨alio de⟩ populo domini regis; (Ricardus) ⟨Thomas⟩ Kirkeby capper, Ricardus (hon) Onethank capper, Jacobus Robson capper et Brianus Gybson questor quilibet manucaptorum sub pena x librarum et dictus Johannes sub pena xx librarum domino regi solvendarum.

xiij^o die Februarii anno supradicto Preceptum quod capias Thomam Gyll de E[bor'] sadler ad sectam Jahanne Carr pro securitate pacis.

xiij^o die Februarii anno supradicto Manucapcio Thome Gyll de E[bor'] sadler quod ipse dampnum corporale non faciet nec fieri procurabit quovismodo in Johannam Carr seu alio de populo domini regis; Johannes Huetson de E[bor'] barker, Johannes Burgh sadler, Thomas Alleyn sadler et Willelmus Hogeson armorer quilibet sub pena x librarum et dictus Thomas sub pena xx librarum domino regi solvendarum.

xiij die Februarii anno regni regis Ricardi tercii primo Preceptum quod capias Willelmum Lapyng de E[bor'] wever alias (dict') laborer ad sectam Thome Fryston capellani pro securitate pacis.

[During the mayoralty of John Newton

arrest Order for the arrest of Thomas Conyers of York, gentleman, also called Thomas Conyes, at the suit of Robert Lille, chaplain and vicar of Bishopthorpe.

26 November 1483 Mainprise of Thomas Conyer of York, gentleman, also called Thomas Conyes, that he should do no harm to Robert Lille, chaplain, under penalty of £20. Innholder William Robynson, weaver Richard Teysdale, searcher Hugh Lytster, and tailor John Skypwith were each bound for £10 as sureties.

the sum of 8 s. 2 d., void because he came for it (Mainprise of William Stenson, clerk, that he should do no harm to John Worsley or anyone else. [Sureties:] Thomas Conzers of York, gentleman; Roger Emson, cobbler; Robert Day, litster; Thomas Riche, hatmaker.)

mainprise for arrest Order for the arrest of Isabel Bolton, widow, formerly of Newall in the parish of Otley, at the suit of John Brown of Farnley in the same parish, 18 December.

arrest, Christmas Order for the arrest of John Ellot of York, yeoman, at the suit of widow Ellen Dalemer.

2 January Merchant Robert Walker, goldsmith Thomas Welles, gentleman Robert Holm, and gentleman John Haystynges came before the mayor and bound themselves for £10 each to ensure that merchant John Peghan would do no damage nor bodily harm to Richard Doweson, clerk, or anyone else, Peghan himself under penalty of £40.

[**f.9v**] *30 January* Order for the arrest of William Harper, son of York cordwainer William Harper, at the suit of the father, to keep the peace.

7 February 1484 Mainprise of searcher John Levetson of Pontefract, Yorks., that he should do no harm to Richard Glover or anyone else under penalty of £20. Cappers Thomas Kirkeby, Richard Onethank, and James Robson, and searcher Brian Gybson were each bound for £10 as sureties.

13 February 1484 Order for the arrest of Thomas Gyll, saddler, at the suit of Joan Carr, to keep the peace.

13 February 1484 Mainprise of saddler Thomas Gyll, that he should do no harm to Joan Carr or anyone else under penalty of £20. Barker John Huetson, saddlers John Burgh and Thomas Alleyn, and armorer William Hogeson were each bound for £10 as sureties.

13 February 1484 Order for the arrest of weaver William Lapyng at the suit of chaplain Thomas Fryston, to keep the peace.]

[**f.10**]   **Jottings and Notes**
          February 1484 X February 1485

De tempore Thome Wrangwyssh maioris civitatis Ebor' anno regni regis Ricardi tercii primo, qui mortuus est [*final three words added in a different hand*]

[During the mayoralty of Thomas Wrangwish in the first year of King Richard III, who is dead.]

(Memorandum that the Thursday next aftir the fest of Saint Mathie in the yere above wryttyn ⟨that is to say the xxvj of the moneth of Feveryer⟩ my said lord the mair com from t)

(Ricardus Thomson)

domini sumus

anno secundo regis Ricardi tercii

Memorandum that the xxij day of Juyl

domini sumus in mundo uniamus corde jocundo [*repeated three times*]

domini sumus in mundo uniamus

[We are lords in the world united by a merry heart.]

[f.10v]   **Arrests and Bonds to Keep the Peace**
                    11 October 1491 plus others undated

xj^{mo} die Octobris anno vij^{me} regis Henrici vij^{mi} Preceptum capias Robertum Stevynson etc., r[espondendum?] Johanni Huton couk pro securitate pacis.

[*entry struck through*] (Manucapcio Roberti Stevenson (yom) de Whiteby in comitatu E[bor'] yoman pro securitate pacis etc., videlicet Willelmus Awn de E[bor'] spicer et Georgius Kirk goldsmyth videlicet quilibet manucaptorum predictorum sub pena x librarum et dictus Robertus (supra) sub pena xx librarum domino regi solvendarum etc.)

partes concordant [*entry struck through*] (Manucapcio Roberti Stevenson de Whiteby in comitatu E[bor'] yoman quod ipse dampnum vel malum corporale non faciet nec fieri procurabit quovismodo in Johannem Hoton ⟨de E[bor']⟩ couk seu alicui alio de populo domini regis videlicet (Th') Willelmus Awn de Ebor' spicer et Jacobus Kirk de eadem goldsmyth uterque manucaptorum sub pena x librarum et dictus Robertus sub pena xx librarum domino regi solvendarum etc.)

Manucapcio Johannis Huton de Ebor' cuc [*incomplete*]

[*11 October 1491* Order for the arrest of Robert Stevynson, answering to John Huton, cook, to keep the peace.

(Mainprise of yeoman Robert Stevenson of Whitby to keep the peace, under penalty of £20. Spicer William Awn of York and goldsmith George Kirk were each bound for £10 as sureties.)

parties are agreed (Mainprise of Robert Stevenson of Whitby, that he do no harm to John Hoton or anyone else, under penalty of £20. Spicer William Awn and goldsmith James Kirk were each bound for £10 as sureties.)

Mainprise of John Huton of York, cook [*incomplete*]]

[f.11]   Reception of Mayor upon Return from Parliament
             26 and 27 February 1484

De tempore Thome Wrangwysh maioris huius civitatis a festo Sancti Blasii anno primo regni regis Ricardi tercii usque idem festum anno regni regis predicti secundo, per unum annum integrum etc. [*3 February 1484 – 3 February 1485*]

[During the mayoralty of Thomas Wrangwish from the feast of Saint Blaise in the first year of Richard III to the following feast, for an entire year.]

metyng the lord mayour at Tadcaster Memorandum that the Thursday next aftir the fest of Saint Mathie in the yere aforsayd, that is to say the xxvj day of the moneth of Februar' in the yere above writtyn, my said lord the mair come to thys cite of York from the parlement of our said sovereyn lord the king; at the wich day Robert Amyas alderman, the commun clerk, the swirdberer (a) and all the seriauntes and officours of my sayd lord the mair attendyd (ap) uppon hym at Tadcastyr and broght hym to the cite afore he had taykyn hys oth and the swird and the mais born afore hym, and by the way (ma) diwyrs of the xxiiij and many odyr of the ⟨most⟩ onest communers mett hym on horsbak by the way and broght hym worshipfully home to hys awn place; and of the morn aftir, that is to say the Fryday the xxvij^{ti} day of the said moneth, he tuke hys oth of mairalte at the commun hall afore all the communs of the sayd cite.

[f.11v]   Return of Richard York from Parliament
              19 and 26 February 1484

Memorandum that the Fryday the xix^{th} day of Februar' in the furst yere of the reing of King Richard the thyrd the parlement of the said king was ffynishid, and (the) Master York was still at London aftir the said parlement ffynyshid to the Fryday then next ffiluyng, that is to say to the xxvj^{th} day of March [*sic*], the which day he tuke hys yorney homward and com home the Ask Wedynsday [*3 March*].

Admission of Chaplain to Chantry Chapel
5 March 1484

admissio et inducio Johannis Ward ad canteriam in capella Sancti Willelmi super pontem Use per Ricardum Toller foundatam Memorandum quod quinto die Marcii anno domini M°cccclxxxiij° et anno regni regis Ricardi tercii post conquestum

Anglie primo tempore Thome Wrangwysh maiore huius civitatis pretextu (cuius) cuiusdem littere presentacionis venerabilis viri Johannis Sandford de Thorp Salvayn, Johannes Warde capellanus admissus fuit ad cauntariam perpetuam in capella Sancti Willelmi super pontem Use per venerabilem virem Ricardum Toller nuper de civitate Ebor' (fecit) f⟨o⟩undatam et in corporale possessionem eiusdem cantarie inductus ut patet sub sigillo officii maioratus predicti.

[*admission and induction of John Ward to the chantry in the chapel of Saint William on Ouse bridge, founded by Richard Toller* On 5 March 1484, during the mayoralty of Thomas Wrangwish, John Warde, chaplain, was admitted to the perpetual chantry founded by Richard Toller in the chapel of Saint William on Ouse bridge, on account of the letters of presentation of the venerable John Sandford of Thorp Salvin, and given bodily possession of the same, as is clear under the seal of the office of mayor.]

Contents of Common Crane
9 April 1484

bona crane Memorandum that ther was in the crayn the ix[th] day of April in the first yere of the reign of King Richard the third vj keys [?] of bras ysshone of theym weyng iij quarterens and vj li. di. C quarter and vij li. of bras vij di. C quarters and xiij li. of led weghtes.

[f.12]   **Arrests and Bonds to Keep the Peace**
                 March 1484

capias iiij° die Marcii anno primo regni regis Ricardi tercii Preceptum quod capias Willelmum Gerrard yoman pro Roberto Walles de civitate Ebor' tailliour et Johanna Ellot uxore Johannis Ellot yoman ad (sect') ⟨sectam⟩ dicti Johannis Ellot (e) yoman.

quarto die Marcii anno primo regni regis Ricardi tercii Preceptum quod capias Willelmum Walls (de) servientem Thome Hausleyn ffyshmonger ad sectam Johannis Marshall de civitate Ebor' ffyshmonger.

supersedeas, vacat quia nunquam fuit sigillatum [*entry struck through*] (Manucapcio Willelmi Walls servientis Thome Hawslyn ffyshmonger quod ipse dampnum corporale non faciet ⟨seu fieri procurabit⟩ Johanni Marshall de Ebor' ffysh-monger seu alicui de populo (domino) domini regis. Willelmus Tayte drapour, Thomas Hawslyn ffyshmonger, Willelmus Dowyr smyth et Willelmus Thomson tapiter videlicet quilibet manucaptorum predictorum sub pena x librarum et dictus Willelmus Walles sub pena xx librarum. Datum vj° die Marcii. Vacat quia nunquam fuit sigillatum (equ) eo quod manucaptores predicti noluerunt obligari.)

vij die Marcii anno primo regis Ricardi tercii, vacat quia postea [*entry struck*

through] (Manucapcio Willelmi Gerrard yoman, Roberti Walleys de civitate Ebor'
tallour et Johanne Ellot uxoris Johannis Ellot yoman ad sectam dicti Johannis Ellot
yoman (quilibet manucaptorum) sub pena x librarum; (Robt') ⟨Johannes Westeby de Ebor' wever⟩, Robertus Coke de Ebor' pewterer, (Thomas Slaw [?] de
E[bor'] merchaunt) Robertus Smyth de E[bor'] smyth, uterque sub pena x librarum
et predicti Willelmus, Robertus et Johanna quilibet eorum sub pena (xx li.) xiij (s.)
librarum vj solidorum viij denariorum, etc.)

[f.12v] *vij die Marcii anno regni regis Ricardi tercii primo* Manucapcio Willelmi
Gerrard yoman, Roberti Walles de E[bor'] taillour et Johanne Ellot uxoris
Johannis Ellot yoman ad sectam Johannis Ellot predicti yoman; Thomas Westeby
de Ebor' wever, Robertus Couke de E[bor'] pewtrer et (Johannes) ⟨Robertus⟩
Smyth de Ebor' smyth quilibet eorum sub pena x librarum et predicti Willelmus,
Robertus Walles et Johanna quilibet sub pena xx librarum.

capias Preceptum quod capias Willelmum Draper ⟨cuver'⟩ et Elezabetham
uxorem eius ad sectam Alicie uxoris Johannis Jakson de Doncastir, viij° die Marcii
anno primo regni regis Ricardi tercii.

capias Preceptum quod capias Laurencium Turnbull de Rippon potter ad sectam
Willelmi Lakford de civitate Ebor' peuterer, viij° die Marcii anno primo regni regis
Ricardi tercii.

ix° die Marcii anno regni regis Ricardi tercii primo Manucapcio Willelmi Draper
cuver' et Elizabethe uxoris eius ad sectam Alicie uxoris Johannis Jakson de
(Pomtfret) ⟨Doncaster⟩; Johannes Awnwyk, Johannes White de E[bor'] cuver',
Willelmus Cokfeld de Cokfeld de E[bor'] goldsmyth et Johannes Spencer, quilibet
sub pena x librarum et predicti Willelmus et Elizabetha uterque xx librarum
domino regi solvendarum.

> [*arrest 4 March 1484* Order for the arrest of yeoman William Gerrard for tailor
> Robert Walles and Joan Ellot, wife of yeoman John Ellot, at the suit of the said
> John Ellot.

> *4 March 1484* Order for the arrest of William Walls, servant of fishmonger
> Thomas Hausleyn, at the suit of fishmonger John Marshall.

> [*writ of*] *supersedeas, void because it was never sealed* (Mainprise of William
> Walls, servant of fishmonger Thomas Hawslyn, that he do no bodily harm to
> fishmonger John Marshall or anyone else, under penalty of £20. Draper William
> Tayte, fishmonger Thomas Hawslyn, smith William Dowyr, and weaver William
> Thomson were each bound for £10 as sureties. Given 6 March. Void because it
> was never sealed and the sureties are not bound.)

> *7 March 1484, void because [of entry that comes] afterwards* (Mainprise of
> yeoman William Gerrard, tailor Robert Walleys, and Joan Ellot, wife of yeoman
> John Ellot, at the suit of John Ellot, under penalty of £13 6 s. 8 d. each. Sureties
> John Westeby, Robert Coke, and Robert Smyth each bound for £10.)

[f.12v] *7 March 1484* Mainprise of yeoman William Gerrard, tailor Robert Walles of York, and Joan Ellot wife of yeoman John Ellot, at the suit of John Ellot, under penalty of £20. Weaver Thomas Westeby, pewterer Robert Couke, and smith Robert Smyth were each bound for £10 as sureties.

arrest Order for the arrest of William Draper and his wife Elizabeth, at the suit of Alice the wife of John Jakson of Doncaster, 8 March 1484.

arrest Order for the arrest of potter Laurence Turnbull of Ripon, at the suit of pewterer William Lakford of York, 8 March 1484.

9 March 1484 Mainprise of William Draper and Elizabeth his wife, under penalty of £20, at the suit of Alice, wife of John Jakson of Doncaster. John Awnwyk, John White, William Cokfeld and John Spencer were bound for £10 each as sureties.]

[f.13]   **Arrests and Bonds to Keep the Peace**
           March 1484

capias Preceptum quod capias Aliciem uxorem Johannis Jakson de Doncastir ad sectam Elezabethe uxoris Willelmi Draper cuverer ix° die Marcii.

ix° die Marcii Manucapcio Willelmi Lakford de Ebor' peuterer ad sectam Laurencii Turnebull de Ripon potter; Johannes Bukler de Ebor' glover, Ricardus Welles de Ebor' escrevener.

ix die Marcii Manucapcio Laurencii Turnebull de Ripon potter (ad sectam Willelmi Lakford de Ebor' peuterer) quod ipse dampnum vel malum corporale non faciet seu fieri procurabit quovismodo in Willelmum Lakford de Ebor' peuterer seu alicui alio de populo domini regis; Ricardus Wynder de E[bor'] peuterer, Johannes Tanfeld de E[bor'] peuterer, Johannes Skipwith de Ebor' taillour et Robertus Calverd de Ebor' shomaker videlicet quilibet manucaptorum predictorum in x libris et predictus Laurencius Turnebull in xx libris domino regi solvendis.

xvij° die Marcii Manucapcio Willelmi Herper filii Willelmi Herper de E[bor'] cord[wainer] quod ipse dampnum vel malum corporale non faciet seu fieri procurabit quovismodo in Willelmum Herper de E[bor'] [seniorem] cord[wainer] seu alicui alio de populo domini regis; Milo Grenebank de E[bor'] cord[wainer], Willelmus Burgeys de E[bor'] capellanus, Henricus Hikes de Ebor' cord[wainer] et Ricardus Jakson de E[bor'] cord[wainer], videlicet quilibet manucaptorum in x libris et idem Willelmus junior in xx libris usque [ad] proximum sessionem pacis proximo etc., domino regi solvendis.

[f.13v] *xvij die Marcii* Manucapcio Alicie uxoris Johannis Jakson de Doncastr' quod ipsa dampnum vel malum aliquod corporale non faciet seu fieri procurabit quovismodo in Elizabetham uxorem Willelmi Draper de E[bor'] cuver' seu alicui alio de populo domini regis; Johannes Brokholes de Ebor' bower, Ricardus Raulyn de E[bor'] cordwaner, Thomas Neleson de E[bor'] smyth et Willelmus Palmer de Ebor' taillour (videlicet) quilibet manucaptorum predictorum in x libris et predicta Alicia in xx libris domino regi solvendis.

xxjº de [*sic*] *Marcii anno primo regni regis Ricardi tercii* Manucapcio Thome Bakhous de Ebor' sawer alias dictus cobler quod ipse dampnum corporale non faciet nec fieri procurabit quovismodo in Willelmum Bowmer de civitate predicta wever seu alicui alio de populo dicti domini regis; Hugo North de civitate predicta tailiour, Robertus Busby de eadem bucher, Robertus Ellerton de eadem tailiour et Johannes Grayson de eadem porter sub pena quilibet manucaptorum predictorum x librarum et dictus Thomas Bakhows sub pena xx librarum domino regi foris-faciendarum.

preceptum Preceptum quod capias dompnum Thomam Chambyr monacum, Johannem Glew de Ebor' pistorem et Henricum Meitcalff (de Ha) yoman Ayrskar' ad sectam Henrici Topham de Ebor' ffullonem [*sic*], xxvjº die Marcii anno primo regni regis Ricardi tercii.

manucapcio Manucapcio (R) Henrici Topham (ffullonem) ffullonis quod ipse dampnum corporale non faciet in dompnum Thomam Chambyr monacum, Johannem Glew et Henricum Meitcalff seu alicui alio de populo domini regis; Christoforus Beyntlay (yoman), Johannes Moy, Johannes Paten, [*blank*] quilibet manucaptorum predictorum sub pena (x)x librarum et dictus Henricus sub pena xx librarum.

[*arrest* Order for the arrest of Alice, wife of John Jakson of Doncaster, at the suit of Elizabeth, wife of William Draper, 9 March.

9 March Mainprise of pewterer William Lakford of York, at the suit of potter Laurence Turnebull of Ripon, sureties John Bukler and Richard Welles.

9 March Mainprise of Laurence Turnebull of Ripon, potter, that he do no harm to pewterer William Lakford or anyone else, under penalty of £20. Pewterers Richard Wynder and John Tanfeld, tailor John Skipwith, and shoemaker Robert Calverd were each bound for £10 as sureties.

17 March Mainprise of William Herper, son of York cordwainer William Herper, that he do no damage nor bodily harm to his father or anyone else, under penalty of £20. Cordwainers Miles Grenebank, Henry Hikes, and Richard Jakson, and chaplain William Burgeys were each bound for £10 as sureties.

[**f.13v**] *17 March* Mainprise of Alice, wife of John Jakson of Doncaster, that she do no harm to Elizabeth Draper or anyone else, under penalty of £20. Bower John Brokholes, cordwainer Richard Raulyn, smith Thomas Neleson, and tailor William Palmer were each bound for £10 as sureties.

21 March 1484 Mainprise of sawyer Thomas Bakhous, also a cobbler, that he do no harm to weaver William Bowmer or anyone else, under penalty of £20. Tailors Hugh North and Robert Ellerton, butcher Robert Busby, and porter John Grayson were each bound for £10 as sureties.

order Order for the arrest of Lord Thomas Chambyr, monk, of fisherman John Glew, and yeoman Henry Meitcalff, at the suit of fuller Henry Topham, 26 March 1484.

mainprise Mainprise of fuller Henry Topham that he do no harm to monk Thomas Chambyr, John Glew, and Henry Meitcalff, or to anyone else, under penalty of £20. Christopher Beyntlay, John Moy, John Paten, and [*blank*] were each bound for £10 as sureties.]

[f.14]   **Arrests and Bonds to Keep the Peace**
                   April–May 1484

preceptum Preceptum (Ricardo) quod capias Ricardum Yonson de E[bor'] taillour ad sectam Johannis Johnson taillour ij^do die Aprilis.

manucapcio Manucapcio Johannis Johnson de E[bor'] taillour quod ipse dampnum vel malum corporale non faciet nec fieri procurabit quovismodo in Ricardum Yonson de E[bor'] taillour seu alicui de populo dicti domini regis; Johannes Kyng de E[bor'] wever, Johannes Thwyng de E[bor'] wever, Ricardus Davys de E[bor'] glover et Johannes Thirleby de E[bor'] capemaker, quilibet manucaptorum in x libris et predictus Johannes in xx libris domino regi solvendis.

manucapcio Manucapcio Ricardi Jonson de E[bor'] taillour quod ipse dampnum vel malum corporale non faciet nec fieri procurabit quovismodo in Johannem Johnson de E[bor'] taillour seu alicui de populo dicti domini regis; Christoforus Bentley de E[bor'] (wever) yo[man], Willelmus Fryston de E[bor'] wever, Willelmus Robynson de Ebor' walker et Robertus (Glovar) Elwald de E[bor'] coriour, videlicet quilibet manucaptorum in x libris et predictus Ricardus in xx libris solvendis domino regi.

xxvij° die Aprilis Preceptum quod capias Johannam Jakson alias dictam Johannam Ewre (alias dictam) ad sectam Emmote uxoris Roberti Lound.

[f.14v] *preceptum* Preceptum quod capias Johannem Bacon de Ebor' cowper ad sectam Johannis Band roper xxviij° die Aprilis.

preceptum Preceptum quod capias Ricardum Blakburn de Ebor' mercerum ad sectam Johannis Cure pro securitate pacis, vij° die Maii.

manucapcio Manucapcio Ricardi Blakburn quod ipse dampnum corporale non faciet nec fieri procurabit quovismodo Johannem Cure seu alicui alio de populo dicti domini regis; ⟨Ricardus⟩ (Ricardos) Russell et Johannes Bailze quilibet manucaptorum predictorum sub pena x librarum et predictus Ricardus Blakburn sub pena xx librarum domino regi forisfaciendarum, vij° die Maii.

preceptum, vacat [*entry struck through*] (Preceptum quod capias Christoforum Bentley, Johannem Ellys et Johannem Patteyn ad sectam Ricardi Blakburn pro securitate pacis viij° die Maii.)

preceptum Preceptum quod capias Ricardum Nicholson de Ebor' clericum alias dictum (Nich') Ricardum Nicholson capellanum (in predicto) pro securitate pacis ad sectam Thome Kyrkby ⟨alias dicti Thome Chalener⟩ de Ebor' shomaker.

manucapcio Manucapcio Ricardi Nicholson de Ebor' clereci alias dicti Ricardi Nicholson capellani quod ipse dampnum corporale non faciet nec fieri procurabit quovismodo in Thomam Kyrkby alias dictum Thomam Chalener de Ebor' shomaker seu alicui alio de populo domini regis; Willelmus Byller clericus, Henricus Hyes shomaker, Johannes Huton potter et Willelmus Carter wynter, videlicet quilibet manucaptorum predictorum sub pena x librarum et predictus Ricardus sub pena xx librarum domino regi forisfaciendarum.

[*order* Order for the arrest of tailor Richard Yonson at the suit of tailor John Johnson, 2 April.

mainprise Mainprise of tailor John Johnson that he do no damage nor bodily harm to tailor Richard Yonson or to anyone else, under penalty of £20. Weavers John Kyng and John Thwyng, glover Richard Davys, and capmaker John Thirleby were each bound for £10 as sureties.

mainprise Mainprise of tailor Richard Jonson that he do no damage nor bodily harm to John Johnson or to anyone else, under penalty of £20. Christopher Bentley, William Fryston, William Robynson and Robert Elwald were each bound for £10 as sureties.

27 April Order for the arrest of Joan Jakson, also called Joan Ewre, at the suit of Emmote, wife of Robert Lound.

[**f.14v**] *order* Order for the arrest of cooper John Bacon at the suit of roper John Band, 28 April.

order Order for the arrest of mercer Richard Blakburn at the suit of John Cure, for the keeping of the peace, 7 May.

mainprise Mainprise of Richard Blakburn that he do no harm to John Cure or to anyone else, under penalty of £20, 7 May. Richard Russell and John Bailze were each bound for £10 as sureties.

order, void (Order for the arrest of Christopher Bentley, John Ellys, and John Patteyn, at the suit of Richard Blakburn, for the keeping of the peace, 8 May.)

order Order for the arrest of clerk Richard Nicholson, also called chaplain Richard Nicholson, for the keeping of the peace, at the suit of Thomas Kyrkby, also called Thomas Chalener, shoemaker.

mainprise Mainprise of clerk Richard Nicholson, also called chaplain, that he do no harm to Thomas Kyrkby also called Thomas Chalener, or to anyone else, under penalty of £20. Clerk William Byller, shoemaker Henry Hyes, potter John Huton, and vintner William Carter were each bound for £10 as sureties.]

[f.15]   Arrest and Bonds to Keep the Peace
May–June 1484

vacat quia per liberam voluntatem Ricardi Blakbourne [*entry struck through*] (Manucapcio Christofori Bentley, Johannis Ellys et Johannis Patteyn quod (ipse) ipsi dampnum vel malum corporale non faciet nec fieri procurabit quovismodo in Ricardum Blakburn seu alicui alio de populo dicti domini regis; Johannes Tyrell de Ebor' wever, Thomas Kechyner de Ebor' tapiter, Thomas Briges de Ebor' ffremason et Ricardus Deen de Ebor' roper, videlicet quilibet manucaptorum in x libris et predicti Christoforus, Johannes et Johannes quilibet eorum xx libris domino regi solvendis.)

Manucapcio (Thome Hesilwod de E[bor'] cartwright) Ricardi Hesilwod filii dicti Thome, Roberti Carlill de E[bor'] whelewright et Ricardi Hall de eadem cartwright et ⟨Willelmi Bishop de E[bor'] whelewright⟩ quod ipsi dampnum vel malum corporale non faciet nec fieri procurabit quovismodo in Margaretam Kelk uxorem Johannis Kelk seu alicui de populo dicti domini regis; Georgius Lokeryk de E[bor'] wever, Johannes Smythson de eadem walker, Johannes Peper de eadem wever et Johannes Metcalf de E[bor'] wever, videlicet quilibet manucaptorum in x libris et predicti Thomas et omnes alii supranominati in xx libris domino regi solvendis.

Preceptum quod capias Johannem Napet de E[bor'] pro securitate pacis ad sectam Thome Ray tapiter.

Preceptum quod capias Willelmum [*incomplete*]

Preceptum quod capias Johannem North capellanum pro securitate pacis ad sectam Thome Wilson.

Preceptum est quod capias Thomam Davyas pro securitate pacis ad sectam Roberti Smyth.

[f.15v] *vacat quia relaxavit* [*entry struck through*] (Preceptum quod capias Ricardum Walshworth de E[bor'] armerer ad sectam Thome Ruke de eadem cobler viij° die Junii.)

Preceptum est quod capias Willelmum Folnetby ad sectam Thome Middylton.

Manucapcio Thome Davyas quod ipse dampnum vel malum corporale non faciet nec fieri procurabit quovismodo in Robertum Smyth seu alicui alio de populo ⟨dicti⟩ domini regis; Edmundus Wright parchemener, Thomas Danson, Johannes Vescy, Willelmus Ramsay cuke, videlicet quilibet manucaptorum in xx libris et (predicti Ed'us, Thomas, Johannes, Willelmus quilibet eorum) ⟨et predictus Thomas⟩ in xx libris domino regi solvendis.

Manucapcio Willelmi North quod ipse dampnum vel malum corporale non faciet nec fieri procurabit quovismodo in aliquem populum ⟨dicti⟩ domini regis; Johannes Leese, Johannes Grethede, Ricardus Froos, Robertus Talbot quilibet manucaptorum sub pena x librarum, et predictus Willelmus North in xx libris domino regi solvendis.

Manucapcio Ricardi North quod ipse dampnum vel malum corporale non faciet nec fieri procurabit quovismodo in aliquem populum dicti domini regis; Johannes Leese, Johannes Grethed, Ricardus Froos, Robertus Talbot, quilibet manucaptorum sub pena x librarum et predictus Ricardus in xx libris domino regi solvendis.

Preceptum est quod capias Johannem Berwyk wauker ad sectam Willelmi North.

Manucapcio pro Johanne Berwyk quod ipse dampnum vel malum corporale non faciet nec fieri procurabit quovismodo in Willelmum North seu alicui alio populo domini regis; Thomas Hesylwod, Johannes Williamson walker, Willelmi [*sic*] (Jakson in Fisshergate) Williamson, Willelmi [*sic*] Mitchell walker, quilibet manucaptorum sub pena x librarum et predictus Johannes in xx libris domino regi solvendis.

[*void at the wish of Richard Blakbourne* (Mainprise of Christopher Bentley, John Ellys, and John Patteyn, that they do no harm to Richard Blakburn or to anyone else, under penalty of £20. John Tyrell, Thomas Kechyner, Thomas Briges, and Richard Deen were each bound for £10 as sureties.)

Mainprise of Richard Hesilwod, son of cartwright Thomas Hesilwod, wheelwright Robert Carlill, cartwright Richard Hall, and wheelwright William Bishop, that they do no damage nor bodily harm to Margaret Kelk or to anyone else, under penalty of £20. George Lokeryk, John Smythson, John Peper, and John Metcalf were each bound for £10 as sureties.

Order for the arrest of John Napet for the keeping of the peace, at the suit of weaver Thomas Ray.

Order for the arrest of William [*incomplete*]

Order for the arrest of chaplain John North at the suit of Thomas Wilson for the keeping of the peace.

Order for the arrest of Thomas Davyas at the suit of Robert Smyth, for the keeping of the peace.

[**f.15v**] *void because released* (Order for the arrest of armorer Richard Walshworth at the suit of cobbler Thomas Ruke, 8 June.)

Order for the arrest of William Folnetby at the suit of Thomas Middylton.

Mainprise of Thomas Davyas that he do no damage nor bodily harm to Robert Smyth or to anyone else, under penalty of £20. Edmund Wright, Thomas Danson, John Vescy, and William Ramsay were each bound for £20 as sureties.

Mainprise of William North that he do no harm to any of the king's subjects under penalty of £20. John Leese, John Grethede, Richard Froos, and Robert Talbot were each bound for £10 as sureties.

Mainprise of Richard North that he do no damage nor bodily harm to any of the king's subjects, under penalty of £20. John Leese, John Grethed, Richard Froos, and Robert Talbot were each bound for £10 as sureties.

Order for the arrest of walker John Berwyk at the suit of William North.

Mainprise for John Berwyk that he do no damage nor bodily harm to William North or to any other of the king's subjects, under penalty of £20. Thomas Hesylwod, John Williamson, William Williamson, and William Mitchell were each bound for £10 as sureties.]

[*Original foliation indicates that the next folio is missing; modern foliation continues unbroken.*]

[**f.16**]   **Bonds to Accept Arbitration**
                 March 1484

[*continued from missing folio*] in xl libris, stare (et) et obedire arbitrio, ordinacioni et judicio Willelmi Skawsby et Petri Cuke ⟨electi⟩ ad arbitrandum pro parte dictorum Johannis Loundesdale ⟨Thome Gray et Johannis Shaw⟩ inter dictum Johannem ex parte una et Willelmum Foulneby ex parte altera de ⟨et⟩ super omnimodis accionibus, sectis, querelis et debatis inter partes predictas habitis a principio mundi usque in diem confeccionis presencium, ita quod arbitrium, ordinacio et judicium dictorum arbitratorum fiant inter partes predictas (citra) infra viij dies proximos etc.

Foulneby Et eodem die prefatus Willelmus Foulneby obligavit ⟨se⟩ domino ⟨nostro⟩ regi in xl libris legalis monete Anglie quod ipse dampnum corporale non faciet nec fieri procurabit in dictum Johannem Loundesdale et quod dictus Willelmus Foulneby stabit arbitrio, ordinacioni et judicio Thome Gray et Johannes Shaw arbitratorum ex parte eiusdem Willelmi ⟨Foulneby⟩, Willelmi Skawsby et Petri Cuke (de) arbitratorum ⟨pro parte⟩ dicti Johannis Loundesdale ad arbitrandum de et super omnimodis accionibus, sectis, querelis, debatis et

demandis inter partes predictas habitis a principio mundi usque in diem confeccionis presencium, ita quod arbitrium, ordinacio et judicium dictorum arbitratorum
fiant et reddantur inter partes predictas infra viij° dies proximos etc.

[[*continued from missing folio*] £40, to adhere to and obey the judgement of
William Skawsby and Peter Cuke, elected as arbiters to determine all actions and
complaints between John Loundesdale and William Foulneby from the beginning of the world to the present day, the arbitration to be made within the next
eight days.

Foulneby And on the same day, William Foulneby bound himself for £40 that he
would do no harm to John Loundesdale or any other of the king's subjects, and
that he would abide by the arbitration and judgement of arbiters Thomas Gray,
John Shaw, William Skawsby and Peter Cuke, who are judging all actions and
complaints the two parties had from the beginning of the world to the present
day, the judgement to be made within the next eight days.]

Delivery of Fish
12 March 1484

Robert Cowper of Cawod etc. Memorandum that the xij^th day of March in the ffurst
yere of the reing of (the reing) King Richard the ffurst [*sic*], Robert Cowper ⟨of
Cawodd⟩ laborer and Johannes Lampwort of Cawod aforsaid com afore Thomas
Wrangwys then beyng mair in to the counsell chambre and swore of ther awn ffre
will apon a boke that tha deliwyrd to Richard Rawlyn and John Barker taillour here
at York at the Salthols iiij^xxxj maysis of rede heryng, the wich (xx) iiij^xxxj maisis the
said Robert and John Lamport rescevyd at Cawod of a (g) kels of William
Handcok.

[f.16v]   Bond to Accept Arbitration
13 March 1484

Johannes Marshall et Johannes Key xiij° die mensis Marcii anno primo regni regis
Ricardi tercii Johannes Marshall cordwener et Johannes Key cordwener obligerunt
se ⟨coram maiore etc.⟩ domino regi in x libris legalis monete Anglie strare [*sic*]
et obedire arbitrio, ordinacioni et judicio Thome Chappman sadler, Willelmi
Harpham cordwener, Thome Kendale et Roberti Nyghtyng ad arbitrandum inter
dictos Johannem Marshall et Johannem Key (c) infra xiiij dies proximos ⟨de et
super omnimodis accionibus, sectis et debatis inter eos habitis⟩ etc., (et si predicti
arbitratores concordare non poterint infra dictos xiiij dies) ita quod ⟨si⟩
arbitrium (sm) et judicium suum non reddant etc., quod extunc (sic) predicti
Johannes Marshall et Johannes Key stabit imperagio unius imparis per dictos
arbitratores seu (l) per dictum maiorem indifferenter electi, ita quod dictus impar
judicium (si) reddat inter partes predictas infra viij dies tunc proximo sequentes sub
pena x librarum (p) forisfaciendarum per ipsum contrarium facientem etc.

[*John Marshall and John Key* On 13 March 1484, cordwainers John Marshall and John Key bound themselves for £10 to abide by and obey the judgement of saddler Thomas Chappman, cordwainer William Harpham, Thomas Kendale and Robert Nyghtyng, arbiters given fourteen days to give judgement on all actions and issues between the two parties. If these arbiters cannot agree, then Marshall and Key will abide by the judgement of an umpire elected by the arbiters or the mayor, and the umpire will have eight further days to render a decision under penalty of £10.]

Lease and Rental Arrangements
16 March 1484

Thomas Wandesford and John Huton Memorandum that the xvjth day of March in the ffurst yere of the reing of Kyng Richard the thyrd Thomas Wandesford and John Huton cuke come in to the counsell chambir of the cite of York a fore Thomas Wrangwysh then beyng mair of the said cite, and the said John Huton then and ther afore the said mair confessid that wher as the said Thomas and Isabell Mawdyslay (on the odir pairte) by thar deid (indent) indentid lete to the said John Huton a place in (Fishgate) Fossgate from the xxiij day of Februar' the xxj yere of the reign of King Edward the iiijth un to **[f.17]** the end of xv yere then next ffoluyng, yeldyng and gyffyng therfor ⟨yerly⟩ duryng the said terme xlv s. if the said Thomas lyffe duryng the said term, that ⟨the said John⟩ (he) shall wele and trewly content and pay every yere to the said Thomas duryng the said term if he liff the ⟨some⟩ (said some) of xlvj s. viij d.

Bond to Accept Arbitration, Resolution of Dispute
17 March 1484

Robertus Bushby et Thomas Auger Memorandum quod xvij° die mensis Marcii anno primo regni regis Ricardi tercii Robertus Busheby de civitate Ebor' bucher et Thomas Auger de Haxby yoman venerunt coram Thoma Wrangwysh maiore civitatis Ebor' et obligerunt se domino regi et uterque eorum obligavit se domino regi in x libris (str) stare et obedire arbitrio, (ar) ordinacioni et judicio Rogeri Laton gentilman, Roberti Walker, Willelmi Deykyn et Petri Cuke (ad arbitrandum) de et super (a) omnimodis accionibus, sectis, querelis, debatis et contraversiis inter dictum Robertum Busheby ex parte una et prefatum Thomam Auger ex parte altera (ita quod arbitrio, ordinacioni et judicio dict') et arbitrium dictorum arbitratorum uterque (d) partium predictarum perimpleverit, ita quod ordinaciones dictorum arbitratorum fiant et reddantur citra (festum) xxviij dies huius mensis Marcii et si dicti arbitratores arbitrium suum non reddant citra dictum diem quod extunc si dictas partes (str) steterunt arbitrio unius imparis per (dictos arbitratores) ⟨maiorem indiferenter⟩ electi infra viij dies tunc proximos sequentes quod etc.

[*Robert Bushby and Thomas Auger* On 17 March, butcher Robert Busheby and yeoman Thomas Auger came before the mayor and bound themselves for £10 to abide by the judgement of Roger Laton, Robert Walker, William Deykyn, and Peter Cuke over all actions and complaints between the two parties. The judgement is to be given within twenty-eight days, or else the parties will abide by the judgement of an umpire elected by the mayor.]

Et postea etc., the said arbitourz made ther award bytwyx the said pairtz that the said Thomas Auger shold deliwyr to the said Robert Bushby the xth day of Aprell then next ffylluyng a hors, a sadyll and a brydill ⟨a sword and a bukler⟩ that he tuke from the said Robert in as gud ⟨condicion and⟩ plite as (the said hors was) in at the tym of the taykyn wer in, or els xxvj s. viij d. for tham, and owyr that tha awardyd that the said Thomas Auger shall gyff [*incomplete*]

[f.17v]   New Chamberlains to Reimburse Predecessors
17 March 1484

ordinacio camerariorum

[ordinance of the chamberlains]

Memorandum that the xvijth day of the moneth of March in the ffurst yere of the reing of King Richard the thyrd in the counsell chamber at the commun hall of the said cite it was ordenyd by Thomas Wrangwysh then beyng mair of the said [city], Mils Meitcalff recorder, William Snawsell, John Tong, Johannes Fereby, William Welles, Robert Amyas, Johannes Newton and William Tod aldermen, Richard Hardsang and William Barker sheryffes, Thomas Catour, William Chymney, Thomas Skotton, William Spence, Robert Gyll, William Tayte, Richard Clerk, Ricardus Marston, Johannes Hagg, Michell White, Johannes Harper, William White and Mils Greynbank of the xxiiij^{ti}, that John Beisby, William Hancok, Robert Johnson and Henry Albone, chamberlayns of thys cite for thys yere, shall content and pay to John Beverlay, Thomas Foulneby and John Shaw, late chamberlayns of thys ⟨cite⟩ at the fest of the Invencion of the Holy Cros callid Saint Elyn day next cumyng eght skor pound of lawfull Ynglish money as parcell of the som that is dew to the said late chamberlayns for soch paymentes as tha maide for the wele of the communalte of this cite in the yere that tha wer chamberlayns of this cite, and ⟨the said viij^{xx} li. so paid⟩ that the resedew of the ⟨said⟩ som that is awyng to tham for the said caus shabe paid by the said chamberlayns now beyng to the said John Beverley, Thomas Foulneby and John Sshaw [*sic*] late chamberlayns at two fest, that is to say at the fest of the Advincul (and) calid Lammes and at the fest of Kyrstynmes next cumyng by evyn porcions; and owyr thys ⟨tha⟩ (it is) ordenyd (by) the sayd day fermly to be kept [f.18] that from hens fforwerd every yere from yere to yere the chamberlayns that ben and shalbe of new chosen chamberlayns shall content and pay to the chamberlayns that next wer afore tham of all soch dewtes as is and shalbe dewe to tham for soch thynges as tha have lad ⟨or shall lay⟩ down for the wele of thys [city] in the tyme that tha wer chamberlayns in the maner and furm insuyng, that is to say the holl som shalbe devyd in thre and payd (and pay by) yerly by the new chamberlayns to the old chamberlayns at the festes of the Invencion of the Holy Cros callid Saint Elyn day, at the fest of Saint Petir callyd Lammes ⟨day⟩ and at the fest of Kyrstynmes ⟨next aftir the old chamberlayns be dischardyd and new chosyn⟩ by evyn porcion uppon the payn of x li. ⟨so oft tyms⟩ to be forfait by hym from hens fforwerd duryng the contrary to thys ordinauns (yf com) as complaynt shalbe made thar of to the mair for the tyme (by) beyng, ⟨the said x li. to be aploid⟩ to the use and behove of the communalte of thys cite.

[f.18v]   Enclosure of Common Land of St. Nicholas Hospital
                  25 February 1484

By the king

Northfeyld belonging to the hospital of Saint Nicholas [final seven words of marginalia written in later, probably seventeenth-century, hand] Trusty and welbelovede we grete youe well, and for asmuch as it ys shewede unto us that their ys a lityll close called the Northfelde belonyng un to our hospitall of Saynt Nicholas in the suburbes of our cite their, which must yerly if it be unsowen lye in common frome the fest of Saynt Michel tharchaungell un to Candelmasse ensewyng, the common wherof is lityll thyng in substance un to you or the commonz of our said cite, as yt is said; we therfor tendyng the well of our said hospitall in that it is of our foundacion, desire and pray youe that ye wilbe agreable that the said close may frome hensforth be kept severall unto our said hospitall at all the seasons of the yere, and ther upon to mak writyng under your common sealle in due forme, wherin ye shall do a merytory dede and un to us full gode pleaser. Yeven under our (sip) signet at our pales of Westm[inster] the xxv day of Februar'.

To our trusty and welbeloved the mair and aldermen of our cite of York

Hospital Given Rights to Common
17 March 1484

Uppon the which writyng shewed unto the commons of this cite oppinly in the common hall the xvijth day of March in the furst yere of the reign of our soverane lord the kyng, it was agred by Thomas Wrangwayssh then beyng mair and all the hole commonalte of this cite that frome hencefforth for the pleser of our said soverain lord the king, sufficient writyng shalbe maid under the common seall of the said cite to the maister of the said hospitale and his successours that he and his successors shall have and hold the said close severally at all tymes of the yere for evere. Wheropon writyng was maid to the said maister of the said (cite) ⟨hospitale⟩ and his successours in forme ensuyng.

[f.19]   **City Grants Common Pasture to Hospital of Saint Nicholas**
                    26 March 1484

Concessio ⟨facta⟩ magistro ac ffratribus et sororibus hospitalis Sancti Nicholai quod bene licebit eis tenere campum vocatum Northfeld' ut suum separalem etc.

hec concessio evacuatur ad instanciam regis Ricardi tercii ad instanciam inhabita-cionum Ebor' et legitime de super facta eidem domino regi tradita et per eum cancellata fuerunt. [Signed] J. Haryngton olim eiusdem regis consilii nunc vero huiusque civitatis consilii ⟨predicti⟩ clericus [marginalia signed with a cross] [*entry struck through*] (Omnibus Christi fidelibus ad quos hoc presens scriptum pervenerit, maior et communitas civitatis Ebor' salutem. Cum nos et predecessores nostri a tempore cuius contra memoria hominis non existat ad nostram libertatem habuerimus communem pasture cum omnibus averiis nostris, quolibet anno a festo Sancti Michaelis archangeli usque ad festum Purificationis Beate Marie Virginis, in uno campo vocato Northfeld' Johanni Wright magistro sive custodi hospitalis Sancti Nicholai extra barram de Walmegate civitatis predicte ac fratribus et sororibus eiusdem hospitalis et successoribus suis spectante prout dictum North-feld' iacet extra barram predictam inter terram Henrici Boynton armigeri vocatam Haworth garthes ex parte orientali et terras Willelmi Gascoign militis et Jacobi Charleton armigeri ex parte occidentali; sciatis nos prefatos maiorem et commu-nitatem ad instanciam excellentis in Christo regis Ricardi tercii Dei gracia regis Anglie et Francie et domini Hibernie remississe, relaxasse et omnino pro nobis et successoribus nostris imperpetuum quietum clamasse prefatis magistro sive custodi ac fratribus et sororibus hospitalis predicte et successoribus suis imperpetuum totum jus et clameum pasture que unquam habuimus, habemus seu quovismodo infuturum habere poterimus in dicto Northfeld' et in qualibet parcella eiusdem, ita quod nec nos nec successores nostri nec aliquis alius nomine nostro aliquod jus seu clameum aut aliquam pasturam in dicto Northfeld' seu in aliqua parcella eiusdem de cetero exigere vendicare seu clamare poterimus infuturum sed de pastura habenda in eadem infuturum simus exclusi per presentes, ita quod bene licebit prefatis magistro sive custodi ac fratribus et sororibus hospitalis predicte et successoribus suis dictum Northfeld' sepibus et fossatis includere et eundem Northfeld' et terram suam separalem erga nos et successores nostros imposterum habere et tenere imperpetuum. In cuius rei testimonium presentibus sigillum nostrum commune apposuimus. Data Ebor' xxvj^{to} die mensis Marcii anno regni regis Ricardi tercii post conquestum Anglie primo.)

[Grant made to the master, brothers, and sisters of the hospital of Saint Nicholas that they be allowed to hold the field called Northfield as their own, etc.

this grant cancelled at the request of King Richard III at the behest of the residents of York; it was given back to the king and cancelled by him. [Signed] J. Haryngton, formerly of the king's council and now clerk of the city council (To all Christ's faithful to whose notice this present letter shall come, greetings from the mayor and commonalty of York. We and our predecessors from time out of mind had the right to common pasture for all our beasts from Michaelmas to the feast of the Purification of the Blessed Virgin Mary in a field called Northfield; this right is given to John Wright, master or warden of the hospital of Saint Nicholas outside Walmgate Bar, to the brothers and sisters of that hospital, and to their successors. This field lay outside of Walmgate Bar between the land known as Haworth garths and belonging to Henry Boynton, esquire, on the east, and lands of William Gascoign and James Charleton on the west. We, the mayor and commonalty, at the request of Richard III, have remised, released and entirely quitclaimed forever for us and our heirs all right and claim to the pasture that we had, have, or in any way henceforth could have, to the master or warden, the brothers and sisters of the hospital, and their successors in perpetuity. So that neither we nor our successors nor anyone in our name may be able henceforth to demand any right or lay any claim to any pasture in Northfield, and so that it be well lawful for the hospital to enclose the pasture with hedges and ditches, we have affixed the common seal to the present grant. Given at York 26 March 1484.)]

[f.19v] Exemptions from Officeholding
27 March 1484

Discharge of John Northeby of all maner of officez etc.

Omnibus Christi fidelibus ad quos hoc presens scriptum pervenerit, maior et communitas civitatis Ebor' salutem. Sciatis nos propter pias et honestas causas nos in Johannem Northeby de E[bor'] bocher moventes ac pro quadam summa pecunie per ipsum Johannem nobis premanibus soluta in relevamen et sustentacionem plurimorum onerum civitatis predicte concessisse per presentes eidem Johanni quod ab hac die in antea ab omni officio et statu electivo in civitate predicta exoneratus existit, et quod de cetero non elegatur nec assumatur in maiorem, custodem, vicecomitem, aldermannum, constabularium nec collectorem taxe sive misse aut aliquod aliud officium sive aliquam (aliq) aliam occupacionem electivam aliquo tempore infuturum contra ipsius voluntatem ponetur nec compellatur per nos seu successores nostros in eadem civitate, et quod ad parliamentum seu parliamenta aut aliquos alios labores forinsecos contra ipsius voluntatem in aliquo compellatur sed de eisdem pro perpetuo sit quietus, ita tamen quod in omnibus et singulis aliis omnibus ad dominum nostrum regem nos que et civitatem predictam singulis futuris temporibus pro toto tempore more suo inter nos una nobiscum contributor sit et partem suam gerens debitam conferat porcionem presenti scriptura in aliqua non obstante. In cuius rei testimonium presentibus sigillum nostrum commune presentibus est appensum. Datum vicesimo septimo die mensis Marcii anno regni regis Ricardi tercii post conquestum Anglie primo.

[The mayor and commonalty of York, to all Christ's faithful to whose notice these presents [letters] shall come, greetings. Let it be known that we were moved for the most honest reasons and a certain sum of money paid by him for the relief of many city burdens, to grant exemption to butcher John Northeby from all civic offices, including the offices of mayor, keeper, sheriff, aldermen,

constable and tax collector, and that he not be compelled to attend parliament or
other labors outside the city against his will, unless he so wishes it. In testimony
of which we affix the common seal, 27 March 1484.]

[f.20] Discharge of (Raulyn Peuterer) ⟨Richard Robynson late of Thyrsk⟩ of all
manere of officez etc.

Omnibus Christi fidelibus ad quos hoc presens scriptum pervenerit, Thomas
Wrangwyssh maior civitatis Ebor', Ricardus York, Willelmus Snawsell, Johannes
Tong, Johannes Fereby, Willelmus Welles, Robertus Amyas, Willelmus Todd,
(Rich) Ricardus Hardsang et Willelmus Barker vicecomes civitatis predicte,
Willelmus Chymney, Thomas Scotton, Willelmus Spence, Willelmus Tayte,
Ricardus Clerk, Ricardus (Hardsang) Marston, Johannes Hagg, Michael White et
Milo Grenebank, salutem. Sciatis nos propter pias et honestas causas nos in
Ricardum Robynson nuper de Thrisk moventes ac eciam pro quadam summa
pecunie per ipsum Ricardum Robynson nobis premanibus soluta in relevamen et
sustentacionem plurimorum civitatis predicte concessisse eidem Ricardo quod ab
die in antea ab ei officio et statu electivo in civitate predicta [ex]oneratus existit, et
quod de cetero non elegatur nec assumatur in maiorem, custodem, vicecomitem,
aldermannum, constabularium nec collectorem taxe sive misse aut aliquod aliud
officium sive aliquam aliam occupacionem electivam aliquo tempore infuturum
contra ipsius voluntatem ponetur nec compellatur per nos seu successores nostros
in eadem civitate, et quod ad parliamentum seu parliamenta aut aliquos alios
labores forinsecos contra ipsius voluntatem in aliquo compellatur sed de eisdem pro
perpetuo sit quietus, ita tamen quod in omnibus et singulis omnibus ad dominum
nostrum regem nosque et civitatem predictam singulis futuris temporibus pro toto
tempore more suo inter nos una nobiscum contributor sit et partem suam gerens
debitam conferat porcionem presenti scriptura in aliquo non obstante. In cuius rei
testimonium sigillum nostrum officii maioratus civitatis predicte presentibus apposuimus. Datum vicesimo septimo die Mercii anno regni regis Ricardi tercii post
conquestum Anglie primo.

[Discharge of Richard Robynson from all civic offices, in the form preceding, 27
March 1484.]

[f.20v]   **Exemption from City Offices**
                     16 March 1484

Disshcharge of Raynald Hall peuterer for all manere of offices etc.

Omnibus hoc scriptum visuris vel audituris maior et (commun') communitas
civitatis Ebor' salutem in Domino sempiternam. Noverit universitas vestra quod
nos considerantes diversas infirmitates in quibus honestus concivis noster Reginaldus Hall alias (dictus) Rawlyn Hall de Ebor' peuterer detentus est necnon propter
alias pias et honestas causas in hac parte nos moventes, et eciam pro decem libris
quas idem Reginaldus in relevamen et sustentacionem plurimorum onerum civitatis

predicte nobis nobis [sic] premanibus solvit quantum in nobis est pro nobis et
successoribus nostris eidem Reginaldo concedimus per presentes quod ab hac die in
antea (in antea) ab omni officio et statu electivo in civitate predicta exoneratus
existit, et quod de cetero non elegatur nec assumatur in maiorem, custodem,
vicecomitem, aldermannum, constabularium nec collectorem taxe sive misse aut
aliquod aliud officium sive aliquam aliam occupacionem electivam aliquo tempore
infuturum contra ipsius voluntatem ponetur nec compellatur per nos seu successores nostros in eadem civitate, et quod ad parliamentum seu parliamenta aut
aliquos alios labores forinsecos contra ipsius voluntatem in aliquo compellatur sed
de eisdem pro perpetuo sit quietus, ita tamen quod in omnibus et singulis aliis
omnibus ad dominum nostrum regem nos que et civitatem predictam singulis
futuris temporibus pro ⟨toto⟩ tempore more suo inter nos una nobiscum
contributor sit et partem suam gerens debitam conferat porcionem presenti
scriptura in aliqua non obstante. In cuius rei testimonium sigillum nostrum
commune presentibus est appensum. Datum xvj die mensis Marcii anno regni regis
Ricardi tercii post conquestum Anglie primo.

[Discharge of pewterer Reginald Hall from all civic offices, in the form
preceding, 16 March 1484, for reason of his illness.]

[ff.21–22 blank]

[f.22v]   **Incomplete and Cancelled Entries**
                 25 April 1484

Prior Sancte Trinitatis et magister gilde (Sancti) Corporis Christi

Memorandum quod xxv^mo die mensis Aprilis anno regni regis Ricardi tercii post
conquestum Anglie primo [incomplete]

Payment for Stone and Lime
8 May 1484

Henry Albayn and Robert Davyson [entry struck through] (Memorandum that thar
was deliwyrd to Henr' Albayn and Robert Davyson mason the viij^th day of May to
by with ston and lym xx s.)

Sale of Poultry in City
8 May 1484

poulters Memorandum that John Hardyng, William Murows, Johannes Dykson
and Johannes Webster poulters had in commaundment the viij^th day of May by my
lord the mair that thay shall sell soch poultre as tha bryng to thys cite acordyng to

the proclamacion of the mair, upon the payn of xl d. to be payd by ichon of thaim duyng the contrary etc.

[f.23]   Bond to Accept Arbitration
27 March 1484

Willelmus Bulmer wever et Thomas Bakhows cobler

Memorandum quod xxvij° die Marcii anno regni regis Ricardi tercii post conquestum Anglie primo Willelmus Bulmer de E[bor'] wever et Thomas Bakhous de Ebor' cobler venerunt coram Thoma Wrangways maiore civitatis Ebor' et obligentur se domino regi in C solidis stare [et] obedire arbitrio, ordinacioni et judicio Johannis Hoton de E[bor'] potter et Ricardi Brigewater de et super omnimodis accionibus, transgressionibus, querelis, debitis, debatis et contraversiis quibuscumque inter partes predictas; et arbitrium, ordinacionem et judicium dictorum arbitratorum utreque partes predicte impleverint citra diem Dominicam in Ramispalmarum, et si dicti arbitratores arbitrium suum non reddant citra dictum diem quod extunc si dicte partes steterunt arbitrio maioris predicti infra iiij°ʳ dies tunc proximos sequentes et quod uterque illorum conservent pacem domini regis citra dictum diem Dominicam ⟨sub pena C solidorum⟩ quod extunc etc. (iij gar')

[On 27 March 1484, weaver William Bulmer and cobbler Thomas Bakhous came before the mayor and bound themselves for 100 s. to abide by the judgement of potter John Hoton and Richard Brigewater over all actions, complaints and crimes between them. The judgement is to be given by Palm Sunday, and if the arbiters cannot agree then the mayor will make a decision within four days. The two parties are to keep the peace until Palm Sunday.]

Incomplete Memorandum
20 May 1484

Memorandum quod xxᵐᵒ die mensis Maii anno regni regis Ricardi tercii post conquestum primo, Johannes Sponer de E[bor'] yoman et Willelmus Hogeson de E[bor'] armorer [incomplete]

[f.23v]   Royal Writ to Excuse Aged Pikemaker from Assize Duty
23 November 1483

Pro Henrico Watson pykmaker quod non ponetur in assisis nec juratis

Ricardus Dei gracia rex Anglie et Francie et dominus Hibernie, maiori et vicecomitibus civitatis Ebor', salutem. Cum de communi consilio regni nostri Anglie provisum sit quod homines sexaginta et decem annorum excedentes non ponantur in assisis, iuratis seu recognicionibus aliquibus, vobis mandamus quod si

Henricus Watson de civitate predicta pykemonger etatem predictam excesserit tunc ipsum Henricum in assisis, iuratis seu recognicionibus aliquibus non ponatis seu poni faciatis contra formam provisionis predicte, et districtionem si quam idem Henricum ea occasione ceperites sine dilacione relaxetes eidem. Teste me ipso apud Westm' xxiijᵒ die Novembris anno regni nostri primo.

Blakwall

[For Henry Watson, pikemaker, so that he not serve on assizes or juries:

Richard, etc., to the mayor and sheriffs of York, greetings. Whereas our royal council has determined that men aged seventy and more are not to be put on any assizes, juries or inquests, we command that if Henry Watson is over that age he be excused from that duty. Witnessed by me at Westminster 23 November 1483. [Subscribed] Blakwall]

Recording of Deeds and Acts of Parliament
4 May 1484

Milo Willstorp et Thomas Metham Memorandum quarto die Maii anno primo regni regis Ricardi tercii Milo Willsthorp armiger habuit duo scripta indentata excepli-ficata [*sic*] sub sigillo officii per Thomam Meitham militem facta prefato ⟨Miloni⟩ (Milonem tenores) tenores quorum patent in registro cum le crucifix desuper in fine eiusdem registri.

acta parliamenti Acta parliamenti edita primo anno regni regis Ricardi tercii irrotulentur in libro cum le crucefix desuper quasi in fine libri.

[*Miles Willstorp and Thomas Metham* On 4 May 1484, esquire Miles Willsthorp had two indented deeds copied under official seal made by Thomas Meitham, knight, the tenor of which is found at the end of the register with the crucifix on it.

act of parliament An act of parliament made during the reign of Richard III is recorded at the end of the book with the crucifix on it.]

[f.24]   Innholders' Contribution to Corpus Christi Pageant
28 April 1484

John Strynger, Robert Shyrley and Androw Blyth that haith taykyn the charge of (brynge) bryngyng furth of the pagient of the inholders

inholders what tha shall pay for pagent sylwyr Memorandum that the xxviijᵗʰ ⟨day⟩ of the moneth of Aprill in the furst yere of the reing of Kyng Richard the thyrd (John Strynger) ⟨William Robynson inholder⟩ Robert Shirley glasier

⟨and inholder⟩ and Androw Blyth wever ⟨and Adam Siggeswik barbour⟩
come a (fore) fore Thomas Wrangwysh then beyng mair of thys cite ⟨of York⟩
and by the assent of all the inholders of thys ⟨said⟩ cite tuke apon them to bryng
furth yerly duryng the term of viij yere then next ffilluyng the pagent of the
coronacion of our lady [blank] pertenyng to the said inholders and also to reparell
the said paghant so that they that holdes inys and (kepys) ⟨haith⟩ no syns (have)
pay as wele ⟨and asmoch yerly⟩ to the reparacion of the said pagent and
brynging furth of the same as the said inholders that haith syns doyth, that is to say
every of them by the yere iiij d., and that also every person that gyrsys horsys of
strangers that comys to thys cite pay in lykwys every yere iiij d. for bryngyng furth
of the said pagiant and and [sic] that also the said (John Strynger) ⟨William
Robynson⟩ Robert Shyrley and Androw Blyth have yerely of the chambyr of thys
cite duryng the said viij yere for bryng furth of the said pagiant acordyng to the
ordinaunce ther of maid, that is to say yerly ij s.

[f.24v]   Names of City Wardens
August 1485 X August 1486

Nomina gardianorum (ten' de Walmgat) anno regni regis (Ricardi) Henrici vij°
(tercii) post conquestum primo:

[Names of the wardens from the first year of the reign of Henry VII:]

Walmgat: Thomas Wrangwyssh, Johannes Harper, Willelmus White, (Willelmus Lame,
Thomas Scotton, Nicholaus Lancaster, Johannes Harper) Thomas Catour, (Thomas Scotton) Willelmus Tayt, (Rogerus Appilby).

Mounkbarr: Willelmus Snawsell, Nicholaus Lancastre, (Willelmus Tod, Johannes Lightlop)
Henricus Williamson, Thomas Fynsh (Johannes Harper, Johannes Ulet).

Bowthom: Johannes Tong, Willelmus Welles, Thomas Allayn, Willelmus Spence, Milo
Grenebank.

Castilgat: (Robertus Amyas) Willelmus Chymney, (Willelmus Chyney Chymney, Johannes
Harper) Ricardus Hardsang [et] Willelmus Barker vicecomites, Ricardus Clerk, Johannes
Gilyot.

Mikyllyth: Ricardus York, Robertus Hancok, (Ricardus Marston) Johannes Hagg,
Nicholaus (Pereson) Vicars.

Posterin de (Skeldergate) Northstrete: Johannes Fereby, Johannes Newton, Michell White
(Willelmus White).

Mayor Orders Aldermen and Wardens to Summon 24 Men to Court
7 May 1484

preceptum factum per maiorem, gardianis pro curia tenenda Thomas Wrangwysh
maior civitatis Ebor', Ricardo York et Roberto Hancok aldermannis, Ricardo

Marston et Johanni Hag, salutem. Ex parte domini regis vobis mando quod venire facias coram vobis in curia wardanrie vestre de Myklyth ibidem tenenda die Veneris proximo futuro post datam presentem xxiiij^{or} probos et legales homines wardanrie vestre predicte et de qualibus parochiis eiusdem wardanrie quatuor homines et constabularii ad audiendum et faciendum ea que eis ex parte dicti domini regis adtunc et ibidem immigentur. Teste prefato maiore apud Ebor' vij^o die Maii anno regni regis Ricardi tercii post conquestum Anglie primo.

Mynskip T[homas Wrangwysh?]

> [*precept made by the mayor, to the wardens holding court* Mayor Thomas Wrangwysh, to aldermen Richard York and Robert Hancok, and to Richard Marston and John Hag, greetings. On behalf of the king, I command you to cause to come [*venire facias*] before you in the court of the ward of Micklegate held next Friday twenty-four good and lawful men of your ward, and four men and the constable from each parish, to listen and to do justice. Witnessed by the mayor at York, 7 May 1484. [Subscribed] Mynskip T.]

[ff.25–25v blank]

[f.26] **Bond to Accept Arbitration**
1 June 1484

Recognitio Ricardi Croklyng et Elezabethe Hamond

Memorandum quod primo die Junii anno primo regni regis Ricardi tercii, Ricardus Croklyng de Ebor' fflech[er] et Elezabetha Hamond venerunt coram Thoma Wrangwysh tunc maiore civitatis Ebor' et obligerunt se et uterque eorum obligavit se domino regi in x libris quod ipsi et eorum uterque stabit et obedierit arbetrio, ordinacioni et judicio Johannis Skelton, Christofori Thomlynson, Thome Tutbac et Thome Wattson litster, arbitratorum inter dictum Ricardum Croklyng ex parte una et ⟨et⟩ dictam Elezabetham ex parte altera indifferenter electorum ad arbitrandum ordinandum et judicandum inter partes predictas de et super omnimodis accionibus, sectis, querelis ⟨et⟩ debaitis et demandis inter partes predictas motis, habitis sive pendentibus racione quacumque a principio mundi usque in diem confeccionis presencium. Et quod partes predictas et eorum uterque arbitrium, ordinacionem et judicium dictorum arbitratorum (perimplient) inter partes predictas ⟨de premissis⟩ fienda bene et fideliter perimpl(a)ent et eorum uterque perimpliet, ita quod arbitrium, ordinacio et judicium dictorum arbitratorum fiant et reddantur in premissis citra diem Dominicam appellatam Trenite Sunday proximo futuram sub pena predicta per ipsum contrarium huius recognissiones facientem etc.

> [Bond of Richard Croklyng and Elizabeth Hamond:
>
> On 1 June 1484, fletcher Richard Croklyng and Elizabeth Hamond came before

the mayor and bound themselves for £10 to abide by the judgement of John Skelton, Christopher Thomlynson, Thomas Tutbac and Thomas Wattson, impartially chosen to determine all actions and complaints moved, had, or pending between them from the beginning of the world to the day these presents are made. The judgement is to be made by Trinity Sunday next coming under the aforesaid penalty.]

[f.26v]   Delivery of Armor
5 June 1484

Delyverd to Richard Walsheforth armorer ij compleit whit hernes except j pare of (gauntlittes) bumbardes and ij par of gantlittes, the vth day of Junii the first yere of K[ing] Richard third and also wantyng a gorget of male.

Bond to Keep the Peace
Undated

Manucapcio pro Willelmo Baker clerico quod ipso aliquod dampnum vel malum corporale non faciet nec fieri procurabit in aliquem populum domini nostri regis; Jacobus Kirk, Nicholaus Maland, Johannes Gilmyn et Thomas Kendell litster sub pena prefati Willelmi xx librarum et cuiuslibet manucaptorum x librarum etc.

[Mainprise for clerk William Baker that he do no damage nor bodily harm to any of the king's subjects under penalty of £20. James Kirk, Nicholas Maland, John Gilmyn and Thomas Kendell were each bound for £10 as sureties.]

Bond to Keep the Peace
14 February 1486

recognitio Memorandum quod xiiij° die Februarii anno regni regis Henrici vij primo, Thomas Wright ffisshmonger venit coram Nicholao Lancaster maiore civitatis Ebor' et obligavit se domino nostro regi in decem libris legalis monete Anglie solvendis eidem domino nostro regi si ipsum contingat imposterum transgressionibus, verbis, operibus vel factis versus Johannem Carter aut aliquem alium de populo domini regis etc.

[*bond* On 14 February, fishmonger Thomas Wright came before the mayor and bound himself for £10 to keep the peace in word and deed towards John Carter and all the king's subjects.]

[f.27] **Delivery of Books and Vestments to Foss Bridge Priest
11 June 1494**

Memorandum that the xj[th] day of Juny the ix[th] yere of the regni regis [*sic*] Henry
vij[th] thes parcels ensuyng tofore the right wurshipfull sir Michaell White mair of the
citie of York wer delivered unto sir Thomas Graunger morn mese prest at Fosse
brigge: in primis mesebouke, a chalez weyng [*blank*], a corperaux with (a case)
layse, a ⟨hole⟩ vestyment of paynted cloth with alb and stolez, a vestyment of
rede burd Alexandre without albe, a vestyment of whyte bustian with an old albe
and stolez.

[f.27v blank]

[f.28] **Orders for Keeping the Peace During Mayoralty of Nicholas Lancaster
February 1485 X February 1486**

Precepta pro securitate pacis et supersideas facta tempore Nicholai Lancastre
maioris civitatis Ebor'

Preceptum est vicecomitibus quod capiunt Willelmum Greve et Katerinam Ive pro
securitate pacis ad sectam dompni Willelmi Pikering etc.

Manucapcio dompni Willelmi Pikeryng quod ipse dampnum corporale non faciet
nec fieri procurabit quovismodo in ullum populum domini regis etc.; Johannes
Fery.

Preceptum pacis contra Ricardum Wardall ad sectam Magistri Willelmi Thomeson
etc.

Manucapcio pro Ricardo Wardall quod ipse dampnum non faciet in dictum
Magistrum Willelmum Thomeson; Thomas Walas, Johannes Dicson.

Capias Johannem Thomeson pro securitate pacis ad sectam Johannis Broket, etc.

Capias Willelmum Cooke pro securitate pacis ad sectam Johannis Newball alias
Smyth, etc.

Manucapcio Willelmi Cooke quod ipse dampnum etc., non faciet in Johannem
Newbald alias Smyth seu cunctum populum domini regis, etc.

Manucapcio Johannis Newbald alias Smyth quod ipse dampnum etc., non faciet in
Willelmum Cooke aut aliquem alium de populo domini regis.

[f.28v] Capias Thomam Yotten pro corporale ad sectam Ricardi Blakbourne de
Ebor', etc.

Manucapcio Johannis Birkhede quod ipse dampnum ⟨vel⟩ malum corporale in Johannem Anderson.

Capias Johannem Anderson pro corporale ad sectam Johannis Birkhede, etc.

Manucapcio dicti Johannis Anderson quod ipse dampnum vel malum aliquod corporale in Johannem Birkhede non faciet etc., videlicet [*incomplete*]

Capias Thomam Carter ad sectam Alicie Lille, etc.

Capias Willelmum Croulle capellanum ad sectam Johannis Ellys shipwright etc.

[Orders for keeping of the peace and [writs of] supersedeas made during the mayoralty of Nicholas Lancastre:

Order that the sheriffs take William Greve and Katherine Ive for the keeping of the peace, at the suit of lord William Pikering.

Mainprise of lord William Pikeryng that he do no harm to any of the king's subjects. John Fery [as surety?].

Order to proceed against Richard Wardall at the suit of Master William Thomeson.

Mainprise for Richard Wardall that he do no harm to Master William Thomeson. Thomas Wallas and John Dicson [as sureties?].

Order to proceed against John Thomeson for the keeping of the peace, at the suit of John Broket.

Order to proceed against William Cooke for the keeping of the peace, at the suit of John Newball alias Smyth.

Mainprise of William Cooke that he do no harm to John Newbald alias Smyth or to anyone else.

Mainprise of John Newbald alias Smyth that he do no harm to William Cooke or to anyone else.

[**f.28v**] Order for arrest of Thomas Yotten at the suit of Richard Blakbourne.

Mainprise of John Birkhede that he do no harm to John Anderson.

Order for arrest of John Anderson at the suit of John Birkhede.

Mainprise of John Anderson that he do no harm to John Birkhede.

Order to proceed against Thomas Carter at the suit of Alice Lille.

Order to proceed against chaplain William Croulle at the suit of shipwright John Ellys.]

[f.29]   **Orders for Keeping the Peace**
                   1485 X 1486

Capias Willelmum Lambe de Ebor' barbour ad sectam [*incomplete*]

Manucapcio domini Willelmi Croulle quod ipse dampnum vel malum aliquod corporale in Johannem Ellys non faciet; Johannes Walker porter, Johannes Priket burneleder et Johannes Steveneson etc., quilibet eorum in x libris et dictus dominus Willelmus in xx libris solvendis domino regi etc.

Capias Johannem Rayner capellanum ad sectam Willelmi Robynson, etc.

Manucapcio dicti Johannis Rayner quod ipse dampnum vel malum aliquod corporale in Willelmum Robynson ⟨non faciet⟩ videlicet Rogerus Fissher, Simon Brigges, Willelmus Post et Thomas Lyvewray etc., quilibet eorum in x libris et dictus Johannes Rayner in xx libris etc., solvendis domino regi etc.

Capias Johannem Watson mynstrell ad sectam Willelmi Plommer etc.

Manucapcio Johannis Watson quod ipse dampnum vel malum aliquod corporale in Willelmum Plommer non faciet nec fieri procurabit; Johannes Topshaw sadler, Willelmus Gilmyn bocher, Ricardus Standisshe et Thomas Knayton etc., quilibet eorum in x libris et dictus Johannes Watson in xx libris.

[f.29v] Capias Willelmum Byngley pro securitate pacis ad sectam Johannis Banes, etc.

Capias Thomam Raper ad sectam Willelmi Hewbanke de Ebor'.

Manucapcio dicti Willelmi quod ipse dampnum vel malum aliquod corporale in Thomam Raper aut aliquem alium de populo domini regis non faciet etc.; Christoforus Bentley, Ricardus Deene, Ricardus Bell et Willelmus Wright etc., quilibet eorum in x libris et idem Willelmus in xx libris.

Capias Thomam Wilson ⟨et Margaretam Wilson⟩ ad sectam Johannis Chapman, etc.

Manucapcio dicti Johannis Chapman quod ipse dampnum etc., in aliquem populum domini regis non faciet etc.; Thomas Fynche, Johannes Bukyll et Thomas Howe etc., quilibet eorum in x libris et dictus Johannes Chapman in xx libris, etc.

[Order to proceed against barber William Lambe at the suit of [*incomplete*]

Mainprise of William Croulle that he do no damage nor bodily harm to John Ellys under penalty of £20. John Walker, John Priket, and John Steveneson were each bound for £10 as sureties.

Order to proceed against chaplain John Rayner at the suit of William Robynson.

Mainprise of John Rayner that he do no harm to William Robynson, under penalty of £20. Roger Fissher, Simon Brigges, William Post, and Thomas Lyvewray were each bound for £10 as sureties.

Order to proceed against minstrel John Watson at the suit of William Plommer.

Mainprise of John Watson that he do no harm to William Plommer under penalty of £20. John Topshaw, William Gilmyn, Richard Standisshe, and Thomas Knayton were each bound for £10 as sureties.

[**f.29v**] Order to proceed against William Byngley for the keeping of the peace, at the suit of John Banes.

Order to proceed against Thomas Raper at the suit of William Hewbanke.

Mainprise of William that he do no harm to Thomas Raper or to anyone else, under penalty of £20. Christopher Bentley, Richard Deene, Richard Bell and William Wright were each bound for £10 as sureties.

Order to proceed against Thomas Wilson and Margaret Wilson at the suit of John Chapman.

Mainprise of John Chapman that he do no harm to anyone under penalty of £20. Thomas Fynche, John Bukyll, and Thomas Howe were each bound for £10 as sureties.]

[**f.30**]   **Bonds to Keep the Peace, Writ of Supersedeas**
                  1 February 1486

Manucapcio Margarete Wilson quod ipsa dampnum vel malum aliquod corporale in Johannem Chapman etc.; videlicet Willelmus Hall, Johannes Robynson et Thomas Walles etc., quilibet eorum in x libris et predicta Margareta in xx libris etc.

Manucapcio Willelmi Pigot quod ipse dampnum vel malum aliquod corporale etc., in aliquem populum domini regis non faciet; Johannes Barwik, Willelmus Notingham, Willelmus Fulford et Ricardus Wright etc., quilibet eorum in x libris et predictus Willelmus in xx libris. Qui quidem Willelmus Pigot primo die Februarii anno regni regis Henrici vij^{mi} primo coram Nicholao Lancastre maiore predicto personaliter comparens breve de supersedeas alias directum vicecomitibus civitatis Ebor' de non molestando eundem Willelmum Pygot occasione alicuius securitatis pacis remanente in cameram concilii dicte civitatis cancellandum restituit. Et deinde dictos Johannem Barwik, Willelmum Notingham, Willelmum Fulford et Ricardum Wright manucaptores dicti Willelmi Pigot in hac parte remisit.

[Mainprise of Margaret Wilson that she do no harm to John Chapman under penalty of £20. William Hall, John Robynson, and Thomas Walles were each bound for £10 as sureties.

Mainprise of William Pigot that he do no harm to any of the king's subjects under penalty of £20. John Barwik, William Notingham, William Fulford, and Richard Wright act as his sureties under penalty of £10 each. On 1 February 1486, William Pigot came before the mayor bearing a writ of *supersedeas* directed to the sheriffs of York, by which he and his sureties had their bonds restored.]

[f.30v blank]

[f.31]   Bonds to Keep Peace
February 1486 X February 1487

Precepta pacis ac supersideas emanant tempore Willelmi Chymney maioris civitatis Ebor' anno regis Henrici vij primo

Preceptum est etc., quod attachias etc., Johannem New etc., ad sectam Johannis Fernour alias Cook etc.

Manucapcio Johannis Newe quod ipse dampnum vel malum aliquod corporale in Johannem Fernour alias Cooke seu aliquem alium populum domini regis non faciet nec fieri procurabit quovismodo videlicet Johannes Holme yoman, Willelmus Caton et Johannes Smyth alias Atkynson videlicet quilibet eorum in x libris et predictus Johannes Fernour in xx libris solvendis domino regi.

[Orders for keeping the peace and writs of supersedeas during the mayoralty of William Chymney during the first year of Henry VII's reign

Order is made, etc. to arrest John New at the suit of John Fernour alias Cook.

Mainprise of John Newe that he do no harm to John Fernour alias Cooke or to anyone else on pain of £20. John Holme, William Caton, and John Smyth alias Atkynson were each bound for £10 as sureties.]

Minstrel and Fisherman Warned to Keep the Peace
1 and 9 September 1486

Memorandum quod primo die Septembris anno regni regis Henrici vij^{mo} (primo) secundo Willelmus Chymney maior etc., monuit eundem Johannem Watson minstrell et districte nomine domini regis precepit eidem quod ipse dampnum aliquod corporale seu gravamen quodcumque in Johannem Comylton de Ebor' minstrell non faciet nec fieri procurabit quovismodo sub pena xl librarum domino nostro regi forisfaciendarum etc.

Memorandum quod ix° die Septembris anno regis Henrici vij secundo Willelmus Chymney maior etc., monuit (An) Johannem Sawnder ffissher et districte nomine domini regis precepit eidem quod ipse dampnum aliquod corporale seu gravamen quodcumque in Willelmum Radcliff merchaunt non faciet nec fieri procurabit quovismodo sub pena xl librarum domini nostro regi forisfaciendarum etc.

[On 1 September 1486, minstrel John Watson was strictly warned and commanded in the king's name that he cause no injury to John Comylton, minstrel of York, under penalty of £40.

On 9 September 1486, fisherman John Sawnder was strictly warned and commanded in the king's name that he cause no injury to merchant William Radcliff under penalty of £40.]

[f.31v]   **Arrests Ordered**
               February 1488 X February 1489

Preceptum est vicecomitibus quod attachiant Marmaducum Clarnax generosum ad sectam Johannis Chapman de Ebor' datum septimo die [*incomplete*]

[The sheriffs are ordered to arrest Marmaduke Clarnax, gentleman, at the suit of John Chapman of York, on the seventh day [*incomplete*]]

Tempore venerabilis viri Roberti Hancok maioris civitatis Ebor'

Preceptum capias Johannem Sissotson de Firthby in parochia de Wistowe in comitatu Ebor' husbondman ad sectam Emmote Botterell.

[During the mayoralty of the venerable Robert Hancok:

Order to arrest husbandman John Sissotson of Firthby in the parish of Westow, Yorkshire, at the suit of Emmotte Botterell.]

Bond to Keep the Peace
2 June 1488

secundo die Junii anno tercio regni regis Henrici vij Manucapcio Johannis Sissotson
de Firthby in parochia de Wistowe in comitatu Ebor' husband[man] quod ipse
dampnum vel malum aliquod corporale predicto Emmoto Boterell vel alicui de
populo domini regis non faciet nec fieri procurabit quovismodo, videlicet Edwardus
Bygod armiger et Ricardus Estwod pistor cuiuslibet eorum sub pena x librarum, et
predictus Johannes Sissotson sub pena xx librarum domino nostro regi forisfaciendarum.

[*2 June 1488* Mainprise of husbandman John Sissotson of Firthby in the parish of
Wistow that he do no harm to Emmotte Boterell or to anyone else under penalty
of £20. Edward Bygod, esquire, and Richard Estwod, fisherman, were each
bound for £10 as sureties.]

[ff.32–33v blank]

[f.34]   Proceedings for Arrests, Bonds to Keep the Peace
**   February 1487 X February 1488**

Precepta pacis et subsideas [*sic*] emanant tempore venerabilis viri Willelmi Todd
civitatis Ebor' maioris anno regni regis Henrici septimi secundo

Preceptum est vicecomitibus quod capiunt per corpus Mathei Conyngham ad
sectam Willelmi Skelton.

Manucapcio Willelmi Skelton quod ipse dampnum vel malum aliquod corporale in
Mattheum Conyngham seu aliquem alium de populo domini regis non faciet etc.;
Thomas Hamblyn, Johannes Frauncesse, Willelmus Tilson et Robertus Jacson
quilibet manucaptorum obligavit se ⟨domino nostro regi⟩ in in [*sic*] x libris et
dictus Willelmus in xx libris de bonis et catallis suis ad opus eiusdem domini regis
levandis.

Preceptum est vicecomitibus quod capiunt Eliam Bell clericum ad sectam Roberti
Horblyn etc.

Manucapcio Elie Bell quod ipse dampnum vel malum aliquod corporale in
Robertum Horblyn vel aliquem alium vel populo domini nostri regis non faciet nec
fieri procurabit quovismodo, videlicet Ricardus Thorneton, Johannes Williamson,
Willelmus Mitford et Robertus Goldsmyth quilibet manucaptorum obligavit se
domino nostro regi in x libris et dictus (Willelmus) Elias in xx libris de bonis et
catallis suis ad opus eiusdem domini regis levandis.

Manucapcio (Rippas) Ed'i Rippas quod ipse dampnum vel malum aliquod corporale in Robertum York (alias) vel aliquem alium de populo domini nostri regis non faciet nec fieri procurabit quovismodo, videlicet Johannes Gudewyn, Johannes Gorrasse, Willelmus Ellerbek et Edmundus Vertee quilibet manucaptorum obligavit se domino nostro regi in x libris et dictus Ed'us in xx libris de bonis et catallis suis ad opus eiusdem domini regis levandis.

Preceptum est vicecomitibus quod capiunt Willelmum Towthorp capellanum ad sectam Ricardi Thorp capellani etc.

[Orders for keeping the peace and writs of *supersedeas* during the mayoralty of the venerable William Todd in the second year of Henry VII's reign

The sheriffs are ordered to arrest Matthew Conyngham at the suit of William Skelton.

Mainprise of William Skelton that he do no damage nor bodily harm to Matthew Conyngham or to anyone else, under penalty of £20 levied of his goods and chattels. Thomas Hamblyn, John Frauncesse, William Tilson, and Robert Jacson were each bound for £10 as sureties.

The sheriffs are ordered to arrest clerk Elias Bell at the suit of Robert Horblyn.

Mainprise of Ellis Bell that he do no harm to Robert Horblyn or to anyone else, under penalty of £20 levied of his goods and chattels. Richard Thorneton, John Williamson, William Mitford, and Robert Goldsmyth were each bound for £10 as sureties.

Mainprise of Ed' Rippas that he do no harm to Robert York or to anyone else, under penalty of £20 levied of his goods and chattels. John Gudewyn, John Corrasse, William Ellerbek and Edmund Vertee were each bound for £10 as sureties.

The sheriffs are ordered to arrest chaplain William Towthorp at the suit of chaplain Richard Thorp.]

[f.34v]   Bond to Keep the Peace, Later Cancelled
9 March and 27 June 1492

Tempore Thome Scotton maioris, ix^mo die Marcii [1492]

Manucapcio Briani Faucet et Reginaldi Jakez quod ipsi (dam) nec eorum alter dampnum vel malum corporale ⟨Petro Fraunk yoman nec⟩ alicui alio populo domini regis non facient nec fieri procurabunt nec eorum alter faciet nec fieri procurabit quovismodo ante proximam sessionem pacis in Guihald civitatis Ebor' tenendam etc., videlicet Johannes Clerk cord[wainer], Johannes Clerk bucher et Johannes Burton bucher videlicet quilibet manucaptorum predictorum sub pena x librarum et predicti Brianus et Reginaldus Jakez sub pena xx^ti librarum etc.

Vacat quia partes predicte concordate sunt et predictus Petrus ⟨postea, scilicet⟩ xxvij^{mo} die Junii anno (v) supradicto, ⟨venit⟩ coram dicto maiore in propria persona et relaxavit sectam suam racione securitatis predicte erga dictos Brianum et Reginaldum et petit ut ut [sic] inde relaxentur et manucaptores predicti exonerentur ad cuius peticiones predicti Brianus et Reginaldus ac manucaptores sui predicti penitus exonerantur etc.

[During the mayoralty of Thomas Scotton, 9 March 1492

Mainprise of Brian Faucet and Reginald Jakez that neither of them do any damage nor bodily harm to yeoman Peter Fraunk or to anyone else, before the next session of the peace is held in the Guildhall, under penalty of £20. John Clerk cordwainer, John Clerk butcher, and John Burton butcher were each bound for £10 as sureties.

[The above is] void because the parties reached agreement and Peter Fraunk came before the mayor and withdrew his suit on 27 June, and asked that the sureties be discharged from their bonds.]

Bond to Assure Presence at Next Sessions of the Peace
10 February 1494

Memorandum quod x^{mo} die Februarii anno regni regis Henrici vij^{mi} etc. nono, Johannes Stevenson ⟨de Ebor'⟩ carpenter [et] Willelmus Dymmet de Huntyngton in comitatu Ebor' wever in propriis personis suis venerunt coram Michaele White maiore civitatis Ebor' in camera concilii dicte civitatis et recognoverunt et eorum alter recognovit se debere Thome Darby (ac) et Johanni Custance vicecomitibus civitatis (Ebor') predicte viginti libras legalis monete Anglie solvendas in festo cathedre Sancti Petri apostoli proximo. Data istius recognitionis die et anno supradicto.

Conditio istius recougnitionis talis est quod si quedam Johanna Turnour de Ebor' spynster in propria persona sua comparuerit coram prefato maiore et sociis suis custodibus pacis etc., ad (p) proximam sessionem pacis in Guihald dicte civitatis tenendam ad respondendum domino regi super hiis que sibi tunc ibidem obicientur quod extra etc.

[On 10 February 1494, carpenter John Stevenson of York and weaver William Dymmet of Huntingdon, Yorks., came before the mayor in the council chamber and bound themselves for £20 to the sheriffs.

The condition of this bond is to assure the presence of Johanna Turnour, spinster of York, before the mayor and his associate keepers of the peace at the next session of the peace held in the Guildhall, to answer the lord king.]

[f.41]   **Delivery of Bill Listing Unauthorised Words**
                    5 May 1488

Die Lune v^to die Maii anno tercio regni regis Henrici vij^mi

Mayor: Robert Hancok. 12: Sir Richerd York k[night], John Tong, John Fereby, Master [Nicholas] Lancastre, William Chymney, John Harper, William White. Sheriffs: George Kirk, Robert Johnson. 24: Thomas Catour, Thomas Allan, William Tayt, Richard Clerk, Miles Grenebank, William Barker, Nicholas Vicars, Roger Appilby, Richard Burrow esquire.

At the which day oon John Calton delyverd a bill of the wordes the which oon Thomas Sturgeon of Lancaster shold say not sounding to the high pleasour and savegard of the kinges person, the tenour of the which bill ensueth [*bill not included*].

[f.41v]   **Treason Spoken Against Earl of Northumberland and Lord Strange**
                     5 May 1488

The same v^th day of May

And apon that both (the) within writen John Calton and Thomas Sturgeon was sent fore tofore the said presentes and the said John Calton shewed the articles of the said bill, (and) the same Thomas Sturgeon answerd and said as to the article that wher Sir Thomas Broghton shold of late aben a Ravenglasse he not that denyed; and as to that that (unto) ⟨at⟩ my lord of Northumberland and my lord Straunge wer all as oon, he denyed not that; and also to the article the which the said John laid ayanest hym that he shold say that the lord Straunge latelie was at Namptewich and thidder cam unto hym many of the gentilmen of Lancasshire and the constablez of the same, he that answerd and shewed it was true.

Item the same day William Thomson was sent for and cam, (wax) was examyned what language he hard Thomas Sturgeon say to John Calton in his house; he said he hard the said Sturgeon say that Sir Thomas Broghton bot late landid at Raven Glasse, to the which he answerd and said that ther wold noon say that bot false harlottes for he knewe that it was contrare, he was of Saynt George ⟨day⟩ ther. Item he hard the said Sturgeon say that my lord of Northumberland and my lorde Straunge wer all oon and wold be, and that we shold have a new chaunge be mydsomer day.

[ff.42–47 blank]

**[f.47v]   Lease of City Tenement to Weavers
7 June 1491**

Memorandum quod (x) vij° die Junii anno regni regis Henrici vij sexto maior et
(communitas) camerarii [?] dimiserunt Johanni Kyng aldermanno textorum et
⟨aliis⟩ textoribus huius civitatis unum tenementum cum pertinentiis super
Toftez proximum lez Pagiant Housez ibidem pro termino xlj annorum, reddendum
inde per annum xvj denarios, ita quod idem textores reparabunt et sustentabunt
dictum tenementum in omnibus durante termino predicto sumptibus suis propriis et
in fine termini bene et sufficienter reparatum dimittent.

[On 7 July 1491, the mayor and chamberlains leased to John Kyng, alderman of
the weavers, and to other weavers of York, a tenement with appurtenances on
the Tofts next to the Pageant House, for a term of 41 years, rendering annually
16 d. The weavers will repair and maintain the tenement during that time at their
own expense.]

[Various jottings follow; folio cropped after following entry]

**Shipman Loses Franchise
20 September 1493**

Memorandum that the Tuesday next after Holy Rode ⟨day⟩ my lord maier
tofore the chamberleyns and other in the counseill chambre opon Ouse brigg for
asmyche as Thomas Wryght shipman which had a ship with colys at the common
stathe and wold not pay and delivere a met colez to the chambre after the auncien
custome of this citie, ⟨for his periury⟩ and contry to his othe at his first
infraunchesyng discharged hym of his franchese fore here after without he make
fyne and come in agayne by redempcion.

**[f.48]   Bond to Keep the Peace
18 September 1487**

Memorandum quod octodecimo die mensis Septembris anno domino millesimo
quadringentesimo octogesimo vij^{mo} et regno regis Henrici septimi ij^{do} [sic]

Manucapcio Willelmi Dighton wirdrawer quod ipse dampnum vel malum aliquod
corporale in Reginaldum Holme seu alicui de populo domini regis non faciet nec
fieri procurabit quovismodo sub pena xl librarum de bonis.

[Mainprise of William Dighton, wiredrawer, that he do no damage nor bodily
harm to Reginald Holme or to any other of the king's subjects, under penalty of
£40.]

Disenfranchisement for Refusal to Deliver Coals to Chamber
17 September 1493

colles Memorandum that the Tuesday next after the fest of thexaltacion of the holy croce the ix[th] yere of regni regis [*sic*] Henry vij[th] within the counseill chambre opon Ousebrigge tofore the chamberleyns and al other comons officers of this citie, for somych as Thomas Wright shipman and fyschmonger havyng a bote with colys at the common stathe and wher of auncien custome of this citie it ⟨is⟩ used that every citicine of this citie ⟨havy⟩ bryngyng any coles to the said stathe to gif ones in avery yere a met colis unto the chambre and ⟨e⟩ of every foreyner as oft tymez as he cometh a met colis, the which met colis to delivere unto the porter to bryng unto the chambre; the said Thomas utterly refused ⟨and denyed⟩ for which denyd contrary ⟨to the said custome and for periury ⟨othe ab⟩ broke⟩ his othe maid at his first enfraunchesyng, my lord maier discharged the said Thomas of his fraunchesyng and that he in no wise shuld occupy within this citie a fraunchestman unto tyme he had maid fyne for his redempcion etc.

[f.48v]   Various Odd Jottings, Practice of Letters and Phrases
**   Undated**

[*The final folio of this volume is very worn and faded, containing only jotted letters and phrases, and splatters of ink.*]

HOUSE BOOK VOLUME 6
1486–1490

HOUSE BOOK VOLUME 6
1486–1490

[f.1]   **Election of Wardens, Attendance Policy, Disclosure of Council Business**
16 February 1486

Liber concilii inchoatus tempore Willelmi Chymney maioris civitatis Ebor' xvj° die mensis Februarii anno domini M°CCCC°lxxxv° et regni regis Henrici septimi primo

> [The book of the council, begun in the time of William Chymney, mayor of York, 16 February 1485 [*sic*], in the first year of Henry VII's reign]

Mayor: William Chymney. 12: William Snawsell, John Tong, John Fereby, William Welles, John Newton, Nicholas Lancastre, Thomas Scotton, John Harpar. Sheriffs: John Beverley, Roger Appilby. 24: Thomas Catour, Thomas Aleyne, William Spense, Richard Clerk, Michael White, William White, Miles Grenebank, Thomas Fynche.

[folio torn and faded on right margin, with loss of two to four words per line as indicated] Assembled hath [elected?] the wardans of evere ward, as in the othre sid of this leef appereth.

absentz and tard' And also that whosoever now being or for the tyme being of this counsaill warned that appears not personally in the counsail within a quarter of an owre after ix of the Mynster clok at everetyme shall pay ij d. And suche as be soo warned and appereth not at any tyme during the said counsail shall pay iiij d. And thofficer not them warning shall pay iiij d. to be leved furthwith by the maier for the tyme being.

discoverede counseill Also that who so ever of the said counsaill that wilfully herafter at any tyme distureth or opyneth to any persone or persones the counsail of the said citie and soo may be . . . by the discretion of the maier and the said counsaill for the tyme being shall pay without pardon or delay to the behove of the citie for every tyme xl s. And who ever of the said counsail laboreth for the relefe of the same or any part therof to paie also xl s., which ordinaunce shalbe executed unto the common clerk, mase berer and undre clerc of the cite for the tyme being. Moreover it is ordigned that the seriaunt to the masez shall se all the stretes clensid bifore Sonday next commyng. And that they shall furthwith commaunde . . . of evere parissh to yeve warnyng to all opyn boldes . . . **[f.1v]** and common chiders and othre misruled people to avode evere parissh out of the citie to the utter partes of the suburbs before Sonday in the secund weke of this Lent; and if they be not avoided be that day to certifie ther names furthwith to the wardans of the ward with there demenaunces and of all othre misruled fro tyme to tyme to thentent that they may see the due reformation herof.

Wardeyns

Walmegate: Thomas Wrangwisshe, Thomas Scotton, Thomas Catour, William Taite, Roger Appilby.

Monkebar: William Snawsell, Nicholas Lancastre, Henry Williamson, Thomas Fynche, John Gylliot.

Bowtham: Johannes Tong, William Welles, Thomas Alan, William Spense, Miles Grenebank.

Castelgate: Robert Amyas, William Chymney, John Harper, Richard Hardsang, William Barker, Richard Clerk.

Mikillith: Richard York, Robert Hancok, John Hagg, Thomas Pereson, Nicholas Vicars.

Posterne of North Strete: John Fereby, John Newton, Michael White, William White.

[*left margin faded and torn, with loss of one to two words as indicated*] . . . *empcion* . . . *counseill* Item that the same day and place it is ordigned that who soo ever he be of this chambre that . . . this counsaill assembled for any mater concernyng the prouffit or worship of the city woll use and effectually shewe his counsaill parcially in favour of any persone or persones . . . the said prouffit or worship and therupon be . . . by the . . . of the said counsaill shalbe for the first and secund tyme be punyshed . . . corretions and arbitrement of the forsaid counsaill and at the third tyme utterly expulsid out of thaccompany of the said counsaill without hope of readmission or reentre unto the same.

[f.2]   **Death of Recorder Miles Metcalf, Prior of Holy Trinity Claims Hospital of Saint Nicholas 29 February 1486**

Monday the xxix° day of February the first yere of the reigne of King Henry the vij[th] [*sic, 1486 was not a leap year*]

Mayor: William Chymney. 12: Thomas Wrangwisshe, William Snawsell, John Tong, John Fereby, William Welles, Nicholas Loncastre, Thomas Scotton, John Harper. Sheriffs: John Beverley, Roger Appilby. 24: Thomas Catour, Henry Williamson, Thomas Aleyne, William Tayte, Richard Clerc, William White, Michael White, Miles Grenebanke, Richard Hardsang, William Barker, John Gilyot, Thomas Fynche.

[*right margin faded with loss of one word per line as indicated*] Assembled in counsaill where [it was] desired by Richard Grene to have in rememberaunce the kinges lettres and the lettres of my lord of Northumberland with othre thinges attemptid herbifore in favour of the said Richard wolling to be admitted to the rowme of recordour of this citie, desiring in consideracion of the premissez and of that at the said rowme is now void by the deth of Miles Metcalf late recordour of the same whome God assole, to accept hyme unto the same shewing that he entendid to do in that part unto theme and the said citie hertly service with due attendaunce and personall aboide within the said citie; unto the which desire it was (desired) answerd that for the absence of Richard Yorke, Robert Hancok and othre aswell aldermen as othre of the counsaill wer absent and the . . . place also at this tyme destitute of . . . ther counsaill lerned, it was thoght necessarye to put in respect thelleccion of a new recordour unto the commyng home of the said Richard York and othre, at the whiche tyme suche a direccion shuld be takyn in this behalve as (by the same) shuld be . . . to reason and stand to the rightes, liberties and lauful accustumes of the said citie, shewing unto the said Richard Grene that by the said continuaunce and delay he shuld never be ferder frome the said office with the . . . premissez; the said Richard shewing hyme self to be content departid.

. . . *hospital of Seynt Nicholas [marginalia appears [f.2v]]* Also the same day and presence the priour of the monastere of the holy Trinitee of this citie of York personally appering before [f.2v] the presence forsaid shewed unto theme that he was truly intitled to have amonges othre thinges the hospitall of Saint Nicholas without the suburbs of the same citie, wherunto he knowing the premissez said that he ententid to entre but desiring therfor to have with hyme the presence of some of some [sic] of the maier seriantes to see the kinges peas kepid in that party; which by the discretion of the said maier and counsaill was grauntid unto the forsaid priour as thing consonaunt to the kinges lawes, right and good conscience.

[f.3] Dispute over Saint Nicholas Hospital
1 March 1486

Wedynsday the first day of Marche in the first yere of the reigne of King Henry vij

Mayor: William Chymney. 12: Thomas Wrangwisshe, William Snawsell, John Fereby, William Welles, Nicholas Lancastre. Sheriff: John Beverley. 24: Thomas Aleyne, William Taite, Richard Clerc, Richard Hardsang, William Barker, Thomas Fynche.

Assembled in counsaill wherby the maier commaunded the kinges lettres direct to the maier and aldermen in favour of the prioure and convent of the Holy Trinitie of York to be opynly red after the tenour ensuyng:

By the king

To our trusty and welbeloved the maier and aldermen of oure citie of York

Trusty and welbeloved we grete you wele; acertaignenyng you that pituous complaint haith be made unto us on the behalve of our welbeloved in God the priour and convent of our monastery of the blessed Trinitie within our citie of York, that where they have beene of tyme passid peasibly possessed and seased of thospitall of Saint Nicholas in the suburbs of the same by virtu of a graunt made therof by the noble prince of blessed memory King Herry the sixt our uncle, by way of eschaung of othre landes enpropred unto our collige of Eton besides our costell of Wyndeshore, as it more evidently appereth by lettres patentes thereof made; the which not withstanding as it is showed unto us oon Master John Wright and othre by crafty invencions interrupte the said priour and convent of there possession in the said hospitall, layyng noo laufull cause or sufficient mater soo to doo, as it is said; we not willing holy chirche to be preiudiced or wronged in the rightes and possessions therof especially places of our fundacion and patronage and remembring also that if the said prior and convent be put frome the possession of the said hospitall they must of reason have [f.3v] concours ayene unto certain levelode that oure said colleige is now possessed of, which wolbe to the gret hurt and damage of the same; and trusting in youre sadnesse and wisedams desire and hertly pray you that at some convenient tyme ye woll doo calle bifore you the said parties and therupon by suche wise weys as ye can use, the cause of differencye by you examined and knowne, ye woll soo procede and take such a direccion herin as the said priour and convent be not preiudiced or wronged in ther right bot that they may have and enioy all that lawe and good conscience shall require in this partie; wherin ye shall doo a worshipfull and meritorious dede and unto us full good pleaser. Yevene undre our signet at our palois of Westm[inster] the iiij day of Fevrier.

Which lettres distinctly red and perfitely understand, it was determyned that the parties named in the said lettres shuld be cald bifore the counsaille and the mater examined of this half the kinges assisse next to be holdyn within the same citie orelles at the tyme of the same assisse. And that in the meane tyme the said prioure and convent if theme list having oone of ther brether with a servaunt or twoo watyng upon hyme or othre discrete persone in ther name shuld make personell abode and tarying in thospitall above writyn, suffering the deputes of my lord the bisshop of Durham ⟨and the deputes of the said Master John Wright⟩ to (he) take away and convey from the said hospitall all such goodes being within the same as may be knowne the goodes of my said lord of Durham ⟨and the said Master John⟩, and over the same to suffer the prest now being ther callid brother to Master John Wright above rehersid ⟨or another discrete prest in his name⟩ to occupie the cure of soule of the chirch of Saint Nicolas parcell of thospitall forsaid ⟨having also oone or two with hyme⟩ unto the tyme of the said next assise with commyng and going to (his) ⟨the⟩ chambre occupied by hyme principally within the said hospitall to take his rest and recreacion within the same for the tyme and in all othre places demeanyng theme quietely and luffingly amonges theme self aswell by night or by day; [f.4] which act and evere part therof [incomplete]

[f.4v]   **Dispute with City Sheriffs, Letters from King Henry and Earl of Northumberland**
               6 March 1486

Monday the vj day of Marche in the first yere of the reigne of King Henry the vij[th]

Mayor: William Chymney. 12: Thomas Wrangwisshe, John Tong, John Fereby, William Welles, Nicholas Loncastre, Thomas Scotton. Sheriff: John Beverley. 24: Thomas Catour, Henry Williamson, Thomas Aleyne, William Taite, Richard Clerk, William White, Michael White, John Hagg, Miles Grenebank, Richard Hardsang, William Barker, John Gilyott, Thomas Fynche.

Assembled in counsaill after communicacion had in the mater of travaux hanging betwix the shereffes of this citie on that oone partie and Roger Laton, William Feyre and othre servauntes to my lord; it was determyned that at such tyme as the said William shuld be at home, which at the making of this act was absent and out of the said citie, the said Roger shuld certifyie the mayre (therfor) therof, and in all hast possible and convenient cause the said William and all othre which made offence ayenst the said shereffes to comme bifore the mayre and the counsaill in the counsaill chamber and ther to submytte themself according to ther demeritez.

Also the same day and place, lettrez direct frome therl of Northumberland unto the maier ⟨and⟩ aldermen of this citie (was) and receyved by that said maier the v day of March now being, was opynly red in the said counsaill after the tenour ensuying, wherupon it was determyned that an awnswer upon the contentes of the said lettres shuldbe [f.5] be [sic] put in respect unto such tyme as Richard York and Robert Hancok knightes at the parlement and othre of the counsaill shuld resort unto the said citie; and that in the meane tyme lettres shalbe direct to therle forsaid shewing unto his lordship the same.

vacat quia postea Also the same day and place the kinges lettres direct unto maire forsaid and by hyme receyved upon Tewesday the vij day of Marche forsaid at nyght of the same day was opynly red.

The tenour of the lettrez above rehersid:

To the right worshipfull and my right hertly biloved ffrend and right trusty and welbeloved ffrendes the maier and aldermen of the citie of York and evere of them

Right worshipfull and right hertly biloved frende and right trusty and welbeloved ffrendez I commaunde me unto you and thaunk you for the perseverant love that I fynd in you at all tymes, wherin I pray you to continue; and where as I am enfourmed that my right hertly welbelovd counsullour Miles Metcalf your record-our is visited with such infirmity that ther is noo liklyhode in hyme but that he is departid by this from this present lif, wherof I am right sory if it had pleased God otherwise, and sith it is soo that ye must have an newe recordour if he be departid, I desire and hertly pray you to graunt unto me the nominacion of such oone unto the said office as I shall appoynt, whoo I trust shall pleas you and of your goodly myndes herin that it woll like you by the berer certifye me in writing; and ye being conformable to thaccomplishing [f.5v] of this my desire and contemplacion ye shall yeve me the more large cause to do that (my) may be consonant to the wele, worship and prouffit of the citie under your conservacion, which I have at all tymes to my powre entendid, that knoweth the blissed Trinitie whome I besech to sende you all thencreas of many good fortunes. Writyn in my castell of Alnewik the xxvj day of (Alnark) Febr'.

Yours to my power, H. Northumberland

[f.6]   Visit of Papal Legate to York
8 March 1486

Wedynsday the viij° day of Marche in the first yere of the reigne of King Henry the vij^th

Mayor: William Chymney. 12: William Snawsell, John Tong, John Fereby, William Welles, John Newton, Nicholas Loncastre, Thomas Scotton. Sheriff: John Beverley. 24: Thomas Catour, Thomas Aleyne, William Tayte, William Spense, Richard Clerk, John Hagg, William White, Michael White, Miles Grenebank, Richard Hardsang, William Barker, John Gilyot.

Assembled in counsaill after the lectour of the kinges lettres directid unto the maier after the tenour ensuying:

By the king

rex Trusty and welbeloved we grete you wele, acertaigneyng you that the right reverand ffader in God the bisshop of Imola legat from the holy see of Rome hath been here within this our realme a certaine season and ministred unto us many singuler and acceptable pleasyrs which of all reason conforemith and bindeth us to owe him the more specially our love and tendre favour; and where as the same bisshop entendith by our licence and sufferance to passe thorough our said realme into Scotland for certaine his besinesse ther, we desiring hyme to bee soo curtesly entretid during his abode in our obeysaunce as he may afterward reapport and ascribe therby honour and nobley to our nacion, pray you hertly that unto the same entent ye woll at his entree intoo our citie of York honourable receve hyme and make hyme suche chere as it apperteyneth, whereby ye shall singularly please us and deserve our especiall thankes. Yevene undre our signet at our palois of Westm[inster] the xxij day of Fevrier.

[f.6v] *receyving of the popes legate with Latyn wordes* It was determyned that the said maier, aldermen and othre of the counsaill, the maier and aldermen in clothyng of violet and the other and othres in like colour or othre sad, shuld receve the popes legat named in the said lettres at the barr of Mikellyth using unto hyme convenient wordes to be utterd in Latyn; and over that cause the thinges herafter writyn to be presentid unto hyme immediately after his lighting; that is to say, ffirst in mayne brede, xij d.; in rede wyne, four galons; in Tyre, oon galon; in Mawmeceye, oon galon; in pikes, iij; in ffressh salmon, oon; in grete elez, twoo.

Wherupon the said legat commyng into the said citie about x of the clok after noone was receyved at the barr forsaid in fourme preceding with good wordes utterd in

Latyn by Master Nicholas Loncastre doctour of civyl [law], oon of the aldermen forsaid (and then after), wherof the tenour ensuyth after thact herof. And then after the present above writyn was honourably conveyed by the comon clerc of the said citie, mase berer and chamberleyns of the same unto the logeyng of the forsaid legat then being within the deans place of the chath[edral] church of York forsaid, unto the which legat (aldermen and counsaill forsaid) the said commune clerc in name of the maire, aldermen and counsaill forsaid usid thies wordes in Latyn:

Salutant te pater clarissime sanctissime apostolice sedis legate huiusce civitatis maior itaque seniores omnes, hec que ferunt isti minuscula tue colendissime dominationi mitissime destinantes ea quamquam minima digne atque animo grato recipere cures instantissime orant.

[The mayor of this city and also all the aldermen greet you, most distinguished father, legate of the most holy apostolic throne; they bring these small greetings, intending them for your most reverend and gentle lordship although of small value, and they beg you that you take care to receive them immediately with grateful and worthy spirit.]

Thies wordes expressid by the said commune clerc unto the said legate in presence of the said deane and many othre men of auctoritee, the forsaid legate using wordes in Latyn yave hertly thankes unto the said maier, aldermen and counsaill, saying he shuld **[f.7]** soo report ther demenaunce and humanitee in this partie unto the kinges highnesse, that his grace shuld be rather inclined graciously to here there peticions to be ministred unto hyme herafter.

Letter from Earl of Northumberland
3 March 1486

Thiez premissez accomplisshed a letter direct frome my lord of Northumberland unto the said maier, shereffes, aldermen and commons was opynly red after the tenour ensuying:

Yours to my powre, H. Northumberland

To the right worshipfull and my right hertly biloved ffrend and right trusty and welbeloved ffrendes the maiour, shereffes and aldermen of the citie of York, the comons of the same, and evere of theme

[R] *littere myse ab erle de Northumbr'* Right worshipfull and right hertly biloved ffrende, and right welbeloved ffrendes, I commaunde me unto you and thanke you for your constant goode hertes loving disposicions to me shewed, wherin I pray you continue. And where as by the desese of my right welbeloved counsaillour Miles Metcalf whome God rest, thoffice of recordourship is now voide, like ye to calle unto your right wise and discrete rememberaunce how that I applied my mynde unto yours when the said office of late was in traverse, and in consideracion therof it pleased you to graunt that the next advoidaunce shuld be at my pleasure, for the

which I thank you as hertly as I can; wherefor I desire and pray you now at the
cummyng of my right trusty and welbeloved servaunt and counsellour Richard
Grene to shew unto hyme your good lordship, masterships, tender wolles and
favours, soo that he to the said office may be lovyngly acceptid and to have it in as
beneficiall and ample wise as the said Miles had, wherin I trust ye shalnot oonely
ministre unto the king our souverain lordes good grace right acceptable pleaser but
also ye shall yeve unto me the more large cause to do thing that may be consenant
to the worship, wele and prouffit of you, for in perfourmans wherof I wolbe as glad
as any man lyving to my powre, that knoweth the blissed Trinitie to whome I
besuch to sende the perseveraunce of love, favour, and amitie amonges you with
thencreas of good fortunes. Writyn in my castell of Alnewik the iij^{de} daye of
Marche.

　　　[letters sent by the earl of Northumberland]

And after the same [**f.7v**] ripely understandid it was determyned that a letter shalbe
direct unto my said lord, bering the tenour herafter folowing:

Reply to Earl of Northumberland Concerning Office of Recorder
9 March 1486

To the right prepotent and our moost especiall and singuler good lord therle of
Northumberland, your moost humble servauntes at our litill powers the maier,
aldermen, shereffes and othre of the counsaill of the citie of York

to therle of Northumberland Right prepotent and our moost especiall and singuler
good lord, we in the moost humble wise recommend us unto your good lordship,
beseching the same to have knowlage that the v day of this present moneth of
Marche we receyved your honourable lettres bering the dait in your castell of
Alnewik the xxvj day of February last past, by the which your lordship desired to
have the nominacion of suche oone as ye wold appoynt to the office of recordour of
this citie; and than after the vij day of the said moneth of Marche we receyved your
othre honourable lettres daited in your said castell the iij day of the forsaid moneth
of Marche, desiring in the same the luffing admission of your servaunt and
counsellour Richard Grene to thoffice forsaid. My lord, true it is that the xxix [*sic*]
day of Febr' forsaid which was the day of the beriall of Milez Metcalf our late
recordour whome God assoile, we assembled in counsaill after certain communicacion had amonges us concernyng thelleccion of an new recordour for certain urgent
causez and consideracions aswell concernyng the liberties and franchesse grauntid
unto the same citie as the puplique wele therof and quietnesse of us and thol
inhabitauntes of the same, it was with good deliberacion determyned, concluded
and ennact remanyng of record in the registres of the said counsaill that thelleccion
of such recordour with all circumstance and othre thinges concernyng the same
shuldbe put in respect to the commyng home of our brethre Richard York et
Robert Hancok absent by auctoritee for the same at this present parlement;
wherfor we in our moost humble wise besuch you to be unto us and the same citie

as ye have bee at all tymes herbifor especiall and singuler good lord in this behalve and all othre thinges concernyng our liberties and fraunchesse forsaid, which saved and kepid with our othes and feithes made unto the observacion of the same, we shall indevour us not oonly at the commyng home **[f.8]** of our said brether bot at all othre tymes and seasons to doo unto you such pleaser and service as for the tyme shall lye in our litill powers, with our daily prayers to God who preserve you right prepotent and our moost especiall and singuler good lord in honour and prosperous state longe tendure with felicitie to his pleaser. Frome York the ix day of Marche.

**[f.8v]   City's Financial Difficulties, Postponement of Election of Recorder
            11 March 1486**

xj day of Marche the yere within writyn

Mayor: William Chymney. 12: Richard York, Thomas Wrangwisshe, William Snawsell, John Tong, John Fereby, William Welles, John Newton, Nicholas Loncastre, Robert Hancok, Thomas Scotton, John Harper. Sheriff: John Beverley. 24: Thomas Catour, Thomas Aleyne, Henry Williamson, William Spense, William Taite, Richard Clerk, Miles Grenebanke, Richard Hardsang, William Barkar.

Assembled in counsaill after communicacion had concernyng thelleccion of a new recordour, and understanding the grete ruyne, decaye and desolacion of the said citie with rememberance of that also at this citie is soo charged with ffee ferme and othre importable to be borne by the same citie without the kinges grace be more benignely shewed unto them, wherof they have singuler hoop and trust so comforhed by the report of Richard York and Robert Hancok late being with his highnesse and by the same gretely comforthhed as they have shewed to the good pleasure of all the said counsaill, yeving theme hertly thaunkes for ther manyfold labours taken in that behalve for the well of the said citie that they be not of powre to bere thordinarye and necessarye charges of the forsaid citie moost specially now after resumpcions of grauntez made by King Richard and othre whome God assoile, and seasing of the paymentes of tolles and othre thinges in late days paid by estraungers and othre resorting unto the said citie for the tyme; wherfor they not thinking necessarie or expedient for theme bot rathre to be denyd in theme to charge the said citie forther with the ffees and curialitee accustumed to be yevene unto the recordour of the said citie, which is bot a charge voluntarye to be had or not had at ther pleasurs after qualitee of causez occurrent for the tyme, which is any such shuld happyn hastly as God defend may be ordured by the discrecion of the said counsaill with assistence and good advise of such ther counsellours as be abiding in the said citie and othre places adioynyng unto the same, with good deliberacion determyned that thact of (ellacio) elleccion of the said recordour shuld be continued unto the next assise or othre tyme of common resorte of ther lerned counsaill unto the forsaid citie.

[f.9 blank]

[f.9v]   **Preparations for King Henry's Visit**
                   16 March 1486

Tuwesday the xvjth day of Marche in the first yere of the yere [*sic*] of Kinge Henry the vijth [*sic, 16 March 1486 was a Thursday*]

Mayor: William Chymney. 12: Richard York, Thomas Wrangwisshe, William Snawsell, John Tong, William Welles, John Newton, Nicholas Lancastre, Robert Hancok, Thomas Scotton, John Harpar. Sheriff: John Beverley. 24: Thomas Catour, William Tait, Richard Clerc, Michael White, William White, Miles Grenebank, Richard Hardsang, John Gilyott, Thomas Fynche.

Assembled in counsaille after certain communicacion had concernyng purviaunce to be made within this citie for the honourable receyvyng of the king if it shall fortune his grace after this fest of Estre to resorte unto the same citie; it was thoght that a wise and thankfull letter shuldbe directid from the said counsaill unto the moost reverend ffader in God my lord archbisshop of York, declaring his diligent acquitall and good lordship shewed unto the said citie and to be conveyed unto the same his lordship by Master John Haryngton in all hast. The tenour of the letter direct unto the said archbisshop folowith herafter and is suche:

To the moste reverende ffader in God and our moost especiall and singuler good lord tharchebisshop of York

Most reverend ffader in God and our moost especiall and singuler good lord, we in our moost humble wise recommend us unto your good lordship, thanking the same in as hertly wise as to us is or may be possible for your manyfold benefices and merciez which ye have shewed at large unto us and this your poore citie at all tymes herbifore and now of late tyme unto our brether Richard York and Robert Hancok, for the whiche we with our bodies and goodes shalbe redie at all tymes to doo you pleaser and service to the uttermost of our litill powers with our daily prayer to God for the continuaunce of your moost reverend prosperitie. Where amonges othre thinges of the bountivousenesse of your good grace shewed unto us and the same your citie, we be enfourmed that it pleasid your said lordship to your peyne **[f.10]** [*bound as [f.19]*] for our comforth, surtie and quietnesse to commaunde that we shuld send (upon) unto you at this tyme somme discrete personne to undrestande your good adviace and pleaser howe we shuld demeane us ayenst this supposid commyng of the king our souverain lord unto this your citie. We not oonely willing according to our dutie to observe your said commaundement bot also for our surtie to be sufficiently instructid how to deal in the premissez saving the kinges pleaser and our dutie unto his grace, with such thinges as hath be shewed unto his highnesse aswell by your said lordship as by bille of humble supplicacion declaring of truthe the evident povertie of the same citie have at this tyme sent unto you your servaunt Master John Haryngton our commune clerk, beseching you not oonely to be soo good lord unto us as to yeve us your good advertisment in this partie, but aswelle to yeve credence unto the said Master John in such thinges as he shall declare unto your forsaid lordship on our behalve in the same, wherby as by othre your moost singuler good lordship shewed unto us and this your said poore citie ye shall bynde us and all othre the poor commoners here to be your continuall oratours and servauntes, most reverend ffader in God and our moost especiall and singuler good lord, Almighty God preserve you in felicitee long to endure to his pleasure. Frome York the xvj[th] day of Marche etc.

Your mooste humble oratours and servauntes, the maier, aldermen, shereffes and othre of the commune counsaille of the citie of York

Craft of Pinners, Intervention of Countess of Northumberland in Election
16 March 1486

pynners Moreover it is aggreed that the auncient ordinaunce of the pynners shalbe observed and kepid as it was bifore the tyme that Nicholas Loncastre was maire of this citie, notwithstanding any act made in the tyme of hyme unto the contrary, and that they shalbe restored to such distressez as was of late taken from theme by the craft of girdlers.

[f.10v] [*bound as [f.19v]*] Also this day it was commond by the maier to be ennact how that my ladye of Northumberland on Sonday last past calling unto hur presence the same maier, Richard Yorke, Thomas Wrangwisshe, John Tong, John Fereby, Thomas Scotton and John Harper in the Frere Austyns in this citie, willid theme that noo thing shuldbe further attemptid in the mater concernyng thelleccion of a new recordour unto the next tyme of hur retourne unto the same citie, notwithstanding any writing to be made unto theme in the meane tyme shewing that she shuld be ther warant and defence in that partie.

[f.11]   King Henry Nominates New Recorder
27 March 1486

Monday callid Blake Monday, the xxvij day of March the first yere of the reigne of King Henry the vij[th]

Mayor: William Chymney. 12: Thomas Wrangwisshe, John Tong, John Fereby, William Welles, Nicholas Lancastre, Robert Hancok, Thomas Scotton, John Harpar. Sheriffs: John Beverley, Roger Appilby. 24: Thomas Catour, Thomas Alan, Henry Williamson, William Spense, Richard Clerk, (John Gilyot) Michael White, William White, Miles Grenebank, John Gilyot, Thomas Fynche.

Assembled in counsaill in the chapitour of the cath[edral] church of Saint Peter of York where the kinges lettres wherof the tenour ensuyth was opynly red:

To our trusty and welbeloved the maire, aldremen and common counsaill of the citie of York

By the king

Welles, Nicholas Lancastre, Robert Hancok, Thomas Scotton. Sheriffs: John Beverley, Roger Appilby. 24: Thomas Cattour, Thomas Aleyn, Henry Williamson, William Spense, Richard Clerc, William Tayte, Michael White, William White, Miles Grenebank, Richard Hardsang, John Giliot, Thomas Fynsh.

Assembled receivid a letter fro the lord Clifford beryng the tennour ensuyng:

To the right worshipfull and my trusty frendes the maier of York with his brether and thinhabitance of the same

Your loving frend H. Lord Clifford and of Westmerland

L. Clifford lettre to attend of the king Right worshipfull and my trusty frendez, I commaund me unto you, and it is so that the kinges grace haith commaundid me to come to his presence to Notingh[a]me, and afor his commyng to York I entende to be with you and to mynistre as myn auncistres haith done here to fore in all thinges that accordith to my dewtie; wherfore I hertely pray you as my trust is in you that ye wol put you in all deligence that ye can deviate to content the kinges grace and the rathor at myn instance and desiere to prepare all thinges ther according to your old custome as may be to the moost worshipe of the citie and to you and me boithe, for I entende to be of as goode will and favour unto the citie and you as any othre of myn aunscytres haith bene before, like as my right trusty servante this berer shall shew you my ferther mynde in that behalve, to whome it like yow to giffe credence, and almighty God preserve you to his pleaser. Writyn at my castell of Skipton the third day of Aprill.

answere maid by master recorder Wherupon the said presence concedering the contentes of the said letter, it was shewid unto oon Karlell, servaunt unto the said Lord Clifford berer of the said letter by the mouthe of John Vavasour seriaunt at the law recorder of the citie that under the king the maier of the said citie is lieutenaunt, (and) haveing full power and auctoritie under the king and lawes to reul and gyde the citie, haveing knawlege by presidences **[f.14v]** remanyng of record in the registre of the said citie in what maner and forme thei shall receive the kinge and how to deame theme to his highnesse in evere behalve, trustyng so to be have theme in that behalve that his grace shalbe wel content and pleasid, and wher it shuld seme to be thought unto the forsaid lord that his auncestres haith had some maner of administracion and reul in the said citie in the commyng of the king unto the same, it was shewid unto the said Karlell to reporte unto the forsaide lord for his aunswere in that matier that by the said presidences or othre wise it can be knawen unto theme that ever eny of the said lord auncistre had eny such administracion or reul within the saide citie, if eny such have had of right the maier and his said brether wold have been as glad of hyme as othre ther predecessours haith been of his auncestres, and therupon hertely commaunding theme unto the forsaid lord desierid hyme to yeve his attendance of the kinges grace according to his deutie and be unto theme and this citie good lord as othre his auncestres haith be herebefore.

[f.14v]   **Dispute between Aldermen, Election of New Alderman**
                 Undated, Spring 1486

Mayor: William Chymney. Deputy recorder: Thomas Asper. 12: Richard York, Thomas Wrangwich, William Snawsell, John Feriby, John Tong, William Welles, Nicholas Loncastre, Robert Hancok. Sheriff: Roger Appilby. 24: Thomas Cattour, Thomas Aleyne, Henry Williamson, William Tayte, **[f.15]** Michael White, Richard Clerc, William Whit, Miles Grenebank, Richard Hardsang, Thomas Fynsh.

Assembled in counsell after communicacion had on the matier of travax hanging betwixt John Harper alderman on the one partie and William Tod lait aldermen now dischargid on the othre partie, for preeminence betwixt theme with good deliberacion determined aswell for the honour of the citie as for a president to be put in rememberance for that which may ensew herafter, that the said John Harper in al thinges shal have preeminence above the saide William Tod at al tymes, and that the same William Tod shalbe commaundid so to accept the said John Harper in evere behalf.

[R] *election of alderman* And also thene after the said maier and aldermen proceding to thelleccion of a new **[f.15]** alderman tobe in the rowmbe of Robert Ameas late alderman deceassid, named, electid and chose William Whit to be alderman in the same rowme, wherupon the same William Whit callid therunto was sworne in forme and maner accustomed in tyme past.

Farm of Skeldergate Tenement
Undated

Mayor: William Chymney. Recorder: John Vavasour. Deputy recorder: Thomas Asper. 12: Richard York, Thomas Wrangwish, John Tong, William Wellis, John Newton, Nicholas Lancastre, Robert Hancok. 24: Thomas Aleyne, Michael White, Miles Grenebank, William Barker, Thomas Fynsh.

Assembled determined that Master John Dalton shalhave to ferme for terme of threskore yeres fro the fest of Saint Michaell archangell next commyng one old and ruyne tenement lying in Skeldergate with charge of wolding and reparacion of the same, paying yerely during the saide terme unto the chamberlains of this citie iiij s., to be maide by indentour with clauses of distresse and reentre unto the same for nowne payment of the said ferm.

[f.15v]   **Plans for King Henry's Reception**
                 Undated, Spring 1486

It is concludit by the maier, his breder aldermen and othre of the common counesell of the citie that thei being in gude hope to fynd the king more gracious soveraine lord unto the forsaide citie by the mediacion of the most reverend fadre in Godd tharchbisshop of York and othre lordes spirituall and temporall of his moost noble counesaill, shewing theime and all thin[ha]bitances therof gretely gladdit and joyed of the commyng of his moost riall persone with othre his nobles unto the saide citie have ordeigned and prepared to receyve the kinges grace in forme felowing, that is to saie:

First, wher the two sheriffes of the saide citie for the tyme being with xx horses haith be accustumed to yeve ther attendance of kinges herbefore resorting unto the citie at Tadcastre brige, being thextremitie of ther fraunches, it is now concludid that not oonly the saide two sheriffes bot aswell two of the aldermen accumpaned with xl horsses shall ther wait on his grace.

Secundly, where the maire and aldermen cled in long gownys of skarlet and othre of the couneseil accumpanyd with thinhabitances of the citie have be accustumed to wait of kinges in lykwise commyng to the citie on horsebak aboute two miles fro the citie, thei be determined that the saide maier and aldermen in like clothing of skarlet, and common couneseill and clerc in violet, chambrelayns in murray, and many of thinhabitances in rede on horsebak shall wait on the king at Bilburgh crose about v miles fro the citie, and othre thinhabitaunces which may not ride or be of power to have rede gownes to yeve ther attendance on foote betwixt Dringhowsis and the citie beside a certaine nowmbre of childrine as shalbe gaddard togiddre aboute Saint James chappell calling joyfully King Henrie after the maner of children.

[f.16] *iij* Thirdly, at the entre of the citie and first bar of the same shalbe craftely conceyvid a place in maner of a heven of grete joy and anglicall armony; under the heven shalbe a world desolaite full of treys and floures, in the which shall spryng up a rioall rich rede rose convaide by viace unto the which rose shall appeyre an othre rich white rose unto whome so being to gedre all othre floures shall lowte and evidently yeve suffrantie, shewing the rose to be principall of all floures as witnesh Barthilmow; and therupon shall come fro a cloude a crowne covering the roses, after the which shall appeir a citie with citisyns with the begynner of the same callid Ebrauk which shall salute the king with wordes felowing in prose and therupon present unto the king the keys of the citie being thenheritaunce of the saide Ebrauk yelding his title and his crowne unto the king as moost glad of hym above al othre.

Ebrauke

> Most reverend rightwose regent of this rigalitie
> Whos primative patrone I peyre to your presence,
> Ebrauuk of Britane I sitt nat this citie,
> For a place (in) to my pleasour of moost prehemynence;
> Herunto I recoursid for moost convenience
> In comforting that by cource of liniall succession
> Myne heires this my citie shuld have in possession.
>
> Of right I was regent and rewlid this rigion,
> I subdewid Fraunce and led in my legence;
> To you Henrie I submitt my citie key and croune
> To reuyll and redresse your dew to defence,

Never to this citie to presume ne pretence
Bot holy I graunt it to your governaunce
As a principall parcell of your inheritaunce.

Please it I besuch you for my remembrance
Seth that I am premative of your progenie,
[f.16v]   Shew your grace to this citie with such abounedance
As the reame may recover in to prosperitie,
And also of your grace gyve not your ee
Oonely to this citie of insufficience
Bot graciously consider therwith and diligence.

It is knawne in trueth of grete experience
For your blode this citie made never degression,
As recordith by the grete hurt for blode of your excellence;
Wherfor the rathre I pray for compassion
And to mynd how this citie of old and pure affeccion
Gladdith and inioith your high grace and commyng
With our concent knowing you ther sufferaine and king.

Fourtly, the king commyng up the stretes shallse the same furnishede with clothis of the best which may begottyn within the citie for the honourment of the same, and at his entrie unto Uuse brigge in theend of the streetes of Skeldergate and North-strete, becauce no gappes shall appeir, shall therbe clothes hangid and a convenient thing divisid wherby if the weder be fair of the lordes before and othre ne before the king schall rayne rose water.

Fiftly shalbe on the hight of Ousebrigge a rioall treyne and therin sodanely appering set togidder in counsail sex kinges crouned betokining the sex Henries, which after the sight had of the king with certaine convenient laisour avisidly shall commyt a ceptour unto Salamon cledd as king, which Salamon shall therupon taking that ceptour and saying the wordes felowing unto the king in prose, yelde unto him the saide ceptour in tokining that in hym is wisdome and justice:

Salomon

Most prudent prince of pruved prevision,
Their primordiall princes of this principalitie
Haith preparate your reame the vij[th] by succession,
[f.17]   Remitting reame als right to your rialtie
Their ar kinges condigne of your consanguinitie,
Ful riall and rightwose in rewle of ther regence
And ful lordly thai execute the lawes of ther legence.

Seth that God moost glorius eternall sapience
Did insence me Salomon of his effluent grace,
Wherfore I am takin as patrone of prudence
To discuse upin conscience ich iudiciall cace,
Revolving how with sapience ye have spent your space
To the tyme of this your misteriusly
Obteyning as moost worthi your right not regosly.

> Now reane ye reule ye your reame rightwosly
> By politike providence as God haith indewid
> To you sufferaunce in sapience submitting me umbly
> Your sage savour sothfastnese haith so be shewid
> In ich judiciall right this reame to be renewid;
> Ye be avisid most worthi by graciouse affluence,
> Submitting to your sufferaunt my septour of sapience.

vj Sextly shal appere in thend of a strete joning on the syde of Ousegate passing into Conyngstrete shalbe a shew and fro the same shall come hailestones to be maid by viace falling on the lordes and othre commyng ne before the king, hailestones to be made by craftes of cumfettes.

vij Sevently shalbe at the common hall a castell appeiring of grete force wherin David as the moost principall shall appeir and he shall with wordes felowing yeld unto the king a swerd of his victorie, ther shalbe in that castell citisyns which after a sight of the king and remembrance of hyme with gude countenaunce shall appeir in clothing of white and greyne shewing ther trueth and hertly affeccion unto the kinge:

[f.17v]   David

> Most prepotent prince of power imperiall,
> Redowtid in ich region of Cristes affiance,
> Your actes victorious be notid principall,
> In maner more noble then Charlis of Fraunce;
> Seth God so disposith of his preordiniaunce
> And right so yeve me might to devyne goodly,
> I David submitt to you my swerd of victorie.

> When I reynid in Judie I know and testify
> That Ebrauuce the noble which subdewid Fraunce,
> In memorie of his triumph this citie did edify
> That the name of his noble shuld have continuance;
> I witnesh that this citie without variaunce
> Was never deflorid be force ne violence,
> Wherfore I have chosyn it for my place to your presence,

> Submitting it with thafforce and trueth to your excellence,
> Beseching your highnese the more for myne instance,
> To this your inheritance tak gracious complacence,
> Seth that it is your citie not filid with dissavaunce;
> Trew and bold to your blode not dreding perturbance
> Which causid moost this citie to be desolate,
> Now reviving in comforth to attaine your asstate.

Eghtly shalbe at thend of Swynegale joning of Staynegate our lady commyng frome hevin and welcome the king in wordes felowing, and therupon ascend ayene in to heven wit angell sang, and ther schall it snaw by craft to be made of waffrons in maner of snaw.

Oure Lady

Henrie seth my sone as thi sufferayne haith the sembly assynyd
Of his grace to be governer for his people protection,
Full specially that thine heier of petie be declinid,
[f.18] I pray the seth thi people haith me mich in affeccion,
My son and my soveraine in whome is eleccion,
Singulerly this citie haith honourd humbely
And maide me ther meane withoutin obieccion
In hope of ther help to have it holy.

[R] *I pray in this space*
What I axk of his grete grace he grantith it gudely
As a beame of all bevtes benyngne,
The his knyght he haith callid victoriously
To convoce and concord this his contrie condigne.

[R] *I shall sew to my sone to send you his grace*
For this citie a place of my pleasing
And have you no drede nor no dowting,
Continuall heir in this reynyng.

[f.18v blank]

[ff.19–19v] [see [f.10]]

[ff.20–20v blank]

[f.21]   **City's Debt to Former Chamberlains**
                2 June 1486

[*entire entry, through [f.22], struck through*] (Friday the secunde day of Junyne the yere of the reigne of King Henry the vij first)

(Mayor: William Chymney. [Deputy recorder?]: Thomas Aspar. 12: Richard York, Thomas Wrangwissh, John Fereby, John Newton, Nicholas Loncastre, Robert Hancok, John Harper. Sheriff: John Beverley. 24: Thomas Catour, Thomas Alan, William Tayte, John Haug, Michael White, Richard Clerc, William Barker, Richard Hardsang.)

(*vacat* Assembled in counsaill hath ordined, stablisshed, statutid and ennactid where the maior and communaltie of this present citie of York be indetted unto George Kirk, Alexander Dauson, Adam Atkynson and John Huton coke late chamberleyns of the same citie in the somme of ffive hundreth sex powndes fourtene shelinges two pens and an half peny due unto theme on and upon thend of ther accomptes in ther behalve yeldid and ending in the fest of Saint Blase last past, which somme of five hundreth sex powndes fourtene shelinges two penns and half a peny John Elwald, William Barkar, Nicholas Vicars and John Hoten potter nowe chamberlayns of the said citie by ordinaunce and auncient custome of the said citie be bondon to have paid and to pay unto the said ⟨late⟩ chamberleyns in the festes of thynvencion of the holy crosse callid Saint Elyn day last past, of Saint Petre callid Lammesse and the nativitie of our lord thene next ensuyng by evyn porcions; and also wher the said John Elwald, William Barker, Nicholas Vicars and John Hoton haith and shall beyre and susteyne before the feste of Saint Blase next commyng othre gret and exceding charges for the said citie and to the use of the same, that the maier, aldermen, sheriffes and common counsaill **[f.21v]** forsaid shall se that the said John Elwald, William Barker, Nicholas Vicars and John Hoton shal have true and indelaied contentacion and reparment in the feste of Saint Elyne next commyng, the feste of Saint Petre callid Lambasse and Cristynmasse thene next ensuyng, of the said five hundreth sex powndes fourteyne shelinges two penys and one half peny. And of all othre somme and sommes of money which shalbe deu unto theme in and upon thend of ther accomptes next to be yeldid in that behalf by evyn porcions, and for the more surtie of the premisses (herof) it is ordigned, statutid, stablished and inactid that the maier, aldermen, sheriffes and common counsaill forsaide shal at the next eleccion of now chamerleyns name and elect such and so mony as shal make the saide payment and contentacion wel and truely unto the forsaide chamerleyns in the saide festes accordingly as othre chamerleyns haith be accustomed to do in such case hertofore without delay upon ther juperdie, which ordinaunce shalbe extendid to al othre to be electid and named chamerleyns of the same citie at eny tyme herafter. And also it is ordigned, statutid, stablished and inactid by the same that if herafter eny chamerleyns do to be named and electid chamerleyns of the same citie for the yere next to come or in eny othre yere thene ensuyng refuse to accept on heme the said office of chamerleyn or to accomplish this present ordinaunce in eny partie therof ⟨as⟩ to hyme by force of the same ordinaunce shall apperteigne, that thene the same so electid chamerleyn shall forfet xl li. to be enployed unto the use of the said citie and to be levied by the mayer for the tyme being without redempcion or pardon of eny part therof as the said maier for the tyme being wol aunswer therfor at his perill; and therupon after the syght and presentment of the same ordinaunce unto William Snawsell and John Tong, William Wells, Thomas Scotton and William Whit aldermen, Roger Appilby sherif, Henrye Williamson, William Spense, Thomas Pereson, Miles Grenebank, John Gilyot and Thomas Fynshe of the said counsaill have expresly consentid unto the ⟨said⟩ ordinaunce and evere part therof willing and ordignyng the same affare as in theme is or may be to be of the same **[f.22]** strengh, force and vertew in evere part as if thei and evere of theme had be present personally and consenting to the making of the same, the day and yere abovesaide. And for the more surtie of the premisses the maier, aldermen, sheriffes and common counsaill forsaid and every of theme unto this act haith subscribid his name or mark with his owne hand:)

[*Signatures, also struck through*]: (Wylliam Chymnay mayre, Richard York, Thomas Wrangwys, John Tong, John Feryby, William Wyllys, John Neuton, Nicholas Loncaster, Robert Hankoc, Thomas Scotton, John Harpar, John Beverlay [and] Roger Apilby vicecomites, Thomas Catour, Thomas Alan, William Tayte, Richard Clerk, Michael White, Milo Grenebank, Recharde Hardsang, William Barkar [*with X mark*], John Gilliott, Thomas Fynch.)

**[f.22v]   Mayor Commands Tailor to Keep the Peace
                   4 June 1486**

Sonday the iiij day of Juyne

Evers Robert Walasse tailour was commaunded by the maier to kep the kinges
peace ayenst Sir William Evers clerc parsone of Alhalowe churche in Peseholme
undre the peyne of iiij hundreth markes to be allevied of his goodes and cattalles.

**King Henry's Letter Nominates New Swordbearer
10 June 1486**

Friday the x day of Juyne [*sic, 10 June 1486 was a Saturday*]

Mayor: William Chymney. Deputy recorder: Thomas Asper. 12: Richard York, Thomas
Wrangwich, John Tonge, John Feriby, William Welles, John Newton, Nicholas Loncastre,
Robert Hancok, John Harper. 24: Thomas Aleyne, William Taite, John Hagg, Richard
Clerc, Michael White, Miles Grenebank, William Barker, Richard Hardsang, John Gilyot.

Assembled in counsell commaundid the kinges lettres to theyme directid to be
discloused and rede after the tennour ensuyng:

By the king

To our trusty and right welbelovid the maier, sheriffes, aldermen and common
counsell of oure citie of York

Trusty and right welbelovid we gret you wele, and for somoche as we be enfourmed
that he which occupieth thoffice of swerdeberer within our citie of York by cause of
his great age and such diseases and infirmities as resten in hyme of liklyhode may
not long occupie and exercise the saide office as it is said, we havyng consideracion
unto the trewe and feithfull hert that oure welbelovid Robert Langston oweth and
berith unto us with thabilitie and hanour that he is of metely for thoccupacion of the
said office, desier therfor and in our herty wise pray you that at such tyme as the
said office shall happyn to be voide be it by deth, cession or left by thoccupiour
therof, ye than wol have the said Robert at the contemplacion of our lettres
therunto before any othre persone recommendid and preferred, as we trust you;
wherin as in our opynion ye shall not onely purvey you of an hable persone to do
you good and worshipfull service bot also for the same greatly please us and
deserve oure herty thankes. Yeven undre our signet at oure manoure of Shene the
iiijth day of Juyne.

Wherupon the said maier, aldermen and **[f.23]** counsellours calling to rememberance how hertofore it pleasid the king to shew unto theyme how his mynde, wol and
pleasur was and shuldbe that thei shuld enioy ther auncheant liberties and costomes
with free eleccion of allmaner ther officers for the tyme notwithstanding any writing

to be maide fro his grace in favour of eny persone herafter; and also how of old tyme it haith be accustomed and ordigned for diverse gret and urgent causes that such as sewed unto the kinge or othre lord for writing to obtigned [*sic*] any office apperteignyng unto the disposicion of the saide maier, aldermen and counsellours, shal never have ne enioy the said office or rowme or othre within the said citie; therfor and for othre causes and consideracions theyme moveing have determined that Robert Langston named in the said lettres shuld never enioy thoffice of swerdeberer or othre office within the said citie; forthermore it is ordigned that frome hensford during the tyme that the said citie shalbe indebtid noo lernyd man shall have eny yerely fee of the said citie except the recorder, common clerc and attorney in the common place, providid alwey that this ordinaunce shall not be extendid to such as be now in possession of fees yeven by the said citie. Also it is ordigned that the testament of Girlyngton shalbe really executid in evere point therof as shall apperteigne before Middesomer next commyng and so fro tyme to tyme herafter according to the true mynde and entend of the same.

Bonds to Keep the Peace
22 June 1486

xxij daie of Juyne

Manucapcio Thome Sklater quod ipse dampnum vel malum aliquod corporale in Margaretam Spenser seu alicui populo domini regis non faciet nec fieri procurabit quovismodo; Rogerus Laton generosus, Ricardus Rawlyn, Thomas Neleson et Thomas Poole, dictus Thomas Sklater obligavit se in xx libris et quilibet manucaptorum predictorum in x libris solvendis domino regi si aliquod dampnum intulit in dictam Margaretam etc.

[f.23v] Riginaldus Holme de Ebor' assumpsit pro seipso quod ipse dampnum vel malum aliquod corporale Roberto Symson, Johanni Symson et Johanni Condall seu alicui populo domini regis non faciet nec fieri procurabit quovismodo sub pena xx librarum de terris et catallis suis ad opus dicti domini regis levandarum, et Thomas Morehous de Ebor' et Johannes Williamson de Ebor' manuceperunt pro eodem Riginaldo pro pace gerendum in hac parte quilibet eorum sub pena x librarum de terris et catallis suis ad opus eiusdem domini regis levandarum.

Robertus Symson de Ebor' assumpsit pro seipso quod ipse dampnum vel malum aliquod corporale Riginaldo Holme seu alicui populo domini regis non faciet nec fieri procurabit quovismodo sub pena xx librarum de terris et catallis suis ad opus dicti domini regis levandarum; Robertus Atkynson et Johannes Gurnard de Ebor' manuceperunt pro eodem Roberto pro pace gerundum in hac parte quilibet eorum sub pena x librarum de terris et catallis suis ad opus eiusdem domini regis levandarum.

Johannes Symson de Ebor' assumpsit pro seipso quod ipse dampnum vel malum aliquod corporale Riginaldo Holme seu alicui populo domini regis non faciet nec fieri procurabit quovismodo sub pena xx librarum de terris et catallis suis ad opus dicti domini regis levandarum; Robertus Atkynson et Johannes Gurnard de Ebor' manuceperunt pro eodem Johanne pro pace gerendum in hac parte quilibet eorum sub pena x librarum de terris et catallis suis ad opus eiusdem domini regis levandarum.

[**f.24**] Johannes Cundall de Ebor' assumpsit pro seipso quod ipse dampnum vel malum aliquod corporale Riginaldo Holme seu alicui populo domini regis non faciet nec fieri procurabit quovismodo sub pena xx librarum de terris et catallis suis ad opus dicti domini regis levandarum; Robertus Atkynson et Johannes Gurnard de Ebor' manuceperunt pro eodem Johanne pro pace gerendum in hac parte quilibet eorum sub pena x librarum de terris et catallis suis ad opus eiusdem domini regis levandarum.

Willelmus Walklyne de Whelldrike assumpsit pro seipso quod ipse dampnum vel malum aliquod corporale Willelmo Wilson seu alicui populo domini regis non faciet nec fieri procurabit quovismodo sub pena xl librarum de terris et catallis suis ad opus dicti domini regis levandarum; Johannes Bell tailiour, Johannes Stokkislay tailiour, Willelmus Whalley tailiour, Robertus Symson walkar de Ebor' manuceperunt pro eodem Willelmo pro pace gerendum in hac parte quilibet eorum sub pena xx librarum de terris et catallis suis ad opus eiusdem domini regis levandarum.

[Mainprise of Thomas Sklater, that he do no damage nor bodily harm to Margaret Spenser or any other of the king's subjects, under penalty of £20, half paid to the lord king and half to Margaret; sureties Roger Laton, gentleman, Richard Rawlyn, Thomas Neleson, and Thomas Poole, each bound themselves for £10.

[**f.23v**] Under penalty of £20, Reginald Holme of York undertakes to keep the peace towards Robert Symson, John Symson, and John Condall, and all other of the king's subjects. Sureties Thomas Morehous and John Williamson bind themselves for £10 each.

Robert Symson undertakes to keep the peace towards Reginald Holme and all other of the king's subjects under penalty of £20. Sureties Robert Atkynson and John Gurnard bind themselves for £10 each on Robert's behalf.

John Symson undertakes to keep the peace towards Reginald Holme and all other of the king's subjects, under penalty of £20. Sureties Robert Atkynson and John Gurnard bind themselves for £10 each on John's behalf.

[**f.24**] John Cundall of York binds himself for £20 to keep the peace towards Reginald Holme and all other of the king's subjects. Sureties Robert Atkynson and John Gurnard of York bind themselves for £10 each on John's behalf.

William Walklyne of Wheldrake undertakes to keep the peace towards William Wilson and all the king's subjects under penalty of £40. Tailors John Bell, John

Stokkislay, and William Whalley, and walker Robert Symson act as sureties for William and bind themselves for £20 each.]

Bond to Accept Arbitration
27 October 1486

Thomas Watson litster de Ebor' assumpsit pro seipso quod ipse stabit et obediet arbitrio, judicio et ordinacioni Ricardi Croklynge et Christofori Thomlynson ex parte dicti Thome ac Willelmi Stubbes et Johannis Ordeux berker ex parte Roberti Yeresley et Katrine uxoris sue, arbitratorum electorum et nominatorum de et super omnimodis accionibus, sectis, transgressionibus et demandis inter partes predictas motis et pendentibus ab origine mundi usque in hodiernum diem videlicet xxvij^{mi} diem Octobris anno regni regis Henrici septimi post conquestum Anglie secundo, ita quod huiusmodi arbitrium, judicium et ordinacio fiant et reddantur per dictos arbitratores citra festum Sancti Andree proximum futurum, et si dicti arbitratores non concordaverint quod extunc idem Thomas Watson stabit et obidiet arbitrio, judicio et ordinacioni Johannis Vavasour servientis domini regis ad legem et imparis per partes predictas in hac parte electi et nominati sub pena x librarum ad opus dicti domini regis de bonis et catallis eiusdem Thome Watson levandarum.

Robertus Yeresley obligavit se in forma predicta.

[Dyer Thomas Watson of York undertakes that he will adhere to and obey the arbitration, judgement and ordinance of Richard Croklynge and Christopher Thomlynson (on the side of the said Thomas) and of barker John Ordeux acting for Robert Yeresley and Katherine his wife, arbiters elected and named to determine all the actions and offences moved or pending between the two parties from the beginning of the world to the present day, namely 27 October 1486, the arbitration to be made and rendered by the coming feast of Saint Andrew. If the arbiters are not able to agree, then Thomas Watson will obey the arbitration and judgement of John Vavasour, serjeant at law to the lord king and umpire between these parties, under penalty of £20 levied on Thomas's goods and chattels.

Robert Yeresley binds himself in the same form.]

[f.24v]   **Assize of Wine**
                10 July 1486

Assisa vini capta in Guihald civitatis Ebor' coram Willelmo Chymney maiore civitatis Ebor' predicte ac aliis aldermannis et vicecomitibus eiusdem die Lune videlicet x° die Julii anno regni regis Henrici septimi post conquestum Anglie primo [*incomplete*]

[An assize of wine held in the city Guildhall in the presence of mayor William Chymney and the aldermen and sheriffs of the city, on Monday 10 July 1486]

[ff.25–25v blank]

[f.26]   **Reimbursement for Repairs to City Tenement**
                 Undated, probably July 1486

Mayor: William Chymney. Deputy recorder: Thomas Asper. 12: Thomas Wrangwishe, John
Fereby, John Tong, William Welles, Robert Hancok, John Harper. 24: Thomas Catour,
Michael White, John Hagg, John Giliot, Thomas Fynch.

Determined that Nicholas Vicars in recompence of xj li. which he shewid hyme to
have expendid aboute necessarie reparacion of a tenement in his holding belonging
to the citie shuld yerely in his ferme have allowed unto hyme vj s. viij d. for the full
peyment of the saide xj li., soo that by the sight of ij of the chamerleins or othre
wise it might be founde that he had maid such reparacion. Wherupon afterward it
was shewid unto the maier and the counsell by Master John Harington common
clerc and by John Elwald and John Huton chamerleins that thei hadd seyin the
reparacion maide by the saide Nicholas Vicars upon the saide tenement and as it
semed unto theyme grete and necessarie reparacion was ther made anenting to a
grete some which the saide Nicolas by his bodily oth affirmed before the saide
maier to be the some of xj li. and more, and therupon it was aggreid that he shuld
have allowance according to the purporte of certain indentours wherof the tenour
ensuyeth herafter.

[f.26v]   **John Hall Summoned Before Mayor and Council**
                 8 July 1486

The viij daie of July

summysis J. Hall John Hall of Stokton personaly appering before my lord the maire
and John Tonge alderman and submitting hym unto my saide lord the maire, my
maisteris aldermen, the sheriffes and common counesellers of this citie for his
(offen) trispas and contempt in beting the common hird of the saide citie,
⟨promisid⟩ to appere personaly before my lord and maisteris at such daie and
place on this half the ffest of Saint Petre callid Lambes as he shalbe commaunedid
and therupon obey and performe such direction and ordinaunce as thei shall mak in
that partie as wele tuching his submission as othre wise in evere behalf under the
peyne of xx li. to be forfet unto the behove of this citie and for the more sevre
accompleshment of the same, Roger Laton squier, William Decan, John Lambe
and Richard Rawlyn haith made theime self pleges for the saide John Hall, evere of
theime binding hym in xx li., to be enployed unto the use of the saide citie in case
that the saide John Hall disobey the direccion and ordinaunce of my saide lord and
maisteris in eny partie therof.

City Sheriffs Ordered to Arrest Three Yorkshiremen
18 July 1486

Preceptum pacis
W. Harome Preceptum est vicecomitibus civitatis Ebor' quod attachiant pro
corpora sua Willelmum Fox de Parva Askham in comitatu civitatis Ebor', Rogerum
Jakson de Clapeham in comitatu Ebor' et Milonem Jakson de eadem si in comitatu
civitatis Ebor' predicte inventi fuerunt vel eorum aliquis inventus fuerit, ita quod
eos habeant in Guihald civitatis predicte coram Willelmo Chymney maiore eiusdem
et sociis suis aldermannis, custodibus pacis et justiciis eiusdem domini regis infra
predictam civitatem, suburbos et libertatem eiusdem ad proximum sessionem pacis
ibidem tenendum ad inveniendum sufficientem securitatem de pace regis gerendum
Willelmo Harome cui de morte et mutulacione membrorum suorum graviter
iniuriatur, et **[f.27]** habeant ibidem tunc hoc preceptum. Teste maiore predicto
apud Ebor' xviij die Julii anno regni regis Henrici septimi primo.

[Order [to keep] the peace

W. Harome The sheriffs are ordered to arrest William Fox of Parva Askham,
Roger Jakson, and Miles Jakson, and to have them before mayor William
Chymney and his associate aldermen, keepers of the peace and justices of the
lord king within the city of York, its suburbs and liberty, at the next session of the
peace, and that they find sufficient surety to keep the peace towards William
Harome and do no injury to him, and **[f.27]** thus they have this order. Witnessed
by the mayor at York 18 July 1486.]

Orders for Sheriffs to Arrest Various Miscreants
July, August, October 1486

Preceptum pacis
W. Curtase Preceptum est vicecomitibus etc., quod attachiant per corpus suum
Willelmum Curtase de Ebor', ita quod eum habeant etc., ad inveniendum
sufficientem securitatem de pace regis gerendum Willelmo Michel de eadem etc., et
habeant ibidem tunc hoc preceptum; teste maiore predicto etc., apud Ebor' ultimo
die Julii anno regni regis Henrici septimi primo.

Preceptum pacis
Preceptum est vicecomitibus etc., quod attachiant Ricardum Mawer boucher, ita
quod eum habeant etc., ad inveniendum sufficientem securitatem de pace regis
gerendum Simoni Michelson laborer cui de morte et mutulacione etc., et habeantur
ibidem etc. Teste etc., xiij die Augusti anno regni regis Henrici septimi primo.

Preceptum pacis
Preceptum est vicecomitibus etc., quod attachiant Ricardum Mawer de Ebor'
boucher ad sectam Johannis Sawer laborer de eadem, datum xxvj^{to} die Augusti etc.
(pace)

Preceptum pacis
Preceptum est vicecomitibus civitatis etc., quod attachiant Ricardum Mawer boucher ad sectam Roberti Michelson laborer, datum xxvj^{to} die Augusti etc.

Preceptum est vicecomitibus etc., quod attachiant Willelmum Barton de Appilton ad sectam Johannis Bilton de eadem, datum nono die Octobris.

Preceptum est vicecomitibus etc., quod attachiant Thomam Peedane laborer ad sectam Nicholai Witton tailiour.

Preceptum est vicecomitibus quod attachiant Willelmum Harper (seniorem) ⟨juniorem⟩ ad sectam Willelmi Harper (filii sui) patris sui.

[Order [to keep] the peace

W. Curtase The sheriffs are ordered to arrest William Curtase of York, so that he find sufficient surety to keep the peace towards William Michel, and that [the sheriffs] have this order. Witnessed by the mayor at York, 31 July 1486.

The sheriffs are ordered to arrest butcher Richard Mawer, so that he find sufficient surety to keep the peace towards laborer Simon Michelson. Witnessed, etc., 13 August 1486.

The sheriffs are ordered to arrest butcher Richard Mawer at the suit of laborer John Sawer, 26 August 1486.

The sheriffs are ordered to arrest Richard Mawer at the suit of laborer Robert Michelson, 26 August 1486.

The sheriffs are ordered to arrest William Barton of Appleton at the suit of John Bilton, 9 October [1486].

The sheriffs are ordered to arrest laborer Thomas Peedane at the suit of tailor Nicholas Witton.

The sheriffs are ordered to arrest William Harper junior at the suit of William Harper, his father.]

**[f.27v]   King Henry's Involvement in Case of John Norman
21 July 1486**

xxj day of Julie

Mayor: William Chymney. Deputy recorder: Thomas Aspar. 12: Thomas Wrangwish, John Ferybe, William Welles, John Newton, Nicholas Lancastre, Robert Hancok, John Harper, William White. Sheriff: Roger Appilby. 24: Thomas Cator, Thomas Aleyne, William Taite,

Richard Clerc, John Hagg, Michael White, Richard Hardsang, William Barker, John Gylliot, Thomas Fynsh.

Assembled in counsaell weir desired by oon calling him self John Pigg servaunt unto the kinges highnes to see hyme disclouse the kinges lettres directid unto John Norman of York in the wordes felowing:

By the king

Welbelovid we grete you weile, and where as it is shewid unto us for verray truth that John Nesfeld delivered hertofore unto your keping certaine goodes to the valoue of foure or fyve hundreth marcas or above which remayne in your handes as it is saide, we for certain causes us moving woll and charge you that forthwith upon the sight of thies our lettres ye deliver al the same goodes unto our servaunt the bringer hereof or elles that ye inmediatly come with hym unto us to shew matier and cause resonable if ye eny can allege why ye aught not thus to doo, not failing herof in eny wise as ye woll awnswere in that behalve at your perill. Yeven undre our signet at our palois of Westm' the xxij daie of Juyn.

To our welbelovid John Norman of our citie of York

And therupon after lectoure of the saide lettres the saide John Pigg considering how the saide maier and counsael at his desire wolling therby to doo singular pleasour unto the king direct their writing unto the said John Norman, **[f.28]** and the same sent with their officer John Nicholson seriaunt at the mase unto Hull, wheir it was shewed that the saide John Norman then was willing hym incontinent upon the sight of the saide writing to have beyn with the saide maier and counsaell to have understand what shuld have be shewid unto him in that partie, and that notwithstanding the saide John Norman apperid not, desired the saide maier and counsaell to se the goodes of the saide John Norman put in savegard unto such tyme the kinges mynd be farthre understand in that partie; wherupon Augnes wif unto the saide John Norman appering before the saide maire and counsell shewid the kinges savegard under the kinges signet bering the tenour ensuyng:

By the king

Henry by the grace of God king of Yngland and of Fraunce and lord of Ireland, to almaner our officers, true liegemen and subgiettes hering or seing thies our lettres and to every of theime, greting. We lat you weit that we of our speciall grace have taken in to our savegard, proteccion, tuicion and defense John Norman of York late attourney unto John Nesfeld squier, al his landes, goodes and catalles; we therfore woll and charge you that ye ne vex ne trouble him in eny behalf for the saide Nesfeld or othre wise, bot that ye suffur the saide John Norman quietly and peasibly to enioy his saide landes, goodes and catalles without disturbance, let or impediment of you or eny of you, as ye wol avoide our grevous displeasour and awnswer unto us at your perilles. Yeven under our signet at our citie of London the viij[th] day of Septembre the first yere of our reigne.

After the sight of the which savegard the saide maier and counsaell denying to accompleshe the desire of the saide John Pigge determined wrote unto the kinges grace a letter after the tenour ensuying:

To the moost high and mighti Cristen prince and our moost redoubtid soverain lord the king, **[f.28v]** [*first line repeated*] we in the moost humble wise recommend us unto your grace with al submission deu unto your magestie; pleas it the same to have knawlege that the xvijth day of this present moneth of July your servaunt John Pigge, shewing by mouth that he had your moost noble lettres direct unto our concitisyne John Norman, affirmed to be your pleasour that the same lettres shuld be deliverd unto hym before us your moost humble subgiettes; we wolling according to our deutie to put us in our ful devours to thaccomplishement of your pleasour in every behalve, yeveing credence unto your saide servaunt, sent oon of our servauntes unto the saide John Norman than being at your towne of Hull, as it was said, with our writing to him directid, by the which we commaundid him incontinent upon the sight of the same writing to be with us to understand such thinges as shuldbe declared unto him at the same his commyng, which John Norman by our saide servaunt culd not be foundon in eny wise; wherupon your forsaid servaunt presenting him before us the xxj day of the same moneth seing that the saide John Norman apperid not toke on hym to disclose your saide moost noble lettres directid to the forsaid John Norman, leveing with us a copy of the same by the which we understode that your saide grace commaundid hym to deliver unto your said servaunt such goodes as he haith of John Nesfeld or els tappeyr before your highnese incontinent upon the recept of the same your lettres, and therupon your saide servaunt on your behalve commaundid us to put in surtie to your behove such goodes as the said John Norman had within this your citie, which moost gracious soverain lord we ne durst take on hus to doo without your especial commaundment unto us in that partie in writing direct, in consideracion of that at Agnes wif of the said John Norman appering before us the said xxj daie of July in presence of your saide servaunt shewid unto us your moost noble lettres of savegard grauntid unto the said John Norman bering the tennour herin closid, declaring ferthre unto us that hur forsaide husband seith the tyme of your moost fortunate reigne was taken in examinacion by diverse of **[f.29]** your moost noble counsael in thinges concerning the saide goodes, and therupon after enpresonment of his persone by diverse daies paied for his savegard in that behalve C marces xv s., as your saide servaunt which diligently haith acquitid hym in the premisses can more largely shew unto your highnese, of whome we besuch to have knawlege what shalbe your pleasour how we farthre shall deal with the saide John Norman if it fortune hym at eny tyme herafter to resorte unto the same your citie, which according to our naturall dueties we shall endevour us to accomplesh to the uttermost of our litil powers, by Goddes grace who ever preserve you moost high and mightie Cristen prince and our moost redoubtid soverigne lord in felicite long to endure. Fro York the xxij day of Julie.

Your moost humble subgiettes the maier, aldermen and common counsael of your citie of York

Orders for Arrests
21 November 1486

Preceptum pacis
Preceptum est quod attachiant Bartholomeum Cammas ad sectam Willelmi Jonson painour xxj (pred') die Novembris.

Precepta pacis
Preceptum quod attachiant Willelmum Johnson ad sectam Bartholomei Cammas.

Preceptum quod attachiant Marmaducum Clarnax ad sectam Johannis Chapman.

[Orders [to keep] the peace

[The sheriffs] are ordered to arrest Bartholomew Cammas at the suit of William Jonson, 21 November.

They are ordered to arrest William Johnson at the suit of Bartholomew Cammas.

They are ordered to arrest Marmaduke Clarnax at the suit of John Chapman.]

[f.29v]   Choice of New Sheriff
Undated, c.July 1486

Mayor: William Chymney. Deputy recorder: Thomas Asper. 12: Thomas Wrangwish, William Snawsell, John Tong, John Feriby, William Wellis, John Newton, Robert Hancok, Thomas Scotton, John Harper, William White. Sheriff: Roger Appilby. 24: Thomas Cator, Richard Clerc, William Taite, Miles Grenebank, Richard Hardsang, William Barkar, John Gilliot, Thomas Fynsh.

Assembled in counsel after communicacion had upon the eleccion of a sherif in place of John Beverlay late oon of the sheriffes of the same citie which deceased the Monday next afore the fest of Saint Marie Magdeleigne, determined that he which shalbe sherif electid in that partie shalbere the charge of the last hole quarter of this present yere in every behalve, ending at the feest of Saint Michael next cumyng, and fro the day of his entre to enioy isshewis and profectes of the same to him as unto oone sherif apperteigning, and therupon the maier and sherif departing out of the counsael, as persons having no voce in eleccion of the said sherif, with oone hole voce electid and named Nicholese Vicars oon of the chambreleyns of the said citie, of his consent promysing to pay unto the prefect of the said citie xl markes, which furthwith was sworne sherif and admittid unto the rowme and place of the said John Beverley which was thelder sherif, never the leis bering his charge as one of the chambreleyns forsaid.

[f.30] **New Sheriff and Chamberlain**
Undated, c.July 1486

Mayor: William Chymney. Recorder: John Vavasour. 12: Thomas Wrangwish, John Tonge, John Feriby, Nicholas Lancastre, Robert Hancok, Thomas Scotton, John Harper, William White. Sheriffs: Nicholas Vicars, Roger Appilby. 24: Thomas Aleyne, William Taite, John Hagge, Richard Clerc, Miles Grenebank, Richard Hardsang, William Barker, John Giliot.

Assembled in counsael determined that Nicholas Vicars late chosyn sherif shalpay [xl] markes by his graunt at the day of his eleccion to be sherif after the maner ensuyng, that is to say incontenently xx markes and in the fest of the nativitie of our lord God xx markes, to be emploed to the belding of the walles or othre wise after the discrecion of the counesael; and also the said counesel, for certaine causes theime meving and specially for that at ⟨it⟩ is not semeing that the said Nicholas Vicars after the fest of Saint Michaell next cumyng when he shall sease of his office of shirifwik shuld occupie as oone of the chambrelayns forsaid whos office is inferiour unto the office of shirif forsaid, have determined that oon shalbe electid chamerleyne, and to be in the inferior place of the said chamerleyne, and therupon electid and named William Pantour plummer to be the same chamerleyne, which sworne and ben admittid promisid to pay incontenent five markes to be employed to the use of the said citie; and forthre the said maier and counsellers of ther one assent and consent have admittid the said Nicholas Vicars of the same counesell to have and enioy the same in as able maner and forme as eny othre which have be sherif herebefore, and therupon he sworne unto the said counesael promised to make a dyner unto the said maier and counesell at his departour out of office of shiriff.

[f.30v] **King Henry Orders Priest Set Free**
31 July 1486

Copie of a letter deliverd fro the kinges grace unto the maire the last day of July ensuyng herafter:

By the king

To our trusty and welbeloved the maier and sheriffes of our citie of York

Trusty and welbelovedd we grete you wele, and where as oon Sir Thomas Metcalf preest for certain misbehavynges surmised to be doon by hym ayenst us contrarie to his dutie and liegeaunce was at our late being at our citie there by our commaundment committed unto prisonne where as yit he remaneth, we for the tendre love which we beer unto thordore of preesthode be content that he be dischargied of his said emprisonnement, and therfor we woll and charge you that upon sufficient suertie by the said Sir Thomas founedon of credible personnes, inhabitauntes of our said citie, in the some of thre hundred poundes, that he at all tymes shalbe furthcommyng tanswere unto us for such thinges as been surmised ayenst him, and that from hensfurth he shalbe to us and al our liege people of good abering, ye incontinently therupon doo him to be sette at his large and libertie without dilay or contradiccion, as our trust is in you, and thies our lettres shalbe your warraunt and sufficient discharge in that behalve. Yeven undre our signet at our palois of Westm' the xx day of Juyll.

Which letter openyd, red and understand by the said maier and sheriffes, Sir Thomas Metcalf preest named in the said letter, Richard Clerc and Thomas Fynsh late sheriffes of the citie of York were boundon after the forme ensuyng, and therupon the said (said) Sir Thomas was dischargied and put to his libertie.

Recogniciones

Thomas Metcalf clericus (et) Ricardus Clerc et Thomas Fynsh de Ebor' coram maiore civitatis Ebor' in propriis personis suis comparientes [f.31] obligaverunt se quilibet eorum obligavit se domino regi in tricentis libris legalis monete Anglie solvendis eidem domino regi vel executoribus suis aut eius certo attornato in festo Sancti Michaelis archangeli proximo futuro post datam presencium sine dilacione ulteriori.

Condicio istius recognicionis talis est quod si prefatus Thomas Metcalf sic fidelis subditus domino nostro Henrico regi Anglie septimo et sic paratus in propria persona sua in civitate Ebor' ante festum Pasche proximum futurum post legalem premunicionem sibi faciendum per maiorem et vicecomites dicte civitatis pro tempore existente vel eorum alterum ad comparentes coram dicto maiore et vicecomitibus et ad videndum super hiis que prefato Thome Metcalf obicientur extunc primus recognicio pro nullo habetur alioquin in suo robore permaneat et effectu.

[Recognizances

Clerk Thomas Metcalf, Richard Clerc, and Thomas Fynsh of York came into the presence of the mayor themselves [f.31] and bound themselves and each bound himself to the lord king for £30, payable to the king or his executors or attorney at the feast of Michaelmas next coming.

The condition of this recognizance is such that if Thomas Metcalf be a faithful subject to our lord king Henry VII and be prepared himself before the coming Easter after legal notice made to him by the mayor and sheriffs to come into their presence, then this bond is null and void in effect.]

This ⟨day⟩ passed under seal oon *venire facias* in the wordes ensuyng:

escaetor Willelmus Chymney maior civitatis Ebor' ac escaetor domini regis infra civitatem predictam, suburbos et libertatem eiusdem, vicecomitibus civitatis predicte, salutem. Vobis ex parte dicti domini regis mando quod venire facitis coram me prefato maiore apud Guihald eiusdem civitatis die Mercurii proximo futuro post datam presencium viginti quatuor probos et legales homines de civitate predicta ad audiendum et faciendum ea que ex parte eiusdem domini regis ad tunc et ibidem iniungentur et habeates tunc ibidem hoc preceptum. Teste maiore predicto ultimo die Julii anno regni regis Henrici septimi post conquestum Anglie primo.

[*escheator* William Chymney, mayor of the city of York and escheator of the lord king within the city, its suburbs and liberty, to the sheriffs of the city, greetings. I command you to cause to come before me in the Guildhall next Wednesday twenty-four worthy and lawful men of the city, to hear and to do all those things I would order and enjoin on them, on behalf of the lord king. Witnessed by the mayor 31 July 1486.]

[f.31v]   Bond to Keep the Peace
Undated

Johannes Roger de Ebor' assumpsit pro seipso quod ipse dampnum vel malum aliquod corporale in Johannem Brouneberde seu alicui de populo domini regis non faciet nec (fe) fieri procurabit quovismodo (Johannes Blenkoo Ricardus Estwod) sub pena xx librarum de terris et catallis suis ad opus dicti domini regis levandarum; Johannes Blenkoo, Ricardus Estwod, Ingro Johnson et Antonius Welburne de Ebor' predicta manuceperunt pro eodem Johanne pro pace gerendum in hac parte quilibet eorum sub pena x librarum de terris et catallis suis ad opus eiusdem domini regis levandarum.

[John Roger of York bound himself for £20 to do no harm to John Brouneberde or to any other of the king's subjects. Sureties John Blenkoo, Richard Estwod, Ingre Johnson and Anthony Welburne are bound for £10 each so that John Roger keeps the peace.]

Inquisition into Lands of Late John Giliot
7 November 1486

Copie of lettres testimonial passid under the maiers seal upon one inquisicion taken by twentie persons appering be force of the writ of *venire facias* forsaide:

Omnibus ad quos presentes littere pervenerint, Willelmus Chymney maior civitatis Ebor' ac escaetor domini regis in comitatu civitatis Ebor' predicte salutem in Domino. Sciatis quod ego escaetor predictus tercio die mensis Augusti anno domini millesimo quadringentesimo octogesimo sexto et anno regni regis Henrici septimi post conquestum Anglie primo in Ebor' predicta virtute officii mei predicti inquisicionem feci et cepi de hiis quorum inquisicio ad officium escaetoris pertinere dinoscuntur per sacramentum viginti proborum et legalium hominum de comitatu predicto, videlicet Johannis Tirrell, Alexandri Dawtre, Henrici Kent, Johannis Craune, Christoferi Bentley, Willelmi Hyndeley, Ricardi Blakborne, Ricardi Crokelyne, Ricardi Thorneton, Thome Forluf, Christoferi Thomlynson, Thome

Welles goldsmyth, Johannis Stokesley, Johannis Bell tailiour, Elie Cure, Willelmi
Lounesdale, Johannis Bawne, Roberti Symson, Thome Bentlay barbour et Thome
del Howne; qui quidam inquisitores jurati dixerunt et presentaverunt tunc ibidem
quod dicta civitas Ebor' fuit antiqua civitas virtute cartarum olim regnum (ali)
Anglie nobilium utique antecessorum domini ⟨nostri⟩ regis qui nunc est longe
ante statutum de terris [f.32] et tenementis ad manum mortuam non ponendum edit
factarum et per diversos reges Anglie antecessores eiusdem domini nostri regis tam
ante dictum statutum quam post illud eciam iniuncte parliamenti confirmat habens
potestatem et auctoritatem condendum leges atque habendum consuetudines et
utendum eisdem infra se, et quod ex consuetudine atque usu stilo et antiquitate
civis contrarii hominis memoria non existit solitum et usitatum fuit in civitate
predicta quod quiscumque subditas domini nostri regis moram trahens in eadem
civitate per suum testamentum et suam voluntatem potuit atque valuit quecumque
terras et tenementa necnon redditus annualis et annutates quascumque de terris et
tenementis suis infra dictam civitatem situatis ad usum cuiuscumque ecclesie,
parochialis. cantarie, hospitalis aut alterius similis loci in Ebor' predicta existen-
tibus eciam [*illegible*] dare et assignare dicto statuto de terris et tenementis ad
manum mortuam non ponendum non obstante, quod quia bone memorie Johannes
Giliot nuper mercator dicte civitatis defunctus in vita sua seisitus fuit ut in dominico
suo de certis terris et tenementis in Fossegate dicte civitatis Ebor' prout insimul
jacent in longitudine a regia strata ibidem ante usque ad Fossatum domini regis et
terram Willelmi Gascoigne militis retro, et in latitudine inter tenementum per-
tinens cantarie Beate Marie fundate in ecclesiam Sancte Crucis in Fossegate in
civitate predicta nuper in tenura Thome Hundemondby nuper de Ebor' ex ea parte
et quedam communem venellam ducentem usque Fossegate predicta retro; que
quidem terre et tenementa cum suis pertinenciis idem Johannes Giliot habuit ex
dono et feoffamento Willelmi Haliday, consanguinii Johannis Haliday filii et
heredis Johannis Haliday quondam de Heslington' generosi defuncti, et sic seisitus
de eisdem testamentum suum et suam ultimam voluntatem condidit et declaravit et
auctoritate dictarum cartarum necnon virtute eiusdem consuetudinis usus stili
atque antiquitates in eadem civitate Ebor' a tempore et per tempus (cuis) cuius
contrarii hominis memoria ut premittitur non existit annuum reddatum quatuor
marcarum legalis monete [f.32v] Anglie exeuntium de omnibus et singulis terris et
tenementis suis predictis ad augmentacionem cantarie Sancti Thome martiris in
ecclesiam Omnium Sanctorum super Pavimentum eiusdem civitatis fundate Willelmo Seton capellano eiusdem cantarie et successoribus suis in dicto testamento
suo et sua ultima voluntate predicta disposuit et legavit habendum et tenendum
predictum annuum redditum prefato Willelmo Seton et successoribus suis predictis
in puram et perpetuam elimosinam imperpetuum; et quod predictus Willelmus
Seton capellanus dicte cantarie eundam annuum redditum quatuor marcarum
racione et pretextu dicte consuetudinis usus stili et antiquitatis atque testamenti et
ultima voluntate predicta ad usum suum et dicte cantarie sue a vicesimo die Julii
anno regni regis Ricardi tercii post conquestum Anglie tercio usque in diem
captionis inquisicionis predicte recepit et habuit, et insuper quod Johannes Giliot
filius et heres dicti Johannis Giliot et executor testimenti sui predicti volens idem
testimentum et predictam ultimam voluntatem prefati probat sui debitam habere
roboris firmitatem per cartam suam primo coram dictis inquisitoribus juratis, et

subsequenter coram nobis atque venerabili viro Johanne Vavasour serviente domini nostri regis ad legem recordatore civitatis et aliis jurisperitiis ostensarii potestatem dedit pro se et heredibus suis prefato Willelmo Seton et successoribus suis capellanis dicte cantarie in defectu solucionis dicti (annu) annui redditus et cuiuslibet parcello eiusdem tociens quociens in terris et tenementis predictis intrandum et distringendum et districciones capiendum ac captas asportandum et penes se retenendum donec de predicto annuo redditum quatuor marcarum et eius arreragiis si que fuerunt eis fuerit plenarie satisfactum; unde ego Willelmus Chimney maior ac escaetor predictus sciens consuetudinem predictam posse stare cum lege itaque eundem Willelmum Seton capellanum et successores suos capella-nos dicte cantarie licite posse eundem annuum redditum **[f.33]** quatuor marcarum in forma predicta annuatim habere et precipere eandem consuetudinem approbans in quantum potui ipsum Willelmi Seton capellanum cantarie predicte pro se et dictis successoribus suis in hac parte ab officio meo in pace dimisi atque dimitto per presentes. In cuius rei testimonium presentibus sigillum officii mei apposui. Date Ebor' quo ad sigillacionem presentium septimo die mensis Novembris anno domini millesimo CCCC^{mo} lxxx^{mo} vj^{to}, et regni regis Henrici septimi post conquestum Anglie anno secundo. [*At the bottom of [f.32] is found the marginalia 'iiij marcas monete legalis ad cantariam Thome martiris in ecclesiam Omnium Sanctorum'.*]

[To all whom these present letters will reach, William Chymney maior of the city of York and escheator of the lord king in the county of the city of York, greetings in the Lord. Be it known that I the escheator on the third day of August 1486 in the first year of King Henry VII's reign, by virtue of my office made and held an inquest pertaining to the office of escheator, for there to be discovered by oath of twenty worthy and lawful men of the aforesaid county, namely John Tirrell, Alexander Dawtre, Henry Kent, John Craune, Christopher Bentley, William Hyndeley, Richard Blakborne, Richard Crokelyne, Richard Thorneton, Thomas Forluf, Christopher Thomlynson, Thomas Welles goldsmith, John Stokesley, John Bell tailor, Elias Cure, William Lounesdale, John Bawne, Robert Symson, Thomas Bentlay barber, and Thomas del Howne; these jurors said and presented that the city of York was an ancient city by virtue of charters of the realm of England and of the ancestors of our lord king, existing long before **[f.32]** mortmain statutes, and that rents and annuities of lands and tenements in York go to the use of the church, parish, chantry, hospital and other similar places; that whereas John Giliot of good memory, former merchant of York now deceased, was while living seised of in his demesne certain lands and tenements in Fossgate in the said city of York, lying in length from the king's highway up to Fossgate in front and the land of William Gascoigne knight behind, and in breadth between a tenement belonging to the chantry of the blessed Mary founded in the church of the Holy Cross in Fossgate (the tenement now in the tenure of Thomas Hundemondby formerly of York) on one side, and a certain common lane leading to Fossgate behind; which land and tenement with its appurtenances the said John Giliot had as a gift and feoffment of William Haliday, kinsman of John Haliday, son and heir of John Haliday, gentleman, late of Heslington, now deceased, and so being seised he willed and declared that by virtue of ancient York custom beyond all memory the annual rent of four marks [f.32v] issuing from each and every of the lands and tenements should go to the additions of the chantry of Saint Thomas the martyr in the church of All Saints Pavement endowed by William Seton chaplain and his successors, Seton and his successors to have and to hold the said annual rent in pure and perpetual alms; and William Seton, chaplain of the said chantry, received and held the said annual rent by reason of the customs and of the will and wish aforesaid, from 20 July 1485 until the day this inquest was held. John Giliot, son and heir of the said John Giliot and executor of his will, confirmed by his charter first in the presence of the said jurors of the inquest, and subsequently before us and also before the venerable John Vavasour, the king's serjeant at law and recorder of the city, and other men of law, that he gave for himself and his heirs full satisfaction to William Seton and his successors in the chantry in default of payment of the rent of four marks; wherefore I, William Chimney, mayor and escheator, knowing the aforesaid custom, am able to abide by the law and assure William Seton and his successors in the chantry the annual rent [f.33] of four marks. In testimony of which I affix the seal of my office. Given at York with the seals of those present, 7 November 1486, in the second year of Henry VII's reign.

four marks of legal money to the chantry of [Saint] Thomas martyr in the church of All Saints]

[f.33v] **Bond to Keep the Peace**
Undated

Ricardus Wardale assumpsit pro seipso quod ipse dampnum vel malum aliquod corporale non faciet nec fieri procurabit quovismodo in Willelmum Tolthrop ⟨capellanum⟩ nec alicui de populo domini regis sub pena xx librarum de bonis et catallis suis ad opus eiusdem domini regis levandarum; Ricardus Coltman et Willelmus Inskip manuceperunt pro eodem Ricardo, uterque eorum sub pena x librarum de bonis et catallis suis ad opus eiusdem domini regis levandarum.

[Richard Wardale undertook on his own behalf to do no injury or bodily harm, nor cause any to be done, to chaplain William Tolthrop nor to any one of the king's subjects, under penalty of £20, to be levied of his goods and chattels. Richard Coltman and William Inskip bound themselves for £10 each on behalf of the said Richard.]

[f.34] **Letters Testimonial for Apprentice Trading on His Own Behalf**
17 July and 4 August 1486

fourt day of August

Catlynson Thomas Catlynson late apprentice unto William Hancok of the citie of York exhibete unto the maier lettres under the seal of the commissarie of the court of York bering the tenour ensuyng, knawleyching the contentes of the same tobe true and his deid by vertew of his oth made upon a booke before the saide maire. Omnibus ad quos presentes littere pervenerint, Thomas Pereson decretorum doctor domini officialis curia Ebor' commissarii generalis, salutem. Sciates quod Thomas Catlynson de Ebor' coram nobis in ecclesiam conventualem Sancti Leonardi Ebor' die, mense et anno infrascriptis personaliter comparens quandam confessionem sponte fecit et juravit in hunc qui sequitur modum. Be it had in mynde that I Thomas Ca[tl]ynson laite apprentice to William Hancok of the citie of York decea[sed ab]oute a fortniet sieth was sent by Robert Hancok alderman and John Elwald oon of the chambreleyns of the said citie unto Hull [with] certaine lyen to be delyverid unto oon John Pall Esterlyng thene being at Hull, to thentent to receyve of the said John Pall othre lyen of like quantite unto the behove of the saide Robert Hancok and John Elwald, which I did; and over that bestowid tene powndes of lauful En⟨g⟩lish money of certaine marchandises boght to the behove of the said Robert of the said John Pall and othre Esterlynges by the speciall desire of the forsaid Robert; and therupon after when I hard say that ther was one callid Ventre, haveing as it was said the kinges chartar and so being under his proteccion, lying in the roide of Grymesby with certaine marchandises to sell, borowde on myne owne trust and to myne owne behove and use tene marces of one Sir John Atkynson othrewise (othrew) called Danby prest of Hull forsaide, with the which tene marces I bought of the saide Ventre two kistes of sogar price thre powndes and tene shelinges, a pipe of white wyne price fyfty shelinges, and thre barellis of assh price sex shelinges and eght penys; which parcelles I b⟨r⟩ought unto the saide citie and the same laide in a place sett in Skeldergate belonging to the prior and convent of Selby and than after sold part of the same, soo that the saide marchandises boght by me of the saide Ventre I bought of myne owne auctoritie without consent, [f.34v] knawlege or ratificacion of (saide) the saide Robert Hancoke, and the same to myne use and profite so haith occupied, manerid and disposid as I may aunswere unto God at the dredefull day of jugement, and so help me God and theis holy evangelistes. Que omnia et singulari vestre universitati tenore presencium innotescimus per presentes quibus sigillum nostrum apposimus. Data et acta Ebor' in ecclesiam predictam xvij° die Julii anno domini millesimo CCCC^mo octagesimo sexto, et anno regni regis Henrici septimi post conquestum Anglie primo.

[So that each and every one of you will be notified by these presents, we affix our seal. Given and enacted at York in the aforesaid church, 17 July 1486, in the first year of Henry VII's reign.]

testimonial Wherupon the said maier at the desire of the said Thomas Catlynson graunt and made to be delivered lettres testimoniall under his seal of maieraltie in this wordes: To all Cristen people unto whome thies presentes shalbe shewid, William Chymney maier of the citie of York sendith greting in our lord God ever lasting; knaw ye for truith that the fourt day of August the yere within writtin Thomas Catlynson lait apprentice unto William Hancoke of the said citie in his propir persone appering before me in the counsael chambre of the same citie exhibete and shewid certaine lettres testimoniall under the seal of the commissarie general of the court of York bering the tenour ensuyng: Omnibus ad quos etc., and therupon incontinent after the open lectour of the said lettres the forsaid Thomas Catlynson knawlegeid the contentes of the same to be true and tobe his deid by vertew of his oth maid in that partie, in witnese wherof I have unto thies presentes sett the sael of myne office of maireltie. Yeven at York forsaid the fourt day of August the first yere of the reigne of King Henry the sevent.

[f.35]   **Delivery of Documents Witnessed**
               5 August 1486 and 7 March 1489

Fift day of August

Thomas Wandisford in his propre persone appering before William Chimney maier of the citie of York in the counseil chamer on Ouse brige within the saide citie in presence of the saide maier deliverd unto Sir William Yngilby knight and Thomas Stillington squier threskore and seventene peassis of evidences, skroullis and munimentes in parchment and paupir part of the same aswele concernyng the saide Thomas Stillington and his right as othre part concernyng the reverend fadir in God Robert Stillington the bisshop of Bathe and othre, delivered unto the saide Thomas Wandisford hertofore by the saide Sir William Yngylby tokepe unto such tyme he shuld demaund of the saide Thomas Wandisford the delivere of the saide evidences, skroullis and munimentes.

[*Added in a later hand:*] And the vijth ⟨day⟩ of March the iiij^{ti} yere of the reign of King Henry the vijth the said Thomas appering tofore John Harper than being maiour confessed and maid knowlige that he resavyd the said evidences, skroules and munimentes of the of the [*sic*] said Sir William the which was unto hym delyverd.

Letter of Attorney for Wine Delivery
6 August 1486

The sext day of August

Laton The maier at the special desire of Roger Laton of York merchaunt sealed a letter of attorney wherof the tenour ensuyth:

Noverint universi per presentes me Rogerum Laton de civitate Ebor' in Anglia mercatorem fecisse, constituisse, ordinasse et loco meo posuisse ac facio constituo, ordino et loco meo per presentes pono dilectos michi in Christo Johannem Squier et Jacobum Mollet de civitate London' in Anglia, predictos mercatores meos veros et legitimos procuratores et attornatos generales conjunctim et eorum alterum (dimidium) per se dimidium et insolidum ad petendum, levandum, colligendum, recuperandum et recipiendum vice et nomine meo quadraginta et octo dolia, unam pipam et dimediam pipe vini mei eiusdem Rogeri contra Deum et justiciam capta per Pi' Ape' [*this abbreviation is not extended and is likely to stand for the personal*

name, perhaps in Gascon or Bordelais, of the person who seised the wine] de civitate
Burdeux Burgensi a quodam nave sive carvella de partibus Britannie vocata
Margareta de Penmark cuius magister erat tempore iniuste capcionis eiusdem
Johannes La Burdeak ac omnia alia et singularia bona et catalla res mercandisas et
debita mea quecumque que michi ab eadem Pi' Ape' aut aliis quibuscumque
personis in quacumque parte mundi extra regnum Anglie predicte existentem
[f.35v] aliquo modo debentur sive a me detinentur; necnon ad prosequendum,
respondendum et defendendum vice et nomine meo in omnibus et singulis curiis et
judiciis eciam ecclesiasticis et secularibus aut iunxtis quibuscumque in omnibus et
singulis causis et negociis placitis, litibus et querelis motis vel movendis coram
quibuscumque iudicibus potestatibus dominis regentibus prepositis vel iusticiariis
seu eorum commissariis qualitercumque motis vel movendis versus prefatum Pi'
Ape' aut alios quoscumque erga quas aliqua accio realis seu personalis michi dat jus
sectam seu defensionem per legem aliquam statutum consuetudinem privilegium
aut ordinacionem quamcumque dantem et concedentem dictis procuratoribus et
attornatis meis conjunctim et dimidium plenam potestatem meam et mandatum
speciale predictum Pi' Ape' ac omnes et singulos debitores meos et detentores
bonorum, catallorum, rerum, mercandisarum et debitorum predictorum ac eorum
et cuiuscumque eorum executores si necesse fuerint vice et nomine meo arrestari,
attachiari et capi ac per res et bona sua distringi faciendum ac in omnibus et singulis
curiis, judiciis, et placitis predictis coram quibuscumque judicibus, potestatibus,
dominis, regentibus, prepositis et justiciariis seu eorum commissariis predictis
implecitandum et contra eos et eorum quemlibet eciam usque ad finalem con-
dempnacionem eiusdem Pi' Ape' ac ceterorum predictorum et eorum cuiuslibet
prosequendum et recuperandum dampna et expensa ac interesse ac execuciones
quecumque petendum et recipiendum ac de receptis et recuperatis acquietanciis
vice et nomine meo predictis faciendum, sigillandum, dandum et liberandum;
necnon condempnatos seu condempnatum ac condempnandos vel condempnan-
dum extra prisonam deliberandum dampna quoque expensas et interesse ac alias
quascumque et soluciones licitos nomine meo subiundum et faciendum cetera quia
omniam et singulam que per me in premissis seu aliquo premissorum debite fieri
possunt pro me et nomine meo plenarie agendum exercendum funendum et
expidiendum a Deo libere et precise prout ego ipse facerem si penes personaliter
interesse ratum et gratum habentem et habitur totum et quicquid dictos procuratores et attornati mei coniunctim vel eorum alter dimidium fecerint aut fecerit
nomine meo in premissis seu aliquo premissorum. [f.36] In cuius rei testimonium
sigillum meum presentibus apposui. Et quia sigillum meum pluribus est incognitum
ideo sigillum honorabilis et discreti viri Willelmi Chimney nunc maioris dicte
civitatis Ebor' presentibus apponi procuram in fidem et testimonium omnium et
singulorum premissorum. Data octavo die mensis Augusti anno domini millesimo
quadringentesimo octogesimo sexto, et anno regni Henrici regis Anglie huius
nominis septum post conquestum primo. Et ego maior predictus ad instanciam et
personalem requisicionem dicti Rogeri sigillum officii mei presentibus apposui,
date in civitate Ebor' predicta die, mense et anno supradictis.

Johannes Harington in legibus bacallarius atque auctoritate apostolica et imperali
notarius publicus dicte civitatis Ebor' consilii clericus premissa fuisse et esse veradico.

.

[Know all men by these presents that I, Roger Laton of York, merchant, have made, established, ordained, and set in my place my beloved in Christ John Squier and James Mollet, merchants of London, to be my true and lawful proxies and attorneys, together and individually, to claim, levy, collect, recover, and receive in my name forty-eight tuns and a pipe and a half of wine taken from me against God and justice by Pi' Ape' [*a contraction of Pierre or Philipe?*] of the city of Bordeaux from a Breton ship or carvel called 'Margareta of Penmark' whose master at that time John La Burdeak was unjustly seized, and each and every good and chattel and items of merchandise belonging to me [**f.35v**] were detained by Pi' Ape. The proxies are to pursue the case and its prosecution against the said Pi' Ape' or anyone else who seised the goods, in secular or ecclesiastical courts, before whatever justices or commissions, so that justice be done, and to make all necessary payments to recover the goods. [**f.36**] In testimony of which I affix my seal. And because my seal is unknown to many, the seal of the honourable and discreet William Chymney, now mayor of York, is also affixed in testimony of each and every of the premises. Given 8 August 1486, in the first year of Henry VII's reign. And I, the aforesaid mayor, at the request of the said Roger, affix the seal of my office, given at York on the day, month and year aforesaid.

John Harington, bachelor of laws and also by apostolic and imperial authority notary public of the said city of York and clerk of the council, verifies this premise.]

Complaint Made to King Henry
28 August 1486

The xxviij[th] day of August passed under seal a letter wherof the tenour ensuyth:

To the moost high and mightie Cristine prince and our moost redoubtid soveraine lord the king

Moost high and mightie Cristened prince and our moost redoubtid souverain lord, we in the moost humble and obidient wise recommend us unto your highnese with as hertly myndes and willis todoo your grace condigne pleaser and service with our bodies and goodes according to our duties as any subgiettes can bee toward ther naturall soverain lord, besuching your saide highnese to have knawleige that we being the moost havie creatours abiding togader in such a citie have sent unto your moost noble and rioall persone the clerc of our poore counsail, the berer herof, whome we moost humble besuch your highnesse forsaide to yeve licence to shewe to the same the cause of our hevinese, and in that behalve to be unto us moost benigne and ⟨gracious⟩ soveraine lord, and we shall daily pray to God to preserve you moost high and mightie Cristened prince and our moost redoubtid soverain lord [**f.36v**] in felicitie long to endure to his pleaser. Fro your citie of York the xxviij day of August.

Your moost humble subgettes the maier, aldermen, comon counseil and the commonaltie of your citie of York

Letters Requesting Remission of Fee Farm
1 September 1486

To my moost especiall gode lord and maisteris the maier, aldermen, sheriffes and other of the counsail of the citie of York

After moost humble and deu recommendacion unto you my lord and maisteris, pleas it you to knawe that this Fryday after my lordes sekenesse, his grete labour and disportes takyn with Sir John Savil, Sir Thomas FetzWilliam, Master Sapcottes, Robert Gren and othre many grete gentilmen toward my lord of Shrowesbury being with hym at my commyng and departing, my saide lord with deligent remembrance of the cause of my commyng, ffirst stodid how to write and to whome and finally addressid two lettres, one to my lord chaunceler and the othre to Maister Secretarie; Master Carnebull sparid not hym self in this matier and after his deligent labour maide unto my lord for my delivere he at my desire haith with his owne pen commendid me and the cause of my riding unto Master Secretarie with whome he may do asmuch as eny of his degre and many above the same liffing, the copies of all thies lettres ensueth herafter. It is wele doone that a letter furthwith be maide unto the saide Maister Carnebull efter the effect of a pauper herin closed and the same to be conveide to him by a sure messinger within vij dais after the receipt herof if eny such be knawne; and elles with John Sponer it is loked after soo soone for diverse causes **[f.37]** which I shall shew unto you at my commyng home by Godes grace which I trust to God shalbe sone and wele to your pleasers, wherunto I shall endevour me with all deligence. My lord chaunceler is at Eely and the king at Wynchestre, and our lord God preserve you right honourable and my (right) speciall good lord and maisters in felicitie long tendure to his pleasour. Fro

Your moost humble servaunt John Harington

Copie of the letter sent to my lord chaunceler

My lord I commend me unto you in myn hertlyest maner, and where ye rather at your instance for the which I hertely thank you and all thei of the citie of York entend you service, the kinges grace knawing the grete ruyne and decay of his saide citie by his lettres patentes graunted to the same all fee ferme therof to hold at his pleaser, yelding yerly unto his highnese xviij li. v s., the which grace of the king bounde theme of the same citie tobe his bedemen and fastened theme faithfully to his highnese, now is assigned for the kinges household Cxx li. parcell of the saide fee ferme contrarie the saide graunt laborid by you; this thing passing the prince and his counceill so soone chaunceed hevieth soore and troubeleth the maier and his brether with othre rulers of the saide citie, by the which and by othre means thei be gretely encombrede, as Maister John Harington this berer clerc of the counseile of the saide citie can shew you, to whome I pray you yef credence, and as ye have be gone with theme for there wele soo continue and the rathre for my sake, wherof I eftsones pray you as hertely as I canne, and almightie Jeshu have you ever in his moost mercifull keping. At my maner of Southwell the first day of Septembre.

Yours during my life Thomas Ebor'

[f.37v] Copie of the letter direct to Maister Secretarie fro my lord archibisshop

Maister Secretarie, I commaund me unto you in myne hertiest maner, and where the kinges grace knawing the grete ruyne and decay of his citie of York by his lettres patentes grauntid to the saide citie all the fe ferme of the same to hold at his pleasour, yelding yerely xviij li. v s., the which grace of the king bounde theme of the saide citie tobe his bedemen and fastined theme faithfully to his (hib) highnesse, now is assigned out of the kinges eschequire for the household by tale made unto Richard Junour of Westm' Cxx li. parcell of the saide fee ferme contrarie to the saide graunt; this thing passing the kinges highnesse and his counceill to some chaungede heveth soore and troubleth the maier and his brethre and rulers of the saide citie, by the which and by othre means thei be gretely encumbrede as Maister John Harington clerc of the counseill of the saide citie can shew you, to whome I pray you yeve credence; and be such meane unto the kinges grace at this tyme that rathre by your labour the saide taile may be called in againe and the saide Maister John soo delivered that he commyng to the saide maier and his brethre before the day of eleccion of new sheriffes of the saide citie, which he can name unto you, may bring theme in writing some thing frome the kinges grace to ther comford, now set in grete hevinesse; wherof I eftsones pray you as hartly as I can and allmightie Jeshu preserve you to his pleasour. At my maner of Southwell the first day of Septembre.

Your lover Thomas Ebor'

[f.38] Copie of Maister Carnebull letter direct to Maister Secretarie

After my deutie with recommendacion unto your good maistership, please it the same to wite that my special loveing frende Maister John Harington this berer haith required me to recommend him with the cause of his commyng unto you, and soo I doo in myne hertiest maner, besuching you for him for thexpedicion of the saide cause, and for the soone sending him hoome, but for the grete trust he haith in your maistership it had bee hard to have coniured hym to have commen to the court as a sewtour; the next tyme I shall write to you to chaunge your style, I trust in God, who have you ever myne especiall good maister in his moost mercifull keping. At Southwell the first day of Septembre.

Yours ever H. Carnebull

[ff.38v–39 blank]

[f.39v]   **Sheriffs Make Payments in Accordance with King Henry's Letters Concerning Fee Farm**
          Undated, c.September 1486

Mayor: William Chimney. Recorder: John Vavasour. Deputy recorder: Thomas Asper. 12: Thomas Wrangwish, John Tong, William Welles, John Newton, Nicholas Lancastre.

Sheriffs: Nicholas Vicars, Roger Appilby. 24: Thomas Aleyne, William Spence, William Taite, John Hagge, Miles Grenebank, Richard Hardsang, William Barkar, John Giliot, Thomas Fynsh.

Assembled in counsail, received and hard redd the kinges severall lettres bering the tenour herafter writtin; and therupon the same redd and understanditt, it was determined that the sheriffes now being and thexsecutours of John Beverley late sherife shuld pay furthwith unto the handes of the chamerleyns threskor poundes to the behove of this citie by force of the kinges lettres patentes made in that behalve, and that the maier and aldermen and counsaile forsaide shuld see that the saide (counsail) ⟨sheriffes⟩ and exsecutours shuldbe kepid harmeles in that behalve in case that thei never have allowaunce of the same in the kinges exchequier at ther acomptes tobe yeldid in that partie; and that also the said sheriffes and executours shuld pay unto the maier nene powndes two shelinges and sex penys to his use as dew unto him at Estre last past as seriaunt at armes so named by the lettres patentes made by King Richard, and that the saide maier shalbe boundon to kepe theme harmeles in that behalve. In witnesh wherof the maier, aldermen, sheriffes and counsailours herafter haith writtin ther names. [*Signatures follow at bottom of folio*: Thomas Aspar, William Chymney mayr, Thomas Wrangwish, Robert Hankoc, John Harppar, Thomas Scotton, Thomas Kater, John Tonge, Thomas Aspar, [*blank*] Wycars, William Taite, W. Barkar, W. Whit, John Gilliott, Thomas Fynch, N. Loncastre, M. Grenbank, Th. Aleyne.]

[f.40]   Royal Letter Pardons Most of Fee Farm
                    12 September 1486

[*This folio was torn on the right edge; the missing piece was incorrectly rejoined to the folio and is one line out of sequence.*]

By the king

To our trusty and welbeloved the maier, aldermen, shiriffes and common counsail of our citie of York

Trusty and welbeloved, we grete you wele, and where as we at our last being at our citie there seing the great ruyne and extreme decay that the same is fallen in, pardoned you in relief thereof all such fee ferme sauf oonly the some of xviij li. v s., the same to contynue duryng our pleaser, it is shewid unto us by our welbeloved Maister John Haryngton clerc of your counsaill how that ye stand in dought and feer whethre our saide graunt shalbe unto you valeable or effectuell by cause of ane assignament maide upon the saide fee ferme of the some of Cxx li. for thexpenses of our household, we assure you how be it that the saide assignement precedid our saide graunte maid unto you, yet our ful entent and mynd is that ye shall fully enioy theffect of the same, and woll that according to our saide pardone ye reteyne stil in your handes your saide fee ferme for this yere and so forth during our pleaser, and we shall othrewise provide for thassignement of our saide household, willing therfore that noon of you dought or feer to take upon him thoffice of sheriffes or other offices of our saide citie, for we shall see our saide graunt to stand ferme and stable wherunto ye may verely trust, and where we assigned certain money of the saide fee ferme to be emploed upon the reparacion of the wallis and othre thinges of our saide citie, we woll and charge you the sheriffes there that such money remanyng in your handes for the saide causes ye doo deliver unto the chamerleins there by theme to be bestowed according to our saide assignement, not leving this undoone as ye entend to please us. Yeven under our signet at our monasterie of Shaftesbury the xij day of Septembre.

[f.40v]   King Henry Orders Peace to be Kept
12 September 1486

By the king

To our trusty and welbeloved the maier, aldermen and sheriffes of our citie of York

Trusty and welbeloved we grete you wele, lating you weit that it haith be shewid unto us how that matiers by means of uniust mayntenaunce and otherwise have be late attained within our citie there by certaine persones whos names our welbeloved Maister John Harington clerc of your counsaill by our commaundement shal shew unto you at large, not oonly to the subversion of our peax and lawes and perturbance of our true subgettes bot also by the same diverse of theme have be put to thextreme daungier and perill of their lives, wherof we be not content nor pleased; wherfore we entending rest and unite to be establisshed amonges our subgiettes especially amonges thincorporates and inhabitaunces of our citie there which we have in favour and tendernesse of our good grace, wol and desire you that calling the persones before you betwix whom the saide contraversies rest, ye woll deligently examine the grounde and occasion of the same, and thereupon by thadvise of your lerned and sad counsaill, and by such ⟨wise⟩ and discrete ways as ye can use, ye woll indevour you to the finiall appesing of the same and establisshment of rest and unite to be had amonges our subgettes there to the good publike and sad governaunce of our saide citie, and if ye fynde any persone obstenate and not confourmable herunto that then ye certifie us of his name and we shall provide such sharp remidy herin according to his demerites as shalbe to the ferefull exemple of all othre, doing your true and effectuall diligence herin as we may evidently perceive and understand the good disposicions that ye have tobeye and please us. Yeven under our signet at our monasterie of Shaftesburie the xij day of Septembre.

[f.41]   Council Clerk Accused of Being a Scot
Undated, after 26 September 1486

Mayor: William Chimney. Recorder: John Vavasour. 12: Richard York, Thomas Wrangwish. Sheriff: Roger Appilby. 24: William Spence, John Hagge, Richard Hardsang, William Barker, John Giliot.

Assembled in counseil received a letter bering the tenour ensuyng:

To the right honorable sirs, the maier, aldermen and comon counseil of the citie of York

Your awne Sir John Aske

Right honorable sirs, I commaund me unto you and thank you for the tender favour that ye have unto my kynseman Master John Harington the clerc of your couneseil, and wher I am informed that he at his late being with the kinges grace understode by his good lordes and maisteris ther that he was reputid to be a Scot, which grew on the report of one Thomas Wharf of [your] citie, whome ye have examyned and ferder entendith to examyne in that behalve, I desire you to have knawlege for truith that the saide Master John was borne in Estryngton besides Houeden of his moder a poore gentil[wo]man whos fader was to my ffader, whome God assoile, at the third and third [sic] degre of consanguinitie, which I wold have comen and shewid unto you in propre person if it had semed to my saide kynseman that I shuld soo have done, and soo I wol at his pleaser herafter. If this sclaunderous report come to the eers of some yongmen of the blode that he is of, it woll grewe theyme, I doubt not, which I pray you desire the saide Thomas Wharfe to remembre. Asfor his ffader, I trust he woll declare hyme unto you to be an Englishman and a poore gentilman borne, thof he never weir taken heir bot for a yoman which he haith been right wele at ease before this, and yit may lif to his honestie, blissid be God, the better, if my saide kynseman his sone faire wel, to whome I pray you for my sake to be more singular good lord and maisters if ye can soo be in eny wise, and our lord God preserve you to his pleasour. Frome Aughton the xxvj day of Septembre.

[f.41v blank]

[f.42]   **Penalty for Striking a City Official, Judgement on Aldermen's Dispute Undated**

[This folio is incorrectly bound after [f.44v].]

Mayor: William Chimney. Recorder: John Vavasour. Deputy recorder: Thomas Asper. 12: Thomas Wrangwish, John Fereby, William Welles, John Newton, Nicholas Lancastre, Robert Hancok, Thomas Scotton, William White. Sheriffs: Nicholas Vicars, Roger Appilby. 24: Thomas Catour, William Taite, (Thomas) ⟨William⟩ Spense, John Hagg, Michael White, Miles Grenebank, Richard Hardsang, William Barkar, John Giliot.

Assembled determined that who soo ever being eny of the incorporates of this citie that violently in his awne defalt drawith herafter eny blode of the maier, aldermen or other of the counseill as the xxiiij[or], recorder, record[er] deputie, common clerc or othre of the saide counseill resiant and abiding within the saide citie, besides amendes deu unto the partie shal pay unto the behove of the citie at every tyme ten powndes without pardon therof.

And also thei thought that John Vavasour recorder *impar* electid betwixt John Harper alderman on the one partie and William Todd laite alderman on the other partie, of almaner of accions, debates, trespasses, contraverses and demandes hanging betwixt the saide parties, shuld yeve award, which therupon awardid, ordenyd and iugied the saide John Harper and William Todd shuld forbeir going [in] procession and making of offering in propre persones unto the Monday in the third weke of Lent in her parich church, as in likewise John Feriby haith promised to doo; after the which Monday the abovewrittin John Harper continewyng alderman shalhave in the saide church and all other places within the liberties of this citie and at all tymes preeminence afore the saide William Tod, remaneing bot a communer; and also that the saide William Todd shuld pay unto the forsaide John Harper in recompence and amendes for his hurt ten powndes with payment of such money as the surgiours shalhave for ther labour in curing of the saide John Harper, which the saide William [f.42v] paide without delay unto the forsaide John Harper; and also that the same John Harper in presence of the maier, aldermen and the common counsell shuld say and soo he saide unto the saide William Tod the wordes felowing, that is to say: 'Maister maier and the maisteris bredren and aldermen, it is so that before this tyme I called William Tod a coyner and a money maker by hardsaw or saying of othre men and none othre wise, notwithstanding I say for certeine that I never knew hym for none nor never understude hyme as oone'. And finially that eithre of theime shuld be fully frenedid with the othre and take handes, which thei did. And the same John Harper at the contemplacion of my lord ⟨C s.⟩ of Northumbreland, the saide John Feriby ⟨lx s.⟩ and the saide maier and his brederne, yafe unto the saide William nene powndes parcell of the saide ten powndes and unto a diner to be made emonges the hole company in confirmacion of the saide aggrement and concorde, the saide John Harper departid with twentie shelinges residewe of the saide ten powndes.

Lease of the Common Crane
13 January 1487

And over this it was determined that William Jacson shuld have the craen to ferme by endentour after the tenour ensuyng, finding two sufficiaunt sureties for him in that partie.

Tenour of thindentour

dimisio de crane This indentour maide in the fest of Saint Hillarie the secund yere of the reigne of King Henrie the sevent; witnesh that the maier and comunaltie of the citie of York haith dimisid and lattin to ferme unto William Jacson of York merchaunt the comon craen belonging unto the saide citie, with all houses and other appurtenaunces therunto belonging to eny wise in as large and ample maner and forme as it haith be dimised and lattin to eny man hertofor, to have and to hold the saide craen with houses and thappurtenaunces unto the saide William and his sufficiaunt deputites frome the daite herof unto thend and terme of ten yeres after the daite of thies presentes, successively felowing, yelding and [f.43] paying yerely for the saide craen with thappurtenaunces unto the saide (craen) maier and comunaltie or chamerleins of the saide citie and ther successours for tyme being during the saide terme of ten yeres aforsaide, at such usuall terme or termes in the yere as the saide ferme of the craen haith be wont to be payed, that is to say in the fest of Saint Petre callid Advincle and the nativitie of our lord God, by even porcions ten markes of laufull English money; and the saide maier and comunaltie shall reparell at ther propre costes and chargies all and every house of office or othre belonging unto the saide craen during the saide terme of ten yeres without eny cost to be maide upon the saide houses by the saide William. Also the saide William willes and grauntes by thies presentes not onely to stand and beir at his propre chargies all maner casualties and infortune of ony thing commyng or happunyng to the saide craen, dischargeing therof the saide maier and comunaltie of the saide infortunes and casualties during the saide terme; and also susteigne and ber at his propre costes and expenses almaner slinges, cabilles, hookes and al othre thinges apperteigning to hemp wair convenient for the saide craen during the terme aforsaide; and soo leve the same in thend of the saide terme providid alway that the saide maier and chamerleins of the saide citie for the tyme being shall aied, succour, and defend the saide William in every thing belonging to the saide craen for the saide terme according to the ancheane ordinaunce and custome maide and continued in that behalve; and that no fraunchest man or woman of the saide citie in eny wise shall colour eny straungers goodes or merchaundises during the saide terme or othre thing wrangfully attempt unto the damage of the saide William, bot the maier for the tyme being shall indevour hym to see a redresse and amendes maide for the same at all convenient [f.43v] tyme when he shalbe desiride by the saide William, and the saide maier and comunaltie shall waraunt and defend the saide craen with houses and thappurtenaunces aforesaide in forme and maner above contened unto the saide William Jacson or his sufficiaunt deputie ayenst almaner persones during the terme of ten yeres aforsaide. In witnesh wherof aswele the seal of thoffice of maioraltie of the saide citie as the seal of the saide William enterchaungeable be put to the parties of thies indentours. Yeven at York forsaide the day and yer above writtin.

Investigation into Possession of Common
Undated

common in the Tangefeld Also after communicacion had in the counsaille chamer at the common hall, it was determined that Master Carnebull shuld have warnyng to shew his evidence whereby he pretendith to have in severaltie a close callid Tanghall, parcell of his prebend of Fridaythorp, before the feste of (Saint) Alhalous next ensuyng; at the which tyme the recorder, resorting unto the citie with certaine oder persons to be named by the discrecion of the counsaille, shall tak avowe of all such grondes aboute the citie as the inhabitance of the same aught to have common in or in severaltie, and therupon by the aviace of the saide recorder to make entresse according, and that unto the saide feste of Alhalous noo thing shalbe attemptid preiudiciall to the saide Master Carnebull touching the forsade Tanghall or othrewise.

**[f.44]   Admission of a New Wait, Recorder Requested for Money
                  4 October 1486**

Mayor: William Chimney. 12: Richard York, Thomas Wrangwish, John Tonge, John
Feryby, John Newton, Robert Hancok, Thomas Scott. 24: Thomas Catour, Miles
Grenebank, Richard Hardsang, William Barker.

Assembled acceptid and admittid Robert Conigilton, one of the waites of this citie,
tobe in the roume of Robert Sheyne being in so grete age and soo decrepid that he
ne may forthre attend thoccupacion of waite forsaide. In consideracion wherof and
of the long continued service that he haith done in the saide rowme by the space of
xl yeres and more, it is determined that the saide Robert Sheyne yerely during his
life and while the said Robert Conigilton shalbe heire waite, shalhave in name of a
pension of the same Robert Conigilton thertene shelinges and (for) ⟨four⟩
penys to be payde wharterly without deley, and forthre that the saide Robert
Sheyne shuld have in his reliefe during his life a house of the commons with charge
of reparacion without eny othre ferme paying for the same.

Also the same day it was determined that a letter shuldbe directed to John
Vavasour recorder after the tenour ensuyng:

To the right worshipfull sir and our right trusty and hertely welbeloved John
Vavasour seriaunt at law, recorder of the citie of York

Right worshipfull sir and our right trusty and welbeloved, we in our moost hertely
wise recommend us unto you, thanking you of your hertely disposicion toward us
and this citie, and for your grete labours and peyns taken at many tymes for the
wele of the same in which behalve we pray you of good continuaunce, and that in
consideracion of that at ye knaw the grete nede which our chamerleines haith of
money to be emploed aboute the reparacion of our walles and othre thinges of
charge of the saide citie, ye wol take such peyne on you at this the commyng of our
brothre Richard York unto the kinges grace, as by the same and help of our saide
brothre we may have hastely word frome you againe to our comford and profit of
the same citie as our verrey trust is in you, that knaweth our lord God who ever
preserve you, right worshipfull sir and our right trusty and welbeloved in felicitie
long to endur. Fro York the fourt day of Octobre.

Your awne the maier and aldermen of the citie of York

**[f.44v]   Lady Fitzhugh's Testimonial for John Harrington
                  30 October 1486**

The thirtie day of Octobre

Mayor: William Chimney. Deputy recorder: Thomas Asper. 12: John Tonge, William
Welles, John Newton, Nicholas Lancastre, Robert Hancok, William White, Thomas

Aleyne. 24: Michael White, Miles Grenebank, William Barker, Thomas Fynch, Nicholas Vicars.

Assembled received a letter bering the tenour herafter ensuying:

To the right worshipfull sirs, the maier, aldermen and common counseil of the citie of York

Aleys Lady FetzHugh

Right worshipfull sirs, I commaund me unto you, and for somuch as Maister John Harington after your departour fro me and my lord, my sone, in the church of York resorting unto me and my saide sone in the Freers Austen soo demeanyd hyme that I and my saide sone and all othre my sones was verey wele content with hyme, I wolling you to knaw the same, desire you if eny persone herafter being in the citie ther wold shew the contrarie or eny thing attempt in that behalve to the hurt of eny persone, that ye wol indeferently and wisely direct the same, shewing for undoubtid that I am as good lady unto the saide Master John as ever I was, and all my sonnes as good lordes and maistirs unto hyme as thei have bene unto hyme in eny tyme past, nought doubting bot he shall soo demean hyme toward us that he shalbe in more singular favour with us then ever he was before this by Godes grace, who ever preserve you to his pleaser. Fro my maner of Tanfeld the xxij day of Octobre.

[f.45] Investigation into Tanghall Commons 31 October and 4 November 1486

[*This folio is bound after [f.47v].*]

the xxxj day of Octobre

Mayor: William Chimney. Deputy recorder: Thomas Asper. 12: Thomas Wrangwish, John Tong, John Fereby, William Welles, John Newton, Nicholas Lancastre, Robert Hancok, John Harper, William White. 24: Thomas Catour, Thomas Aleyne, John Hagge, William Taite, Miles Grenebank, William Spence, Michael White, Richard Clerc, William Barker, John Giliot, Thomas Fynsh, Nicholas Vicars, Roger Appilby.

Assembled in counseil concludid that an abstinence shuld be had of entre unto the common which is pretendid to be had in Tonghall unto the end of the next moneth, and all othre groundes wherin eny comon is pretendid, and that the serchours shuld be movid to be content with the same shewing that John Sponer upon Friday or Saturday next commyng shall for the good directing of the premisses be send to London to the recorder with a letter to the recorder and instruccions to be made unto hyme after the tenour ensuyng herafter; and that in the mean tyme communicacion shulbe had with the commoners dwelling next unto such groundes as was in travax to understand ther myndes in that partie; wherupon the saide comoners movid by Thomas Scotton, Roger Appilby and othre therunto assigned consentid that like abstinence shuld be had unto the fest of Saint Andrew next commyng.

To the right honorable Sir John Vavasour seriaunt at law recorder of the citie of York

Right honourable sir, we commaund us unto you and thank you in our moost hertely maner for the grete peyns which ye have taken and dayly takith on you for the wele of this citie; sir, the commoners heir callith soo to have entrie of ther comon, we have with great labours entreatid thame to be content to forbere unto the fest of Saint Andrew, shewing unto thame that in the meane tyme we shal have your presence heir or at the leist your hole counseil and mynd in writing under what forme we shall take entriee; wherfore we hertely besuch you to see and ripely examen such instruccions as we have yeven in writing to the berer herof to be shewed unto you; and therupon if ye may in eny wise therof it be to your peyne and losse dispose you to be heir before the saide fest of Saint Andrew, ye shall never doo thing of greter pleaser to us **[f.45v]** and the hole comunaltie; and if ye may not in all goodly haist to certifie us by writing soo clerely that this berer nede have no credence unto us aswele tuching the good spede of the pardone of our fee ferme as of the entre unto our saide common which we cannot (entred) entrete the comoners to forbere longar than to the saide fest of Saint Andrew, all be it we and all thei as ye knaw wele be disposed to doo what we goodly may in favour of Master Carnebull specially and othre also in whos groundes we claime common. If our brothre Master York be with you, we besuch you to commaund us hertly unto hyme and pray hyme of his help and good aviace in this behalve, wherunto we trust, that knaweth our lord who preserve you. Frome York the fourt day of Novembre.

Your awne the maier, aldermen and comon counsell of the citie of York

Instruccions yeven to the messager which shall resort frome the citie of York to Master Recorder of the same:

First desire to knaw of hyme how he haith spedede in the citie matier touching the kinges graunt made to the citie, and if it be sped to send word certaine of the same furthwith if eny come heder before the commyng home of the saide messager.

If it be not finally sped sollicit diligently frome tyme to tyme the saide Master Recorder and Master York for the hasty speid of the same if the king be at London or if the speide therof may be had ther in his absence and elles by ther good aviace and writing to be sent unto the court to the kinges secretarie or othre after their wise discrecions to labour for a final conclusion in that behalve. Master Asshby of the signet haith the registour conteignyng the last letter sent frome the king to this citie in that matier; **[f.46]** he is wise and luffeing, and with Master Secretarie may doo moost in that behalve unto whome Master Harington haith writin a letter tuching the premisses, to thintent if the case require, that the saide massager may have a cause to present hyme self to the saide Master Asshby if the saide Master Recorder and Master York seyme he shall soo doo besides ther writing to be made in that behalve.

no [illegible] article Secundly shew unto the saide Master Recorder and Master

York how that the comoners of this citie, calling to remembrance the good and luffeing wordes spokyn unto theyme in the name of the hole counseil by the mouth of Master Recorder, desiring an abstinence of entre of eny ther common kept in severaltie unto this fest of Alhalous, shewing that then thei shuld indoubtidly by his good aviace and help have peaxable entrie, without in the meane tyme thinges might be foundon and shewid by the contrarie parties why thei might not to have such comon, now the saide comoners haith desirid of the saide counseil that thei may have the saide comon. It is knawne that such lettres as was directid frome this citie to Master Carnebul in that behalve remaneth yit in Suthwell by cause of his absence to hyme not shewid; considering therfore how the said abstinence of entre unto this fest of Alhallous was taken moost specially for favour of the saide Master Carnebull, in consideracion of the good maistership and singular favour that he haith oftentymes shewid to this citie, the saide counseil with the consent of the comoners wolling to doo forther pleaser unto the saide Master Carnebull specially and othre in whos groundes thei have comon, and also being desiorous restfully to have ther right haith consent that a like abstinence of entre shalbe had unto the fest of Saint Andrew; wherfore desire ye the saide Master (Carnebull) Recorder and Master York to speke with the saide Master Carnebull if he be ther and othre as it shall seyme unto theme in preventing of such compleintes as peraventour herafter may be made contrarie the truth to the hurt of some of the saide counseil or othre of the citie to the kinges highnesse, the lordes or othre of his noble counseil or to the saide Master Carnebull to provoke hyme to displeser without cause.

[f.46v] Thirdly, bring certaine word in writing frome the saide Master Recorder if he (can) ⟨come⟩ not in proper person hider before the saide fest of Saint Andrew, whos presence the saide counseil and comoners desierith to have before the saide fest, how, when, and in what maner thei shall entre with all othre circumstance required in that behalve to thintent that no thing shalbe attemptid contrarie the kinges peax and his (h) lawes to the growge or displeasour of eny person.

This premisses shewid by the sight of this pauper unto the saide Master Recorder and Master York doo after ther commaundement, shewing unto theyme as ye wisely can by mouth what ye knaw to be shewid ferthre for the haisty accomplisshment of the same; and therupon dispose you homewarde in all goodly haist.

[f.47]   **Fee Farm Rescued from Royal Household**
              12 November 1486

[*This folio was torn and the missing piece rejoined incorrectly to the right margin, one line out of sequence.*]

the xij^th day of Novembre

The maier and his brethern received a lettre sent frome the recorder (and), Maister York, Thomas Henrison and George Skalby bering the tenour ensuyng:

To all Cristen people to whos notice thies presentes shall come, William Chimney maier of the citie of York sendith greting in our lord God everlasting. Seith it is meritorie by the declaracion of the truith to provoke Christen people to thexecucion of elimose and othre dedes of charitie, I therfor the saide maier wolling to releve povertie of evere indegent creature, acertain your universitie that John Whitfeld which haith by divers yeres been conversaunt and abiding within the saide citie of peaxable and true conversacion is fallen by sinistre fortune ⟨and gret sekenes⟩ into such feblenesse of his body and povertie that without the succour of othre he may not defending his naturall life pay his debtes nor without more haistie succour be shewid unto him kepe his personne frome durance of impresonment ayenist the prosecucion and suytes of his creditours; wherfore pleas it you of your charitie the nathre for this my true testimonie and declaracion to accept and receive the saide John unto your gracious favour and hyme releve in wey of pitie and charitie with your elimose, by the which ye shall doo unto God as in myne opinion thing of grete merite, causing me, my brethre aldermen and othre of the forsaide citie in such case herafter to shew at your desier similable pleasour. Yeven under the seal of office of maieraltie of the saide citie the xij day of Januare the secund yere of the reigne of our soverain lord the king Henrie the sevent.

To all Cristen people to whos notice thies presentes shall come, William Chimney maier of the citie of York, aldermen, shiriffes and commen counesellours of the same sendith greting in our lord God everlasting. For somoch as by the ordour of reasone and band of charitie evere personne being in auctoritie or callid to honour above othre is boundon by true testimonie (state and degre in case of nede conveniently required) to declare the innocencie of his nebour being of inferior condicion, state **[f.59]** and degre in case of nede conveniently required, we therfore wolling all ambiguitie and slaunederous fame laboring as it is saide ayenist our welbeloved conciticyne Roger Brokholis to be laide apart and the verey truith to be manifest and knawne in thinges concernyng his demeanaunce ayenist certain pleges and suerties of one Robert Porte late of York forsaide, certifie your universitie that the saide Roger after deu and laufull processe had and continued in the shiriffes court of the saide citie recovered ayenist the forsaide suerties in an accion of trespase.

[f.59v]   Violent Behaviour of Minster Vicars
Undated, c.January 1487

Mayor: William Chimney. Legal advisors: Thomas Middilton, Edmund Thwaites, Thomas Asper. 12: William Welles, Nicholas Lancastre, John Harper, William White. Sheriffs: John Beysby, John Shaw. 24: Thomas Catour, Richard Clerc, John Hagg, Thomas Aleyne, Michael White, William Taite, Miles Grenebank, Richard Hardsang.

It ⟨was⟩ is thought in counesell taken by the saide maier, aldermen, shiriffes and common counesellours of the citie of York, that wher certain vicars of the church of York with othre lately assembled riotously to the nowmebre of xxx personnes or moo within the saide citie, and therupon walking thrugh the citie by nyght hurt certaine personnes of the same citie, and also wher certain personnes of the clouse of York assembled theme in grete nowmbre in maner of warre and therupon commyng into the citie shot many arrous ayenist the sheriffes and ther foulkes commyng with theme for the conservacion of the peax, and hurt George Essex and othre waiting of the saide shiriffes, emanges othre thing shuld be taken as a common matier of the saide citie soo tobe examined and concludid; and that Roger Laton, the wif of Thomas Rich with othre of the saide citie, fyndyng theme grevid in this behalve shalhave warnyng to prepare ther particuler compleintes, and the same shew unto my lord of Northumbreland and his counesell, by this too take such direccion as shalbe thought moost convenient.

[f.60]   **William Todd as Alderman**
          31 January 1487

The last day of (Fevru) Januar'

Mayor: William Chimney. Deputy recorder: Thomas Asper. 12: Thomas Wrangwish, William Snawsill, John Fereby, William Welles, Nicholas Lancastre, (William) ⟨Thomas⟩ Scotton, John Harpour, William White.

Assembled in counesell after communicacion had of Thomas Wrangwish and John Harpour at the instant labour and desier of my lord of Northumbr[eland] shewid unto theyme by the mough of Sir William Gascoigne in open counesell, ther being the personnes here writtin, and Sir Hugh Haistinges, Thomas Middilton and Edmund Thwaites to abide the ruell and ordinaunce, arbitrament and jugement of my saide lord in and of almaner of accions, debates, demaundes, trespasses and querelles hanging eny wise betwixt theyme or outhre of theyme and William Tod; the saide Sir William promitting that the saide William shuld abide the same, concludid that the saide William Todd by the avodaunce of the rowme of eny alderman be in deid an alderman and tobe furthwith reputid and taken in evere behalve, and therupon incontinent Thomas Scotton wolling for divers causes leve his rowme desiered to be exonerate of the same his rowme, and (inde) in deid ther surrenderid in the same, which was ther admittid, wherby immediately the saide William Todd was alderman of the citie as in like wise he was in tyme past.

[f.60v blank]

[f.61]   **Bonds, Arbitrations, Appraisal of Goods**
          Undated

Johannes Golan et [*blank, with some erasures making the line illegible*] arbitratores inter Johannem Lowas, Jacobum Link, Milonem Harwom, Thomam Graa, Alexandrum Dauson, citra festum Natalis Domini. Et si etc., tunc unius imperis etc., citra P[ascham?] in x libris etc.

[John Golan and [*blank, etc.*] arbiters between John Lowas, James Link, Miles Harwom, Thomas Graa, Alexander Dauson, [to make a judgement by] Christmas. And if, etc., then an umpire [will be elected, and make a judgement] by Easter [*?*], [under penalty of] £10, etc.]

[*Remaining entries are written upside down on the folio, and are faded and illegible in places*] . . . bonorum Ade Siggeswik qui debet xl marcas [*blank*] Thomas Chapman, (Thomas) ⟨Johannes⟩ Robynson, Thomas Johnson, Johannes Blakey – Memorandum that thies persones shall prayse thie(s) goodes of Adam Sigeswik and after as thei be praysed William Jacson and his brethre in law shall take and recive for the somme of xl markes if thei woll extend therunto ⟨and the residue to pay in money if thei wol not so extend⟩. And if then Adam Sigeswik thinke the goodes praysed to hys prouffit and that then be more necessary for hyme, than the said (William) Adam shall pay unto the saide W[illiam] Jacson and his brethern the said xl markes in money, and they to (a) allowe hyme for pay out of the said xl markes in money iiij markes. And aswele the said William and his brethern as the said Adam byndes thamself and othre of theme in x li. of lawfull Inglessh money to be leveyd of ther goodes and catalles to thuse and prouffit of this citie, that thay and eithre of theme shall bide with praysing of the saide goodes without any contiridiccion etc.

By indentura etc., quod Willelmus (Barbar) ⟨Barton⟩ carpenter filius Johannis Barton unius filiorum Johannis Barton nuper de Ebor' skyner defuncti [*illegible*] etc., Roberto Hancok et Johanni Thibpeny etc., ad termino xv annorum (reddendo inde) pro [*2 lines illegible*]

Colyers Thomas Clepnail bower, Georgius Essex, Johannes Huton, Johannes Clerk, (Georgius Essex), arbitratores inter Robertum Bowman et Ricardum Bowlyn promiserunt stare et obedire se etc., in xx libris, ita quod arbitrium etc., fiant etc., citra festum Sancti Andree etc., et si non concordant tunc eligent imparem inter se etc., ita etc., fiant etc., citra festum Natalis Domini etc.

[By indenture, etc., that William Barton, carpenter, son of John Barton, one of the sons of John Barton, formerly of York, skinner, now deceased, to Robert Hancok and John Thibpeny, etc., for a term of fifteen years [*illegible*]

Colyers Bower Thomas Clepnail, George Essex, John Huton, John Clerk, arbiters between Robert Bowman and Richard Bowlyn, promise to adhere to and obey etc., for £20, that the said arbitration be made by the feast of Saint Andrew, and that if the arbiters cannot agree an umpire will be elected, and [his judgement to be made] by Christmas.]

[ff.61v–62v blank]

[f.63]   **Newly-Elected Officers Take Oaths**
                 16 February 1487

The book of counesell and a[id?] begone in the tyme of the right honourable
William Todd maier of the citie of York in the fest of Saint [*blank*] the xvj day of
Februarie the secund yere of the reigne of King Henrie the sevent

William Todd maier assembled in the common hall with certain his breder
aldermen, shiriffes and common counesellours then being present, the hole
communaltie after the auncient custome usid in the saide citie, the aldermen and
counesellours forsaid weyre callid by name as herafter ensuyth, besids the
serchours of every craft which also was callid.

12: Richard York, Thomas Wrangwish, William Snawsill, John Tong, John Fereby, William
Welles, John Newton, Nicholas Lancastre, William Chimney, Robert Hancok, John
Harpour, William White. Sheriffs: John Beasby, John Shaw. 24: Thomas Catour, Thomas
Aleyne, Henry Williamson, William Spence, Richard Clerc, William Taite, John Hagg,
Michael White, Thomas Pereson, Miles Grenebank, Richard Hardsang, William Barker,
John Giliot, Thomas Fynsh, Nicholas Vicars, Roger Appylby.

Assembled in the saide hall ther being also present Thomas Asper recorder deputie
and Master John Harington c[lerk] **[f.63v]** the saide counesell after the maier,
aldermen, counesellours and clerc forsaide had taken ther theyre oth accustomed,
the commons presentid unto the saide maier a bill of supplicacion wherof the
tenour ensuyth, and therupon the same red; John Haistinges squier at the mase,
John Strangwish swerd berer, John Fery, Thomas Massingham, John Sponer and
John Nicolson seriauntes at the mase, weyre sworne in forme accustumed, [and]
Henrie Barbour was admittid seriaunt at the saide masse.

[ff.64–67v blank]

[f.68]   **Citizens to Keep King's Peace, Unfranchised Glasier Pardoned**
                 2 March 1487

The ij^do day of March

Mayor: William Todd. Deputy recorder: Thomas Asper. 12: Thomas Wrangwish, John
Tong, John Fereby, Nicholas Lancastre, William Chimney, John Harper. Sheriffs: John
Beasby, John Shaw. 24: Thomas Aleyne, William Spense, William Taite, Richard Clerc,
John Hagg, Michael White, Miles Grenebank, William Barker, Thomas Fynsh, Nicholas
Vicars.

Being assembled in counsell the maier commaundid streitly on the kinges behalve
John Marshall ther being present to kep the kinges peax for hyme and his ayenist
Richard Williamson and all othre the kinges people.

[*A hand drawn in the left margin points to this entry.*] [*R*] *glasier* Also that William Craenburgh, for his offense in that he haith occupied within the citie as a fraunchestman in his craft of glasier not being fraunchest, shalbe pardoned at the instance of my lord of Northumber[land] unto whome he haith done service, with that at he shall furthwith admittid a fraunchest man, paying for the same according to the custome of the saide citie in tymes past xxj s., and over that pay and content xx s. equally tobe dividid to the citie and to the craft of glasiers for his upset in the same craft and never the leas dispose hyme to dwell on the common rent.

Also the saide maier commaundid on the kinges behalve Richard Williamson and John Williamson ther and then being present, that thei and eithre of theyme for theme and theirs shuld kep the kinges peax ayenist the saide John Marshall, William Marshall and John Yons ande all othre the kinges people.

[f.68v]   Arrests, Bonds to Keep the Peace
3 and 15 March 1487

Preceptum est vicecomitibus civitatis Ebor' quod attachiant Matheum Cunnyngham ad sectam Willelmi Skelton, date iij° die Marcii.

Willelmus Skelton assumpsit pro seipso quod ipse dampnum vell malum aliquod corporale in Matheum Cunnyngham seu alicui de populo domini regis non faciet nec fieri procurabit quovismodo sub pena xx librarum de bonis et catallis ⟨suis⟩ (eiusdem Willelmi) ad opus eiusdem domini regis levandarum; Thomas Hamlyne, Johannes Frauncisse, Willelmus Tilson et Robertus Jacson wright manuceperunt pro eodem Willelmo, quilibet eorum sub pena x librarum de bonis et catallis suis ad opus eiusdem domini regis levandarum.

Preceptum quod attachiant Eliam Bell ⟨presbiterum⟩ ad sectam Roberti Horblyne.

Elias Bell assumpsit pro seipso quod ipse dampnum vel malum aliquod corporale in Robertum Horblyne vel alicui de populo domini regis non faciet nec fieri procurabit quovismodo sub pena xx librarum; Ricardus Thorneton, Johannes Williamson, Willelmus Mitforth, Robertus (Huchonson) ⟨Goldsmyth⟩ sumpserunt pro eodem, quilibet eorum sub pena x librarum.

xv° die mensis Marcii anno regni regis Henrici vij secundo, Georgius Blovet et Johannes Bailey personaliter comparuerunt coram Willelmo Todde maiore civitatis Ebor' et obligerunt se in iiij libris legalis monete Anglie solvendis ad usum communitatis civitatis Ebor' quod ipsi stabunt et perimplebunt laudum et iudicium Johannis Gaunt, Johannis Hopkynson, Johannis Robynson tailyour et Thome Chapman arbitratorum indifferenter electorum inter eosdem, de et super omnimodis controversiis inter eisdem pendentibus ita **[f.69]** quod huiusmodi laudum feratur inter eisdem citra Dominicam in Ramispalmarum proximam futuram post datam huius recognitionis.

recognitio Thome Watson et Johannis Pereson litsters, partes concordate sunt et vacat recognitio [*entry struck through*] (xix° die mensis Marcii anno regni regis Henrici vij^{mi} secundo, Thomas Watson de Ebor' litster et Johannes Pereson de eadem litster personaliter comparentes coram Willelmo Todde maiore civitatis Ebor' in Guilhada eiusdem obligaverunt et eorum alter obligavit se domino nostro regi in C libris legalis monete Anglie levandis de bonis et catallis eorundem Thome et Johannis ac eorum alterius ad opus maioris et communitatis civitatis Ebor' predicte, de stando, parendo et perimplendo laudum, iudicium et decretum Johannis Stokesley, Thome Wharf bower, Johannis Bell et Johannis Hogeson couper, civium civitatis predicte arbitratorum per dictum maiorem indifferenter nominatorum et electorum in, de et super omnibus et omnimodis controversiis, demandis et querelis inter eosdem Thomam et Johannem qualitercumque exortis, motis sive pendentibus a principio mundi usque in hanc diem, ita quod huiusmodi laudum, iudicium et decretum ferantur inter dictos Thomam et Johannem citra Dominicam in Ramispalmarum proximam futuram post datam presentis recognitionis. Et si huiusmodi arbitratores citra Dominicam predictam inter se ⟨non⟩ concordare nec partes ad concordiam et pacem ducere poterunt prefati Thomas et Johannes obligaverunt (se et) et eorum alter obligavit se in summa predicta levanda ut supra de stando et parendo laudum et iudicium de et super omnimodis controversiis predictis unius imparis per dictum maiorem in hac parte nominandi et eligendi, ita quod idem impar laudum et iudicium sua in premissis inter partes predictas ferat citra vigiliam sacre Pasche extunc immediate sequentis.) Et moniti fuerunt prefati Thomas et Johannes ac eorum alter monitus fuit per dictum maiorem tunc ibidem ⟨et postea post arbitrium⟩ et ex parte domini nostri regis quod ipsi ⟨de cetero⟩ et eorum alter versus ⟨alterum⟩ custodiant ⟨et custodiat ipse⟩ pacem eiusdem domini nostri regis sub pena forisfacture summe xx librarum superius nominate.

[The sheriffs are ordered to arrest Matthew Cunnyngham at the suit of William Skelton, 3 March.

William Skelton undertook that he would do no harm to Matthew Cunnyngham or to any other of the king's subjects, nor cause them any harm, under penalty of £20 levied of his goods and chattels; sureties Thomas Hamlyne, John Frauncisse, William Tilson and Robert Jacson bound themselves on behalf of William for £10 each.

They are ordered to arrest Elias Bell, priest, at the suit of Robert Horblyne.

Elias Bell undertook that he would do no harm to Robert Horblyne or to any other of the king's subjects, nor cause them any harm, under penalty of £20; sureties Richard Thorneton, John Williamson, William Mitforth, and Robert Goldsmyth went to bail for him, each under penalty of £10.

On 15 March 1487, George Blovet and John Bailey personally came before mayor William Todde and bound themselves for £4 payable to the use of the commonalty of York that they would abide by the judgement of John Gaunt,

John Hopkynson, tailor John Robynson, and Thomas Chapman, arbiters impartially elected between them, over all controversies lying between them, **[f.69]** their judgement to be made by Palm Sunday next coming after the date of this bond.

bond of Thomas Watson and John Pereson, dyers, the parties are agreed and the bond is void (On 19 March 1487, dyers Thomas Watson and John Pereson came before mayor William Todde in the Guildhall and bound themselves for £100 to stand to and carry out the advice and judgement of John Stokesley, bower Thomas Wharf, John Bell, and cooper John Hogeson, citizens of the city of York and arbiters impartially named and elected by the mayor concerning all controversies and actions risen forth, moved or lying between the two parties from the beginning of the world to this day, the said judgement to be made by the next Palm Sunday after the date of this bond. And if the arbiters are not able to agree, then Thomas and John are bound to obey the judgement of an umpire named and elected by the mayor, whose judgement is to be given by the eve of Easter immediately following.) Thomas and John were each advised by the mayor that they were to keep the lord king's peace under penalty of forfeiture of £20.]

[f.69v]   Bond to Accept Arbitration
21 March and 26 April 1487

recognitio Rogeri Brokholles et Johannis Hopkynson, vacat quia partes concordate sunt ut patet Rogerus Brokholles de Ebor' bower et Johannes Hopkynson de eadem venerunt personaliter coram Willelmo Todde maiore civitatis Ebor' xxj° die mensis Marcii anno regni regis Henrici septimi post conquestum Anglie secundo, et recognoverunt se debere domino nostro regi xl libras legalis monete Anglie levandas de bonis et catallis prefatorum Rogeri et Johannis ad usum et opus dictorum maioris et communitatis, de stando, parendo et perimplendo laudum, iudicium et decretum Elie Cure, Ricardi Croklyn, Thome Blylye et Willelmi Jacson arbitratorum per dictum maiorem inter partes predictas indifferenter electorum et nominatorum de et super omnibus et omnimodis accionibus, querelis, debatis et demandis inter eos qualitercumque exortis, motis, habitis sive pendentibus a principio mundi usque in diem confeccionis presencium, ita quod huiusmodi laudum etc., feratur inter partes predictas per dictos arbitratores citra Dominicam in Ramispalmarum proximam futuram post datam predictam. Et in casu quod dicti arbitri [*sic*] inter se non concordare nec partes huiusmodi ad pacem ducere poterunt citra Dominicam predictam tunc partes predicte obligarunt se et eorum alter obligavit se in xx libris etc., levandis ad opus predictorum maioris et communitatis de stando et parendo laudum etc., maioris predicti imparis de et super premissis per partes predictas electi; ita quod idem impar ferat laudum suum in hac parte citra Cenam Domini vocatam Shive Thursday extunc proximam sequentem etc.

arbitrium Et prefati arbitri personaliter comparentes coram dicto maiore xxvj° die mensis Aprilis anno predicto in camera civitatis Ebor' (coram) laudum, iudicium et decretum sua tulerunt in hac forma quod prefatus Rogerus Brokholles cum libera amicitia deliberabit et resolvet prefato Johanni Hopkynson de summa per ipsum obtenta in curia dictum Johannem sine dilacione aliquali xj solidos viij denarios que quidem laudum etc., prefatus Rogerus tunc ibidem emologavit et rationem habuit tunc ibidem presentibus tunc ibidem Thoma Asper legisperito, Johanne Catour et Johanne Custance camerariis modo quia Johanni Robynson clerico notario publico etc.

[*acknowledgement of Roger Brokholles and John Hopkynson, void because the parties are agreed, as is clear* Bower Roger Brokholles of York and John Hopkynson came personally before the mayor William Todde on 21 March 1487, and bound themselves in £40 to stand to and carry out the judgement of Elias Cure, Richard Croklyn, Thomas Blylye and William Jacson, arbiters impartially chosen and named by the mayor over all and every of the actions, suits and demands arisen, moved, had, or lying between Roger and John from the beginning of the world to the day these presents [bonds] are made, the judgement to be given by Palm Sunday next coming. And in case the said arbiters are unable to agree and lead the parties to peace by Palm Sunday, then the said parties will bind themselves for £20 to obey the judgement of an umpire elected by the mayor, his judgement to be given by Shrove [*sic*] Thursday next following.

arbitration The aforesaid arbiters came personally before the mayor 26 April in the council chamber and brought their judgement, namely that Roger Brokholles in free friendship will deliver and pay to John Hopkynson the sum of eleven shillings eight pence without delay that Roger agreed to, by man-at-law Thomas Asper, chamberlains John Catour and John Custance, and John Robynson clerk and notary public.]

**[f.70]   Meeting with Thomas Davyson Planned
            13 March 1487**

(Mercurii) Wedynsday the xiij^th day of March [*sic, 13 March 1487 was a Tuesday*]

Mayor: William Tod. Recorder: John Vavasour. Counsellor: Thomas Asper. 12: John Feryby, John Tong, William Wells, John Newton, William Chymney, John Harper. Sheriffs: John Beseby, John Shaw. 24: Thomas Catour, William Spense, Richard Clerc, William Taite, John Gilyot, Thomas Fynche, Nicholas Vicars. Absent: [12:] Richard York, Thomas Wrangwissh, William Snawsell, Nicholas Lancastre, Robert Hancok, William White; [24:] Thomas Alain, Henry Williamson, John Hagg, Michael White, Miles Grenebank, Roger Appilby.

Assembled in counsaill it was determyned that Thomas Davyson shalbe commond with at his commyng to this citie for ij roulez which he had frome the chambre.

[f.70v blank]

[f.71]   **Arrest, Bond to Keep the Peace**
                    26 March 1487

xxvj die Marcii

Preceptum est vicecomitibus quod attachiant Henricum Archer, Thomam Lenyng et Johannem Markyngton ad sectam Willelmi Hyncecliff capellani.

Eodem die ydem (Willelmus Hyn')

Idem Willelmus Hynscliff assumpsit pro se ipso quod ipse dampnum vel malum aliquod corporale Henrico Archer, Thome Lenyng et Johanni Markyngton non faciet nec fieri procurabit quovismodo sub pena xx librarum; Rogerus Laton, Johannes Lounesdall et Johannes [blank] assumpserunt pro eodem Willelmo quilibet eorum sub pena x librarum de bonis et catallis suis ad opus domini regis levandarum.

Eodem die

Johannes Markyngton assumpsit pro seipso quod ipse dampnum vel malum aliquod corporale Willelmo Hynscliff capellano non faciet nec fieri procurabit quovismodo sub pena xx librarum; Johannes Sponer, Willelmus Maundevill et [blank] assumpserunt pro eodem quilibet eorum sub pena x librarum etc.

[The sheriffs are ordered to arrest Henry Archer, Thomas Lenyng and John Markyngton at the suit of chaplain William Hyncecliff.

On the same day

The same William Hynscliff bound himself to do no damage nor bodily harm to Henry Archer, Thomas Lenyng, and John Markyngton, nor cause any harm to be done to them, under penalty of £20; sureties Roger Laton, John Lounesdall and John [blank] bound themselves on behalf of William for £10 each.

On the same day

John Markyngton bound himself to do no damage nor bodily harm to chaplain William Hynscliff, nor cause any harm to be done to him, under penalty of £20; sureties John Sponer, William Maundevill and [blank] each bound himself for £20, etc.]

[f.71v blank]

[f.72]   **Bonds to Accept Arbitration**
               27 March 1487

xxvij^{mo} die Marcii anno regni regis Henrici septimi secundo Thomas Coke vinter et Robertus Rede personaliter comparuerunt coram Willelmo Tod maiore civitatis Ebor' ⟨et obligaverunt se in xx^{ti} libris legalis monete Anglie solvendis ad usum communitatis⟩ quod ipsi stabunt et perimplebunt laudum et iudicium Willelmi Robynson, Roberti Shirley, Johannis Nordouse barker (J) et Johannis Crake arbitratorum indifferenter electorum inter eosdem de et super omnimodis controversiis inter eosdem pendentibus, ita quod huiusmodi laudum feratur inter eosdem citra Dominicam in Ramispalmarum proximam futuram post datam huius recognitionis etc.

vacat quia partes concordate sunt [*entry struck through*] (Eodem die Willelmus Hynsecliff capellanus et tota ars le skynners personaliter comparuerunt coram eodem maiore et obligaverunt se in xx^{ti} libris legalis monete Anglie solvendis ad usum communitatis quod ipsi stabunt et perimplebunt laudum et iudicium Thome Gray, Georgii Kirk, Willelmi Barker merchaunt et Roberti Johnson arbitratorum indifferenter electorum inter eosdem de et super omnimodis controversiis inter eosdem pendentibus, ita quod huiusmodi laudum feratur inter eosdem citra Dominicam in Ramispalmarum proximam futuram post datam (presentium) huius recognicionis etc.) Arbitri tradiderunt laudum inter partes predictas in scriptis ut patet infra et sic recognicio presens est vacua etc.

Manucapcio pro Willelmo Towthorp capellano quod ipse dampnum vel malum aliquod corporale Ricardo Thorp tapiter vel alicui alio de populo domini regis non faciet nec fieri procurabit quovismodo; Johannes Stokesley, Bartramus Dawson, Thomas Topshaw et Johannes Burkhede quilibet manucaptorum obligavit se in x libris et prefatus Willelmus in xx libris legalis monete Anglie solvendis et levandis ad opus (dict') communitatis civitatis Ebor' de bonis et catallis eorundem etc.

[On 27 March 1487, vintner Thomas Coke and Robert Rede personally appeared before mayor William Tod and bound themselves for £20 payable to the use of the commonalty, that they would abide by the judgement of William Robynson, Robert Shirley, barker John Nordouse, and John Crake, arbiters impartially chosen [to decide] all controversies pending between them, the said judgement to be made by Palm Sunday next coming after the date of this bond.

void because parties are agreed (On the same day chaplain William Hynsecliff and all the craft of the skinners personally appeared before the mayor and bound themselves for £20 that they would abide by and carry out the judgement of Thomas Gray, George Kirk, merchant William Barker, and Robert Johnson, arbiters impartially elected [to decide] all disputes pending between them, this judgement to be made among them by Palm Sunday next coming after the date of this bond, etc.) The arbiters handed over their commendation in writing as is clear within and this present bond is void.

Mainprise for chaplain William Towthorp that he do no damage nor bodily harm to weaver Richard Thorp or to any other of the king's subject; sureties John Stokesley, Bartram Dawson, Thomas Topshaw, and John Burkhede each bound himself for £10 and the aforesaid William [bound himself] for £20.]

[f.72v]   **Testimonial of Woman's Good Character**
                28 March 1487

Declaracio bone fame Elizabetha Ricardby uxor Thome Panyerman de Filey

To all true Christen people to whos notice thies presentez shal comme, William Todde maier of the citie of York sendith greting in our lord everlasting. And where it is a thing right meriterioux and acceptable unto God to testifye the truthe in evere thing doubtfull and in especiall the innocency of any persone diffamed of any cryme, whereby ther good name shuld perissh without evident declaracion of the truthe in that behalve, knawe ye therfor for truthe that the xxviij day of this present moneth of March the yere of the reigne of our souverain lord King Herry the sevent the secunde, William Tait, Richard Hardsang, Roger Appilby, John Custance, Thomas Chapman, Robert Yeresley, Thomas Barbour, John Robynson, William Ratcliff, George Blevet, John Smyth, John Tailyour, John Rand, Richard Ruddok, Robert Smyth, William Wynter, William Beene, William Leedes, John Marshall, Herry Ledes and Robert Abell, cociticyns of the said citie of York being personnez of good name and fame and worshipfull conversacion, appering bifore me the said William Todde maier, the chamberleyins and othre ministres of the said citie in the counsaill chambre, ther have reportid and affermed and sworne of the holy evangelistes and upon ther fidelities, truthe and honesties that they have knawne Elizabeth Ricardby now wif to Richard Panyerman of Filey herbifore by the space of viij yeres togadder and more, dwelling with Richard Parke late of York decesid ffisshmonger, and after his decese with Margarete his wife, by all the which tyme the said Elizabeth at all tymes was reputid an honest madyn, clene of body, true of handes and tong and in all thinges appertigneyng to hur womanhode a madyn of honest conversacion and good disposicion, never notid of any cryme or othre thing sinistre; which the said persones with all othre honest neghbours theraboutes wolbe redy as they say to testifye in court or out of court, at any place or tyme when cum they shalbe therunto required; wherfor I the maier forsaid require you to accept, repute and take(n) the said Elizabeth in your favours according to hur meritiez and womanly disposicion forsaid as she is right well worthy to be taken, and the rather at the contemplacion of thies our lettrez testimonialles. Yevene at the citie of York forsaid under the seall of myne office and the severall sealles of the persones above writyn, the day, moneth and yere above writyn.

[f.73]   **Report of Earl of Lincoln's Treason**
                31 March 1487

Thappeching of James Taite and his confession made upon the same

Master Thomas Karlill personally appering bifore William Todde, maier of the citie of York, Sir Robert Rither sheriff of the shire ther, Thomas Aspar recordour deputie, Richard York, John Tong, John Newton and William Chymney aldremen, Thomas Catour, William Taite, Michael White, Richard Hardsang, William Barkar and Nicholas Vicars of the commune counsaill of the said citie, assembled in counsull the last day of March the secunde yere of the reigne of our souverain lord King Herry the sevent, shewed and deliverd unto the said maier a bill writyn with thand of the said master Thomas Karlill bering the tenour ensuyng:

James Taite said to Master Karlill and Sir William Artas parson of Saynt Elyn at the walles and to Sir George Mede and to John Lokyrmose, that therle of Lincoln wold giff the kinges grace a brekefast as it was enfourmed hyme by the servaunt of the said erles, and also that Sir Thomas Malleverey wold take his part with many othre moo, and when the king was at York that the erle afforsaid wald have goone over the walles to Robyn of Redesdall to take his part. Thies wordes was said the xxx^ti day of Marche the ij yere of King Herry the vij to me ⟨the⟩ said Thomas Karlill and to the witnesse afforsaid at iiij of the clok at after nowne within his owne place in the said parisshing of Saint Elyn of York.

Wherupon the said James callid personally to awnswer to the contentes of the same, desired to have a clerk to hyme assigned to write what he wold say in that partye aswell concernyng such thinges as he hard as his langage uttred unto the said Master Thomas in that behalve, which he had assigned to hyme. And therupon the said James or [sic] the departour of the said maier, aldremen and commune counsaill from ther counsaill chambre in his proper persone apperid bifore theme, and to the said maier delyverd a bille of his answere signed with his hand bering the tenour herafter wrytyn:

I James Tayte rade to Retford and upon oure Laidy Day last past as I comme homeward in Doncastre I hit with vij horssez of straungers and ther was amonges them a white horsse led shewing me by a merchaunt [f.73v] servaunt that it was that was in saddell of that horsse gold and silver; than I herd that said soo and askid hyme fro whyne he comme and he said froo London, than an othre of the same merchaunt men askid me wheder ther was any deth within this citie or not, and I said nay, than I shewed unto hyme that I shuld knawe oone of the company by his horsse, he asking me where and howe I shuld knawe this horsse, and I said agane that I knewe hyme in York the last tyme the kinges good grace was ther, for I trowe that he was my lord of Lincolne hobye, for with me was he loged; than this man shewing to hyme my sayng, he comme bak unto me and askid me howe I fore and askid me where I knewe this horsse, and I said he was my lord of Lincolnes, and he bad me say the truthe, and I wist well than that by that same watch word he was my lord of Lincolne horsse; and than I askid hyme howe my lord of Lincolne fore and askid hyme where he was, and he tald me as far furth as he culd undrestand that he was departid from the kinges grace; and I askid hyme wheder to the see or to the lond and he said, 'I trowe he nede not goo to the see, for he hath frendes enogh upon the lond'; and I shewed unto hyme agane that my lord had many good frendes in this cuntree as farfurth as I knew, and I said that bicause have more undrestonding of his communicacion; than he shewing unto me, 'thowe shall see not long too that John of Lincoln shall yeve theme all a brekefast that oweth hyme noo luff nor favour'; I asking hyme that my lord of Northumberland and he stode in condicion, he said agane 'he dothe both litill for us, therfor we sett litill by hyme, for thou shall here tell that right good gentilmen shall take my lordes part. Can ye oght tell me howe farr I have to Sir Thomas Malleverey place, for we must have hyme writing orelles send it hyme'. Then I askid hyme if he wold to York and he said, 'nay, I must to Hull, and if I come to York I shall call upon you'. I comme than to Wentbrig to an in, and spird for thiez merchauntes that wold ride forward to York, and the good man of the house told me that they wer sleping in ther beddes and thiddre I come twise to spire [f.74] after theme. And I desired the hostler for to tell me where he was that rode of the hoby, and had not he bene I had ther tarid longer, than I departid from hyme; and than I met betwix Daryngton and Wentbrig a man that was bowne to the servaunt of my lord of Lincolne that lay at Wentbrig in his bed, and I toke knowlage to that same man for he was somtyme of his company, for he said he had sent for hyme in grete hast with a man that was with hyme hired for to goo for hyme, and I come stregh to York. Than thies same merchauntes of London come unto York and a servaunt of theires shewed me that they shuld mete the prioure of Tynmouthe at the signe of the boore in York. And I come to Master Karlell shewing unto hyme all maner of thinges that I had hard, as is afforsaid, bicause of my discharge and for saving of the othe that I maid to God and the king, and in noone othre wise bycause he was oone of the kinges chapleyns, this servaunt of my lord of Lincolne that shewed me this by the way as I come froo Doncastre hight Saunder. And I shewed unto Mastre Karlill the last tyme the king was here that two felows that dwelt aboute Middelham said that here is good gate for us to Robyn of Redesdall over the walles; and this I said and noo word more, litill nor mekill, and the same two felows resortid to my lord of Lincolne houshold and come thiddre to mete and drink.

This doone, the said maier, aldremen and counsaill sent to oone John Hoton, hostler at the signe of the boore within the said citie, where the priour of Tynmouthe was lately loged, to undrestand if he of the same persones or such othre had any knowlage; which personally appering bifore the said maier, aldremen and counsaill affirmed that on Monday last past a servaunt of the priour of Tynmouthe accompayned with iij persones commyng out of the south parties and the said priour was ther logid the said Monday. Wheropon it was determyned by the said maier, aldremen and counsaill that aswell the said James as the said John Huten with the said Master Thomas Karlill and an officer of the said citie shuld be sent with the commyssions abovesaid unto my lord of Northumberland to take furthre examinacion in that partie, and therupon to undrestand [f.74v] his pleasure in the same. And that also furthwith oone shuld be sent with the copies of the said confessions unto the king to shewe the same unto his grace and to have knawlage of his pleaser therin and othre thinges, wherewith his highnesse woll charge the said maier, aldermen, counsaill and communaltie of the said citie which they wolbe redye to perfourme according to ther duties.

Mayor Writes to Earl of Northumberland
31 March 1487

Copie of the letter directid unto therle of Northumberland

To the right prepotent and my moost especiall and singuler good lord therle of Northumberland

Right prepotent and my moost especiall and singuler good lord, I commaunde me unto your good lordship, and by Herry Barbour the berer send unto you such thinges as hath be doone bifore me and certain my brether, wherby ye shall undrestand such direccion as hath be taken amonges us here. Albeit I have sent John Sponer oone of our officers unto your said lordship, which is assigned to ride unto the kinges secretary with the copie of such thinges as we have sent unto you, to present unto the kinges grace, if it seme to your lordship it shal soo bee; and elles I am determyned to folow therin your pleaser froo I may undrestand the same, which I besuch you that I may by writing to be delyvered unto the said John Sponer, wherby I may content the myndes of my brethre by whose avice it was determyned that the premisses shuld be shewed unto the kinges highnesse forsaid. And as touching the furthre examinacion of an Thomas Karlill and othre more largely named in the othre writing sent unto your lordship, I trust to knawe the pleasoure of your lordship by the said Herry Barboure. And our lord preserve you, right prepotent and my moost especiall and singuler good lord in felicitie long to endure. Frome York the last day of Marche.

Your moost humble servaunt at his litill powre, William Todde, maire of the citie of York

[f.75] **Letter to Bishop of Exeter, King's Secretary**
31 March 1487

Copie of the letter directid to the kinges secretary

To the right reverend ⟨ffader in God⟩ and my right especiall and singuler good lord the bisshop of Excestre the kinges secretary

Right reverend ⟨fader in God⟩ and my right especiall and singuler good lord, I commaunde me unto you with hertly thaunkes for your good lordship shewed unto this poore citie at all tymes, moost specially at such tymes as Maister John Haryngton hath be with you in mateirs of the same, for the which ye have bondon us to your continuall service. Sir, after certain reportes maid unto me concernyng langage shewed to be uttred by oone James Taite of this citie, I calling unto me certain of my brether and othre of the counsaill of this citie, have examined the matier this day as apperith more at large in a bill herin cloused, besuching you to shew the same unto the kinges grace, and therupon undrestand furthre his pleasure therin, which and all othre I shalbe glad and redye to accomplisshe to thuttermast of my powre during my lif by Goddes grace, and that ye woll yeve credence therin furthre unto this berer. And our lord God preserve you right reverend and my right especiall and singuler good lord in felicitie. From York the last day of the month of Marche.

Youre moost humble servaunt and bedeman William Todde, maier of the citie of York

**[f.75v]   Earl of Northumberland Responds Concerning Earl of Lincoln and Peace Within City
3 April 1487**

Tewesday the third day of Aprile

Mayor: William Todde. 12: Richard York [*list incomplete*]

Assemblid in counsaill, a lettre direct from therle of Northumbreland to the maire and his bretherne aldremen was redde after the tenour ensuyng:

To the right worshipfull and my right hertly biloved frend the right trusty and welbeloved frendes the maier of the citie of York and his brethre aldremen of the same and evere of tham

Right worshipfull and right hertly biloved frende and right trusty and welbiloved frendes, I commaunde me unto you, and thanke you for your curtasse writinges and message to me at this tyme sent, which I have right well conceyved; and where as in part of your instruccions ye certifye me of the departour of therl of Lincolne, I yisterday by the kinges moost noble lettrez to me directid was acertayned of the same, and where as ye aske myne advice in shewing the departour of the said erle unto the kinges highnesse, I remitte that unto your discrecions and wisdams. Furthermore I pray you to shew your faithfull diligence for thestablisshment of the good rule and peax of that citie, and to cause sure watche to be made within the said citie, and also in subduyng all ryot and riotous langage by any persone committed contrary to the well of the king our souverain lord and this his realme if any suche can be fonden to see tham punyshed. And in the perfourmans of the premissez or in any othre thing that I may doo for the wele of you or of that citie, ye therin shall fynde me your good lord to my powre, that knoweth the blissed Trinitie who conserve you. Writyn in my maynour of Lekynfeld the first day of Aprill.

Your owne to my power, Herry Northumberland

[ff.76–77v missing, but original pagination indicates no folio missing]

[f.78]   **Mayor's Letter on Behalf of Roger Brokholls**
                  Undated, c.April 1487

The copie of a lettre direct to Sir Hugh Hastinges knight frome the maier in the favour of Roger Brokholles

Right honourable and worshipfull sir, I commaunde me unto you, and where hertofore upon certain credence shewed unto me upon the behalve of my lord and yours by a gentilman callid Roger Kelke servaunt unto his lordship, I have enprisonned oone of oure cociticyns and neghbours callid Roger Brokholles sith Sonday last past, to his grete hevynesse, hurt and discomfurth. Sir, soo it is that aswell diverse of my brether of the chambre as othre right worshipfull and many honest commoners of this citie here, marvilling gretely of his long inprisonment without bale and mayneprise, not knowing such cause why soo to bee, hath and doth make daily importune labour and grete instance for his deliverance in that partie, offering certain of themself to be bondon in a thousand poundes that the said Roger at all tymes herafter shalbe furthcommyng to awnswer unto any thing which shalbe laide or obiect ayenst hyme by what persone it be in any behalve, which offer as yit I have refused; and that not oonly hath set theme bot also othre commons of this citie in a grete sisme and rumour, to me a thing right perliouse and importable. Wherfor I besuch your mastership to shewe the premissez unto my lordes lordship and his noble counsaill in such wise as the said Roger may be let to bale and maynprised undre the fourme abovesaid, orelles that I may be certified by his right noble lettres of such heynouse cause why he ne oght soo to bee, that I may shew the same unto the said commoners for myne acquitall herin and ther appesing, for it is thoght here that if any freman of this citie be enprisonned for any cause or thing commyt by hyme, except it be ayenst thastate and dignitie royall or felony, may and oght to be mayneprised undre such surtye. Master Hastinges, I woll doo no preiudice unto the porest of the commons here standing as I stand, for an hundreth powndes, remembring the othe which I have takyn and in especiall in this my begynnyng in thoffice of mairaltye. And therfore I besuch you remember the premissez soo they touche me right negh, and that I may be certified therupon by the berer herof in all hast possible.

From York etc., your etc., William Todde maier of the citie of York

[f.78v]   **Earl of Northumberland Blames Brokholls and Others for Attacking**
                  His Servant
                  3 April 1487

Copie of a letter direct ffrom therle of Northumberland unto the maier etc.

To the right worshipfull and my right hertly biloved frende and right trusty and welbiloved frendes the maiour of the citie of York and his bretherne aldermen of the same, and evere of theme

Right worshipfull and right hertly biloved frende, and right trusty and welbeloved frendes, I commaunde me unto you, and thanke you of your curtasse writing and luffing disposicion, which I welle undrestand by your lettres sent unto (th) me by my right trusty servaunt Roger Kelke, and where as Robert Symson servaunt to Master William Beverley brought unto me certain lettres from the kinges high-nesse, comaunding me by vertu of the same after due prouff hadd for the title of the said Master William concernyng thospitall of Well, depending in traverse betwix hyme on that oone parte, and Sir John Nicholson parsone of Wathe on the othre partie, that I shuld see the said Master William wer put in possession in the said hospitall, I entending thaccomplisshment of the kinges pleaser sent my right trusty chapleyne Master John Curwever with the said Robert Symson berer of the said lettres for the perfourmans of the kinges pleaser in this behalve; and they going for thexecuting of the same at my sending, oon Roger Waunesford and Joseph Ughtred, with othre riotous persones and misdoers, lay in wait of the said Robert in Conyngstrete within the citie of York, where as ye have the rule, and hyme grevously hurt and woundid to the juperdie of his lif; wherfor on the king our souverain lordes behalve I charge you and on myne require you to cause due inquisicion tobe had after the fourme of the kinges lawes, soo as the verrey truthe of this mater may be foundon and presentid; and for the consideracion that Roger Brokholles aided, confortid and conveid the said misdoers and in especiall the said Roger Waunsforth, soo that by his meanes he skaped that he might not be attachid, and as hidderto noo certayne knowlage had whider the said Robert Symson will lif or noo of the said hurtes, I therfor on the behalve of oure said souverain lord charge you and on myn will you that the said Roger Brokholles be kept in sure warde, as ye woll aunswer at your perill unto the pleaser of his highnesse be furthre shewed unto you eithre by his grace or me; and where it is allegid for thexcuse of the said Joseph Ughtred that he shuld not be oone of the said misdoers, he hath confessid afore me such as by the same it may be well understand he was oone of thoccasioners of **[f.79]** of [*sic*] the said ryot and affraye, and soo of right he hath deservyd to be punisshid. That knoweth the blissed Trinitie who conserve you. Writyn in my maynour of Lekynfeld the iij day of April.

Your hertly lover Herry Northumberland

Mayor Responds to Earl's Letter
13 April 1487

Copie of a letter direct to therl of Northumberland from the maier etc.

To the right prepotent and my moost especiall and singuler good lord my lord of Northumberland

Right prepotent and my moost especiall and singuler good lord, in the moost humble wise I commaunde me unto youre good lordship, and have sent unto the same by this berer the prest which your servauntes toke and broght to me, and where I have enlargid Roger Brokholles supposing by such thinges as was shewed unto me that I therby shuld have pleasid you, knowing nowe the contrary by your noble lettres to me directid; wherupon I have takyn agane in too my warde the said Roger and ther shall kepe hyme to I have further understand your pleaser in that partie. My lord, truthe it is that the same Roger largely excusith hyme of any langage contrary his dutie aswell touching the kinges highnesse as your lordship, desiring me to be the meane unto your lordship that ye woll wotsave to suffice hyme to present hyme unto the same, and therupon to take his excuse; and over this diverse of my neghbours to the nombre of ij or iij C at diverse tymes hath be with me for thenlargeing of the same Roger, and cannot welbe content with his inprisonment in this case saving your pleaser. Wherfor my lord at the reverence of God and the rather that my neghbours may knowe that your lordship at my poore prayer and moost humble supplicacion in this partie wille suffre hyme to be enlarged, whereby I shalbe of better power to doo your service as my mynd is to doo, wotsave that the said Roger may be at this fest of Estre enlarged, and therupon boundon at such day as ye woll appoynt to come unto your said lordship to make his declaracion in the premisses, which he shalbe redie to doo, and I shalbe [f.79v] your continuall bedeman, redy during my lif to doo you pleaser and service after my litill power, by Goddes grace who ever preserve you, right prepotent and my moost especiall and singuler good lord to your continuall comforth. Fro York the xiijth day of April.

Your humble servaunt William Todde maier of the citie of York

Mayor's Letter Testimonial for City Hosteler
Undated, c.April 1487

Copie of a letter testimonial for William Maunsell

To all true Christen people to whos notice thies presentez shalcom, William Todde maier of the citie of York sendith greting in our lord God everlasting, and where by the lawes of almighty God evere true Christen man his bondon to relees by the way of elmose and charitie ther neghbour fallen to extreme povertie and indigence by losse of his goodes or othre wise, knawe ye therfor for certain howe hertofore our welbeloved cociticyn William Maunsell, late osteler at the signe of the swan within the said citie, had deliverd unto his keping a ffardell with certain stuff in the same, which he knew not, by oon John Borowe loged at the in of the signe of the saide swan, and therwith was charged.

[ff.80–80v blank]

[f.81]   **Inquisition into Holdings of the Late Sir Brian Stapleton**
                     14 June 1486 and 11 April 1487

Stapilton

Inquisicio capta apud Ebor' in comitatu civitatis Ebor' in Guihald eiusdem civitatis

die Mercurii proximo ante festum Pasche videlicet xj° die mensis Aprilis anno regni
regis Henrici septimi post conquestum Anglie secundo, coram Willelmo Todde
maiore civitatis Ebor' ac escaetore dicti domini regis, de diem clausit extremum
eidem escaetori directa in hec verba: Henricus Dei gratia rex Anglie et Francie et
dominus Hibernie dilecto et fideli suo maiori civitatis sue Ebor' ac escaetori suo in
eadem civitate, salutem. Quia Brianus Stapilton nuper de Carleton in comitatu
Ebor' miles qui de nobis tenuit in capite diem clausit extremum ut accepimus tibi
precipimus quod omnia terras et tenementa de quibus idem Brianus fuit seisitus in
dominico suo ut de feodo in balliva tua die quo obiit, sine dilacione capias in
manum nostram et salvo custodiri facias donec aliud inde preceperimus, et per
sacramentum proborum et legalium hominum de eadem balliva tua per quod rei
veritas melius sciri poterit diligenter inquiras quantum terrarum et tenementorum
idem Brianus tenuit de nobis in capite tam in dominico quam in servicio, in dicta
balliva tua dicto die quo obiit, et quantum de aliis per quod servicium et quantum
terre et tenementa illa valeant per annum in omnibus exitibus et quo die idem
Brianus obiit et quis propinquior heres eius sit et cuius etatis. Et inquisicionem inde
distincte et aperte factam nobis in cancellaria nostra sub sigillo tuo et sigillis eorum
per quos facta fuerit sine dilacione mittas et hoc breve. Teste me ipso apud Westm'
xiiij° Junii anno regis Henrici primo.

[An inquest *diem clausit extremum* held at York in the county of the city of
York in the Guildhall, the Wednesday before Easter, namely 11 April 1487, in
the presence of William Todde mayor of the city of York and escheator of the
lord king, directed to the said escheator in these words: Henry by the grace of
God, etc., to his beloved and faithful mayor of his city of York and escheator
in the same city, greetings. Whereas Brian Stapilton, formerly of Carleton in
the county of York, knight, who held of us in chief, has died as we understand,
we command you that you take into our hands without delay all lands and
tenements of which the same Brian was seised in his demesne as of fee in your
bailiwick on the day that he died, and that you cause them to be safely kept
until we command you otherwise, and that by the oath of worthy and lawful
men of your same bailiwick by whom the truth of the matter can be better
known you diligently inquire how much land and tenements the same Brian
held of us in chief both in demesne and in service in the same bailiwick on the
said day on which he died, and how much of others and by what service and
how much those lands and tenements are worth yearly in all issues, and on
what day the same Brian died and who is his next heir and of what age. And
the inquisition thereof, clearly and openly made, you do send to us in our
chancery without delay under your seal and the seals of those by whom it has
been made and with this writ. I myself being witness at Westminster 14 June
1486.]

[ff.81v–82v blank]

[f.83]   **City Asks King for Help in Rebuilding Defences and Arming Castle**
              23 April 1487

Copie of a letter direct unto the kinges highnesse ffrom the maier, aldremen, shereffes and commune counsaill of the citie of Yorke

To moost highe and mighty Christen prince and our moost redoubtid souverain liege lord, the kinge

Moste high and mighty Cristen prince and oure moost redoubtid souverain liege lord, we in oure moost humble wise recommendes us unto youre moost royall magestye, besuching almightye God to send your grace good and prosperoux lif with thabboundaunces of perseveraunt fortunes. Pleasit the same to be acertayned we er and evermore shalbe your true and feithfull subgiettes redye tobbey with our bodis and godes any your high commaundementes aswell for the safegard of youre moost royall persone as this youre realme, and in especiall in sure preservyng of this youre citie unto youre grace singulerly ayenst all othre entending the contrary. Albeit, souverain lord, youre said citie is soo gretely decayed aswell by falling downe of the walles of the same and by taking downe of youre castell ther by King Richard and as yit not reedified as othre in diverse wise that without the same bee more largely manned may ne cannot wel be kept ayenst youre ennymes and rebelles, if they shuld as God defend approche and move werre ayenst the same; and also howe your said citie is not inhabit by the whiche ther is not half the nombre of good men within your said citie as ther hath beene in tymes ⟨past⟩; wherfor it wold pleas youre moost noble grace if the case require that your said ennymes approche unto the same, to provide and ordain that your true citicyns therof may be conveniently assisted and releved at your propre costes and charges, wherby we trust to God to withestand your said ennymes and kepe this your said citie unto you, souverain lord; and where also your said citie is not well furnesshed with artilment and stuff of ordnaunce for the more diffence of the same, as it hath beene hertofore, soo it hath beene charged of lait in that behalve, we besuche your moste noble grace that some of your ordnaunce and artilment of werr might be sent hidder to the same entent, which wer a thing unto us of grete comforth and make us encouraged the more largely to withstand your said ennymes. Furthre to the berer herof John Vavasour your seriaunt at the lawe and our recordour, we besuch your moost noble grace to yeve credence in such thinges as shall showe unto the same upon our behalve concernyng the premissez. And the blissed Trinitee preserve you most highe and mighty Cristen prince and oure moost redoubtid souverain liege lord evere in felicitee. From your said citie the xxiij day of April the secunde yere of your moost gracioux reigne.

Your moost humble subgiettes and true liegemen, the maier, aldremen, shereffes and commune counsaill of your citie of York

[*A hand drawn in the left margin points to this entry*.] And also for so moche as Robert Serle elect to be oone of the moremastars of this citie wold not take upon hyme the charge therof, as his felewe did callid William Dekyn, it was yevene hyme in strait commaundement by the said mayre that he shuld ⟨not⟩ occupie as a ffraunchest man within the same, and to pay to the commune use of thes citie in name of a forfet for his desobedience in that behalve xx li.

[f.85]   Bonds and Arrests
Undated, c.April 1487

Serl [*R*] *murage, sur premunicionem* Robertus Serl de Ebor' ffletcher assumpsit pro seipso ac Thomas Brigges mason et Robertus Denton ffletcher de Ebor', predicti assumpserunt et quilibet pro se assumpsit pro dicto Roberto quod idem Robertus Serl comparebit coram domino maiore et aldermannis civitatis Ebor' quibuscumque vocatus fuerint ad obediendum mandatis suis in materia concernente reparacionem murorum eiusdem civitatis sub pena xl librarum pro eisdem et eorum quolibet camere civitatis predicte solvendarum.

Preceptum est vicecomitibus quod capiunt Ricardum Knaresburgh ad sectam Ricardi Beleby ad essendum ad proximam sessionem pro pace gerenda erga eundem Ricardum.

Knaresburgh [*R*] *vacat* Ricardus Knaresburgh generosus personaliter comparens coram Willelmo Todde maiore civitatis Ebor' assumpsit pro seipso in quadraginta libris necnon Thomas Scotton de Ebor' merchaunt, Thomas Alan de eadem bakar, Ricardus Thorneton de eadem spicer et Johannes Norman de eadem merchaunt personaliter ut supra comparens coram dicto maiore assumpserunt et quilibet eorum assumpsit in xx^{ti} libris legalis monete Anglie solvendis domino nostro regi et ad opus eiusdem de bonis eorundem et cuiuslibet eorum levandis quod ipse Ricardus Knaresburgh dampnum vel malum aliquod corporale in Ricardum Beleby generosum se[u] aliquem alium de populo dicti domini regis non faciet nec fieri procurabit per se vel suos quovismodo infuturum.

partes concorde sunt et ideo dimissi sunt manucaptores Et postea idem Ricardus Beleby in propria persona sua coram maiore predicto et remisit accionem suam versus dictum Ricardum Knaresburgh, et ideo dimissi sunt manucaptores predicti presentibus tunc ibidem [*remainder of line, c.4 words, illegible*]

capias Preceptum est vicecomitibus civitatis Ebor' quod attachiant per corpus suum Ricardum Karlell ad sectam Ricardi Davyas yeoman etc., essendum coram maiore etc., ad proximam sessionem etc.

capias Preceptum est eisdem vicecomitibus quod attachiant Ricardum Davyas yeoman ad sectam Ricardi Karlill laborer ad veniendum ut supra etc.

supersedeas, Davyas Idem Ricardus assumpsit pro seipso in xx^{ti} libris necnon

Thomas Spicer, Thomas Robynson, Johannes Stevenson et Christoforus Lodestok cives civitatis Ebor' assumpserunt et quilibet eorum assumpsit in x libris legalis monete Anglie solvendis domino nostro regi et ad opus eiusdem de bonis eorundem et cuiuslibet eorum levandis quod ipse Ricardus Davyas dampnum vel malum aliquod corporale in Ricardum Karlell laborer seu alicui alio de populo dicti domini regis non faciet nec fieri procurabit pro se vel suos quovismodo infuturum.

[*Serl, murage, under notice* Fletcher Robert Serl of York bound himself, and mason Thomas Brigges and fletcher Robert Denton of York each bound himself on behalf of Serl, that Serl would appear before the lord mayor and the aldermen whenever called to obey an order concerning repair of the city walls under penalty of £40.

The sheriffs are ordered to arrest Richard Knaresburgh at the suit of Richard Beleby to be at the next session to keep the peace towards Beleby.

Knaresburgh, void Richard Knaresburgh, gentleman, personally appeared before mayor William Todde and bound himself for £40, and also merchant Thomas Scotton, baker Thomas Alan, spicer Richard Thorneton, and merchant John Norman appeared before the mayor and each bound himself for £20, that Knaresburgh do no damage nor bodily harm to Richard Beleby, gentleman, or to any other of the king's subjects.

the parties are agreed and the sureties are dismissed And later, the same Richard Beleby personally [came] before the mayor and remitted his action against Richard Knaresburgh, and the sureties are dismissed.

arrest The sheriffs are ordered to arrest Richard Karlell at the suit of yeoman Richard Davyas, being before the mayor at the next session [of the peace].

arrest The sheriffs are ordered to arrest yeoman Richard Davyas at the suit of laborer Richard Karlill, coming as above, etc.

[*writ of*] *supersedeas, Davyas* The same Richard bound himself for £20, and also Thomas Spicer, Thomas Robynson, John Stevenson and Christopher Lodestok, citizens of York, each binds himself for £10, to assure that Richard Davyas do no damage nor bodily harm to laborer Richard Karlell or to any other of the king's subjects.]

[f.85v]   **King Henry Thanks City for Loyal Support**
                 1 May 1487

Tewesday the first day of May

Mayor: William Todde. 12: Richard York, Thomas Wrangwisshe, John Tong, John Fereby, John Newton, Nicholas Loncastre, Robert Hancok. Sheriffs: John Beseby, John Shawe. 24:

John Hagg, Richard (Barkar) Hardsang, William Barkar, John Gilyot, Thomas Fynche, Nicholas Vicars.

Assembled in counsaill, the kinges noble letters was redde after the fourme ensuyng:

To oure trusty and welbiloved the maier, shireffes and aldermen of our citie of York

By the king

Trusty and welbiloved we grete you wele, latting you wit that by sundry reportes made unto us, we undrestande the faithfull diligence and ⟨wise⟩ weys that ye have used in couraging and stirring our subgiettes of our citie there and othre for thobservyng and keping of ther truthes and due obbeysaunce unto us, as to endevour tham to the resistence and withstanding of our rebelles and traitours if they arrive in thoos parties and approche our said citie; ffor the which your faithfull acquitail and true demeanyng we ⟨hert⟩ thanke you hertly, praying you that like as ye have worshipfully begonne and doone ye woll persever and continewe in the same, and ye ⟨my⟩ may be assured we shalnot forget your constant ⟨feith⟩ trouthe and faithfull service in this partie, but soo remembre it as ye shall thinke it right welbestowed to your wele herafter. Yevene undre oure signet at our citie of Coventre the xxviij day of April.

[f.86]   Mayor Makes Arrest at King's Command
3 May 1487

Copie of a letter direct to the kinge frome the maier:

To the moost high and mighty Cristen prince and my moost redoubtid souverain lord the king

Most high and mighty Cristen prince and my moost redoubted souverain lord, in my moost humble wise I recommend me unto youre moost noble grace, and have receyved your moost graciouse letters to me direct the first day of this instant moneth of May yevene at your citie of Coventre the xxvij day of April, of the which I am right joyus that it wold please your highnesse soo graciously to write unto me your poore subgiet in that behalve; and according to the contentes therof I shal endevour me as I have begonne and doon within this your citie here to the uttermost of my powre to persever and continewe in the same as accordith to my naturall dutie and liegeaunce as your true and faithfull subgiet redy tobbey any your high commaundementes aswell with my bodye as goodes at any tyme herafter. And where othrewise ye yave me in commaundement in the same your gracious letters to attache oon Browne within this your said citie abiding, which I have perfourmed and hath hyme in my sure warde and keping souverain lord, soo it is that the said Browne on the tyme he was attached was and as yit he is soo evidently seek that he ne may without grete juperdie of his lif travell on horsse or foote toward your highnesse furthwith; wherfor I send unto your good grace the berer herof to understande your furthre pleaser therin. And if it shall please the same to have hyme conveyd in suche state as he is, I shall perfourme youre high commaundement in that behalve according to my dutie in all goodly hast after perfite knowlage therof. Most high and mighty Cristen prince and my moost redoubtid souverain lord, the blissed Trinitie preserve you in felicitie, prosperus lif with thabboundaunce of good fortunes. From your citie of York the third day of May the secund yere of your moost noble reigne.

Your moost humble subgiet William Todde, maier of this your citie of Yorke

[f.86v] Recorder Reports that King Will Supply City with Guns and Help Against Rebels
1 May 1487

Copie of a letter direct from the recordour as herafter ensuyth:

To my right honorable lord the maier of the citie of York, my masters his brethre aldermen of the same, and the commune counsaill of the same citie, be this deliverd

Right honourable lord and masters, I commaunde me unto you, latting you have knowlage that the kinges grace is well pleased and content for your due obbeyng of his last lettre and for the keping of his intent of the same and for your politik guyding of the citee. Affore my commyng to the kinges grace at Coventre oon of your maters was determyned, and a servant of the kinges riden with writing and money to Sir Richard Tunstall, Sir John Savell, Sir Robert Rither sheref of Yorkshire, Sir Edmund Hastinges, Sir John Nevill, Sir Rauff Bigod and Sir Marmaduc Constable to assist your citie and the communaltye of the same, in caas that the kinges ennymees approche thiddre. I send you a letter to William Tunstall for gonnys from the king, and also an othre letter to Sir Richard Tunstall for the well of the citie; send furth ij servauntes of yours with bothe the same letters, and ye woll have any gonnez at Scarburgh; ye must cary them at your cost and charge, and this is the kinges commaundement. And on Saint Philip day and Jacob the popes bulles were proclamed at Coventre by my lord archbisshop of Canterbury and v othre bisshoppes undre stole, accursing all them that holdith ayenst the kinges title. The king is gretely accompaigned and hath yit noo certain knowlage when his ennymees woll take ther shipping. As for any othre tidinges take credence to the berer of this lettre. The blessed Trinitie have you in his keping. Writyn at Coventre the first day of May. I fforgat not your ffraunchesse and liberties and that the knightes that the king intend to send to the citie in caas that his ennymees approche thiddreward to be undre the rule of my lord the maier, the which is the kinges liuetenaunt ther and he to have the chefe guyding undre the king. As to this desire the king and all his counsail was well pleased and content therwith.

Your servaunt John Vavasour your recorder

**[f.87]   King Orders Delivery of Ordnance from Scarborough
30 April 1487**

Copie of the kinges letter direct as ensuyth herafter:

To our trusty and welbeloved the maier, shiriffes and aldremen of our citie of York
and to the commune counsaill of the same

By the king

Trusty and welbiloved we grete you wele, and have receyved your letters bering
dait the xxj day of the last moneth, and herd your credence uppon the same by our
trusty servaunt John Vavasour oon of our sergiauntes at the lawe and your
recordour, whereby we perceve well that accordingly to your duties ye be unto us
true and faithfull subgiettes, for the which we tendirly thanke you and pray you of
your good continuance in the same. And where as ye desire to have assistence of us
at oure costes and charges etc., knowe ye that on the commyng to us of youre said
recordour we hadd writyn to diverse gentilmen that they with ther company shuld
addresse theme to our citie ther and have sent to them money for the same entent,
as we trust ye shall shortly perceve by experience. We send to you also certayn our
letters endorced to our trusty and welbeloved William Tunstall, constable of our
castill of Scardeburgh, chargeing hyme by the same to deliver by indentures unto
you twelve serpentynes, som more some lesse, of diverse sortes garnysshed with
chambre and powder therunto according, ye making the costes and charges for the
cariage therof, as by the copie of the said letters herin encloused ye may undrestand
more at large. And asfor the discharge in oure eschequir that ye desire to have
there for certeyne our fefermes of oure said citie, we seeing well the true acquitaill
ye be of with (our) your good devours, diligence and hertines anempst us, be
content to send and write that of the same ffee ferme ye shalhave due allowaunce in
all goodly hast as apparteyneth. Assure your self that ye no shall doo unto us
service nor pleaser that we shall forget, but remember the same to your welles and
honoures in tyme to comme. Yeven undre our signet at oure citie of Coventre the
last day of April.

**[f.87v]   City to Listen to King's Messenger
29 April 1487**

Copie of a lettre of credence direct from the kinges grace

To oure trusty and welbiloved the maier, aldremen, shereffes and commons of our
citie of York

By the king

Trusty and welbiloved we grete you wele, and send unto you oure full trusty
servaunt and chapeleyne Master William Creton to shewe to you our mynde in

certayne thinges. We pray you that unto hyme ye yeve full credence in that he shall sey to you on our behalve. Yevene undre our signet at our citie of Coventre the xxix day of Aprill.

[f.88]   **Arrest, Bond to Keep the Peace**
                  Undated, c.April–May 1487

Hesshdale Preceptum est vicecomitibus civitatis Ebor' quod attachiant pro corpora sua Ricardum Bradye yoman et Thomam Bradye bakar ad veniendum etc., ad inveniendum sufficientem securetatem pacis versus Elizabetham uxorem Rogeri Hesshdale de Ebor' baker etc.

Bradye Thomas Brady de Ebor' baker assumpsit pro seipso in viginti libris necnon Cuthbertus Brownelesse dyer, Johannes Sawnderson ffissher, Edmundus Diconson wever et Rogerus Sawer coverletwever, cives civitatis Ebor', predicti assumpserunt et quilibet eorum assumpsit in x libris legalis monete Anglie pro prefato Thoma (quod ipse dampnum vel malum) solvendis domino nostro regi ⟨et⟩ ad opus eiusdem de bonis et catallis eorundem et cuiuslibet eorum levandis, quod ipse Thomas dampnum vel malum aliquod corporale (therf) Elizabethe uxori Rogeri Hesshdall de Ebor' predicto baker non faciet nec fieri procurabit pro se vel suos quovismodo in futurum.

[*Hesshdale* The sheriffs of the city of York are ordered to arrest yeoman Richard Bradye and baker Thomas Bradye to come etc., to find sufficient surety to keep the peace towards Elizabeth, wife of Roger Hesshdale of York, baker.

Bradye Thomas Brady of York bound himself for £20, and also dyer Cuthbert Brownelesse, fisherman John Sawnderson, wever Edmund Diconson, and coverlet-weaver Roger Sawer, citizens of York, each bound himself for £10 on behalf of Thomas Brady, that he do no damage nor bodily harm to Elizabeth, wife of Roger Hesshdall, baker of York, nor cause any harm to be done in the future.]

King's Letter Concerning Rebels from Flanders
4 May 1487

Copie of the kinges lettrez direct as ensuyth:

To oure trusty and welbeloved the maier, aldremen and commune counsail of our citie of York

By the king

Trusty and welbeloved we grete you wele, and for somoche as we have certain knowleige in sundry wise that our rebelles bene departid out of Flaundres and goon westwardes, it is thoght by us and by oure counsaill that ye shal not nede to have any strength or company of men of werre for this season to ly amonges you, and therfor we pray you that ye woll have sad regard to the good rule and sauf keping of oure citie ther to thappesing of rumours and correcting of evel disposed folkes, with sending unto us of your newes from tyme to tyme, and assure your self that for this true acquitail ye have beene of unto us, wherin we pray you to continewe, we shalbe soo good and gracious souverain lord unto you as of reason ye shalhave good cause to thinke the same for wel employed. Yevene undre our signet at oure citie of Coventre the iiij^c day of May.

[f.88v]   **Argument in York Minster**
                 7 May 1487

Monday the vij day of May

Mayor: William Todde. 12: Richard York, Thomas Wrangwisshe, John Tong, John Feriby, John Newton, Nicholas Loncastre, William Chymney, Robert Hancok, John Harper, William White. Sheriffs: John Beseby, John Shawe. 24: Thomas Catour, Michael White, Richard Clerc, Miles Grenebank, Richard Hardsang, William Barkar, John Gilyot, Nicholas Vicars, Roger Appilby.

Assembled in counsaill, it was shewed unto the said maier and counsaill by John Hastinges squire at the mase howe oone John Cure of York walkar said unto hyme the day bifore in the Mynster, the mayre and his brethern beyng togadder in counsaill behynd Saint Christofor [altar], 'Loo John Hastinges, loo, hath not the mayre and his brethre lattyn yone knight come hidder to be our captayne? By Goddes body, I wold they wer all hanged for therof they wold suffer it, in faith we wolnot'.

Also it was shewed by Richard Borowe squire howe oone Robert Cook of York pewterer shuld say to hyme in the Mynster on Sonday last past in this fourme, 'Master Borowe, will ye suffre thies knightes that is commyn hidder to be captayns? By Goddes body, if ye woll suffre them we wilnot, ffor we shall lyg it on ther fflesshes or evene'. And the said Richard Borowe said to the said Robert Cook, 'Hold thy peas, lewed felowe, for wer not for that connysaynt that tha beres, if my lord mayre wol doo any thing for the kinges grace, I shall cause the[e] to be enprisonned for thies wordes'.

[f.89]   **Bonds to Keep the Peace**
                Undated, c.May 1487

Cure [R] *maynprise sur premonicio* Johannes Cure de Ebor' walkar coram Willelmo Todde maiore civitatis Ebor' in camera concilii dicte civitatis personaliter comparens assumpsit pro seipso in C libris necnon Robertus Symson, Johannes Williamson, Willelmus Thomeson et Henricus Toppan cives et walkers in eiusdem civitate comparentes personaliter loco predicto et coram prefato maiore et aliis, assumpserunt et quilibet eorum assumpsit pro dicto Johanne Cure in xl^{ta} libris legalis monete Anglie solvendis et levandis tam de bonis et catallis dicti Johannis Cure quam manucaptorum suorum superius nominatorum ad usum et proficium domini nostri regis, quod ipse Johannes Cure aliquo tempore infuturum super premunicionem littera sibi facta si gaudeat viribus suis personaliter comparebit et in omnibus paratus erit ad respondendum quibuscumque rebus seu materiis que sibi et adversus eum quovismodo obicientur ex parte dicti domini regis seu alterius cuiuscumque, et quod decetero habebit se magis pacifice tam in verbis quam in factis sub pena predicta.

Cook [R] maynprise sur premunicio Robertus Cook de Ebor' pewterer coram prefato maiore loco predicto personaliter comparens assumpsit pro seipso in C libris necnon Johannes Ordows pewterer, Robertus Preston glaiser, Willelmus Sawer ffoundour et Johannes James pewterer, cives dicte civitatis Ebor' comparentes personaliter loco predicto et coram prefato maiore et aliis, assumpserunt et quilibet eorum assumpsit pro dicto Roberto Cook in xl^{ta} libris legalis monete Anglie solvendis et levandis tam de bonis et catallis dicti Roberti Cook quam manucaptorum suorum superius nomina-torum ad usum et proficium domini nostri regis, quod ipse Robertus Cook aliquo tempore in futurum super premunicionem littera sibi facta si gaudeat viribus suis personaliter comparebit et in omnibus paratus erit ad respondendum quibuscumque rebus seu materiis que sibi et adversus eum quovismodo obicientur ex parte dicti domini regis seu alterius cuiuscumque, et quod decetero habebit se magis pacifice tam in verbis quam in factis sub pena predicta, etc.

[*Cure, mainprise under notice* Walker John Cure of York appeared personally before mayor William Todde in the council chamber and bound himself for £100, and also Robert Symson, John Williamson, William Thomeson and Henry Toppan, citizens and walkers, appeared personally and bound themselves on Cure's behalf for £40 each, that Cure is to behave most peaceably at all times in the future in both words and deeds and will be prepared to answer any and all things and materials on behalf of the lord king or any other.

Cook, mainprise under notice Pewterer Robert Cook appeared personally before the mayor in the same place and bound himself for £100, and also pewterer John Ordows, glasier Robert Preston, founder William Sawer, and pewterer John James appeared personally and each bound himself on Cook's behalf for £40, that Cook is to behave most peaceably at all times in the future both in words as in deeds under the aforesaid penalty.]

[f.89v] **Mayor's Testimonial for City Skinner**
9 May 1487

Copie of a letter testimonial for Nicholas Bowlee

Bowlys To all tru Christen people to whos notice thies presentz shal com, William Todde maier of the citie of York sendith greting in our lord God everlasting, and where evere man is bondon by the due ordour of the lawe of God to socour and relef by way of elmose his neghbour fallen to extreme povertie by misfortune of this fallible world, knaw ye for certain howe of law oure welbeloved conciticyn Nicholas Bowles skynner deliverd unto oone Thomas Scot skynner of Ripon, of verray trust and faith which he bereth towardes hyme, asmoch stuff of ffurrez as did amounteth to the somme of twenty markes and more, supposing noon othre bot to have bene iustly content and paid for the same by the said Thomas, wherwith he as a persone never entending to pay and content the said Nicholas for the said furrez is goone ⟨and⟩ departid out of this his naturall cuntre, not known to the said Nicholas where he is, to his utter undoyng and impoverisshment without your liberall elmose be shewed unto hyme in this partie. Pleasit therfor the same in tendre consideracion of the premissez and of that at the said Nicholas may inhabit here amongest us and mayntigne and uphold his household as he hath doone hertofore, bering his charges as othre citicyns of this citie, at such tyme as he shol come amongest you for his releef in this behalve at the reverence of God and in the way of charitye to succour, help and releef hyme with your elmose forsaid, and the rathre at this my prayer and instance, wherby undoubtid ye shall doo unto God a thing right acceptable and also cause the said Nicholas to be your continuall bedeman for the same. In witnesse wherof unto thies presentz I have put the seal of myne office of mairaltie. Yeven at the citie of York the ix day of May in the ij^d yere of the reigne of our souverain lord King Herry the sevent.

[f.90]   New Chamberlains Reimburse Predecessors, Death of Former Mayor William Wells
11 May 1487

Friday the xj day of May

Mayor: William Todde. 12: Richard York, Thomas Wrangwissh, ⟨John Tong⟩, John Fereby, ⟨John Nauton⟩, ⟨Nicholas Loncastre⟩, William Chymney, Robert Hancok, John Harper, William White. Sheriffs: John Beasby, John Shawe. 24: Thomas Catour, William Tayte, Richard Clerk, Richard Hardsang, William Barkar, John Gilyot, Thomas Fynche, Nicholas Vicars.

[R] fo. xxj° Assembled in counsaill, it was determyned that the chamberleyns now being shall take upon them the charge of the chambre as othre chamberleyns hath doone tofore, and to pay and content the old chamberleyns of ther dutye due unto them in and upon thend of ther accomptes, and for ther more ease in that partie it shalbe in ther chose wheder to have ij othre chamberleyns chosen to them or noo. And elles to forfeit ichoone of them xl li. according to thordinaunce therupon made in the tyme of William Chymney late mayre of this said citie. [*The marginalia refers to the original foliation of the entry beginning on the modern [f.21] in Book Six.*]

And over this it was determyned that writing shuld be maid unto the kinges grace shewing the heynouse deth of William Welles late mayre and alderman of this citie to obteigne his letterz of commission to enquire upon the same etc.

Memorandum that John Tong and Nicholas Lancastre aldermen was insert amonges ther brethre above writyn upon owne desire. And also John Newton and William White send to by the mare commaundement ratified the act above writyn.

**[f.90v]   City Informs King of Former Mayor's Murder and Scarborough's Failure to Deliver Ordnance
14 May 1487**

Copie of the (kinges) letter direct to the kinges grace from the mayre and his brethre

To the moost high and mighty Cristen prince and our moost redoubtid souverain liege lord the king

Most high and mighty Cristen prince and our moost redoubtid souverain lord, we in our moost humble wise recommend us unto your (good) highnesse, thanking your moost noble grace in that it hath pleased the same at our moost humble peticion late maid unto your said grace so graciously too remember us, in that ye have sent hidder for our assistence and releef, aswell in consideracion of the grete ruyne and decay of this your said citee as the taking downe of your castell ther and as yit not reedified, your right trusty and welbiloved knight for your body Sir Richard Tunstall, your chapleyne Master William Creton, and othre honourable gentilmen well accompaigned, which hath soo demeanyd them here that we and all othre weldisposid people of the same be right wel content with them and by ther commyng and abode here gretely comforthed and enioyed, whom we besuch your highnesse to have in the tendre favour of your grace for the same, certifying furthre your highnesse howe, according to your moost drad commaundement contigned amonges othre thinges in your moost noble lettrez yevene at your towne of Huntyngton the xx^{ti} day of April, we have kept due watche and warde for the surty of this your said citie, aswell by day as by night, and from tyme to tyme, and soo we shall continue unto we have othrewise in commaundement from your said grace; and where, souverain lord, our welbeloved brothre William Welles late mayre of this your said citie [*1479–80*] and alderman of the same, being at your said watch as wardan and ruler therof, to (y)our grete hevynesse and discomforth was striken to deth by oone John Robson milner and citicyn of this your said citie, whom we have in sure ward to be inquired of according **[f.91]** to your lawes and punysshed after his demeritiez in example of all othre; and for so mooch as we ne may without the hurt of the wif of our said brothre take upon us within the yere to make processe concernyng the punysshment of the said John Robson without your moost noble lettres of commission be unto us directid in that partie, we therfor besuch your moost noble grace for soo moch as that heynouse dede was commyt on our said brothre, standing oone of the justices of your peas within your said citie and occupied the same tyme in your service as wardan of your watch at Bowthom barre, it wold pleas your grace the rather to be enclined to graunt the said commission in the moost laufull and large fourme accustumed in such caas herbifore aswell for treson as felony, if it soo shalbe fondon laufully soo that the said heynouse dede may be punysshed aswell in example of all othre herafter as for the more surtye of your justices of peax and wardeyns within this your said citie for the tyme being herafter. And where, souverain lord, othrewise othrewise [*sic*] at our moost humble peticion it pleased your grace to addresse your moost noble lettrez unto William Tunstall squire, your cunstable of your castell of Scardeburgh, for xij serpentynes with chambre and powder garnysshed sufficiently for the same, to have be delyvered by indentour to this your citie for the more diffence therof, as it did appere more at large in the copie of your said lettrez to us sent in that behalve, wher upon we sent for the same, and we be aunswerd souverain lord by your said constable that ther is not iiij serpentynes within your said castell and soo as yit we be not purved, wherfor we besuch your moost noble grace othrewise too provide for ordnaunce so to be sent to this your said citie for the more defence of the same. Moost high etc. From this your cite of York the xiiijth day of May.

Your moost humble, true and ffeithfull subgiettes, the maier, aldermen, shereffes and commune counsaille of your citie of York

**[f.91v]   King Writes that Rebels Will Not Attack City
                    15 May 1487**

Thewesday the xv^{ti} day of May, the kinges lettres was red in the Guihald before the communaltye as ensuyth:

To our trusty and welbeloved the mair, aldremen and communaltie of our citie of York

By the king

Trusty and welbyloved we grete you wele, and have undrestand by manyfold reportes made unto us theffectuel devoir and grete besinesses that ye put you in for the good provision and preparacion of vitaill and othre stuf for suche men of worship and their retenues as we late commaunded to goo thidder for the surtye and defense of our citie ther if our rebelles had arrived nigh thoos parties, for the which as we for many othre causes have (othre) doon we thanke you hertely, and thus by your truthes and good myndes daily to us contynued ye have assured the favour of our good grace unto you, like as ye shall fynd in effect in such pursutes as ye shall make unto us herafter, lating you wit that seing our rebelles, as we be acertayned, bee departid westwardes, we have licenced suche personnes as we commaunded to make ther repare thiddre to depart thens for a season and to resort to you ayene if the caas shall so require, and also our cousin therl of Northumberland entendeth hastily to be in the cuntrey nigh unto you, which we doubt not wol gladly assist and strength you at all tymes if ye desir hym so to bee. Yeven undre our signet at our castell of Kenelworth the viijth day of May.

[f.92]   **Examination of Chamberlains' Accounts, Regulations for the Craft of Ropers**
21 May 1487

Monday the xxj day of May anno regni regis Henrici vij° ij°

Mayor: William Todde. Deputy recorder: Thomas Aspar. 12: Richard York, Thomas Wrangwisshe, John Tong, John Fereby, Nicholas Lancastre, William Chymney, Robert Hancok, John Harper. Sheriffs: John Beseby, John Shawe. 24: Thomas Alan, William Tait, Richard Clerc, Michael White, Miles Grenebank, Richard Hardsang, William Barkar, Nicholas Vicars.

Assembled in counsaill upon a peticion contigned in a bill exhibit to the mare by the communaltie, it was determyned that ij aldermen that not occupied thoffice of mairaltye, ij of the xxiiijᵗⁱ and iiij of the moost sadde and honest commoners of this citie, taking to them ij auditours, shall examyn and serche all thaccomptes of chamberleyns sith the tyme of the marialtie of William Holbek, late mayre of this citie etc. [*Holbeck was last mayor 1472–73*]

[*A hand drawn in the left margin points to this entry.*] *pro le ropers and hayresters* Item the same day past a bill of peticion made by ropers and hasters, the tenour wherof is that every roper and haster commyng to this cite and woll set up as a maister within the same citie, in making ropes, kilne hares, teildes or eny othre thing pertenyng or belonging to the said craft of ropers and haisters, shal pay at his first setting up xiij s. iiij d., the on half to the use of the commonaltie tobe resavyd by the handes of the chaumberleyns for tyme being, and the othre half to the supportacion of the charges of the said ropers and harsters.

Item in the same it is past that every forent commyng ⟨to⟩ this cite selling ropes, kilne hares, teildes, sye or eny othre thing to thame belonging be contributory to the said ropers and haisters in paing of pagent silver.

Item that it be not leful to eny roper within this cite and libertiez of the same from hensforth to wirk eny maner stuffe ne ropes, kilne heris or eny othre thing to that craft belonging, to eny other man not being of the same craft to retale ayane apon payne of forfating of vj s. viij d. *camere et arte tociens quociens*.

[f.92v]   **Murdered Alderman Replaced, Widow Not Charged for Pageant Contribution, King Orders Prisoners to Steward of Pontefract**
22 May 1487

Tewesday the xxijᵗⁱ day of May

Mayor: William Todde. Recorder: John Vavasour. Counsellor: Thomas Aspar. 12: Richard York, Thomas Wrangwisshe, John Tong, John Ferebye, John Newton, Nicholas Lancastre, William Chymney, Robert Hancok, John Harper.

Assembled in counsaill elect and named John Gilyot merchaunt, oone of the xxiiij^{ti}, in oone of the aldremen in the rowme and place of William Welles late aldreman of the same, which John tooke his oth and rowme in that behalve accustumed.

Also it was aggreed that my lady Lambe, late wif to William Lambe aldreman and a widowe, during the tyme that she standes widowe, shall not be chargid with thoffice of padgiant master in irenmonger craft. And for hur more ease in that behalve, she hath yevene ⟨to⟩ (of) the commonaltye of this citie vj s. viij d.

And also the same day was opynned and red the kinges severall letters direct as herafter ensuyth:

To our trusty and welbiloved the maier and aldremen of our citie of York

By the king

Trusty and welbiloved we grete you wele, lating you wit that it is commyn unto our knowlege how that a certain persone of our citie ther not fering God nor the daungier of our lawez late cruelly murdred a brothre of ⟨you⟩ for doing and executing [f.93] his office, whom for the said offence ye have in prison; wherfore we not willing such odious offensez to passe unpunysshed, woll and desire you and also charge you that incontinently upon the receipt herof ye doo send surely and saufly the said personne unto your trusty and welbeloved counseillour and knight for your body Sir Richard Tunstall, steward of our hounour of Pomitfrete, whome we have commaunded to convey hyme unto us, to thentent that we may have hyme in examinacion upon his said demeanyng; and in like wise, we woll that ye doo send unto the said ⟨Sir⟩ Richard aswell the personne remaynyng ther in ward for his unsitting and outeragious langage had unto you in the presence of our trusty and welbiloved chapleyne Master William Creton, as oone Roger Layton, soo that he may doo them to be brought unto us for to be examyned of such thinges as shalbe declared ayenst tham at ther commyng unto our presence, and that ye leve not this undoone as we may evidently perceve the wille and desire that ye have to please us. Yevene undre our signet at our signet [sic] at our castell at Kenelworth the xvj day of May.

Memorandum that this letter was writyn and endoced tofore the sight of the letter direct unto the kinges grace from the maier and his brethern as is tofore writtyn, as apperith more at large in othre the kinges letters herafter ensuyng:

By the king

To our trusty and welbiloved the maier and aldermen of our citie of York

Trusty and welbiloved we grete you wele, and bifore the commyng of your lettrez specifyng amonges othre thinges your desire to have a commission which we send unto you by this berer, we had endoced unto you our othre letters which the said berir shall delyver unto you, wherfor and for somoch as if it be thought unto you not according for lak of auctoritie or othrewise to correct such personnez as in our former lettres be comprised, we then pray you ensue and accomplissh **[f.93v]** our mynd expressed in the same, and for your fast luffing disposicion anempst us we shall rest your favourable souverain lord in any your reasonnable desires for your wele and honnour. Yevene under our signet at our castell of Kenelworth the xvij[th] day of May.

Upon the which letters it was determyned that the kinges mynd shuld be perfourmed specified in his former letters for certain consideracions them moveing, and that writing shuld be made unto his grace from the maier, aldremen, shereffes and commune counsaill of this citie subscribed with all ther handes in maner and forme folowing:

To the moost high and mighty Christen prince and our moost redoubtid souverain liege lord the king

Most high and mighty Cristen prince and our moost redoubtid souverain liege lord, we in our moost humble wise recommend us unto your highnesse, and have receyved of late aswell your gracious lettres of commissions which we have and shall pute in full execucion after the contentes therof, as othre your moost noble lettrez missives to us direct, and according to your moost drad commaundment in the same we have sent unto the right worshipfull Sir Richard Tunstall your counsaillour and knight for your body at Pomitfret, John Robson milner which late haynously committed the deth of our brothre William Welles, with oone John Cure walkar whom we had in bale for certain his unsitting langage uttred in our Guildhall bifore your chapleyne Master Creton at his last being ther, to be conveyed unto your highnesse by your said knight; and where by the same your moost noble lettrez we had in commaundement to attache oone Rogier Layton and hyme to have sent with the othre abovewrityn unto your said knight, souverain lord, we upon the sight of the same did put us in our uttermost devours to have attached hyme, and as yet we ne can atteyne soo to doo, for soo moch as he is departid from this your citie and unknowne to us where he is; albeit souverain lord if the said Rogier resort at any tyme herafter unto the same we shall perfourme your high commaundement in that **[f.94]** behalve as accordith with the dutye of our liege lord; and for asmuch as we doubt that labour shalbe made unto your highnesse for the said John Robson at his commyng unto the same for his acquitall anempst that haynouse dede by certain persones entending the subversion of us and this your chambre, if the same shuld passe unpunisshed as God defend we send unto your moost noble grace oone of the chamberleyns of this your said citie, son in lawe unto our late brothre William Welles and berer herof, to shewe the verey truthe of the deth of the said William Welles, ayenst any senistre reportes tobe maid unto your highnesse contrary the same, and furthre our myndes concernyng the premissez unto whom we besuch your moost noble grace to yeve credence. And the blessed Trinitie preserve you, moost high etc.

Your moost humble subgiettes: William Todde, maier; John Vavasour, recordour;

Richard York, Thomas Wrangwissh, John Tong, John Fereby, John Newton, Nicholas Lancastre, William Chymney, Robert Hancok, John Harper, John Gilyot [aldermen]; John Beseby, John Shawe, shereffes; Thomas Catour, Thomas Alan, William Taite, William Spense, Richard Clerk, John Hagg, Michael White, Milez Grenebank, Richard Hardsang, William Barkar, Thomas Fynch, Nicholas Vicars, Roger Appilby [members of the 24].

[f.94v] Examination of Chamberlains' Accounts
28 May 1487

Monday the xxviij day of May

Mayor: William Todde. Recorder: John Vavasour. 12: Thomas Wrangwisshe, John Tong, John Fereby, Nicholas Lancastre, William Chymney, Robert Hancok, John Harper, John Gilyot. Sheriff: John Beseby. 24: Thomas Alan, William Tait, Richard Clerk, Michael White, Miles Grenebank, Richard Hardsang, William Barkar, Thomas Fynch, Nicholas Vicars.

Assembled first in counsaill in the counsaill chambre within the Guildhall and after bifore the more part of the serchours of the citie in the same, where it was than and ther aggreed by the said serchours for asmoch as it was determyned by the maier, aldermen and commune counsaill that a serch and a vieu shuld be takyn of all the chamberleyns accomptes sith the tyme of William Holbek late maier of this citie, that the chamberleyns nowe being shuld pay the old chamberleyns of the last yere as othre of old tyme hath be wont to be paid and hath bene used amonges them, and that the forsaid accomptes shuld be examyned by ij of such aldremen as hath not beene maierez, and ij of the commune counsaill for the chambre, and iiij of the moost sadde and honest personez of the communaltye of this citie of (or) the commons, namyng amonges tham ij indifferent auditours, wheropon the said serchors askid a deliberacion to Friday next folowing to appoynt such iiij persones with auditours tofore said.

[f.95] Bond to Accept Arbitration
Undated

(Alex') ⟨Ricardus⟩ Davyas de Ebor' glover et Ricardus Karlell de eadem scoler assumpserunt et (quilibet) ⟨alter⟩ eorum assumpsit se in xx libris de stando et parendo laudum, arbitrium et judicium Thome Watson, Thome Kendall, Christofori Thomelynson et Willelmi Herryson arbitratorum inter prefatum Ricardum Davyas ex una parte et Ricardum Karlell ex parte altera, de et super omnibus accionibus, debatis et controversiis pendentibus, electorum et nominatorum, ita quod huiusmodi arbitrium etc., fiant et reddantur inter partes predictas citra festum sancte Trinitatis proximum futurum etc., concordatur arbitrio quod Ricardus Karlill solvet vicecomitibus civitatis Ebor' pro affraia et le blodowne facta inter ipsum et dictum Ricardum Davyas etc.

[Glover Richard Davyas of York and scholar Richard Karlell bound themselves and each bound himself for £20 for adhering to and obeying the advice, arbitration and judgement of Thomas Watson, Thomas Kendall, Christopher Thomelynson and William Herryson, arbiters elected and named between Davyas on the one side and Karlell on the other, concerning all actions and controversies pending between them, this judgement being made and rendered by the next coming feast of Holy Trinity, it being agreed that Karlill pay the city sheriffs for the affray and bloodshed between him and Davyas.]

King Cooperates in Punishing Alderman's Murderer
3 June 1487

Witsonday in the chapitour house of the cathedral churche of York

Mayor: William Todde. Recorder: John Vavasour. 12: Richard York, Thomas Wrangwissh, William Snawsell, John Fereby, John Newton, Nicholas Lancastre, William Chymney, Robert Hancok, John Harper, William White, John Gilyot. Sheriffs: John Beseby, John Shawe. 24: Thomas Alan, William Tayte, Richard Clerc, John Hagg, William Spense, Miles Grenebank, Richard Hardsang, William Barkar, Thomas Fynche, Nicholas Vicars, Roger Appilby.

Assembled in counsaill where the kinges lettrez deliverd by John Stokdall, oone of the chamberleyns of this citie, directed as ensuyth, was discoused and red after the tenour ensuyng:

To our trusty and welbiloved the maier and aldremen of our citie of York

By the king

Trusty and welbiloved we grete you wele, and where as we late directid unto you our especiall lettrez for the sure and sauf sending unto our trusty and welbiloved counseillour and knight for our bodye Sir Richard Tunstall of oon John Robson that lair ther cruelly [f.95v] murdred a brothre of yourez to our grete displeaser, and after that sent unto you our lettres of commission to sitte and inquire of the said offence and to procede to thexecucion of the said murdour, it is soo that ye setting apart thauctoritie of the said commission have sent the said offendour unto us, wherfor we woll and commaunde you to send us word by writing whethre ye may procede ther to thaccomplisshment of our said commission and to the full punisshment of the said persone, and if ye may soo doo and desire us by your writing to have hyme thiddre, we shall send hyme ayen unto you to thentent that the ministration of justice ayenst hyme according to his demeritiez which we woll that ye in all wise put in full execucion, and in the meane season we shall see hyme surely and saufly to be kept without grace or pardonne, and if any personnez reseaunt amonges you woll presume to interrupte or let you in ministracion of justice in this partie, we woll than that ye doo them to be attached and sent surely unto us, and we shall soo provide for ther punisshment as all othre shall take example and fere to doo or attempt any such thinges herafter. Yeven undre our signet at our castell of Kenelworth the last day of May.

Wherupon it was determyned by all above writtyn that they shuld mete agayne in counsaill at the brig the morowe after at ij of the clok to examyn more ripely the contentes of the said letters and therupon to write unto the kinges grace according to his high commaundement.

[f.96]   Council Asks King that Murderer Be Tried at York
4 June 1487

Monday iiij day of Juyn

Mayor: William Todd. Recorder: John Vavasour. 12: Richard York, Thomas Wrangwissh, William Snawsell, John Tong, John Fereby, John Newton, Nicholas Lancastre, William Chymney, Robert Hancok, John Harper, William White, John Gilyot. Sheriffs: John Beseby, John Shawe. 24: Thomas Catour, Thomas Alan, William Spense, William Tayte, Richard Clerc, John Hagg, Miles Grenebank, Richard Hardsang, William Barkar, Nicholas Vicars. Absent: Michael White, Thomas Fynch, Roger Appilby.

Assembled in counsaill determyned that writing shalbe maid unto the kinges grace in fourme folowing:

To the moost high and mighty Cristen prince and our moost souverain liege lord the king

Most high and mighty Cristen prince and our moost redoubtid souverain liege lord, we in our moost humble wise recommend us unto your moost noble grace, thanking your highnesse of your moost noble lettres to us direct yevene at your castell of Killingworth the last day of May, which is to our moost singuler comforth for that we knowe your grace woll execute youre lawes and cause misdores to be punysshed according to ther demeritiez; souverain lord, as for the murdour of our brothre William Welles at your sute your lawes wilnot suffre John Robson takyn for the same to be arreyned to the yere and day be past, albeit the wif of the said William Welles saith that she woll sue a bille of appele bifore us ayenst the said John in the case we arreyne hyme by the vertue of (our) your said commission, and in the case she soo woll doo we woll according to justice procede ayenst the said Robson upon the commission of gaol delyverer and of hur bille of appele, if it shall pleas your highnesse to send the said Robson downe unto us agayne and therupon to doo execucion as your lawes shall require. And the blissed Trinitie [f.96v] preserve you, most high and mighty Cristen prince and our moost redoubtid souverain liege lord in his blissed gouvernaunce. From York the iiij day of Junyn etc.

Your moost humble subgiettes, the maier, aldremen, shereffes and commune counsaill of your citie of York

Earl of Northumberland Asks for Help Against Rebels, Chamberlains Reimburse Predecessors
6 June 1487

Copie of a lettre direct from therl of Northumberland to the maire etc., as ensuyth:

To the right worshipfull and my right hertly biloved ffrend and right welbiloved frendes the maier of the citie of York, the aldermen and shireffes of the said citie and to the commons of the same

Right worshipfull and my right hertly biloved frend and right welbiloved frendes, I commaunde me unto you, and thanke you for the constant loving disposicions that I have foundon in you, wherin I pray you to persever, and where as the king our souverain lordes rebelles bene landed in Fourneys at the pile of Fowdray upon Monday last past, which God helping I entend to resist and for the same entent wolbe in the citie of York toward them upon Sonday next commyng, therfor I desire and pray you to cause provision of vitrull tobe redy ayenst that tyme for such people as shall come and be ther with me; also that ye incontinent after the sight herof woll provide for the sure kepinge and saufgard of the said citie, and that suche persones as ye goodly may forbere, the city kept, if it woll pleas you, they may accompany me in ther best and moost defensible array to do the king service for thentent afforsaid. And I pray you to yeve credence unto my right trusty servaunt Richard Burgh squire concernyng the premissez, and to do thing that may be for your welez I wolbe as glad as any man doing to my power that knoweth the blessed Trinitie, whome I besuch to send you all good fortunez. Writyn in my maynour of Lekingfeld the vj day of Juyn.

Your loving frend H. Northumberland

Which letter was oppynly red bifore the maier, aldremen and commune counsaill of (of) the citie of York, first in the counsaill chambre within the Guilhall and after bifore all the comons of the said citie in the said Guilhall ther assembled, where and when [f.97] aswell the said maier, aldremen, shereffes and commune counsaill forsaid as the said commons was aggreed eithre to othre holding up ther handes that they wold kep this citie with ther bodiez and goodes to thuttermast of ther powerz to the behove of our souverain lord the king ayenst any his rebelles entending to entre the same.

[R] *chamberleyns* And also the said comons then and ther wer aggreed that the chamberleyns now being shall content and pay the old chamberleyns of such duties as be due unto theme at thend of ther accomptes yeldid in the fest of Saint Blaise the yere of the reigne of King Herry the vij[th] ij[d].

Letter to Mayor from Lambert Simnell and Followers
8 June 1487

Copie of a letter direct to the maire etc., from the lordes of Lincoln, (of a) Lovell and othre late landed in Fourneys in the name of ther king calling hymself King Edward the vj^t

By the king

To our trusty and welbiloved the maiour and his brethren and communaltye of our citie of York

Trusty and welbiloved we grete you wele, and forsomoch as we beene commen within this our realme not oonely by Goddes grace to atteyne our right of the same but also for the relief and well of our said realme, you and all othre our true subgiettes which hath bene gretely iniuried and oppressid in default of nowne ministracion of good rules and justice, desire therfor and in our right hertly wise pray you that in this behalve ye woll show unto us your good aides and favourez, and where we and such power as we have broght with us by meane of travayle of the see and upon the land beene gretely weryed and laboured, it woll like you that we may have relief and ease of logeing and vitailles within our citie ther, and soo to depart and truly pay for that at we shall take, and in your soo doing ye shall doo thing unto us of right acceptable pleaser, and for the same find us your good and souverain lord at all tymes herafter, and of your disposicions herin to acertain us by this bringer. Yevene undre our signet at Masham the viij day of Juyn.

[f.97v]   City Informs Earl of Northumberland of Simnell's Letter and Denies Rebels' Requests, Earl Promises His Help
8 June 1487

(The copie of) Which letter was immediately sent to therl of Northumberland for to see and a copie of the same was sent to Sir Richard Tunstall and an othre deliverd to Master Payne to shewe it to the kinges grace. And furthwith the maire, aldremen, shereffes and commune counsaill of the citie of York assembled in counsaill in the counsaill chambre within the Guildhall, departid from the counsaill and commaunded and was aggreed that evere wardan shuld be in harnesse and reise his warde and kepe due watch that noo persone shuld have entre into the said citie bot such as bee true liegemen unto our souverain lord the king Herry the sevent. And the said maier incontinently by thadvise ⟨of⟩ his bretherne aldremen, shereffes and commune counsaill forsaid sent in message unto the said lordes of Lincoln and Lovell iij of the chamberleyns, yeving theme in commaundement to shew unto the said lordes that my lord the mayre, my masters his bretherne aldremen, the shereffes, commune counsaill with thool communaltye of the citie of York beene finally determyned that he which the said lordes callid ther king, they nor none of ther retinew or company entending to approch this citie shuld have any entre in to the(im) ⟨same⟩, bot to withstand them with ther bodies and goodes if they wold atteyne soo to doo.

And the same day a letter was direct from therl of Northumberland unto the maier etc., as herafter foloweth:

To the right worshipfull and my right hertly beloved frend and right trusty and welbiloved frendes the maiour of the citie of York, the shireffes and his brethern of the same

Right worshipfull and right hertly biloved frend and right trusty and welbiloved frendes, I commaunde me unto you, and not oonely thanke you for your luffing disposicions perseverantly shewed unto me but specially for the faithfull guyding and true disposicions shewed for your provedent and sure ordring of the king our souverain lordes citie undre your rule for the surtie and conservacion of the same to his moost high pleaser, praying you as effectually as I can therin to shewe your faithfull endevours with all diligence as ye have doone, and if the caas require [**f.98**] that occasion be to the contrary herof, I therof certified who God helping wolbe at Poklington to morowe at evene, shalnot rest ther but be with you the same nyght, like as worshipfull this berers, chapleyns unto the kinges highnesse, kan shew unto you, to whom I pray you to yeve credence; and upon Sonday next commyng I wol not fail to be with you at the farrest and to fore if ye think it requisite, that knoweth our ffader celestiall whome I besuch to be your everlasting protectour. Writyn in my manour of Lekyngfeld the viij^{th} day of Juyn.

Your lovyng ffrend, H. Northumberland

City's Account of Lambert Simnell's Rebellion
8–17 June 1487

The processe of the batell beside Newark in the third yere of the reigne of King Henry the vij^{th} Satterday the viij^t day of Juyn [*sic, 8 June 1487 was a Friday*] the yere of the reigne of our souverain lord King Herry the sevent at after none of the same day the chamberlayns sent in message unto the lordes of Lincolne and Lovell and othre herbifore named, come in at Mikylgate barre and ther shewed unto my lord the mayre and othre his brethren being present howe the said lordes and ther retinewe was departid over Brugh brig and soo streght suthward not entending to come negh this citie to ⟨do⟩ any preiudice or hurt unto the same. And incontinently after ther commyng, the lord Clifford sent word unto my lord maier that he might come in with his folkes and retinewe for to assiste and support the maier and the communaltye of this cite if any of the kinges ennymes wold approche unto the same; wherunto the mayre consentid and grauntid that he shuld soo have his entree and causid all the stret of Mikelgate to be garnysshed with men in harnesse to the nombre of DC personez and moo. And within the space of an howre after receyved the said Lord Clifford at Mikilgate barr with CCCC personnez of ffoot men and horsmen in to the said citie and sent unto hyme a present of wyne and [*blank*] according to his honour.

And upon Trinitie Sonday at none my lord of Northumberland with many knightes and lordes of this cuntree cam **[f.98v]** to this citie. And the same day at afternowne the Lord Clifford toke his iourney towardes the kinges ennemyes lying upon Bramham more and loged hymself that night at Tadcastre, but the same night the kinges ennemyes lying negh to the same towne cam upon the said Lord Clifford ffolkes and made a grete skrymisse ther into so moch that he with such folkes as he might get retourned to the citie agane. And at that same skrymisse wer slayne and maymed diverse of the said towne and thinhabitantes ther were spoled and robbed. And the gardewyans and trussing coffers of the Lord Clifford was taken of the brig by misfortune and had unto the othre partie.

Also upon the Tewesday after therl of Northumberland, Lord Clifford and many othre nobles accompanyd with vj M^l nombred departid suthward toward the kinges grace at xj of the clok, and anone after his departour the lordes Scropes of Bolton and Upsall constreyned as it was said by ther ffolkes cam un horsbak [to] Bowthom barr, and ther cried 'King Edward' and made asalt at the yates, bot the comons being watchmen ther well and manly defendid tham and put tham to fflitht. And incontinently the maire upon knowlage therupon accompaned with a C persones in harnesse made his proclamacion thrugh out the citee in the name of King Herry the sevent, chargeing all maner of ffraunchest men and othre reseaunt within this citie furthwith to be in harnesse and attend upon the wardans, and that evere wardan shuld kepe his ward at his juberdy, and that all maner of (u)straungers in **[f.99]** harnesse shuld depart furth of the citee at the south gate under the payne of forfatour of his harnesse and his body to prison. Therl of Northumberland having knowlage herof, being within vj milez of the citie, sent in message unto the maier and desired hyme that he might come and entre the citie agane for diverse consideracions and causes hyme moveing. Wher(for)upon the maier by thadvise of his brethre sent Master Vavasour recordour and iij of his bretherne aldremen with othre of the counsaill of this citie accompayned with xij horsse in message unto the said erl, shewing how he shuld be welcome to the said citie and asmany as he wold undretake wer the kinges true liegemen, and ⟨caused⟩ all the strete of Mikelgate to be garnisshed with men in harnesse to the nombre of iiij M^l.

And incontinently therupon, the said erl, the Lord Clifford and othre many nobles accompayned with iiij M^l men and moo was thankfully receyved unto the said citie and ther continued to Thursday Corpus Christi day, and the same day at noone hastly the said lordes toke ther journey towardes the north parties.

[R] *proclamacion of the differyng of Corpus Christi play* Upon Corpus Christi evene proclamacion was made thrugh the citie that the play of the same for diverse consideracions moveing my lord maier, my masters aldremen and othre of the commune counsaill (that the play of Corpus Christi) shuld be differd unto the Sonday next after the fest of Saint Thomas of Canturbury, and than after it was differd to the Sonday next after the fest of Saint Petre callid Advincle because bicause [*sic*] of the kinges commyng hidder.

The Satterday next after the fest of Corpus Christi the king lying with a grete powre divyded in thre hostez beyond Newark the wayward of the same, in the which therl of Oxford, the Lord Straunge, Sir John Chyney, therl of Shrewesbury and many othre to the nombre of x M^l [**f.99v**] met with the lordes of Lincoln and Lovell, with othre many noblez aswell of Ynglisshmen as Irisshmen and othre to the nombre of xx M^l, of the more beyond Newark, and ther was a soore batell, in the which therl of Lincolne and many othre aswell Ynglisshmen as Irissh to the nombre of v M^l wer slayne and murdred; the Lord Lovell was discomfetid and ffled with Sir Thomas Broghton and many othre, and the child which they callid ther king was takyn and broght unto the kinges grace and many othre in grete nombre, which was juged to deth at Lincolne and othre places theraboute etc.

And upon Sonday by iij of the clok in the mornyng tidinges came to my lord maier from the feld, howe Almighty God had sent the king victorye of his ennymies and rebelles, and therupon my lord maier taking with hyme his brethre aldremen with thool counsaill of this citie upon certain knowlage of the victory forsaid shewed by the mouthe of a servaunt of Master Recordour commyng streught from the said feld, cam to the cathedral church of York and ther caused all the ministres of the same to make lovinges to our saveour for the tryumphe and victory forsaid, singing solemplye in the high qwere of the said church the psalme of *Te deum laudamus* with othre suffragies.

[f.100]   New Chamberlains Named, One Too Poor to Hold Office
23 June and 17 July 1487

Satterday in the vigil of Saint John Baptiste at the Guildhall

Mayor: William Todde. Recorder: John Vavasour. 12: Richard York, Thomas Wrangwisshe, John Tong, John Feriby, John Newton, Nicholas Loncastre, William Chymney, Robert Hancok, John Harper, John Gilyot. Sheriffs: John Beseby, John Shawe. 24: Thomas Catour, Thomas Alan, William Spense, Richard Clerk, Henry Williamson, Richard Hardsang, Miles Grenebank, Thomas Fynch, Nicholas Vicars.

Assembled in counsaille within the counsaill chambre [and] ther electid and named John Norman merchaunt and Thomas Chapman sadler chamberleyns of this citie tobe adioyned to the othre named and electid in the fest of Saint Blaise last past.

[R] *Chapman* And also the xvij^t day of the moneth of July next after the fest abovewrityn, it was aggreed by all the counsaill here writtyn that Thomas Chapman of new elect oone of the chamberleynes of this citie for diverse causes and consideracions shalnot be named nor electid to bere thoffice of sheref of the same or any othre office or charge within the same during the terme of x yeres next folowing and fully tobe complete. And if it be thoght and supposed by any of the counsaill of the chambre of this citie at any tyme within the terme of x yeres forsaid that the said Thomas hath growne in goodes by the which he might atteyne to bere thoffice of sheref here, yit never the lesse if the said Thomas present hymself ij days to fore thelleccion of the shereffes bifore the maier, his bretherne aldremen and the commune counsaill of this citie forsaid for the tyme being, and ther by othe shewe his insufficiencye in that behalve, that then he shalbe spared frome the said office or charges during the terme of x yeres and fully to be complete.

Present at this latter act the persones above writyn except of the commune counsaill Thomas Catour, William Spense, and Richard Hardsang, and in ther absence after was present William (Barkar) Tayte and William Barkar at the making of the same.

[f.100v]   Arrests and Bonds to Keep the Peace
Undated, c.June–July 1487

Capias Johannem Martyn de Ebor' glayser ad sectam Roberti Preston.

Capias Ricardum Walshworth de Ebor' armorour ad sectam Roberti Dowe.

Capias Thomam Appilby portam ad sectam Willelmi Lowdan.

Capias Margaretam Johnson ad sectam Elizabethe Scot.

Capias Johannem Kirkby capellanum ad sectam Willelmi Lutton.

Capias Thomam Grene capellanum ad sectam Thome Conyers.

Capias Johannem Braideley et Johannem Aleyne ad sectam Willelmi Duket.

Capias Thomam Walshworth, Willelmum Walshworth et Johannem Walshworth ad sectam Johannis Helperby.

supersedeas Johannes Kirby capellanus assumpsit pro seipso in xx libris necnon Johannes Atkynson, Robertus Baynes, Willelmus Barton et Roulandus Fallowefeld assumpserunt et quilibet eorum assumpsit pro prefato Johanne Kirkby in x libris ⟨de bonis suis levandis⟩ quod ipse dampnum ⟨vel⟩ malum aliquod corporale in Willelmum Lutton non faciet nec fieri procurabit quovismodo etc.

supersedeas Willelmus Lutton assumpsit pro seipso in xx libris ac eciam Johannes Deny, Johannes Pitcher, Johannes Marshall et Johannes Wynd assumpserunt et quilibet eorum assumpsit pro dicto Willelmo Lutton in x libris de bonis et catallis suis et eorum cuiuslibet levandis ad opus et utilitatem communitatis civitatis Ebor' etc., quod ipse dampnum vel malum aliquod corporale in Johannem Kirkby capellanum seu aliquem alium de populo domini nostri regis non faciet nec fieri procurabit quovismodo etc.

supersedeas Margareta Johnson assumpsit pro seipso in xx libris necnon Johannes

Russell, Hugo North et Johannes Lullay assumpserunt et quilibet eorum assumpsit
pro dicta Margareta in x libris de bonis et catallis suis et eorum cuiuslibet levandis
ad opus et utilitatem communitatis civitatis Ebor' etc., quod ipse dampnum etc., in
(Margaret') Elizabetham Scot seu alicui alio de populo domini nostri regis non
faciet nec fieri procurabit quovismodo etc.

supersedeas Johannes Bradeley assumpsit pro seipso in xx libris necnon Johannes
Fidler, Johannes Fatting, Robertus Da(v)y et Edmundus Cawthorn assumpserunt
et quilibet eorum assumpsit pro dicto Johanne in x libris levandis de bonis et suis
catallis eorum quia cuiuslibet ad opus et utilitatem communitatis civitatis Ebor'
etc., quod ipse dampnum etc., in Willelmum Duket seu alicui alio de populo
domini nostri regis non faciet nec fieri procurabit quovismodo etc.

[Arrest of John Martyn of York, glasier, at the suit of Robert Preston.

[*The remaining seven entries in this section follow the same form.*]

[*writ of*] *supersedeas* Chaplain John Kirby bound himself for £20, and also John
Atkynson, Robert Baynes, William Barton and Roland Fallowefeld each bound
himself on Kirby's behalf for £10 levied on their goods, that Kirby would do no
damage nor bodily harm to William Lutton nor cause any harm to be done.

[*writ of*] *supersedeas* William Lutton bound himself for £20, and also John Deny,
John Pitcher, John Marshall and John Wynd each bound himself on Lutton's
behalf for £10 levied on their goods and chattels [payable to] the work and the use
of the commonalty, that Lutton would do no damage nor bodily harm to chaplain
John Kirkby nor to any other of the king's subjects, nor cause any harm to be done.

[*writ of*] *supersedeas* Margaret Johnson bound herself for £20, and also John
Russell, Hugh North and John Lullay each bound himself on Margaret's behalf
for £10 levied of their goods and chattels to the work and use of the community,
that Margaret do no damage etc. to Elizabeth Scot nor to any other of the king's
subjects, nor cause any harm to be done.

[*writ of*] *supersedeas* John Bradeley bound himself for £20, and also John Fidler,
John Fatting, Robert Day and Edmund Cawthorn each bound himself on
Bradeley's behalf for £10 levied of their goods and chattels to the work and use of
the community, that Bradeley do no damage etc. to William Duket nor to any
other of the king's subjects, nor cause any harm to be done.]

**[f.101]   Chamberlain Gains Windmill
               22 June 1487**

Custance

[R] *upset de milners* Memorandum that the xxij^{ti} day of Juyn ⟨anno regni regis

Henrici vij secundo⟩ the right honourable and worshipfull William Todde maier of the citie of the citie of [sic] York in the counsaill chambre upon Ouse brig admitted John Custance, one of the chamberleyns of the said citie, with the consent and assent of the serchours of the milners ⟨of the said citie ther present⟩ to hold and occupye a commune wynd milne, soo that he set into the same a suffisaunt and ane able milner that can well and truly serve the kinges people at all such seasons as they shall have recourse (for) to the same for grynding of any maner of graynes. And therupon his said admission he paide incontinently unto the craft of milners and to the chambre equally tobe devided according to thordinance of the same craft iij s. iiij d. Present ther and than at his said admission ⟨John Catour⟩ Conan Gossep chamberleyns, John Robynson notary, and many othre.

Arrests and Bonds to Keep the Peace
Undated, c.June 1487

Capias Ricardum Wilson husband[man] ad sectam Thome Girdler de Furnasse.

Manucapcio Ricardi Wilson quod ipse dampnum vel malum aliquod corporale in Thomam Girdler seu aliquem alium de populo domini nostri regis non faciet nec fieri procurabit quovismodo videlicet dictus Johannes Garnet capellanus, Thomas Bailyey.

Capias Robertum Flaxton de Ebor' bucher ad sectam Roulandi Brice de eadem bucher.

Manucapcio pro Roulando Brice quod ipse dampnum vel malum aliquod corporale in Robertum Flaxton seu aliquem alium de populo domini nostri regis non faciet nec fieri procurabit quovismodo; Willelmus Garion, Johannes Gilmyn, Willelmus Wright et Willelmus Helperby quilibet eorundem manucepit in x libris et predictus Roulandus in xx libris levandis (ad) de bonis eorundem ad opus domini nostri regis.

Capias Robertum Baok, Willelmum Baok capellanum et Thomam Bek ad sectam Johannis Birkhede merchaunt etc.

Capias Thomam Dicson, Ricardum Bullasse et Ricardum Dicson ad sectam Johannis Orom etc.

[Arrest of husbandman Richard Wilson at the suit of Thomas Girdler of Furness.

Mainprise of Richard Wilson, that he do no damage nor bodily harm to Thomas Girdler nor to any other of the king's subjects nor cause any harm to be done; [sureties] the said John Garnet, chaplain, and Thomas Bailyey.

Arrest of Robert Flaxton of York, butcher, at the suit of Roland Brice, butcher of York.

Mainprise for Roland Brice, that he do no damage nor bodily harm to Robert Flaxton nor to any other of the king's subjects nor cause any harm to be done; William Garion, John Gilmyn, William Wright and William Helperby each bound himself for £10, and the said Roland bound himself for £20, levied of their goods, to the work of our lord king.

Arrest of Robert Baok, chaplain William Baok, and Thomas Bek, at the suit of merchant John Birkhede.

Arrest of Thomas Dicson, Richard Bullasse and Richard Dicson at the suit of John Orom.]

[f.101v]   King Orders Service of Thanksgiving for Victory
                16 June 1487

Copie of the kinges lettres direct as herafter foloweth:

By the king

To our trusty and welbeloved the maire of our citie of York

Trusty and welbeloved we grete you wele, and forsomoch as it hath liked our blissed salveour to graunte unto us of his benigne grace the triumphe and victorye of our rebelles without deth of any noble or gentilman on our part, we therfore desire and pray you and sithen this said victorye procedeth of hyme and concernyth not oonely the wele and hounour of us but also of this our royme, nathelesse charge you that calling unto you in the moost solempne churche of our citie ther your brethren thaldremen and othre, ye doo lovinges and praisinges to be yevene to our said salveour after the best of your powers. Yevene undre our signet at our towne of Newerk the xvj day of Juyn.

Arrests and Bonds to Keep the Peace
Undated, c.June 1487

Orom Manucapcio Johannis Orom quod ipse dampnum vel malum aliquod corporale in aliquem populum domini regis non faciet nec procurabit fieri quovismodo; Willelmus Burgesse capellanus et Johannes Custance uterque eorum assumpsit pro dicto Johanne in x libris et prefatus Johannes in xx libris levandis de bonis et catallis eorundem et cuiuslibet eorum ad opus domini regis etc.

Capias Johannem Gose ad sectam Johannis Sargiant etc.

Capias Willelmum Byngley skynner ad sectam Willelmi Skelding shomaker etc.

Manucapcio Willelmi Skelding quod ipse aliquod dampnum in Willelmum Byngley non faciet etc., videlicet dictus Willelmus Skelding in xx libris necnon Johannes Hastinges armiger, Georgius Lokrik wever, Ricardus Bewik shomaker et Robertus Swan trimer, quilibet eorum manucepit pro dicto Willelmo in x libris quod ipse dampnum non faciet ut supra etc.

Capias Thomam Appilby porter ad sectam Willelmi Lowdan.

Willelmus Lowdan assumpsit pro seipso in xx libris necnon Thomas Glover bower et Alexander Ambler assumpserunt pro dicto Willelmo in x libris levandis etc., quod nullum dampnum faciet alicui populo domini regis etc.

[*Orom* Mainprise of John Orom, that he do no damage nor bodily harm to any of the king's subjects nor cause any harm to be done; chaplain William Burgesse and John Custance each bound himself on Orom's behalf for £10, and the said Orom bound himself for £20, levied of their goods and chattels.

Arrest of John Gose at the suit of John Sargiant.

Arrest of William Byngley, skinner, at the suit of shoemaker William Skelding.

Mainprise of William Skelding, that he do no damage to William Byngley, under penalty of £20; [sureties] John Hastinges, knight, weaver George Lokrik, shoemaker Richard Bewik and trimmer Robert Swan each bound himself on Skelding's behalf for £10 that he would do no damage as above.

Arrest of porter Thomas Appilby at the suit of William Lowdan.

William Lowdan bound himself for £20, and also bower Thomas Glover and Alexander Ambler bound themselves on Lowdan's behalf for £10 levied etc., that he would do no harm to any of the king's subjects.]

[f.102]   **Bonds to Accept Arbitration**
           5 October 1487

v° die mensis Octobris anno regni regis Henrici vij tercio

Barkar, Kirkby et Johnson; vacat recognitio quia partes concorde sunt [*entire entry struck through*] (Johannes Barkar de Ebor' tailyour assumpsit pro seipso in xx libris ex una parte ac Thomas Kirkby et Willelmus Johnson assumpserunt pro seipsis ex altera parte in xx libris levandis de bonis et catallis suis ad opus domini regis etc., quod ipsi et eorum quilibet stabit et obediet laudo, ordinacioni et iudicio Johannis Thomeson, Thome Beene, Johannis Hogeson et Willelmi Stubbez ffletcher arbitratorum inter partes predictas per dominum maiorem indifferenter electorum et nominatorum in, de et super omnimodis accionibus tam realibus quam personalibus, sectis, demandis et querelis inter easdem partes occasione cuiuscumque rei vel cause a principio mundi usque in diem confeccionis presentium recognitionum, exortis, motis et pendentibus et eadem ex utraque parte perimplebit, ita quod huiusmodi laudum, ordinacio et iudicium fiant et reddantur inter partes predictas citra festum Sancti Wilfridi archiepiscopi proximum futurum.)

vᵒ die Octobris anno regis Henrici vij tercio

Burton, Ripplingham Magister Willelmus Burton clericus assumpsit pro se ipso in xx libris ac Willelmus Taite et Nicholaus Regent assumpserunt et alter eorum assumpsit pro (se) prefato Magistro Willelmo in x libris, necnon Ricardus Ripplingham clericus assumpsit pro seipso in xx libris ac Johannes Blessing et Hermanus Goldsmyth assumpserunt et alter eorum assumpsit pro prefato Ricardo in x libris levandis de bonis et catallis eorundem et cuiuslibet eorum ad opus domini nostri regis, quod ipsi Magister Willelmus et Ricardus et eorum alter stabunt et obedient ac stabit et obediet laudo, ordinacioni et iudicio Milonis Harwom, Willelmi Robynson, Ricardi Wynder et Thome Braderig arbitratorum inter partes predictas per dominum maiorem indifferenter electorum et nominatorum in, de et super omnimodis accionibus tam realibus quam personalibus, sectis, demandis, debatis et transgressionibus inter easdem partes occasione cuiuscumque rei vel cause a principio mundi usque in diem confeccionis presentium recognitionum, exortis, motis et pendentibus et eadem perimplebunt et alter eorum perimplebit, ita quod huiusmodi laudum etc., fiant inter partes predictas citra festum (Omnium Sanctorum proximum futurum) Sancti Andree apostoli proximum futurum.

H. R.

[*Barkar, Kirkby and Johnson; bond void because parties are agreed* (John Barkar of York, tailor, bound himself for £20 on the one side, and Thomas Kirkby and William Johnson bound themselves on the other side for £20, levied of their goods and chattels to the work of the lord king, etc., that they and each one of them would adhere to and obey the advice, ordinance and judgement of John Thomeson, Thomas Beene, John Hogeson and fletcher William Stubbez, arbiters between the said parties elected and named by the lord mayor, in, of, and over all actions both real and personal, all suits and actions between these parties, of whatever thing or cause arisen from, moved, or pending between them, from the beginning of the world to the present day, this judgement to be made and rendered by the next coming feast of Saint Wilfrid the archbishop.)

5 October 1487

Burton, Ripplingham Master William Burton, clerk, bound himself for £20, and also William Taite and Nicholas Regent each bound himself for £10 on behalf of Master William, and also clerk Richard Ripplingham bound himself for £20, and John Blessing and Herman Goldsmyth each bound himself on Ripplingham's behalf for £10, that the said Master William and Richard Ripplingham would adhere to and obey the advice and judgement of Miles Harwom, William Robynson, Richard Wynder and Thomas Braderig, arbiters impartially named and elected by the lord mayor over all actions both real and personal, and all suits, actions and trespasses between the said parties of whatever cause, from the beginning of the world to the present day, this judgement to be made by the next coming feast of Saint Andrew the apostle.]

[f.102v] **Bonds to Accept Arbitration**
26 October 1487

Stok, Asshton, Pikard, Nayler Memorandum quod xxvj° die mensis Octobris anno regni regis Henrici vij tercio, Thomas Stok de Ebor' skynner assumpsit pro seipso in x marcis necnon Ricardus Asshton assumpsit pro seipso in x libris ac eciam idem Ricardus assumpsit pro Johanne Pikard et Johanne Nayler de Ebor' predicta skynners ⟨et pro alter eorundem⟩ in x libris levandis de bonis et catallis eorundem et cuiuslibet eorum ad opus domini nostri regis quod ipsi Thomas, Ricardus, Johannes et Johannes et eorum quilibet stabunt et obedient ac stabit et obediet laudo, ordinacioni et iudicio Willelmi Todde militis maioris civitatis Ebor' ac Georgii Kirk et Roberti Johnson vicecomitum eiusdem, arbitratorum inter prefatos Thomam Stok et Ricardum Asshton ex una parte et ⟨eundem (prefatum) Thomam Stok et⟩ dictos Johannem Pikard (et) Johannem Nayler et [*sic*] altera parte indifferenter electorum, in, de et super omnimodis accionibus realibus et personalibus, sectis, demandis et querelis inter partes predictas a principio mundi usque diem confeccionis presentium recognitionum, motis, exortis et pendentibus et eadem laudum, ordinacionem et iudicium ex utraque parte perimplebunt, ita quod huiusmodi laudum, ordinacio et iudicium fiant et reddantur inter partes predictas per dictos arbitratores citra festum Sancti Martini in yeme proximum futurum post datam predictam.

H. R.

Brise, Flaxton Memorandum quod xxvj° die mensis Octobris anno regni regis Henrici vij^mi tercio Roulandus Brise de Ebor' bowcher et Robertus Flaxton de eadem bouchre coram Willelmo Todde milite maiore civitatis Ebor' personaliter comparens assumpserunt et alter eorum assumpsit pro seipso in xx libris levandis de bonis et catallis eorundem et alterius eorum ad opus domini nostri regis quod ipsi Roulandis et Robertus et eorum alter stabunt et obedient ac stabit et obediet laudo, ordinacioni et iudicio Willelmi Garton, Johannis Robynson, Willelmi Helperby et Ricardi Tebbe arbitratorum inter prefatum Roulandum ex una parte et dictum Robertum ex altera parte indifferenter electorum et nominatorum in, de et super omnibus accionibus realibus et personalibus, sectis, demandis et querelis inter partes predictas a principio mundi usque datam predictam motis, exortis et pendentibus et eadem laudum etc., perimplebunt et perimplebit, ita quod huiusmodi laudum etc., fiant et reddantur inter partes predictas per dictos arbitratores citra festum Sancti Martini proximum futurum post datam predictam. Et in casu quod dicti arbitratores inter se non concordare (poterint) nec partes huiusmodi ad pacem traducere non poterunt tunc prefate partes stabunt et obedient laudo, ordinacioni et iudicio Willelmi Todde militis maioris civitatis predicte imparis in hac parte indifferenter inter easdem electi in, de et super permissis, ita quod huiusmodi laudum etc., fiant etc., per dictum imparem citra festum Sancti Andree apostoli proximum futurum post datam predictam.

H. R.

[*Stok, Asshton, Pikard, Nayler* On 26 October 1487, skinner Thomas Stok of

York bound himself for £10, and also Richard Asshton bound himself for £10, and also the same Richard bound himself for £10 for skinners John Pikard and John Nayler, levied of their goods and chattels, that the said Thomas, Richard, John and John and each one of them would adhere to and obey the advice and judgement of William Todde, knight, mayor of York, and of George Kirk and Robert Johnson, sheriffs of York, arbiters between Thomas Stok and Richard Asshton on the one side and the same Thomas Stok and said John Pikard and John Nayler on the other side, arbiters impartially elected in and over all actions both real and personal, suits and disputes between the said parties from the beginning of the world to the present day, the said judgement to be made and rendered by Martinmas next coming.

Brise, Flaxton On 26 October 1487, butchers Roland Brise and Robert Flaxton each bound himself before Sir William Todde mayor of York for £20 levied of their goods and chattels that they would adhere to and obey the advice and judgement of William Garton, John Robynson, William Helperby and Richard Tebbe, arbiters impartially elected and named over all actions both real and personal, suits and disputes moved, arisen, or pending between them, this judgement to be made and rendered by the next coming Martinmas. And if the said arbiters are unable to agree then the parties must keep the peace and obey the judgement of Sir William Todde, mayor of the city and elected as umpire between the parties, his judgement to be made by the next coming feast of Saint Andrew.]

**[f.103] Master of Mint Relinquishes Old Coining Irons
28 June 1487**

delivere of the old coyneing yryns unto the citie of London Be it had in mynde that the xxviij day of Juny in the secund yere of the reigne of King Herry the vij[th], Thomas Graa master of the mynt within the palois garth of the citie of York deliverd unto William Todde maier of the citie of York a bagg of ledder contigneing (viij) ⟨xij⟩ old conyng iryns, that is to say iiij standers and viij trusselles, the which bagg the said William Todde maier sealid and deliverd to the handes of John White coigner, to deliver unto the Chequour at London, and from thens to bring newe gravene iryns agane from the said Eschequour unto the said citie of York.

**Bonds to Keep the Peace
Undated, c.June 1487**

Flaxton Manucapcio pro Roberto Flaxton quod ipse dampnum etc., in Roulandum Brise seu aliquem alium de populo domini regis non faciet nec fieri procurabit quovismodo, videlicet Ricardus Croklyn et Thomas Welles quilibet manucaptorum assumpsit pro seipso in x libris et prefatus Robertus assumpsit pro seipso in xx libris levandis ad opus domini nostri regis de bonis eorundem etc.

Hewar Robertus Hewar de Ebor' shomaker assumpsit pro seipso in xx libris necnon Johannes Tenaunt, Thomas Kirkby shomaker, (Thoma) Johannes Kirkby poynter et Johannes Downe pursor assumpserunt et quilibet eorum assumpsit pro prefato Roberto in x libris levandis de bonis et catallis eorundem et cuiuslibet eorum ad opus domini nostri regis, quod ipse Robertus pro se vel suos dampnum vel malum aliquod corporale in Robertum Bullok seu aliquem alium de populo domini nostri regis non faciet nec fieri procurabit quovismodo.

supersedeas pro Byngley Willelmus Byngley de Ebor' skynner assumpsit pro seipso in xx libris necnon Ricardus Asshton skynner, Henricus Wressill et Thomas Stok assumpserunt etc., quilibet eorum assumpsit pro dicto Willelmo in x libris levandis ut supra quod nullum dampnum faciet Willelmo Skelding shomaker nec alicui etc.

[*Flaxton* Mainprise for Robert Flaxton, that he do no damage etc., to Roland Brise or to any other of the king's subjects, nor cause any harm to be done; Richard Croklyn and Thomas Welles bound themselves for £10 on Robert's behalf, and Robert bound himself for £20.

Hewar Shoemaker Robert Hewar of York bound himself for £20, and also John Tenaunt, shoemaker Thomas Kirkby, painter John Kirkby, and purser John Downe each bound himself for £10 levied of their goods and chattels, that Robert would do no damage nor bodily harm to Robert Bullok or to any other of the king's subjects.

[*writ of*] *supersedeas for Byngley* Skinner William Byngley of York bound himself for £20, and also skinner Richard Asshton, Henry Wressill and Thomas Stok each bound himself on behalf of William for £10, that he do no harm to shoemaker William Skelding or to anyone else.]

[f.103v]   Mayor Delivers Coining Irons
19 July 1487

delyvere of the coigneyng yryns of the citie of York unto Thomas Gray Memorandum that the xix[th] day of July in the secunde yere of the reigne of King Herry the sevent, Thomas Graye goldsmyth maister of the mynt at the palays of the moost reverend ffader in God tharchbisshop of York, personally appering bifore William Todde maier of the citie of York in the chambre upon Ouse brig, presentid unto hyme a bagg of leder sealed, contigneing in the same iiij standers and viij trusselles beryng the peny coigne sent unto hyme furth of the kinges Eschequour as he shewed; the which bagg my lord maire receyved at thandes of the said Thomas and delyverd unto hyme the said iiij standers and viij trusselles and reservyd the bagg which thei wer in unto hyme self for soo moch as ther was a holle in the side of the said bagg at the which the said iryns was takyn furth etc.

City Spicer Acknowledges Debt
16 November 1487

Thorneton, Talbot Richard Thorneton of York spicer personally appering bifore Sir William Todde knight maier of the citie of York in the counsaill chambre of the same the xvj^th^ day of Novembre in the iij yere of the reigne of King Herry the vij^t^, confessid and knowlegid hymself to be indettid unto Robert Talbot of York walkar iiij li., to be paid to the said Robert in fourme folowing, that is for to say ij days bifore the fest of Saint Thomas thappostil next commyng, xx s.; in the fest of the purificacion of our ladye next after, xx s.; in the fest of Pasche then next folowing, xx s.; and in the fest of Witsonday next after that, xx s. of laufull Ynglisshe money without any further delay.

H. R.

[f.104]   **Lease of Garden, Bond to Keep the Peace**
                  20 July 1487

Stokesley Vicesimo die Julii anno regni regis Henrici septimi post conquestum Anglie secundo, Johannes Stokesley de Ebor' sissor venit personaliter coram Willelmo Todde maiore et camerariis infra cameram concilii et cepit de eisdem maiore et camerariis unum ortum iacentem extra portam de Walmegate prout iacet inter terram monialarum de Clementhorpe ex parte orientali et terram Henrici Albone ex parte occidentali, habendum et tenendum dictum ortum prefato Johanni a festo Purificacionis Beate Marie Virginis proximo futuro post datam presentium usque ad finem et terminum decem annorum extunc proximo sequentium et plenarie complendorum, reddendo inde annuatim prefatis maiori et camerariis seu custodibus pontis Use qui pro tempore fuerunt ij solidos vj denarios ad terminos Pentecostes et Sancti Martini per equales porciones primo termino incipienti in festo (Sancti) Pentecostes proximo futuro etc.

Sawnder et Smyth Johannes Sawnderson ffissher et Johannes Smyth de Ebor' ffissher assumpserunt et alter eorum assumpsit (st) se stare arbitrio, laudo et iudicio Thome Armyn et Johannis Stokesley pro parte dicti Johannis Saunderson ac Johannis Awkland et Thome Barbour pro parte Johannis Sawnderson [*sic*], predicti ⟨arbitratores⟩ de et super omnibus accionibus inter eosdem pendentibus etc., et hoc sub pena xx librarum levandarum ad opus domini regis etc., ita quod huiusmodi laudum etc., fiant et reddantur per huiusmodi arbitratores citra festum Sancti Michaelis proximum futurum.

[*Stokesley* On 20 July 1487, tailor John Stokesley of York came personally into the presence of mayor William Todde and the chamberlains within the council chamber and leased from the mayor and chamberlains a garden lying outside Walmgate Bar and lying between the land of the nuns of Clementhorpe [priory] on the east side, and land of Henry Albone on the west side; John is to have and to hold the garden from the feast of the Purification of the Blessed Virgin Mary next coming after the date of these presents [bonds], to the end of a term of ten years fully completed, rendering yearly to the aforesaid mayor and chamberlains or to keepers of Ouse bridge 2 s. 6 d. in equal portions at Pentecost and Martinmas, beginning next Pentecost.

Sawnder and Smyth Fishermen John Sawnderson and John Smyth of York each bound himself for £20 to adhere to the arbitration and judgement of Thomas Armyn and John Stokesley on the part of the said Saunderson, and John Awkland and Thomas Barbour on the part of John Sawnderson [*sic*], the arbiters to determine all matters pending between them, the judgement to be made and rendered by the next feast of Michaelmas.]

[f.104v]   Preparations for King Henry's Visit
27 July 1487

Thursday the xxvij day of July [*sic, 27 July 1487 was a Friday*]

Mayor: William Todde. Recorder: John Vavasour. 12: Richard York, John Tong, John Fereby, John Newton, Nicholas Loncastre, William Chymney, Robert Hancok, John Harper, William White, John Gilyot. Counsellor: Thomas Asper. Sheriffs: John Beseby, John Shawe. 24: Thomas Catour, Thomas Alan, Richard Clerk, William Tayte, Thomas Fynch, Nicholas Vicars.

Assembled in counsaill, it was shewed by John Sponer sergiaunt at the mase late sent in message unto the kinges secretary with certain writing and credence, how the kinges grace entendith God speding to be at this his citie here upon Monday next commyng betwix iiij and v of the clok at afternone the same day accompaygned betwix xij or xv thowsand men, and to tary and make his abode there frome the said Monday to the Thursday in the morneyng. And that my lord the mayre with his brethren aldremen and the commune counsaill of this citie in there moost goodly array as merchantes and citicyns shuld receyve his grace into the citie according to thauncient custome of the same. And also that the play of Corpus Christi shuld be made redy ayenst Lammesse day, for asfar as he culd perceve by the kinges secretary forsaide it shuld please his highnesse to here it the same day. Which premissez shewed the said John Sponer with thankes yevene for his acquitall therin departid with licence frome the said counsaill. Wherupon it was determyned that my lord mayre, my masters thaldremen his brethre clothed in scarlet and the commune counsaill in cremesyn and othre wise goodly arrayed, shuld receve the kinges highnesse into this his citie without Mikillyth barre standing on rowe bifore Saint Thomas house ther, and that Master Recordour shuld use thies wordes ensuyng unto the kinges grace there in the name of my lord mayre, my masters aldremen, shereffes, commune counsaill and thool body of this citie:

recorder wordes, and speach of our recorder Moost high and mighty Christen prince and our moost drad souverain liege lord, the maier, aldremen, **[f.105]** shereffes and commune counsaill with thool body of this citie as your true and faithfull subgiettes welcome your moost noble grace unto this your citie with due lovinges unto almyghty God for the grete fortune ⟨and noble tryumphe and victory⟩ it hath plased his godhede to graunt unto your highnesse at this tyme in subduyng of your ennymies and rebelles, besuching almighty God to continewe you in the same.

And that within the barre in Mikilgate of eithre side the strete shall stand the communaltye of evere craft in ther best array without any staffes bering, with due obeysaunce making unto (the k) his grace, and crying of 'King Herry'.

Also it was determyned then and ther that proclamacions shuld be maid thrughe out the citie incontinently after departour of the counsaill in forme folowing:

Oyes thrise: My lord mayre and shereffes of this citie straitly chargeth and commaundeth on the behalve of our souverain lord the king, that evere commune vitailler of this citie, that is for to say bakers, brewers, bowchers, ffisshers, vinters, cookes and inholders have redy within them vitaill suffisaunt for such company as shall attend here upon our souverain lord the king at his commyng hidder upon Monday next ensuyng or at any tyme of thissidre, aswell for man as for best, during such season as it shall please his highnesse to make his abode here and in his retourne agane unto the same, and that evere vitailler sell noo maner of vitaill but such as is holsome both for man and best, and sell after suche price and to kepe the true assise, as shalbe set upon the same by my lord mayre as clerk of the market within this citie at the commyng of the kinges grace unto the same, upon the payne of forfaytour of a C s., to be raised of evere commune vitailler failing in this behalve and his bodye to prisone. And that all rede wyne, claret and white be sold for x d. a galon and noo derrer under the payne above said.

[f.105v]   King Orders Men Fed at Fair Price
            5 June 1487

Copie of a proclamacion sent from the kinges grace undre thalf seal as herafter foloweth:

Henricus Dei gracia rex Anglie et Francie et dominus Hibernie, universis et singulis vicecomitibus, maioribus, ballivis, constabulariis ac omnibus aliis officiariis et ministris nostris ubique constitutis ad quos presentes littere pervenerint, salutem. Mandamus vobis quod statim post visum presencium in singulis locis infra ballivas vestras et cuiuslibet vestrum tam infra libertates quam extra V magis videritis ex parte nostra presentes proclamaciones fieri factas in hec verba:

[Henry by the grace of God, etc., to each and every of the sheriffs, mayors, bailiffs, constables and all other of our officers and ministers wheresoever appointed to whom these present letters reach, greetings. We command you that immediately upon looking at these [letters] you cause to be made in each and every one of your bailiwicks and within the five liberties of your city our present proclamations in these words:]

For asmoche as the king our souverain lord accompayned with grete multitude of his nobles and subgiettes of this his realme entendith in short tyme to passe thrugh thies parties for the repressing and subduyng of the maliciouse purpose of his grete rebelles and enemyes, and for that that his highnesse ne his said company in noo wise shuld be destitute or wantyng of vitaill for man or horsse, he straitly chargith and commaundith evere vitailler and all othre his subgiettes dwelling in evere towne and place where his said highnesse and his said company shall come, to purvey and make redye plenty of brede and ale and of othre vitall aswell for hors as for men at resonable price in redy money therfor to them and evere of them truly to be contentid and paide as they and evere of thame truly tobe contentyd and payed as they and evere of thame entend the well of his moost royall persone and of this his realme and to avoide his grevous displeaser and indignacion. Et hoc sub particulo incumbenti nullatenus omittatis. Teste meipso apud Kenelworth quinto die Junii anno regni regis secundo.

[And none of the details pertaining to this are to be omitted by any means. Witnessed by myself at Kenilworth, 5 July 1487.]

[f.106]   Royal Proclamation to Keep Peace While King Henry in City
Undated, c.June–July 1487

Copie of a proclamacion sent from the kinges grace unto my lord mayre by the kinges herbingers to be proclamed thrugh the citie

The king our souverain lord straitly chargith and commaundeth that noo maner of man of whatsoever astate, degree or condicion he be, robbe, dispole any dispale any [sic] church ne take out of the same any ornament therto belonging, ne touche nor set hand on the pix wherin the blessid sacrament is contigneyd, nor yit robbe ne dispoile any maner of man or woman upon payne of dethe; and also that no maner personne ne personnes whatsoever they be make no querell to any man ne(c) sease, vexn ne trouble any man by body or goodes for any offense or by colour of any offense hertofore doone or committed ayenist the royall magistie of the king our souverain lord without his auctoritie or special commaundement yevene unto hyme or them that soo dothe in that behalve upon payne of deth. Also that noo maner of persone whatsoever he be ravisshe(d) noo religiouse woman nor mannes wif, doughter, mayden ne noo mannys ne womans servaunt, nor take ne presume to take any maner of vitaill, horsemet or mannes mete without paying therfor the resonable price therof assised by the clerc of the market or othre the kinges officers therfor ordigned upon payne of deth.

herbingers Also that noo maner of persone ne personnes whatsoever they be take upon theme to loge themself nor take noo maner of logeing ne herbigage but suche as shalbe assigned unto hyme or them by the kinges herbigeours, nor dislogge noo man nor chaunge noo logging after that he be assigned with thadvise and assent of the said herbigeours upon payne of enprisonment and to be punysshed at the wille of our saide souverain lord. Also that noo maner of man whatsoever he be make noo maner of quarell with any othre man for noo maner of cause olde ne newe ne make noo maner affraye within the ⟨⟨ooste⟩⟩ (ost) ⟨oost⟩ ne without, upon payne of enprisonment and to be punysshed according to his trespasse and defaute, and if ther happen any such querell or affraye to be made by any evil disposed personnes that than noo maner of man for any acquentance or felishop that they be of take noo part with noo suche misdoers in any such affrayes or querelles upon payne of enprisonment and to be punysshed [f.106v] at the kinges will, but that evere man endevour himself to take all such misdoers and bringe theme to the marshalles warde to be punysshed according to ther desertes. Also that noo maner of personne whatsoever he be hurte, trouble, bete nor lett noo maner of personne, man, woman or childe bringing any vitaill unto the kinges oste upon payne of enprisonment and his body to be at the kinges wille. And over this that every man being of the retinewe of our said souveraine lord at the first sowne or blast of the trumpet doo saidell his horse, at the secunde doo bridell, and at the third be redyn on horsbak to awayte upon his highnesse upon peyne of enprisonment. Also that noo maner of personne whatsoever he be make noo skryes, showtinges nor blowing of hornes in the kinges oste after the watche be sett upon payne of enprisonment and his body to be at the kinges wille; and also that noo vacabunde nor othre folowe the kinges oste but suche as be reteyned or have maisters within the same upon payne of enprisonment and to be punysshment in example of othre, and noo comon woman folowe the kinges ostes upon payne of enprisonment and openly to be punysshed in example of all othre. Also whansoever it shall please the kinge our souverain lord to commaunde any of his officers to charge any thing in his name by his high commaundement or by the commaundement of his constable or marshall, that it be observed and kept upon payne of enprisonment and his body tobe punysshed at the kinges pleaser.

[f.107]   King Henry Visits City
              30 July–28 August 1487

The secund tyme of the comyng of the kinges grace Herry the vij[th] unto this his citie

The Monday the xxx[th] day of the moneth of July the kinges grace accompayned with many lordes and nobles of his realme and ther retinew to the nombred of x thowsand men in harnesse with his baner displayed cam to the citie of York about iiij of the clok at after none the same day and at Saint Thomas hospitall without Mikelgate barre my lord mayre, Master Recordour with all aldremen and counseillours of this citie in ther moost goodly maner and aray like citicyns receyved his moost royall persone into this citie with wordes ensuyng utterd by the mouthe of Master Recordour forsaid:

speach of Master Recorder Moste high and mighty Christen prince and our moost drad souverain lige lord, your true and faithfull subgiettes the mayre, aldremen, shereffes and common counsaill, with thool body of this your citie in ther moost humbly wise welcomes your moost noble grace unto the same, yeving due lovinges unto almighty God for the grete fortune, noble trihumpe and victory which it hath pleased his godhede to graunt unto your highnesse in subduyng your rebelles and ennymes at this tyme, besuching almighty God to continewe your moost noble grace in the same.

my lord maiour did bere the mace before the king Which wordes the kinges grace receyved thankfully and soo rodd furth thrughe the citie, my lord mayre bering the mase bifore his highnesse (unto th) on horsbak unto the paloys beside the cathedral church of York. On Weddynsday after [*1 August*] in the fest of thadvincle of Saint Petre, the play of Corpus Christi by the kinges commaundement was played thrugh the citie and his grace hering the same in Conyingstrete at Thomas Scot house. Thursday after [*2 August*] in the mornyng Roger Layton squire was juged at the Guildhall to be heded for certain poyntes of treason committed by hyme ayenst the kinges highnesse. And of Satterday next after [*4 August*] at ij of the clok at after none the said Roger was heded upon the Payment and his body and hede beryd togidder in his parissh church of the Holy Trinitie in Gotheromgate. The same Satterday and Thursday before [*2 August*] Thomas Metcalf gentilman and oone Tempesse was juged by Sir John Troubleveile knight marshall to be heded in like wise, bot after they obtagned ther pardones upon the kinges grace. In the vigill of Saint Petre callid Advincle [*1 August*], the king dubbed my lord **[f.107v]** mairer callid William Todde and Richard York alderman knightes. Monday after [*6 August*] the kinges grace accompaigned with many lordes and nobles of this his realme toke his journey toward Durham and Newcastell, and from thens retourned within the space of xiiij days commyng by Burghbrig and soo streght unto Pomifrect, unto the which my lord mayre, iiij aldermen accompayned with lx horsse cam unto the kinges grace shewing unto (the the) his highnesse certain maters concernyng the well and prouffit of this citie, of the which they hadd a perfite aunswer and his grace right well content with ther commyng, and so retourned agayne unto this citie upon the Sonday after the fest of Saint Bartilmewe [*26 August*].

Assault on City Shoemaker
26 August 1487

submysion The same Sonday at night certaine gentilmen and yomen belonging unto thabbot of Saint Mary Abbey maide affray and asalt upon oone Borowdall shomaker dwelling in Staynegate ayenst thordinaunce of this citie, ffor the which the said abbot not knowing of the said affray nor willing to ratifie the same, sent unto my lord maier and his brethre aldremen and othre of the counsaill assembled in counsaill, the said gentilmen and yomen upon the Tewesday next after [*28 August*] to shewe ther dealing and to submitte theme self if they had oght offendid ayenst the kinges peas and libertie of this citie.

[f.108]   Earl of Northumberland Provides Venison Feast
10 September 1487

the fest of venyson and wyne yevene to the maier and commonaltie by therl of Northumberland The right prepotent and right noble lord therl of Northumberland for his entier affeccion and luff which he did and dothe bere unto this citie of York and in consideracion of the good zele and true hertes which thinhabitants of the same hath ever borne towardes his lordship, of his owne mere motion gaf unto my lord maire, his bretherne aldremen and commune counsaill (and) viij warantes for viij bukkes and v markes of money to be disposid in solace and recreacion of them and of the honest commoners of the said citie; which as it apperteyneth was thankfully receyved and the said warrantes put in execucion and sped; and forsomoch as the said v markes wold not suffice nor extend to half the costes of the said recreacion, it was thoght that the guild of Saint Christofor shuld susteigne the superpluss, which did amount the somme of vj li., soo that by the same and the residue of the said markes left (of) ⟨over⟩ thexpences and lauboures about the speding of the said warrantes and othre thinges necessary in that behalve, with the said bukkes, my lord mayre, my masters thaldermen his brethre, the commune counsaill with othre gentilmen of Aynesty, and sex hundreth of the moost honest commoners of this ⟨said citie⟩ had a worshipfull recreacion, solace and disport, with brede, ale, venyson rost and bakyn with rede wyne suffisiaunt without any thing paing for the same, bot onely thankes unto the said right prepotent and right noble lord, and the said guild of Saint Christofor. In the Guildhall of of [*sic*] the said citie the Monday x day of Septembre in the iij yere of the reigne of our souverain lord King Herry the vijth.

HR

[f.108v]   Visit to King Henry at Pontefract, Fee Farm Grant, Crimes During Royal Visit
24 and 25 August, 3 September 1487

Veneris ffestum Sancti Bartholomei apud Guihald

Mayor: William Todde. Recorder: John Vavasour. 12: Richard York, Thomas Wrangwissh, John Tong, John Fereby, John Newton, Nicholas Loncastre, William Chymney, John Harper, William White, John Gilyot. Sheriffs: John Beseby, John Shaw. 24: Thomas Alan, William Spense, William Tayte, Richard Clerc, Michael White, Miles Grenebank, William Barkar, Thomas Fynche, Nicholas Vicars, Roger Appilby.

Assembled in counsaill determyned that my lord mayer, Master Recordour, Sir Richard York knight, William Chymney, John Harper, John Gilyot aldremen, Thomas Fynch and Nicholas Vicars accompayned with xl horsse shuld ride unto the kinges grace to Pomifret for certain urgent maters concernyng the puplique wele of this citie to be shewed unto his highnesse ther er his departour furth of this north cuntree.

sheryffes, lx li. parcell of the kinges gefyng to the sherifes Also the same day the commune seall was grauntid by all the communes assembled in the Guilhall unto John Beseby and John Shawe, shereffes, for ther indempnitye and surtye enempst the payment of lx li. grauntid unto the said citie by the kinges grace of the ffee ferme of the same.

Dauson submysion Also the same day it was aggreed by all above writyn that for such offence as Alexander Dauson committe ayenst this citie in latting in oone Roger Layton, standing oute of the kinges grace and late put to execucion for certain his demereties ayenst his highnesse, in to the said citie at suche tyme as his rebelles approched unto the same, and also for so moche as the said Alexander did purchasse the kinges writing ayenst (the s) my lord mayre surmising **[f.109]** wrong suggestions in the same ayenst hyme, shuld submitte hymeself unto my lord maier and (payesse) to the use of the communaltye pay upon grace and othre pardone x li.

Robert Hancok alderman, John Hagg and Richard Hardsang assembled in counsaill the iij day of Septembre affermed thact above writtyn enempst Alexander Dauson.

Pountefecte Satterday after the fest of Saint Bartilmewe [*25 August*] my lord maier accompayned with his brethre aldremen and othre above named to the nombre of lx horssez rode to the kinges grace to Pomifrect where they wer right worshipfully receyved and of the kinges grace hertly welcomed. And after certaine urgent maters shewed unto his highnesse concernyng the puplique wele of this citie, retourned unto the said citie purchasing amonges othre thinges the kinges severalles writinges as the tenour therof ensueth, the Sonday next after [*26 August*].

Residents of Ainsty Should Help Defend City
26 August 1487

York Henry by the grace of God king of England and of Fraunce and lord of Irland, to our trusty and welbeloved the maier and his bretherne of our citie of York and to the commune counsaill of the same, greting. For asmoche as we be credibly enfourmed that the wapentake of Aynesty adioynyng unto our said citie is within the precincte and boundes of the ffraunchises of the same as parcell of the countye therof, whereby the reseauntes and inhabitauntes within the same aught of right to be redy in obeyng and attending upon you whan ye shall call upon theme for ther assistence in the defense and tuicion of our said citie if the caas require, we therfor tendring the well and surtie of the same woll that according to your auctoritie ye on oure behalve yeve straitly in commaundement unto all **[f.109v]** knightes, squires, gentilman and all othre reseauntes and inhabitauntes of and within the said wapentake to be attending and assisting unto you for the defence and saufgard of our said citie when the caas shal require, upon the perill that may ensue, and that ye faile not thus to doo, as ye woll aunswer unto us at your perilles. Yevene undre our signet at our castell of Pountefrete the xxvj day of August the third yere of our reigne.

Aynesty Henry by the grace of God king of England and of Fraunce and lord of Irlande, to all knightes, squires, gentilmen and othre reseauntes and inhabitauntes of and within the wapentake of Aynesty adioynyng unto our citie of York, greting. Forasmuche as we be credibly enfourmed that the said wapentake is within the precincte and boundes of the ffranchises of our said citie as parcel of the cuntye therof, whereby ye and every of you aught of right to be redy and obedient unto the maire there whan he shall warne and calle you to thassistence and defense of our said citie when the caas shall require, we therfor tendring the wele and surtie of the same woll and commaunde you that whansoever the said maire and his bretherne shall call upon you for your assistence in the defence and tuicion of our said citie, ye be according to your dutie setting apart all reteyndres and attendance upon othre persones and commaundementes of our wardeyns of our marches towarde Scotland and of our shireffes of our countie of York for the tyme being, helping, attending, obeying, and assisting in al thinges as it apperteyneth without obstacle or contradiccion, as ye woll answer therfor unto us at your perilles. Yevene undre our signet at our castel of Pomifreit the xxvj day of August the third yere of our reigne.

[f.110]   City Merchant Pays Fine
10 September 1487

Satterday the xth day of September [*sic, 10 September 1487 was a Monday*]

Dauson Alexandre Dauson merchaunt personally appering bifore William Todde knight maier of the citie of York in the counsaill chambre within the Guildhall of the same, bringing with hyme Master Robert Este, chamberleyne of the cathedral church of York, laide downe tofore the said maier for such offence as had committe, as more at large apperith in an act within writyn, x li. by thandes of the said Master Este, of the which my lord maier toke unto hyme agane at [the] contemplacion of thool counsaill v markes and of my lord deane and the chapitour of the cathedral church of York laboring for hyme in that behalve five nobles, and at thespecial request of the chamberleyns ther being present twenty shelinges, so that he paide clere to thuse of the communaltie foure poundes.

[f.110v]   Council Pays Annuity to Franciscan Friary
21 September 1487

In the fest of Saint Mathew the xxj day of Septembre anno regni regis Henrici vij tercio

Mayor: William Todde knight. Recorder: John Vavasour. 12: Richard York, Thomas Wrangwissh, William Snawsell, John Tong, John Fereby, John Newton, Nicholas Loncastre, William Chymney, Robert Hancok, John Harper, William White, John Gilyot. Sheriffs: John Beseby, John Shawe. 24: Thomas Catour, Thomas Alan, Henry Williamson, William Tait, John Hagg, Richard Hardsyng, William Barkar, Thomas Fynch, Nicholas Vicars, Roger Appilby.

[R] *Frerez Minours* Assembled in counsaill at the counsalle chambre within the Guildhall, determyned that the wardan and brethern of the house conventuall of Frerez Minours within the citie of York, wherof the mare and commonaltie of the same for the tyme being standes patronez and ffoundours in consideracion therof and of the povertie and nowne hanour in the which they be of at this tyme, and also

for singing of (an) ⟨twoo⟩ annuel obites with masse, dirige and othre suffraiges
with dailez prayers for the prosperoux lifes of the maire and commonaltie forsaid
liffing and for ther (sea) soulez when they be past this transitory life and of all
Christen soules an annuel pension of xx s. over and above such somme of money as
shalbe offerd by the said maire, his bretherne aldermen, the commune counsaill
and othre of the communaltie at ther pleaser the daye of the said massez. And that
iiij of thaldermen above writyn, that is to say Sir Richard York, Thomas
Wrangwissh, John Tong and John Fereby, shall have communicacion with the said
wardan and his brethern for a convenient place to be assigned unto the said maire
and his brethern within ther placez at such tymes as shall resort to the same at ther
pleasours. And therupon writing to be made according to the premisses etc.

[f.111]   **New Sheriffs and Their Sureties**
                21 September 1487

shereffes In the said fest of Saint Mathew, George Kirke merchaunt and Robert
Johnson groyser was elect to bere and occupie thoffice of shereffes for yere
ensuyng.

Manucaptores pro Georgio Kirk: Robertus Hancok aldermanus, Ricardus
Hardsang.

Manucaptores pro Roberto Johnson: Nicholas Lancastre, Nicholas Vicars.

Arbitration Decided for Hull Merchant and City Widow
14 October 1487

Satterday xiiij^th day of Octobre [*sic, 14 October 1487 was a Sunday*]

Thaward yevene betwix John Birdsall and Kateryna Pikard herafter foloweth:

Birdsall, Pikard William Todde knight maier of the citie of York, George Kirke
and Robert Johnson sheriffes of the same, arbitours betwix John Birdsall of
Kingeston opon Hull merchaunt of that oone partie and Katerine late wif of
William Pikard decesid of that othre partie, in and upon all and almaner accions
personelles and realles, sutes, querelles, debates and demaundes hanging betwix
the said parties by reason of any mater or cause frome the begynnyng of the world
unto the day above writyd, indifferently named and elect, after and upon mature
examinacion of such mater of controversy and variance as did depend betwix the
said parties, awardeth and juggeth in fourme folowing: That the said parties and
eithre of theme shall rest with such coste as they have maide in and [of] the said
maters, and that the said Katerine shall pay unto the said John Birdsall or his
certaine attourney xl s. of laufull Inglisshe money in full payment of iiij li. upon an
obligacion in the which the said William was bondon unto the said John Birdsall
(for) with Nicholas Risshworth decesid, and also that the said obligacion upon the

payment of the said xl s. shalbe canseld and such parcelles of money as bee contignened in this det boke of the said William Pikard enenst the said John and surmised to be due by hyme shalbe taken furth of the same and noo furthre demaunde therof to be made by the said Katerine or any othre in hur name.

HR

[f.111v]   Macebearer's Annuity, Lease of City Land, Members for Parliament
16 October 1487

Monday after the fest of Saint Wilfride, that is to say the xvj day of Octobre anno regis Henrici vij tercio [*sic, 16 October 1487 was a Tuesday*]

Mayor: William Todde knight. 12: Thomas Wrangwisshe, John Fereby, Nicholas Lancastre, William Chymney, Robert Hancok, John Harpar, William White, John Gilyot. 24: Thomas Catour, Thomas Alan, William Taite, John Hagg, Richard Hardsang, William Barkar, Nicholas Vicars, Roger Appilby.

Fynche Assembled in counsaill determyned that Thomas Fynche laite seriant at the mase belonging to the maier in consideracion of his good service which he did as long as he occupied the same office and also of his impotencye and age at this tyme, shalhave an annuitie of xx s. (to be perceyved yerely) and a house of Barkar Hill late grauntid unto Robert Burgesse decesid, and the said Thomas for the said ffee and house shall yeve his attendance upon the more maisters or rent maisters of the said citie for the tyme being in any thing concernyng ther charge and office, and the said Thomas to have the said ffee and house to be upholdyn and repareld at his proper costes and chargez and soo to be left, as long as any more masters or rent maisters shall occupie within the said citie. And where the said Thomas had a graunt of the said ffee of xx s. and the house abovewrityn in the days of the right worshipfull John Newton laite maire of this citie [*1483–1484*] and hath his patent made of xxvj s. viij d. and soo hath receyved the same evere yere sith contrary the graunt abovesaid, it was determyned by all abovewrityn that the said Thomas shuld lese the prouffit of his graunt of this yere and not enter to any ffee taking unto the fest of Pasche next ensuyng.

Turnebull Also it was determyned that oone Turnebull telar shalhave by lese a tenement in Walmegate late in tholding of Roger Appilby for the terme of x yeres, yelding yerely for the same to the maire and commonaltie of this citie for the tyme [**f.112**] being at ij usuell termez in the yere by evene porcions x s., and the said Turnbull to reparell and uphold the said tenement at his propre costes and charges during the terme of x yeres forsaid and in thend of the same soo sufficiently to lese it, as it appereth more at large in the said lese etc.

knightes of the parliamentes Also the same day Nicholas Lancastre and John Gilyot aldremen wer named and elect tobe at the kinges parlement for this citie as knightes for the same.

[f.112v]   **Bond to Accept Arbitration**
              7 November 1487

Lefton, Alan, Alan et Wilkynson, vacat hec recognitio [*entry struck through*]
(Memorandum quod septimo die mensis Novembris anno regni regis Henrici
septimi post conquestum Anglie tercio, Thomas Alan de Ebor' bakar et Thomas
Wharf de eadem bower necnon Thomas Chapmen de eadem sadler et Willelmus
Highfeld generosus coram Willelmo Todde milite maiore civitatis Ebor' personaliter comparentes prefati Thomas Alan et Thomas Wharf assumpserunt et eorum
alter assumpsit pro Ricardo Lefton de Ebor' cutler, Thoma Alan de eadem sadler
et Johanne Alan de eadem baker in xx libris, ac prefati Thomas Chapman et
Willelmus Highfeld assumpserunt et eorum alter assumpsit pro Johanne Wilkynson
de (eadem) Ebor' predicta cutler in xx libris legalis monete Anglie levandis de
bonis et catallis tam prefatorum Ricardi Lefton, Thome Alan et Johannis Alan ac
Johannis Wilkynson quam prefatorum Thome Alan, Thome Wharf, Thome
Chapman et Willelmi Highfeld et eorundem cuiuslibet ad opus domini nostri regis,
quod ipsi Ricardus Lefton, Thomas Alan et Johannes Alan (ex) ⟨de⟩ parte una
et Johannes Wilkynson ex parte altera stabunt et obedient laudo, ordinacioni et
iudicio Thome Foulneby, Alexandri Dauson, Johannis Stokesley et Willelmi
Stubbez arbitratorum in, de et super omnibus et omnimodis accionibus tam
realibus quam personalibus, sectis, demandis et querelis ac transgressionibus
quibuscumque inter partes predictas a principio mundi usque in diem confeccionis
presentium recognitionum occasione cuiuscumque rei vel cause exortis, motis et
pendentibus indifferenter per dominum maiorem predictum nominatorum et
electorum, ita quod huiusmodi laudum, ordinacio et iudicium fiant et reddantur
inter partes predictas per dictos arbitratores citra festum Epiphanie proximum
futurum post datam predictam, et si dicti arbitri citra dictum diem inter se ⟨non⟩
concordare nec partes huiusmodi ad pacem in, de et super premissis ducere possint
tunc prefati Ricardus Lefton, Thomas Alan et Johannes Alan ac Johannes
Wilkynson et eorum quilibet stabunt et obedient laudo, ordinacioni et iudicio
prefati domini maioris imparis inter partes predictas in, de et super premissis
nominati et eosdem laudum, ordinacionem et iudicium pro parte sua debite
perimplebunt et perimplebit eorum quilibet, ita quod **[f.113]** laudum, ordinacio et
iudicium sua fiant et reddantur inter partes predictas per dictum imparem citra
festum Sancti Hillarii proximum extunc sequentem.)

                                                        (HR)

(Et preceptum fuit partibus predictis per dominum maiorem ex parte domini nostri
regis quod gerant et custodiant pacem inter se pro se et suis et non transgradiatur
unus quisque alio verbo vel facto citra festum predictum etc.)

Partes predicte concordate sunt et veredictum arbitratorum supradictorum inferitur
infra ut patet ibidem vacat recognitio hec et cancellatur.

preceptum pacis Et preceptum est per dominum maiorem ex parte domini nostri
regis partibus supradictis quod tam prefatus Ricardus Lefton pro se et suis versus
Thomam Alan et Johannem Alan quam ipsi Thomas et Johannes versus dictum

Ricardum custodiant et gerant ac custodiat et gerat (pacem) eorum quilibet pacem dicti domini regis sub pena v marcarum levandarum de bonis et catallis forisfacientur in hac parte ad opus dicti domini regis et civitatis Ebor'.

[*Lefton, Alan, Alan and Wilkynson, this bond void* (On 7 November 1487, baker Thomas Alan of York and bower Thomas Wharf, and also saddler Thomas Chapmen and William Highfeld gentleman, appeared before mayor William Todde, and Alan and Wharf each bound himself for £20 on behalf of cutler Richard Lefton of York, saddler Thomas Alan, and baker John Alan, and the aforesaid Thomas Chapman and William Highfeld each bound himself for £20 on behalf of cutler John Wilkynson, that the said Richard Lefton, Thomas Alan and John Alan on the one side, and John Wilkynson on the other side will adhere to and obey the advice, ordinance and judgement of Thomas Foulneby, Alexander Dauson, John Stokesley and William Stubbez, arbiters impartially elected by the mayor over all actions both real and personal, and all suits and trespasses moved or pending between the parties, their judgement to be made and rendered by the coming feast of Epiphany; and if the arbiters are unable to agree, then the parties will obey the judgement of the lord mayor chosen as umpire over all these matters, his judgement to be given by the coming feast of Saint Hilary.)

(And the lord mayor ordered on behalf of the lord king that the parties keep the peace among themselves and they would not offend in word or in deed until the aforesaid feast.)

The aforesaid parties are agreed and the verdict of the aforesaid arbiters is placed within as is clear, and this bond is void and cancelled.

order [for the keeping] of the peace It is ordered by the lord mayor on behalf of the lord king that Richard Lefton is to keep the peace towards Thomas Alan and John Alan, and that they are to keep the peace towards Richard Lefton, under penalty of five marks forfeited of their goods and chattels, for the service of the lord king and of the city of York.]

Bond to Accept Arbitration
13 November 1487

Bowman et Bowlye, vacat recognicio quia partes concordare sunt Memorandum quod xiij° die mensis Novembris anno regni regis Henrici septimi post conquestum Anglie tercio, Robertus Bowman et Ricardus Bowlye personaliter comparentes coram Willelmo Todde milite maiore civitatis Ebor' assumpserunt et eorum alter assumpsit pro seipso in xx libris legalis monete Anglie levandis de bonis et catallis eorundem et eorum alterius ad opus domini nostri regis et usum civitatis sue predicte quod ipsi et eorum alter stabunt et obedient laudo, ordinacioni et iudicio Thome Chapman et Georgii Essex pro parte dicti Roberti Bowman, necnon Johannis Huton et Johannis Clerk pro parte dicti Ricardi Bewly, arbitratorum electorum et nominatorum in, de et super omnibus et omnimodis accionibus tam realibus quam personalibus, sectis, demandis et querelis ac transgressionibus quibuscumque inter partes predictas, a principio mundi usque in diem confeccionis presentium recognitionum occasione cuiuscumque rei vel cause exortis, motis et pendentibus, ita quod huiusmodi laudum, ordinacio et iudicium fiant et reddantur inter huiusmodi partes per dictos arbitratores citra festum Sancti Andree apostoli proximum futurum post datam predictam, et si dicti arbitri citra festum predictum inter se concordare aut partes ad pacem in, de et super premissis ducere non poterunt, tunc prefati Robertus et Ricardus et eorum alter stabunt et obedient ac stabit et obediet laudo, ordinacioni et iudicio unius imparis per dictos arbitratores elegendi et nominandi in prefatas partes in, de et super premissis et eadem laudum, ordinacio et iudicium pro parte sua debite perimplebunt et perimplebit eorum alter; ita quod laudum, ordinacio et iudicium sua fiant et reddantur inter partes predictas per dictum imparem citra festum Natalis Domini proximum extunc sequentem.

HR

[*Bowman and Bowlye, bond void because parties were agreed* On 13 November 1487, Robert Bowman and Richard Bowlye personally appeared in the presence of Sir William Todde, mayor of the city of York, and each bound himself for £20 levied of their goods and chattels that they and each of them would adhere to and obey the advice, ordinance and judgement of Thomas Chapman and George Essex on the side of the said Robert Bowman, and of John Huton and John Clerk on the side of the said Richard Bewly, arbiters elected and named in, of and over each and every action both real and personal, all suits and trespasses moved or pending between the said parties from the beginning of the world to the present day, this judgement to be made and rendered by the said arbiters by the feast of Saint Andrew next coming; and if the said arbiters are unable to agree, then Bowman and Bowlye will abide by the judgement of an umpire named by the arbiters, his judgement to be made by next Christmas.]

[f.113v]   **Bonds to Accept Arbitration**
            21 November 1487

Lowas et Kirk, vacat hec recognitio quia arbitratores non concordare nec impar in hac parte [*entry struck through*] (Memorandum quod xxj° die mensis Novembris anno regis Henrici septimi post conquestum Anglie tercio, Johannes Lowas de Tadcastre generosus et Jacobus Kirk de Ebor' goldsmyth coram venerabili viro Willelmo Todde milite maiore civitatis Ebor' in camera concilii eiusdem personaliter comparentes assumpserunt et eorum alter assumpsit pro seipso in x libris quod ipsi et eorum alter stabit et obediet laudo, ordinacioni et iudicio Johannis Golan et Milonis Harwom ex parte dicti Johannis Lowas ac Thome Graa et Alexandri Dauson ex parte prefati Jacobi Kirk ⟨arbitratorum inter easdem partes⟩ nominatorum et electorum in, de et super omnibus et omnimodis accionibus tam realibus quam personalibus, sectis, demandis et querelis inter easdem partes, a principio mundi usque in diem confeccionis presentium recognitionum occasione cuiuscumque rei vel cause motis, exortis sive pendentibus, ita quod huiusmodi laudum, ordinacio et iudicium fiant et reddantur inter partes predictas per dictos arbitratores citra festum Natalis Domini proximo futurum post datam presencium, et si dicti arbitri citra dictum festum inter se concordare nec partes ad concordiam ducere non poterunt tunc prefati Johannes et Jacobus et eorum alter stabit et obediet laudo, ordinacioni et iudicio in, de et super premissis unius imparis per dictos arbitratores indifferenter inter eosdem nominandos et eligendos et eadem ⟨ex utraque⟩ (pro) parte (sua) perimplebit, ita quod huiusmodi laudum, ordinacio et iudicium fiant et reddantur inter partes huiusmodi per dictum imparem citra festum Epiphanie extunc proximum sequentem.)

Baxter, Stede et Grayson [*entry struck through*] (Memorandum quod dicto die et anno Willelmus Baxter et Johannes Stede ex una parte et Johannes Grayson de Ebor' porter ex altera parte coram domino maiore predicto personaliter comparentes assumpserunt et quilibet eorum assumpsit pro seipso in x libris legalis monete Anglie levandis de bonis et catallis (eorundem) et cuiuslibet eorum ad opus domini regis et civitatis sue Ebor' quod ipsi et eorum quilibet stabunt et obedient ac stabit et obediet laudo, ordinacioni et judicio Petri Cook, Johannis Stokesley, Johannis Gaunt et Elie Cure arbitratorum inter partes predictas in, de et super omnibus et omnimodis accionibus tam realibus quam personalibus, sectis, demandis et querelis inter easdem, a principio mundi usque in diem confeccionis presencium occasione cuiuscumque rei vel cause exortis, motis et pendentibus indifferenter electorum et nominatorum et eadem laudum, ordinacionem et judicium perimplebunt et eorum quilibet perimplebit, ita quod huiusmodi laudum, ordinacio et iudicium fiant et reddantur per dictos arbitratores inter partes predictas citra festum Natalis Domini proximum [**f.114**] futurum post datam presencium, et preceptum est prefatis Willelmo, Johanni et Johanni et eorum cuilibet per dictum dominum maiorem ex parte domini regis predicti ut teneant et custodiant pacem inter se sub pena x librarum usum communitatis civitatis predicte applicandarum et de bonis ingressum faciant in hac parte levandarum sine pardonacione aliquali. Partes sunt concordate ut testantur Petrus Cooke et Johannes Gaunt atque Willelmus Baxster superius nominatus coram domino maiore.)

[*Lowas and Kirk, this bond void because the arbiters did not agree nor did the umpire* (On 21 November 1487, John Lowas, gentleman, of Tadcaster, and James Kirk of York, goldsmith, came before the venerable Sir William Todde, mayor of York, in the council chamber and each bound himself for £10 that they would adhere to and obey the advice, ordinance and judgement of John Golan and Miles Harwom on the side of John Lowas, and of Thomas Graa and Alexander Dauson on James Kirk's side, these arbiters named and elected over all actions both real and personal, all suits and disagreements moved, arisen, or pending between the said parties, from the beginning of the world to the present day, this judgement to be made by next Christmas, and if the arbiters are unable to agree then John and James will obey the judgement of an umpire named and elected by the said arbiters, and his judgement to be made and rendered by the feast of Epiphany next following.)

Baxter, Stede and Grayson (On the said day and year, William Baxter and John Stede on the one side, and porter John Grayson of York on the other side came

before the lord mayor and each bound himself for £10 that they would abide by
and obey the advice and judgement of Peter Cook, John Stokesley, John Gaunt
and Elias Cure, arbiters impartially named and elected over all actions both real
and personal, and all suits and disagreements arisen, moved or pending between
them from the beginning of the world to the present day, this judgement to be
made and rendered by the said arbiters by the Christmas [f.114] after the present
date; and it is ordered by the said lord mayor that William, John and John hold
and keep the peace among themselves under penalty of £10. The parties were
agreed as was witnessed by Peter Cooke and John Gaunt and also William
Baxster named above before the lord mayor.)]

Bonds to Keep the Peace
5 December 1487

Quinto die mensis Decembris anno regni regis Henrici septimi tercio in camera
consilii civitatis Ebor'

Annotson, Annotson, Hubberd Willelmus Annotson de Askham in comitatu
civitatis Ebor' husbandman assumpsit pro seipso in xl libris necnon Christoforus
Annotson et Robertus Huberd de eadem husbondman assumpserunt et eorum alter
assumpsit pro prefato Willelmo in xl libris legalis monete Anglie levandis de bonis
et catallis eorundem et cuilibet eorum ad opus et utilitatem communitatis civitatis
Ebor' quod prefatus Willelmus omni tempore in futuro dominis viribus gaudeat
paratus erit et comparebit personaliter coram maiore civitatis Ebor' pro tempore
existente ad respondendum quibuscumque rebus et materiis que sibi obicientur per
quoscumque personas ex parte domini nostri regis seu alterius persone cuiuscumque nomine suo racione et pretextu alicuius communicacionis habitis inter eundem
Willelmum et Thomam Barrey de Ebor' wever.

Barray, Annotson Thomas Barrey de Ebor' wever assumpsit pro seipso in xl libris
necnon Ricardus Blakburn de Ebor' mercer, Ricardus Clerke tanner, Johannes
Hall tanner, Willelmus Hert wever et Henricus Toppan walker de Ebor' assumpserunt et eorum quilibet assumpsit pro prefato Thoma Barrey in xl libris legalis
monete Anglie levandis de bonis et cattallis eorundem et cuiuslibet eorum ad opus
et utilitatem communitatis civitatis Ebor' quod prefatus Willelmus omni tempore in
futuro domini viribus gaudeat paratus erit et comparebit personaliter coram maiore
civitatis Ebor' pro tempore existente ad respondendum quibuscumque personas ex
parte domini nostri regis seu alterius cuiuscumque persone nomine suo racione et
pretextu alicuius communicacionis habitis inter eundem Thomam et Willelmum
Annotson de Askham husbandman.

[The fifth day of the month of December in the third year of the reign of king
Henry VII, in the council chamber of the city of York

Annotson, Annotson, Hubberd Husbandman William Annotson of Askham,
Yorkshire bound himself for £40, and also Christopher Annotson and hus-

bandman Robert Huberd of the same place each bound himself on behalf of the said William for £40, that William at all times in the future will be prepared and will appear before the mayor of York responding to any things and materials whatsoever, obeying the lord king or others in his name, by reason and pretext of any communication had between the same William and weaver Thomas Barrey of York.

Barray, Annotson Weaver Thomas Barrey of York bound himself for £40, and also mercer Richard Blakburn of York, tanners Richard Clerke and John Hall, weaver William Hert and walker Henry Toppan each bound himself on behalf of Barrey for £40, that Thomas at all times in the future will be prepared and will appear before the mayor of York, responding to those people acting on behalf of the lord king or others in his name, by reason and pretext of any communication had between the same Thomas and William Annotson of Askham, hus-bandman.]

[f.114v]   Bonds to Keep the Peace and Accept Arbitration
13 November 1487

Huton, Biller [*entry struck through*] (Johannes Huton de Ebor' potter et Magister Willemus Biller clericus noterius publicus xiij° die mensis Novembris anno regni regis Henrici septimi post conquestum Anglie tercio comparentes personaliter coram Willelmo Todde milite maiore civitatis predicte infra hospicium suum ibidem assumpserunt et eorum alter assumpsit pro seipso et suis amicis et familiaribus in centum libris legalis monete Anglie necnon Thomas Graa de Ebor' predicta goldsmyth et Johannes Elwald de eadem merchaunt assumpserunt et eorum alter assumpsit pro dicto Johanne et Magistro Willelmo ac suis familiaribus et amicis predictis in centum libris consimilis legalis monete Anglie levandis tam de bonis et catallis prefatorum Thome Graa et Johannis Elwald quam dictorum Johannis Huton et Magistri Willelmi Biller ad opus et utilitatem maioris et communitatis civitatis predicte quod ipsi nec eorum alter per se vel suos dampnum nullum vel malum aliquod corporale in Johannem Holme yoman aut aliquem alium de populo domini nostri regis non faciet nec fieri procurabit quovismodo etc.)

Holme Johannes Holme yoman xiij° die mensis Novembris anno regni regis supradicto personaliter comparens coram maiore predicto infra hospicium suum predictum assumpsit pro seipso ac suis amicis et familiaribus in centum libris legalis monete Anglie necnon Willemus Nelson gent' et Johannes Paynter gent' assumpser-unt et eorum alter assumpsit pro dicto Johanne Holme ac suis amicis et familiaribus predictis in centum libris consimilis legalis monete Anglie levandis tam de bonis et catallis prefatorum Willelmi Nelson et Johannis Paynter et alterius eorundem quam dicti Johannis Holme ad opus et utilitatem dictorum maioris et communitatis civitatis predicte quod ipse per se vel suos nullum dampnum vel malum aliquod corporale in Johannem Huton de Ebor' potter aut Magistrum Willelmum Biller clericum notarium publicum de eadem nec eorum alterium aliquem alium de populo dicti domini regis non faciet nec fieri procurabit quovismodo etc.

Huton, Biller, Holme Johannes Huton de Ebor' potter et Willelmus Biller clericus notarius publicus ex una parte et Johannes Holme yoman ex altera parte assumpserunt et quilibet eorum assumpsit pro seipso in centum libris legalis monete Anglie levandis de bonis et catallis eorundem et cuiuslibet eorum ad opus dictorum maioris et communitatis quod ipsi et eorum quilibet stabit et obediet laudo, ordinacioni et iudicio venerabilium virorum Thome Allan, Michaelis White, Ricardi Hardesang (et) **[f.115]** et Thome Fynche arbitratorum in, de et super omnibus et omnimodis accionibus tam realibus quam personalibus, sectis, demandis, controversiis, transgressionibus et querelis inter partes predictas, a principio mundi usque in diem confeccionis presentium recognitionum occasione cuiuscumque rei vel cause spiritualis vel temporalis habitis, motis sive pendentibus indifferenter inter easdem partes electorum et nominatorum, ita quod huiusmodi laudum, ordinacio et iudicium fiant et reddantur per dictos arbitratores inter partes predictas citra festum Epiphanie domini proximo futurum post datam predictam.

arbitrium Et in casu quod dicti arbitratores in, de et super premissis inter se concordare nec partes huiusmodi ad concordiam ducere minime poterunt, tunc tam prefati Johannes Huton et Willelmus Biller quam dictus Johannes Holme, et idem Johannes, Willelmus et Johannes et eorum quilibet pro parte sua stabit et obediet laudo, ordinacio et iudicio in, de et super omnibus et singulis premissis reverendorum virorum domini decani ecclesie cathedralis beati Petri Ebor' et Magistri Willelmi Poteman canonici residenciarii eiusdem imparis inter partes predictas super eisdem indifferenter electi et nominati, ita quod laudum, ordinacio et iudicium sua fiant et reddantur per eosdem inter easdem partes citra festum Sancti Hillarii extunc proximum sequentem etc.

supersedeas pro Birkhede, vacat ex assensu presentium [*entry struck through*] (Johannes Birkhede de Ebor' merchaunt assumpsit pro seipso in xx libris necnon Johannes Catour de eadem merchaunt, Milo Harwom de eadem westmentmaker, Willelmus Baxster de eadem girdler et Bertramus Dawson de eadem hoyser assumpserunt et quilibet eorum assumpsit pro dicto Johanne Birkehede in x libris levandis ad opus et utilitatem domini nostri regis quod ipse Johannes Birkhede nullum dampnum vel malum aliquod corporale in aliquem populum dicti domini regis faciet vel fieri procurabit quovismodo etc.)

supersedeas pro Baok, vacat ex assensu presencium [*entry struck through*] (Willelmus Baok capellanus personaliter comparens coram Willelmo Todde (maiore) milite maiore civitatis Ebor' assumpsit pro seipso in xx libris necnon Johannes Robynson tailyour, Georgius Blevet, Cuthbertus Brownelesse et Johannes Watton ffissher assumpserunt et quilibet eorum assumpsit pro dicto Willelmo Baok in x libris levandis de bonis et catallis eorundem et cuiuslibet eorum ad opus et utilitatem domini nostri regis quod ipse Willelmus Baok nullum dampnum vel aliquod malum corporale in Johannem Birkhode aut aliquem alium de populo dicti domini regis faciet nec fieri procurabit quovismodo etc.)

[*Huton, Biller* (On 13 November 1487, potter John Huton of York and Master William Biller, clerk [and] notary public, appeared personally before Sir William

Todde, mayor of the city, within his townhouse, and each bound himself and his friends and household members for £100, and also goldsmith Thomas Graa of York and merchant John Elwald each bound himself on behalf of John [Huton] and Master William etc. likewise for £100, levied on their goods and chattels, that neither of them will damage nor do bodily harm to yeoman John Holme nor to any other of the king's subjects, nor cause any harm to be done.)

Holme On the same day, yeoman John Holme personally appeared before the mayor in his townhouse and bound himself and his friends and household members for £100, and also William Nelson and John Paynter, gentlemen, each likewise bound himself on behalf of John Holme etc. for £100, that no damage nor bodily harm would be done to potter John Huton of York nor to Master William Biller, nor to any other of the king's subjects.

Huton, Biller, Holme Potter John Huton of York and William Biller clerk [and] notary public on the one side, and yeoman John Holme on the other side, each bound himself for £100 levied of their goods and chattels that they will adhere to and obey the advice, ordinance and judgement of the venerable Thomas Allan, Michael White, Richard Hardesang [f.115] and Thomas Fynche, arbiters elected and named in, of and over each and every action both real and personal, all suits, controversies and trepasses had, moved or pending between the said parties from the beginning of the world until the day these presents [bonds] were made, in all things spiritual or temporal, the said judgement to be made and rendered by the feast of Epiphany coming after the date abovementioned.

judgement And in case the said arbiters are unable to agree, then Huton, Biller, and Holme will adhere to and obey the judgement of the most reverend lord dean of the cathedral of Saint Peter, York, and of Master William Poteman, residentiary canon of the same church, elected and named as umpires, their judgement to be made by the feast of Saint Hilary next coming.

[*writ of*] *supersedeas for Birkhede, void by the assent of those present* (Merchant John Birkhede of York bound himself for £20, and also merchant John Catour, vestmentmaker Miles Harwom, girdler William Baxster, and hosier Bertram Dawson each bound himself on behalf of Birkhede for £10, levied to the work and use of our lord king, that Birkhede do no damage nor bodily harm to any of the king's subjects.)

[*writ of*] *supersedeas for Baok, void by the assent of those present* (William Baok, chaplain, personally appeared before Sir William Todde, mayor of York, and bound himself for £20, and also tailor John Robynson, George Blevet, Cuthbert Brownelesse, and fisherman John Watton each bound himself on Baok's behalf for £10 levied of their goods and chattels to the work and use of our lord king, that Baok do no damage nor bodily harm to John Birkhode or to any other of the king's subjects, nor cause any harm to be done.)]

[f.115v]   **Bonds to Accept Arbitration**
                   Undated

Cravene Johannes Cravene de Ebor' generosus personaliter comparens coram
Willelmo Todde milite maiore civitatis Ebor' assumpsit pro seipso in decem libris
legalis monete Anglie levandis de bonis et catallis eiusdem Johannis ad opus et
utilitatem domini nostri regis quod ipse stabit et obediet in alto et basso laudo,
ordinacioni et iudicio domini maioris predicti necnon aldermannorum, conciliano-
rum et legisperitorum civitatis predicte in, de et super omnimodis causis et materiis
ac rebus quibuscumque per eundem Johannem contra jura et iusticiam ac libertates
dicte civitatis qualitercumque perpetratis et ex parte eorundem maioris, aldermannorum, consiliariorum et legisperatorum civitatis predicte versus eundem
Johannem exponendis et eadem laudum, ordinacionem et iudicium pro parte sua
debitis in omnibus et per omniam perimplebit.

Smyth, Harman Harmanus Goldsmyth de Ebor' goldsmyth assumpsit pro seipso in
x libris necnon Johannes Smyth de eadem ⟨assumpsit pro seipso⟩ (barbour) et
Henricus Smyth de eadem barbour (assumpserunt et eorum alter) assumpsit pro
(seipso in x libris) dicto Johanne quod prefati Harmanus et Johannes (st) et eorum
alter stabit et obediet laudo, ordinacioni et iudicio Johannis Huton et Johannis
Elwalde pro parte dicti Harmani necnon Johannis Stokdall et Thome Foulneby pro
parte dicti Johannis Smyth arbitratorum in, de et super omnibus et omnimodis
accionibus tam realibus quam personalibus, sectis, demandis et querelis inter
prefatum Harmanum ex una parte et supradictum Johannem Smyth ex parte altera,
a principio mundi usque in diem confeccionis presencium occasione cuiuscumque
rei vel cause exortis, motis et pendentibus inter easdem partes electorum et
nominatorum, ita quod huiusmodi laudum, ordinacio et iudicium fiant et reddantur
inter partes predictas per dictos arbitratores citra festum Sancti Hillarii proximum
futurum, et in casu quod dicti arbitratores inter se concordare aut partes huiusmodi
ad pacem in, de et super premissis minime ⟨ducere⟩ poterunt citra festum
predictum, tunc prefati Johannes Smyth et Harmanus Goldsmyth et eorum alter
stabit et obediet laudo, ordinacioni et judicio unius imparis per dominum maiorem
civitatis Ebor' inter partes predictas nominandi et eligendi et eadem laudum,
ordinacio et iudicium parte predicta et earum altera perimplebunt et perimplebit,
ita quod laudum, ordinacio et iudicium dicti imparis in, de et super fiant et
reddantur inter partes predictas per eundem citra festum conversionis Sancti
(Palu') Pauli extunc proximum sequentem.

                                                                          HR

[*Cravene* John Cravene of York, gentleman, personally appeared before Sir
William Todde, mayor of York, and bound himself for £10 levied of his goods
and chattels to the work and use of our lord king, that he will adhere to and obey
totally the advice, ordinance and judgement of the lord mayor and also the
aldermen, councillors, and legal advisors of the city, in, of and over all causes
and things against law and justice and the liberties of the said city, howsoever
perpetrated by Cravene and shown to him by the mayor, etc.

Smyth, Harman Goldsmith Herman Goldsmyth of York bound himself for £10, as did John Smyth of York, and barber Henry Smyth bound himself on John's behalf, that Herman and John would abide by and obey the judgement of John Huton and John Elwalde on Herman's side, and John Stokdall and Thomas Foulneby on John Smyth's side, arbiters named and elected in, of and over all actions both real and personal, suits and complaints between Herman on the one side and John Smyth on the other side, from the beginning of the world to the day these presents [bonds] were made, the said judgement to be made and rendered by the coming feast of Saint Hilary; and in case the said arbiters are unable to agree and lead their parties to peace, then Smyth and Goldsmyth will obey the judgement of an umpire named and elected by the lord mayor of the city, whose judgement is to be made and rendered by the feast of the Conversion of Saint Paul next coming.]

[f.116 blank]

**[f.116v]   City Asks King to Remit Fee Farm
                Undated, Autumn 1487?**

To the king our souverain lord

copia bille suplicacionis porecte regi maiestati Sheweth mekely unto your noble grace your true subgiettes and liegemen the maier, citicyns and communaltie of your citie of York, that where in your parlement holden at Westm[inster] the vij day of Novembre the first yere of your moost noble reigne, it was ordaygned and stablisshed by auctoritie of the same parlement among othre thinges that an Cxxj li. iij s. iiij d. shuld be takyn of the ffee ferme of the citie of York to be applied towardes the payment and contentacion the expensez of your moost honourable houshold by assignement therof to be made by the thesaurour of England for the tyme being to the tresaurer of your said houshold for the tyme being, as in the said act among othre is contigned at large; and where afterward moost redoubtid souverain lord ye by your graciouse lettres patentes bering dait at Westmynster the xviij^th day of Juyn the first yere of your moost noble reigne, for certain consideracions moving your grace in the said letters patentes specified of your said grace speciall gaff and graunted to your said subgiettes by the name of mauer and citicyns of the said citie and ther successours lx li. yerely to you appertigneing of the said fee ferme of an Clx li., to be had and perceyved to the said maier and citicyns and ther successours at the festes of Estre and Saint Michael archangell by evene porcions by thandes of the shereffes of the said citie for tyme being during your high pleaser, and that aswell all shereffes of the said citie than being and after to be shuld be as the said maier and citicyns and ther successours of the forsaid lx li. yerely ayenst your grace and your heires shuld be quyte and discharged during your said pleaser; and furthremore by the same lettrez patentes of your said grant ye remised and released aswell to the said maier and citicyns and ther successours as to the said shereffes and ther successours and to the citicyns of the said citie, all the residue of

parte sua, stabunt et obedient ac stabit et obediet laudo, ordinacioni et iudicio Johannis Stokesley, Ricardi Croklyn, Elie Cure et Thome Wharf arbitratorum inter partes predictas indifferenter electorum in, de et super omnibus et omnimodis accionibus tam realibus quam personalibus, sectis, demandis et querelis inter partes easdem occasione cuiuscumque rei vel cause a principio mundi usque in diem confeccionis presentium recognitionum motis, exortis sive pendentibus, ita quod huiusmodi laudum, ordinacio et iudicium fiant et reddantur inter partes predictas citra Carniprivium proximum futurum. Date vj° die mensis Februarii anno regni regis Henrici vij^{mi} tercio.

[*Blakbourne, Saxton; bond void because parties are agreed* Richard Blakbourne, Richard Clerc, Henry Toppan, Thomas Barray and William Thomeson on the one side, and John Saxton, Richard Kilbourne, Thomas Kitchynner and William Howbank of York on the other side, personally appeared before Sir William Todde, mayor of York, in the council chamber, and each bound himself for £100 levied and paid of his goods and chattels to the work and use of our lord king, that the same Richard Blakbourne, Richard, Henry, Thomas and William Thomeson, and each of them on his part, and the said John Saxton, Richard Kilbourne, Thomas and William will adhere to and obey the advice and judgement of John Stokesley, Richard Croklyn, Elias Cure and Thomas Wharf, arbiters impartially elected in, of and over each and every action both real and personal, all suits and complaints moved, arisen or pending between the said parties from the beginning of the world to the day these presents [bonds] are made, this judgement to be made and rendered by the feast of *Carniprivium* next coming. Given on 6 February 1488.]

Taward betwix Birkhede and Bayok (T) [*incomplete*]

[f.121]   Craftsmen Fear Being Made Moremasters
14 February 1488

[*R*] *submysion* Memorandum that the xiiijth day of February in the third yere of the reigne of our souverain lord King Herry the sevent in the counsaill chambre within the Guyldhall of the citie of York, James Lounesdall of the same hoyser and Thomas Knolles of the same draper, severally appering bifore Sir William Todde knight maier of the citie of York, chamberleyns of the same, and othre, fering themself to be elect and named moremasters of the said citie, of ther free wolles not constreyned by any persone, consetitid (and), grauntid and putte themeself ther lettrez of exempcion and discharge undre the commune seal of this citie forsaid, and such sommez of money as they and eithre of theme paid and content to thuse of the communaltie of the same to the rule, disposicion and jugement of the right honourable and worshipfull my lord maier, my maisters aldermen (and), shereffes and commune counsaill of this said citie, they to dispose ther said personez, lettrez and money according to reason and good conscience, rather than to be named or electid any of the said moremasters, (and also the said day and yere) the said Jamez and ever protestyng that they might be repaid ther saide money etc.

[f.121v]   **King Orders Peace Be Kept, Rioters Be Punished**
            3 June 1488

By the kyng

Trusty and welbelovyd we grete you wele, nat doubtyng bot that your wysedoms
can remembre and wele considre that the use and entreteiyng of sad rule and good
governaunce in every cite and towne furst and principally pleaseth God and
establissheth perfite rest and tranquillitie, eicrissheth and encreaseth love, causeth
plentie and habundance and lawes to have thare due courses, iustice to bee
indifferentlie ministred and executed, the universall weale alwey enhauncyng and
flowryng by thies behalves, and by the contrary use and way ensewen commocions,
striffes, debates, povertie and miserie and many othre inconvenientes; the perill
and daunger whereof must of reason be arrected and layed to the charge of thoo
persones havyng rule and auctorite, where any mysgovernauncez be haunted if by
thare omissions and negligences thoffendours be suffred to renne in boldenesse
unpunysshed; and forasmuch as we have and bere as good mynde and large
affeccion to all our true subgettes and be desirous of the comon wele of this our
realme as ever did eny our noble predecessours, God be our juge, therfor we write
unto you at this tyme desiring and stratelie comaunding you to endevour you
fromhensforth by your best wisedoms and diligences to see that gude rule and
substanciall guyding be firmelie had and effectually felowed in all places within
your iurisdiccion havyng ful gude and wise awaite contynuelly that if eny
vacabundes, riotours or ungudelie disposed (personnes) or ungudelie disposed [*sic*]
personnes resciaunt or repairing amonges you presume or tak apon thame to make
eny embraciaries, affrayes or debates by colour or boldnesse or lyvereys or
otherwise or to sowe any sedeciouse langage, arreise any rumours or forge or
contrive newes or tidinges of us or eny estates of this our land or of othir withoute
the same to abuse and blynde our innocent subgettes, provoking and endusing
theym to renne or falle into rebellian and disobeisaunce in subversion of all gude
rule pollicie, ye than failnot to attach and committe to sure warde withoute baile or
delyverance all tho that ye shall fynde gilty or suspect in the premissez, and to
certefie us thare names with the specialtie of thare offences to thentent that we may
gyff you for your gude acquitall our special thankes and shew therapon our forther
pleasour for thare due and laufull punycion, latting you wite that if it cam to our
eires and perfite knowlage that if ye suffre such misruled people using eny unsitting
langage or reising any rumours or offending in eny poyntes above rehersed to
escape you unponysshed contrarie to your dutie both enenst God and us, we shall
so sharpelie lay it to your blame and charge with punysshement according as shalbe
to the feirfull president **[f.122]** and grevuse example of all other our subgettes and
officers disobeissance to execute our like and special comaundmentes, which
thinges therefore we (av) advise you to call and take to herte accordinglie. Yeven
under our signet at our castell of Wyndesore the iij^d day of Juyn.

To our trusty and welbiloved the mair and shireffes of our citie of York

[f.122v]   Members for Parliament Chosen, Abatement of Tax Requested, Discharge from Holding Civic Office
31 December 1488

Ultimo die Decembris

Mayor: Richard Hancok. 12: Richard Yorke knight, Thomas Wrangwish, John Fereby, Master Nicholas Lancastre, William Chymney, William Todd knight, John Harper, William White, John Gylliot. Sheriffs: Thomas Foulneby, Thomas Gray. 24: Thomas Allan, Thomas Catour, William Tayte, Richard Clerk, William Barker, Miles Grenebank, Thomas Fynch, Roger Appilby.

parlement At the which day the said presence wer assembled in the counsell chambre apon Ousebrig, and there and then the kinges writ for the somones of his hight courte of parliament was openlie red, and forsomuch as efter the recept of the said writ ther is noon countie tofore the first day of the said parliament, therfor all above of oon assent and consent and for the kinges high pleasour and also for that at noon lak shalbe put unto the cite, hath nominate and chosen (ter) tobe cocitesyns for the cite at the said parliament the right wirshupful sirs Sir Richerd Yorke and Sir William Todd knyghtes.

And also the same day ⟨it⟩ is determyned and agreid that ther shalbe thre lettres writen and maid for the abatement of the tax etc., to my lord chaunceler, my lorde tresorer, and to the lorde privey seall.

And also the same day it was shewed by the maiour as toching John Boon som tyme inhabiting within this cite and nowe dwelling in Doncastre, that the same John Boon so that he myght curtaslie be (inte' intoeth' intaewhit) ⟨delt⟩ with for a fyne tobe yeven to the behufe of the commonaltie for his discharge during his naturall lieff of eny office bering within this cite, he wold and proposeth to (inhabiting) inhabet hym self within this cite ayane, and so it is determyned that my lorde the maiour and ij or iij aldermen shal common with the said John and to bring the same John as for as the may for the common wele.

[ff.123–124v blank]

[f.125]   Arrests and Bonds Made During the Mayoralty of Robert Hancock
Undated, 3 February 1488 X 3 February 1489

Precepta pacis et supersedeas tempore venerabilis viri Roberti Hancok maioris civitatis Ebor'

Capias Ricardum Ewen ad sectam (Willelmi) Thome Tirrell.

supersideas pro Tirrell et [illegible] anno regni regis etc. [entry struck through]
(Thomas Tirrell assumpsit pro seipso in xx libris necnon Johannes Hagg, Willelmus

Tirrell, Johannes Pyr et Johannes Nicholson yoman assumpserunt et quilibet eorum assumpsit pro dicto Thoma in x libris levandis de bonis eorundem et ad opus domini nostri regis etc., quod ipse dampnum vel malum etc., alicui de populo dicti domini regis non faciet nec fieri procurabit quovismodo etc.)

Memorandum quod inunctum est per dominum maiorem Willelmo Lowdan et Thome Appilby et eorum alteri ex parte domini nostri regis quod alter versus alterum non transgrediatur verbo, opere vel facto de inceps sub pena tociens quociens iij solidos viij denarios camere civitatis Ebor' ⟨et arte diligente⟩ applicandum et solvendum per ipsum quo sic transgrediatur etc.

Capias Willelmum Harper de Ebor' scoler ad sectam Willelmi Harper de eadem shomaker.

Preceptum capias Nicholaum (v) Brantyngham unum vicarium bedernie ad sectam Johannis Huchonson.

[Orders [for the keeping] of the peace and stays of proceedings during the mayoralty of Robert Hancok:

Arrest of Richard Ewen at the suit of Thomas Tirrell.

[*writ of*] *supersedeas for Tirrell and [illegible] in the year of the reign of the king etc.* (Thomas Tirrell bound himself for £20, and also John Hagg, William Tirrell, John Pyr and yeoman John Nicholson each bound himself on Tirrell's behalf for £10 levied of their goods to the work of our lord king, etc., that Tirrell do no damage nor harm etc., to any of the king's subjects, nor cause any harm to be done, etc.)

Be it remembered that it is commanded by the lord mayor to William Lowdan and Thomas Appilby and others on behalf of the lord king that neither trespass against the other in word, act or deed, under penalty of 3 s. 4 d. to the chamber of the city paid by the craft after each trespass.

Arrest of William Harper of York, scholar, at the suit of shoemaker William Harper.

Order for the arrest of Nicholas Brantyngham, a vicar of the Bedern, at the suit of John Huchonson.]

[ff.125v–126v blank]

[f.127]   Incomplete Entry
16 February 1488

Memorandum that the xvjth day of February in the third yere of the reigne of our souverain lord King Herry the vij^t, the right worshipfull sir Thomas Wrangwissh aldremen appering [*incomplete*]

[f.127v]   Delivery of Writ, Bonds to Keep the Peace, Payments to Bridge Keepers
20 October 1488

Memorandum that John Lowes of Tadcastre seriant at armes etc., deliverd a writ of *diem clausit extremum* therof mortem domini Willelmi Gascoigne unto my lord mayre the xx day of Octobre.

Willelmus Annotson de Askam husband[man] assumpsit pro seipso in xl libris necnon Christoforus Annotson et Robertus Hubberd (assumpserunt) de eadem husbandmen assumpserunt et eorum alter assumpsit pro eodem Willelmo in xl libris legalis etc., levandis etc., ad opus communitatis etc., quod prefatus Willelmus omni tempore ⟨proximo⟩ futuro ⟨omnis viribus gaudeat et comparatur⟩ paratus erit (ad tenendum) personaliter coram maiore civitatis Ebor' pro tempore existente ad respondendum quibuscumque rebus et materiis que sibi obvietur per quascumque personas ex parte domini nostri regis seu alterius cuiuscumque persone non suo durante vita ⟨sue⟩ naturale prefati Willelmi.

Thomas Barra de Ebor' wever assumpsit pro seipso in xl libris; Ricardus Blak-bourne ⟨mercer⟩, Ricardus Clerk barkar, Johannes Hall tanner, Willelmus Hart wever et Henricus Toppan assumpserunt etc., in xl libris levandis ut supra etc., quod ut supra etc.

Item solutiones camerariis per custodes pontis Fosse – v li.

Item solutum eisdem per Christoforum [*faded*] – iij s. iiij d.

[Husbandman William Annotson of Askham bound himself for £40, and also Christopher Annotson and Robert Hubberd, husbandmen, each bound himself on William's behalf for £40, levied, etc., to the work of the commonalty etc., that the aforesaid William at all times in the future will be prepared to come personally before the mayor to respond to whatever things and materials that turn up by whatever persons on behalf of our lord king or any other person during the natural life of the said William.

Weaver Thomas Barra of York bound himself for £40; mercer Richard Blak-bourne, barker Richard Clerk, tanner John Hall, weaver William Hart and Henry Toppan bound themselves etc., for £40 levied etc., as above.

Item, paid to the chamberlains by the keepers of Foss bridge – £5.

Item, paid to the same by Christopher [*faded*] – 3 s. 4 d.]

Attendance List
16 February 1488

Sabbati festum Sancte Julianne

Mayor: William Todde knight. Mayor elect: Robert Hancok. 12: Richard York knight, Thomas Wrangwissh, William Snawsell, William Chymney, Nicholas Loncastre, William White. Deputy recorder: Thomas Asper. Sheriffs: George Kirk, Robert Johnson. 24: Thomas Catour, Thomas Alan, William Spense.

Attendance List
February–March 1488

Lune in [*faded, 2^d semana?*] xl^c

Mayor: Robert Hancok. Recorder: John Vavasour. 12: Richard York knight, William Chymney, John Harper. 24: Thomas Catour, Thomas Alan, William Tayte, Richard Clerc, Miles Grenebank, Richard Hardsang.

[f.128]   Bonds to Accept Arbitration
3 January and 18 February 1489

Memorandum quod tercio die Januarii anno quarto regni regis Henrici septimi in camera consilii venerunt personaliter coram Roberto Hancok maiore civitatis predicte tam Willelmus Mas[on?] vynter quam Henricus Toppan ffullour in propriis personis suis et recognoverunt debere domino regi xl libras legalis monete Anglie quod ipsi et uterque eorum stabunt et perimplebunt ordinacioni, arbitrio et iudicio Thome Wellis goldsmyth, Thome Smyth cord[wainer], Ricardi Crokelyn et Christofori Thomlynson arbitratorum indiferenter electorum de et super omnibus et omnimodis accionibus tam realibus quam personalibus inter partes predictas habitis, motis sive pendentibus a principio mundi usque in diem confeccionis presencium, ita quod eadem ordinacio, arbitrium et iudicium fiant et reddantur inter partes predictas per dictos arbitratores citra festum Sancti Willelmi archiepiscopi proximum futurum, et quod dicte partes in medio (ter) tempore gerent pacem domini regis inter se sub pena xl librarum partium forisfaciendarum deficientium.

Memorandum quod xviij° die Februarii anno iiij^{to} regni regis Henrici septimi in camera consilii civitatis Ebor' venerunt personaliter coram Johanne Harper maiore eiusdem civitatis 〈Thomas〉 (Thomas) Asenby barbour et (mrli) Magister Willelmus Burton in propriis personis suis et recognoverunt se debere domino regi

C solidos legalis monete Anglie ad ipsi et uterque eorum stabunt et perimplebunt
ordinacioni, arbitrio et iudicio Willelmi Tayte, Petri Coke, Elie Cure et [blank]
Robynson wever arbitratorum per dictum maiorem indiferenter electorum de et
super omnibus et omnimodis accionibus tam realibus quam personalibus inter
partes predictas habitis, motis sive pendentibus a principio mundi usque in diem
confeccionis presencium, ita quod eadem ordinacio, arbitrium et iudicium fiant et
reddantur inter partes predictas per dictos arbitratores citra Dominicam proximam
post terciam septimanam xlme proximam futuram, et quod dicte partes in medio
tempore gerent inter se pacem domini regis sub pena predicta partium forisfaciendarum deficientium, etc.

[On 3 January 1489, vintner William Mas[on?] and fuller Henry Toppan
appeared personally in the council chamber before mayor Robert Hancok and
bound themselves to owe the lord king £40 that they and each of them will adhere
to and obey the ordinance, arbitration and judgement of goldsmith Thomas
Wellis, cordwainer Thomas Smyth, Richard Crokelyn and Christopher Thomlynson, arbiters impartially elected over all actions both real and personal had,
moved or pending between the said parties from the beginning of the world to
the day these presents [bonds] were made, the said judgement to be made and
rendered by the next coming feast of Saint William the Archbishop, and that in
the meantime the said parties should keep the lord king's peace under penalty of
the £40 to be forfeited.

On 18 February 1489, barber Thomas Asenby and Master William Burton
appeared personally before mayor John Harper in the council chamber and
bound themselves to owe the lord king 100 s. that they would adhere to and carry
out the ordinance, arbitration and judgement of William Tayte, Peter Coke,
Elias Cure and [blank] Robynson, weaver, arbiters impartially elected by the
mayor over all actions both real and personal had, moved or pending between
the said parties from the beginning of the world to the days these presents
[bonds] were made, this judgement to be made and rendered by the Sunday after
the third week in Lent next coming, and in the meantime the said parties are to
keep the lord king's peace towards each under under the aforesaid penalty to be
forfeited.]

[f.128v]   **Bonds to Accept Arbitration**
                12 and 21 March 1489

Memorandum quod xij^{mo} die Marcii anno iiij^{to} regni regis Henrici septimi
Conorandus Gossep et Robertus Burnet in propriis personis suis venerunt personaliter coram Johanne Harper maiore civitatis Ebor' et recognoverunt se debere
domino regi xx^{ti} marcas bone et legalis monete Anglie de bonis et catallis suis
levandas etc., quod ipsi et uterque eorum perimplebunt ordinacioni, arbitrio et
iudicio Johannis Elwald, Alexandri Dauson, Johannis Robynson et Willelmi
Barker arbitratorum per dictum maiorem indiferenter electorum ad (al) arbitrandum et tractandum inter partes predictas de omnibus transgressionibus.

recognitio inter Ricardum Clerk et Willelmum Hughbank Memorandum quod xxj°
die Marcii anno iiij^{to} regni regis Henrici septimi coram Johanne Harper maiore
civitatis Ebor' in camera consilii eiusdem civitatis venerunt personaliter tam
Ricardus Clerk tanner quam Willelmus Hughbank tanner et recognoverunt se
debere domino regi x libras legalis monete Anglie ad opus domini regis de bonis et
catallis suis levandas, quod ipsi et uterque eorum stabunt et perimplebunt
ordinacioni, arbitrio et judicio Johannis Ordeux, Thome Watson, Adam Atkynson
et Thome Lewlyn arbitratorum tam ex parte dicti Ricardi Clerk quam ex parte
predicti Willelmi Hughbank indiferenter electorum de et super omnibus et
omnimodis transgressionibus, litibus, causis, contraversiis et aliis quibuscumque
inter eos habitis, motis sive pendentibus a principio mundi usque in diem
confeccionis presencium, ita quod eadem ordinacio, arbitrium et judicium inter
partes predictas fiant et reddantur inter partes predictas citra Dominicam in
Ramispalmarum proximum fututurum [*sic*], et quod dicte partes gerent pacem
domino regi inter se sub pena predicta in medio tempore.

[On 12 March 1489, Conorand Gossep and Robert Burnet came personally
before mayor John Harper and bound themselves to owe the lord king twenty
marks of legal English money levied of their goods and chattels, etc., that they
would carry out the ordinance, arbitration and judgement of John Elwald,
Alexander Dauson, John Robynson and William Barker, arbiters impartially
elected by the mayor to arbitrate and deal with all trespasses between the parties.

bond between Richard Clerk and William Hughbank On 21 March 1489, tanners
Richard Clerk and William Hughbank came before mayor John Harper and
bound themselves to owe the lord king £10 of legal English money levied of their
goods and chattels, that they would adhere to and carry out the judgement of
John Ordeux, Thomas Watson, Adam Atkynson and Thomas Lewlyn, arbiters
impartially elected over all trespasses and controversies had, moved or pending
between the said parties from the beginning of the world to the day these
presents [bonds] were made, this judgement to be made and rendered by Palm
Sunday next coming, and the parties are to keep the peace in the meantime.]

**[f.129]   Earl of Northumberland Asks for Troops Against Scotland, City Walls
        to be Repaired
        17 and 22 April 1488**

Acta et processus concilii tempore ⟨venerabilis viri⟩ Roberti Hancok maioris,
festum Sancte Juliane, videlicet xvij° die Februarii anno regni regis Henrici vij^{mi}
tercio [*sic, the feast of Saint Juliana falls on 16 February*]

[Acts and proceedings of the council during the time of the venerable Robert
Hancok mayor, the feast of Saint Juliana, namely 17 February in the third year of
the reign of Henry VII]

Die Lune xxij^{do} die Aprilis anno tercio regni regis Henrici vij [*sic, 22 April 1488 was a Tuesday*]

Mayor: Robert Hancok. 12: Sir Richard Yorke knight, Thomas Wrangwissh, John Tong, John Fereby, John Newton, Master Nicholas Lancaster, William Chymney, Sir William Todde, John Harper, William White. Counsellor: Thomas Asper. 24: Thomas Catour, Thomas Alleyn, John Hag, William Spence, William Tayte, Michael White, Richard Clerk, Miles Grenebank, Richard Hardsang, Nicholas Vicars, Roger Appilby, John Shawe.

Wer the same day assembled in the counsell chaimbre of Ousebrig and ther and then a lettre that cam from the right noble lord therle of Northumberland direct to the aforsaid maiour and the aldermen his brethern, the tenour whereof foloweth:

To my right hartily bilovyd frende the maiour of the cite ⟨of York⟩ and to my right trusty and welbeloved frendes his bredern aldermen of the same

Right wourshupfull and right hartely biloved and right trusty and welbelovyd frendes, I recommaund and comaund me unto you, and I have auctorite and commaundment from the kynges highnes to prepare sertan men, archers, for aide to be had to the kyng of Scotland for wages, and for the same to understand of you and other gentilmen what men ye woll make redy to take the said wages towardes the accomplisshement of the kynges mynde in that bihalve, and therapan that I may be asertayned from you in all hast possible as ye entend the pleasour of the kynges highnes and as my special trust is in you, and the blissed Trinite be your conservatour. Writen in my castell of Werkworth the xviij day of Aprill.

Your lovyng frend H. Northumberland

Item the same day it is agreid by thassent and consent of all abovesaid that Thomas Thirland shalbe recontent of x li. which by him is laid down to the reparacions of the wallez according to theffect and ordynaunce therof maid etc., to hym or his assigney in that behalf etc.

[f.129v]   Bond to Accept Arbitration, Arrest of Chaplain
April 1488

recognitio [c.1 word torn] die Aprilis Johannes Birkehede milner et Ricardus Frase milner venerunt personaliter coram reverendo viro Roberto Hancok maiore et recognoverunt se (v) debere domino regi ⟨xl libras⟩ quod stabunt et uterque eorum stabit ⟨et perimplebit⟩ ordinacioni, judicio et arbitrio Thome Topshawe saddiller, Johannis Esheweray cord[wainer], Rolandi Hilton et Radulphi Peti arbitratorum inter partes predictas indiferenter electorum de et super omnibus et omnimodis accionibus, querelis, debatis et demandis inter ipsos motis, habitis sive (spectantibus) ⟨pendentibus⟩ a principio mundi usque in diem ⟨confectionis⟩ presencium que quedam summa (cause) concessere solvere ad festum (Pasche) Pentecostes sub pena illorum deficientium in premissis de bonis et catalis suis levanda.

Preceptum capias dompnum Nicholaum Topshawe capellanum ac unum mona-
chorum domus Sancte Trinitatis Ebor' ad sectam magistri Elie Bell clerici.

[*bond, April* Millers John Birkehede and Richard Frase came personally before
mayor Robert Hancok and bound themselves to owe the lord king £40 that they
would adhere to the ordinance and judgement of saddler Thomas Topshawe,
cordwainer John Esheweray, Roland Hilton and Ralph Peti, arbiters impartially
elected over all actions and complaints moved, had or pending between the said
parties from the beginning of the world to the present day, payment to be made
by the feast of Pentecost.

Order for the arrest of lord Nicholas Topshawe, chaplain and monk of Holy
Trinity, York, at the suit of Master Elias Bell, clerk.]

[f.130]   **King's Letter Read, Ordnance Keeper Examined, Guest's Words
              Repeated
              17 June 1488**

xvij° die Junii anno tercio regni regis Henrici vij^{mi}

Mayor: Robert Hancok. 12: Richard Yorke knight, John Tong, John Newton, Master
Nicholas Lancastre, William Chymney, Master William Todd, William White, John Gylliot.
Recorder *locum tenens*: Thomas Asper. Sheriffs: George Kirke, Robert Johnson. 24:
William Spence, William Tayte, Richard Clerk, John Hagg, Michael White, William Barker,
Roger Appilby.

At the which a lettre was red tofore the said presence which by the kinges grace was direct
to the maiour and shireffes of this cite, which lettre is registerd in the xviij leif tofore
preceding etc. [*see above, [f.88]*], (ar) and apon that it was thoght necessary the same
lettre tobe red tofore the seircheours of this cite shortlie for certan consideracions etc.
Item the same day the copy of a indentour of a annuall fee to be paid to John Craven etc.,
was red tofore the said presence which the same day was thoght that he shold be
examyned apon such artilirie of werr the which tofore this was delyverd to [his] handes to
kep, and also that he have doon his dewtie according to theffect of the said indentour, that
than he so examyned by the said maiour and two aldermen and no defalt in hym found, he
to have his fe and other comprehendit in the same indentour, and if he have not and that
laufully proved, tobe discharged for eny fe or other herafter to be paid to the said John
Craven etc. Item the same day John Bell taillour was sent for tobe examyned what that he
hard an estranger say in his house which was gest with hym, he confessed and said that
herd the same estranger and his gest say.

[f.130v]   **City Asks Archbishop of York for Help with King's Tax
              23 June 1488**

The copy of a lettre direct unto the (righ) most reverent fadder in God tharchebisshop of York, from the maiour of the cite of Yorke, shireffes, aldermen and the
common counsell of the same

Most reverend fadder in God and our most especial and singuler gude lorde, we in our most humblie wise recommendes us unto your gude lordship, thankyng the same in as hertelie wise as to us or may be possible for the manyfoldes benefices and merites which ye have shewed at large unto us, and to this your pore cite at all tymes herbifore for the which we with our bodies and goodes shalbe redy at all tymes to do you(r) pleasour and service at the uttermost of our powers, with our daylie prayers to God for the contynuance of your most prosperus state. Sir, pleas it your gude lordship to have knowlige that considering nyghnes of tyme of payment of the oon halfendell of the tax late grauntid to our sovereyn lorde the king with the forvent desire the which we have to pleas his grace according to our naturall dewtes, natwithstanding the greit povertie, ruyne and decae of this said cite, wherby we have be the rather induced to mak effectuall levy of the said tax, and therfor also hath put it in reall suretie to be had when the (caur) case shall require of the oon partie, and on the other partie calling to mynde the common opynion of men here supposing that our said sovereyn lorde of his greit benignitie wol remit and fully pardon us and other of this northparties the same tax with that also that we be credable enfourmed that in the cuntries aboutes us here as yit no levy is maid of the same, we have sent up the berer herof to John Vavesour the kinges seriant at the lawe our recorder, for thexecucion of certan thinges thinges [sic] consernyng the publiquiance wele of this your cite emonges whom we have desired hym of the consideracions above writen tobe mean to the kinges grace or som of his most noble counsell that we may have perfite knowlige of the pleasour of his said grace in the premissez, whether disposed to have redy payment of the said tax or to have it kept in our handes to his pleasour forther understand in that behalf, or if it shall so content his highnes which God (knowe) graunt nowe to pardon the same, which we trust his grace (wo) wolbe inclined as san to do unto us in consideracion of the said poverite, ruyne and decae, as unto eny other his sugettes in thise parties, wherfor we in our most humblie wise besecheth your gude lordeship nat onelie by your most honorable lettres tobe direct to the kinges grace or som of his most noble counsell [illegible] to labour for theffectuall accomplisshement of our said desire, bot aswele to shewe unto the said berer your best advise in that behalf for the comforth and suretie of us in the same, wherby as herbifore ye have don in grett thinges ye shall surelie fasten us and the pore inhabitantes here to your contynuall service with our prayers to God duryng our lyves by the grace of the same who preserve you, most reverend fadder in God and our most especial and singuler gude lorde in felicitie with encreise of goode fortunez long to endour to his pleasour. Writen at your cite of York the xxiij day of Juyn.

Your most humblie beidmen and servauntes at thare pore power the maiour, shireffes, aldermen of your cite of Yorke

To the most reverend fadder in God and our most especial and singuler gude lorde tharchbisshop of York primate of England

[f.131]   **City Asks Recorder for Advice on King's Tax**
                24 June 1488

To the right wirshupful sir John Vavasour, oon of the kinges seriantes at the lawe
and recorder of the cite of Yorke.

Right wirshupful sir, we recommend us unto you, desiryng you to call unto your
remembraunce howe we tofore this hath writen unto you shewing the greit decae,
ruyne and povertie of the cite of Yorke and the kinges sugettes within the same, we
doubt not bot ye understand the same no man better, wherfor the cause of this our
writing to you at this tyme is this: we prepare us in gadering of the kinges tax by the
commaundment of his collectours more largelie and hastelie than the cuntre doeth,
for the which the hole commonaltie and the kinges sugettes (thare) aforsaid
marvels much, we so deill saing they trust remembring thare greit povert the king of
his most benivolent grace wold be as gude and gracious lorde unto tham and to us
as to eny other place within this his realme; ffor which cause and for all our weles,
we hertelie desire and pray you tobe gude mean for us all unto the said kinges grace
so that we myght understand his gracius mynde, for we ben as fereful for his greit
displeasour as eny other his sugettes within this his realme; wherfor Master
Recorder howe we shalbe demeaned in the premissez we herteley desire and pray
you of your most best and faithful advise and counsell, and all that to this berer in
thinges that he shall shew unto you upon our behalve to yiff credence and for your
curtas lettre the which ye of late and send ⟨us⟩ in the which we understand by
your greit diligence and labour it hath taken and gude speid for which and other
your greit and effectuall ⟨labour⟩ in this behalf by the grace of God at your next
commyng home to deserve it at your pleasour who preserve you. In hast from
Yorke the xxiiij day of Juyn.

By the maiour, shireffes, aldermen and the hole counsell of the citie of Yorke

Preceptum capias Ricardum Stodert nuper de Skipwith in comitatu Ebor' yoman ad
sectam Elie Bell (clerico) clerici.

[Order for the arrest of Richard Stodert, formerly of Skipwith, Yorkshire,
yeoman, at the suit of clerk Elias Bell.]

[f.131v]   **Arrests and Bonds to Accept Arbitration**
                 Undated, Summer 1488

Preceptum capias Thomam Stokdale capellanum ad sectam Magistri Willelmi
Burtan (m).

Preceptum capias Robertum Hertlington de Clyfton iuxta Ebor' in comitatu Ebor'
laborer ad sectam Nicholai Edwyn wever.

concordate sunt [*entry struck through*] (Magister Nicholaus Lancastre doctor

Preceptum capias Ricardum Brain de Ebor' mercatorem ad sectam Roberti Wilde shirman.

Manucapcio pro Johanne Smyth bocher et Anicia uxore eius quod ipsi nec eorum uterque dampnum vel malum aliquod corporale Henrico Pulley et Johanne uxori eius vel alicui alii de populo domini regis non faciet nec fieri procurabit (p) quovismodo videlicet predictus Johannes Smyth in xx libris, et quilibet manucaptorum sub pena x librarum, videlicet Johannes Northeby bocher, Johannes Suttan mason, Rolandus Brise bocher et Robertus Heworth cord[wainer] domino regi forisfaciendarum.

Manucapcio Cuthberti Brounlesse de civitate Ebor' litster quod ipse dampnum vel malum aliquod corporale Michaeli White tinctori aut alicui de suis vel aliquo alio de populo domini regis non faciet nec fieri procurabit quovismodo videlicet (quilibet manucaptorum in C libris) ⟨predictus (Cul) Cuthbertus manucepit pro seipso in C marcis, et super hac⟩ Johannes Robynson taillour et Thomas Chapman saddiller venerunt personaliter coram Roberto Hancok adtunc maiore civitatis Ebor' et ⟨devenerunt plegios pro predicto Cuthberto ac⟩ recognoverunt se debere domino regi C libras de bonis et catallis suis levandas ad opus domini regis si predictus Cuthbertus Brounlesse temptaverit (aut) pacem domini regis versus dictum (Willelmum) ⟨Michaelem⟩ White vel suos aut illam procuraverit etc.

Preceptum capias Henricum Stansfelde de (Eland) ⟨Rastrik⟩ in parochia de Halifax' gent[leman] ad sectam Johannis Wilkyn yoman.

[Order for the arrest of labourer John Brereclyff of Temple Saint John next to Copmanthorpe, Yorkshire, at the suit of Roger [*blank*], servant of Richard Vavesour.

Order for the arrest of Richard Brain, merchant of York, at the suit of shearman Robert Wilde.

Mainprise for butcher John Smyth and Anicia his wife, that they (neither of them) do no damage or bodily harm to Henry Pulley and Joan his wife, or to any other of the king's subjects, under penalty [for John Smyth] of £20; the sureties, each binding himself for £10, include butcher John Northeby, mason John Suttan, butcher Roland Brise, and cordwainer Robert Heworth.

Mainprise of dyer Cuthbert Brounlesse of York, that he do no damage nor bodily harm to dyer Michael White nor to any other of the king's subjects, nor cause any harm to be done, under penalty of £100; and also tailor John Robynson and saddler Thomas Chapman came personally before mayor Robert Hancok and became sureties on behalf of Cuthbert, binding themselves for £100 levied of their goods and chattels, that Cuthbert try to keep the peace towards Michael White.

Order for the arrest of Henry Stansfelde of Rastrick in the parish of Halifax, gentleman, at the suit of yeoman John Wilkyn.]

[f.133] **Election of Sheriffs, Opening of Common Lands**
21 September 1488

Die Dominica in festo Sancti Mathie apostoli anno iiij° regni regis Henrici vij^{mi}

Mayor: Robert Hancok. Recorder: John Vavesour. 12: Richard Yorke knight, Thomas Wrangwisshe, William Snawsell, John Fereby, Master Nicholas Lancastre, William Todd knight, John Harper, William White, John Gilliot. Sheriffs: George Kirke, Robert Johnson. 24: Thomas Allan, William Tayte, William Spence, John Hagg, Michael White, Miles Grenebank, Richard Hardesang, William Barker, Thomas Fynche, John Beisby, John Shawe.

Ad quem diem omnes prescripti ex unanimi assensu et consensu eligerunt Thomam Folnetby mercatorem et Thomam Graa aurifabrum vicecomites civitatis Ebor' ad occupandum officium vicecomitis infra eandem civitatem secundum consuetudinem eiusdem pro anno sequenti.

Item the same day it was agreid by the said presencs that all tho that have eny closyng or other holding within this libertie closed and aught at this Michaelmesse next tobe laid open in peseable wise, that the fermours opyn ther yates of thare fermoldes to thentent that no hurt be don apon the whikfall belonging to the same, and also that noon inconvenient efter that ne groge be had to the said fermours by eny cocitecyn of this said wirshupfull cite bot by reason of the openyng the coceticyns to have thare (thar) common etc.

> [On this day all the abovewritten unanimously elected merchant Thomas Folnetby and goldsmith Thomas Graa sheriffs of the city of York, to hold the office according to custom for the following year.]

[f.133v] **City Orders Opening of Common Land**
29 September 1488

Die Lune in festo Sancti Michaelis archangeli anno iiij^{to} regni regis Henrici septimi

Mayor: Robert Hancok. Recorder: John Vavesour. 12: Richard Yorke knight, John Fereby, Nicholas Lancaster, William Chymney, William Todd knight, John Harper, William White, John Gylliot. 24: Thomas Catour, William Tayte, Richard Clerk, John Hag, Richard Hardesang, William Barker, John Shawe.

Tangfelde At the which day all abovesaid determyned ⟨and concludet⟩ that such common as the communaltie of this cite of right aught to have in the Tangfeld, Hallfeld and other, that the ⟨same⟩ commonaltie shall in peseable wise withoute eny insurrection or riot kepe ther possession and at the common sergiantes shall in curtaswise go to every fermour and keper of every closer and othre and shew thame that this present day at xij of the clok to opyn (the) the yates of thare fermoldes to thentent that the commonaltie may enter into the same to have ther common acording to ther right.

[f.134]   **Aged Swordbearer Retires**
                  19 October 1488

xix° die Octobris

Mayor: Robert Hancok. 12: Richard Yorke knight, William Snawsell, John Fereby, b–Master Nicholas Lancaster, a–John Newton, William Chymney, John Harper, John Gilliot. 24: Thomas Catour, William Tayte, Richard Clerk, Miles Grenebank, Roger Appilby, John Shawe.[*Lower-case letters indicate correct order of precedence.*]

[R] *John Strangwisshe swordbearer* [*marginalia in later, probably seventeenth-century, hand*] At the which day (it was) John Strangwisshe swerdberer to the maiour cam personalie tofore the said presence and thare and then humblie shewed hym self howe that he was greitlie aged and also in greit sekenysse and other diseissez, by reason of the which he was not able for the wirshop of this wirshupful cite to do service in the said office of swerdberership, and ther surrendert the same office unto the said my lorde maiour and other above writen to put into the same such a gentilman as mybht be to the pleasour of thaym and for the wirshup of this said cite, shewing over that he trusted for his contynuance in the said office thai woldbe and stand his gude lord and maisters and to the same he humblie desired thame, and apon that my said lorde maiour and maisters ⟨considering the premissez⟩ determyned that the ⟨said⟩ John Strangwish for his gude service and attendaunce tofore this by hym doon in the said office and also his humblie surrendour of the same office, that what (Gentl') gentilman shall occupie next in the said office of swerdberership shall during (his) the naturall lieff of the said John Strangwish yeld and pay yerelie owte of the hole ffe belonging to the said office of swerdberership xxvj s. viij d. of lauful money of England at foure tymes of the yere accustomed by the handes of the chaumberleyns for tyme being, to be paid to the said John Strangwish or his assigney during his naturall leff, and if sobe the said gentilman the which next the said ⟨to⟩ the office shalbe admitted by the visitacion of God or otherwise ⟨of his mere motion⟩ to be discharged of the said office, that than the next gentilman that shalbe admitted to the said office to bere the said pencion to the said John Strangwish during his naturall lieff.

[f.134v]   **Selection of New Swordbearer, Instructions on Payment of King's Tax**
                  20 October 1488

xx^mo die Octobris

Mayor: Robert Hancok. 12: Richard Yorke knight, John Fereby, John Newton, Nicholas Lancaster, William Chymney, John Harper, William White. 24: Thomas Catour, Thomas Allan, William Tayte, John Hagg, ⟨Michael White⟩, Miles Grenebank, Richard Clerk, Richard Hardesang, John Shaw. Sheriffs: George Kirke, Robert Johnson.

Wer assembled in the counsel chambre apon Ousebrig and thare and than aswele John Strangwish late swerdberer as Humfrey Maners of newe admit unto the same, and there and then the said Humfrey Maners agreid hym to (cam) content and pay to the said John Strangwish a yerelie pencion of xxvj s. viij d. (during) by yere during the season and tyme that he shall occupie the same office of swerdberership, the same pencion to rest quarterlie in the hondes of the chaumberleynes for tyme being, that is to say vj s. viij d. every quarter of the hole fe due to the ⟨said⟩ Humfrey Maners by reason of his said office.

To the right wirshupful the maier and his brethern aldermen of the citie of York

Right wirshupful I recommend me unto you, and like it you to wit I have receyved your lettrez and also herd the credence shewid unto me on your behalve by my frende Vavesour your recorder, and where as at this tyme the kynges grace is content and paid by you of that one half of the xvme for the cite of Yorke except xxx li. wherof ye desire to have alouaunce, therunto it hathnot ben accustomyd that eny alouaunce shold be had therof unto the ful payment of the hole xvme, and ye nede not to mystrust the kynges ⟨grace⟩ highnes therin for he is gracious sovereyne lorde unto you and so hath ben sith the begynyng of his noble reign, and therof therbe eny service that I can do for you and the wele of the said cite, I wold be right glad after my litell power to do it, that knoweth God who preserve you. At Westmynstre the xiiij day of Octobre.

Your Dynham

[f.135]   Alderman Suspected of Seditious Words
25 October 1488

xxv° die Octobris

Mayor: Robert Hancok. 12: Richard Yorke knight, Thomas Wrangwish, John Fereby, John Newton, Master Nicholas Lancastre, William Chymney, William White. Counsellor: Thomas Asper. 24: Thomas Allan, William Tayte, Richard Clerk, John Hagg, Michael White, Richard Hardesang, William Barker. Sheriffs: George Kirke, Robert Johnson.

the honour or hurt of the said Sir Robert Plompton knyght At the which day it was shewed by Thomas Davyson and Roland Robson the saing of the right wirshupful Sir Robert Plompton knyght of the sediciouse saing of John Harper one of the aldermen of the cite of Yorke, which saing shuldnot sound to the hanour of the said Sir Robert Plompton; the said maiour understonding the said saing examyned every man of the ⟨said said⟩ ⟨same⟩ saing whether by there othez they ⟨or eny of thayme⟩ ever hard the said John Harper within the counsell chambre, in the counsell or elswhere, have eny such language or saing as the ⟨said⟩ said Thomas and Roland shewed; they and every of ⟨thame⟩ by hym self ⟨expreslie⟩ said of ther faith and holydom that they ne noon of thaym never herd within the counsell chambre, in the counsell ne elswhere ⟨ne other which should sound (to the) ayanest⟩ any such saing ne language of the said John Harper and that they er and wolbe redy that to aprove ⟨of⟩ as right and lawe woll.

[f.135v]   Sir Richard York Sent to King's Council
19 October 1488

xix die Octobris anno iiij^{to} regni regis Henrici vij^{mi}

Mayor: Robert Hancok. 12: Richard Yorke knight, Thomas Wrangwish, John Fereby, John Newton, Master Nicholas Lancastre, William Chymney, William White, John Gylliot. Counsellor: Thomas Asper. 24: Thomas Catour, Thomas Alan, Richard Clerk, Richard Hardesang, Roger Appilby. Sheriffs: George Kirke, Robert Johnson.

Wer assembled in the counsell chaimbre apon Ousebrig and ther and then determyned of oon assent and consent that right wirshupful Sir Richerd Yorke knyght sitold ride up to London to this greit and honorable counsell now to be holden at Westm[inster] the xth day of Novembre next commyng according to thentent of kinges lettres missives direct to the maiour, his brethren aldermen and other the common counsell of the same cite, as in the same lettres more planelie doeth appere, taking apon the day to his costes and charges vij s. during the seasen that he shall attend apon the said counsell.

[f.136]   Bonds to Keep the Peace
11 November 1488

Johannes Person de Ebor' dyer venit in propria persona sua coram Roberto Hancok maiore civitatis Ebor', Thoma Wrangwish et Magistro Nicholao Lancastre aldermannis eiusdem civitatis custodibus pacis et justiciis domini regis de pace conservanda infra libertatem civitatis die Martis in festo Sancti Martini episcopi et confessoris anno quarto regni regis Henrici septimi in camera consilii civitatis predicte et recognovit se debere eidem domino regi centum marcas bone et legalis monete Anglie solvendas et levandas de omnibus bonis et catallis, terris et tenementis suis si dictus Johannes Person erga Willelmum (Wel') White aldermannum civitatis predicte (et) ⟨vel⟩ suos familiares per insurrecciones aut congregaciones illicitas aut per minas, insidias seu aliquo alio modo quod in lesionem seu perturbacionem pacis cedere valeant.

Willelmus White tinctor (ac) ac unus aldermannorum civitatis Ebor' venit in propria persona sua coram Roberto Hancok maiore civitatis Ebor', Thoma Wrangwish et Magistro Nicholao Lancastre ⟨aldermannis⟩, custodibus pacis et justiciis domini regis de pace conservanda infra libertatem civitatis predicte, die Martis in festo Sancti Martini episcopi et confessoris anno quarto regni regis Henrici septimi in camera consilii civitatis predicte et recognovit se debere eidem domino regi centum marcas bone et legalis monete Anglie solvendas et levandas de omnibus bonis et catallis, terris et tenementis suis si dictus Willelmus per se vel suos erga Johannem Person tinctorem vel suos familiares amodo transgrediatur aut pacem perturbaverit per insurrecciones, confideraciones aut congregaciones illicitas aut per minas, insidias seu (l) aliquo modo que in lesionem seu perturbacionem pacis cedere valeant quovismodo.

[Dyer John Person of York came personally before mayor Robert Hancok and aldermen Thomas Wrangwish and Master Nicholas Lancastre, keepers of the peace and justices of the lord king in the liberty of this city on Tuesday the feast of Saint Martin 1488, and bound himself to owe the king one hundred marks of legal English money levied of all his goods, chattels, lands and tenements, and allow to happen no insurrections or illegal gatherings against alderman William White or his household members, or threats, plots or any other means that breach or disturb the peace.

William White, dyer and one of the aldermen of the city of York, came personally before mayor Robert Hancok and aldermen Thomas Wrangwish and Master Nicholas Lancastre, keepers of the peace and justices of the lord king on Tuesday the feast of Saint Martin 1488 and bound himself for one hundred marks that he would not disturb the peace against dyer John Person or any of his household by way of insurrections, confederations or illegal gatherings or through threats, plots, or any other way that breaches the peace.]

[f.136v] Accusations of Seditious Language
4 December 1488

Memorandum the iiij^th day of Decembre the fourt yere of the reign of King Herry the vij^th, Thomas Sturgeon of Lancastr' set in the Kidcote of Yorke for certain sediciouse language ayanest our said sovereyn lorde was apon the kinges grace shewid by the right wirshupful sir Sir Richerd Yorke knyght delyverd of the said prison and the said Sturgeon apon the holy evaungelist sworn in the counsell chambre tofor Robert Hancok maiour, Sir Richerd York, Thomas Asper and diverse other tobe and stand true lige man unto our said sovereyn lord etc., and so departed at his arge [?]. And Thomas Folnetby and Thomas Gray than being shireffes of this wirshupful citie ayanest our sovereyn lorde aforsaid and all other of forther keping of the body of the said Sturgeon clerelie tobe discharged.

Item the same day, presence and place was sent for ⟨oon Jamez Tayte founder⟩, he in his propre person examyned what wordes he hard a gentilwoman callid Maistres Worsley say in his house etc., he answerd and said that the said gentilwoman sayd in the variaunce betwix Sir George Nevill and William Highfeld that ther was noon that tuke the ways and favour with the said Highfeld and Biller bot such that wold have the erle of Northumbreland to were the garland, and (apon) ⟨a⟩ that ⟨was treuth⟩ he vouched hym to the recorde of Thomas Wright potter and melemaker and Richerd Wighman potter, cocitesyns of Yorke, which Thomas Wright was the same day at efternoon sent for and examyned as toching the said sediciouse saying, and he tofor the said maiour (wh) with in ⟨his⟩ house and ther and then by the comaundment of the said maiour, Thomas Asper being present with other, said and confessid that he hard noon such wordes by the said gentilwoman said etc., and that he at all tymez wolbe redy at his pore power to approve.

[f.137] Item the same day incontinent efter the same Thomas Wright examyned what he hard the said gentilwoman say of the premissez, the said Richerd Wightman was sent for and then he said and confessed that he hard the said gentilwoman say that noon wold tak the way (with maister) ayanest Maister Nevill bot such as wold the erle of Northumbreland shold were the garland, he answerd and said shortlie to hir it was fer said and semyd hir not to have eny such language.

[f.137v]   **Attendance List**
                     December 1488

[*blank*] die Decembris

Mayor: Robert Hancok. 12: Richard Yorke knight, John Fereby, William Todd knight, William White, John Gylliot. Counsellor: Thomas Asper. 24: Thomas Allan, William Tayte, John Hag, Richard Clerk.

[f.138]   **Selection of New Chamberlain**
                     January 1489

[*blank*] die Januarii

Mayor: Robert Hancok. 12: Nicholas Lancastre, William Chymney, John Harper. Counsellor: Thomas Asper. Sheriffs: Thomas Foulneby, Thomas Graa. 24: ⟨Thomas Catour⟩, Thomas Allan, William Tayte, William Spence, Richard Clerk, John Hagg, ⟨Thomas Fynch⟩, William Barker, Robert Johnson.

At the which day forsomuch as John Gaunt late chosyn oon ⟨of⟩ the chaumberleyns of this wirshupfull cite now departed unto the mercy of God, it was shewed (unto) by the mouth of the said maiour (th) oon Thomas Hauslyn ffisshemonger, so that he myght be forborn of ferther bering of the office of chaumberleynship that for this last payment which draweth (xxx) xxxiij li., that he woldbe of (good be) will to content and pay the same sowme.

confirmed page 152b [marginalia at bottom of folio in later, probably seventeenth-century, hand]

[f.138v]   **Accounts of Present Chamberlains**
                     2 February 1489

ij^{do} die Februarii

Mayor: Robert Hancok. 12: Thomas Wrangwish, John Fereby, Master Nicholas Lancastre, William Chymney, John Harper, William White. Counsellor: Thomas Asper. Sheriffs: Thomas Foulneby, Thomas Graa. 24: Thomas Allan, Henry Williamson, William Spence, William Tayt, Michael White, ⟨Richard Clerk⟩, Richard Herdesang, William Barker, Miles Grenebank, Thomas Fynch, John Shawe, Robert Johnson.

At the same day it is agreid that the chaumberleyns of this yere, that is to say Peris Coke and other his ffelowez, shall resave and presave withoute delay of the next chaumberleyns elect for this next yere xxxiij li., the which is assigned by thame to pay to John Stokdale oon of the chaumberleyns for John Gaunt late decessid and one of the chaumberleyns with the said Peris and other at the ffest of the Invencion of the Crosse next commyng, and as for other money laid doun by the said John Gaunt, his executours to tak it up of the next chaumberleyns at the other two days of payment next the said ffest ensuyng.

[f.139]   **Unauthorised Opening of City Gates, Repayment of Citizen with Discharge from Officeholding**
4 February 1489

iiij^{to} die Februarii

Mayor: Robert Hancok. Mayor elect: John Harper. 12: Thomas Wrangwissh, John Fereby, Master Nicholas Lancastre, William Chymney. Counsellor: Thomas Asper. Sheriffs: Thomas Foulneby, Thomas Gra. 24: Thomas Catour, Thomas Allan, Henry Williamson, William Tayt, Richard Clerk, John Hagg, Michael White, Miles Grenebank, Richard Herdesang, John Shawe, Robert Johnson.

(Whe) Wer assembled in the counsell chambre apon Ousebrig, and there and then it was openyd and shewed by the mouth of the said Robert Hancok maiour that where he apon Saynt Blaise day in the mornyng sent John Sponer oon of the seriantes to the maise comaunding hym forto go to Boutham barre and to shet the greit yates of the same and ⟨to⟩ leve opyn the wekid therof, to thentent that the kinges people myght have ther passage and repassage, and ther apon the same John went to the same barre and fulfilled the maiour comaundment, and apon that efter the said greit gates so shet oon Thomas Wandesford gentleman with othre with hym ⟨cam⟩ and toke the keis withoute licence of the same officer and opynned the same gates; and for that offence furthwith the said Thomas Wandesford was sent for, cam personalie tofore the said presence and the premissez laid unto hym by the mouth of Thomas Asper, he answerd and said that he with John Metcalfe and othre went (unto) ⟨towardes⟩ the barre of Boutham, he seyng the barre stakyn demaundet John Sponer what was the reason the barre was stakyn, he answerd and said that it was the maires comaundment, the same Thomas seing keis lying apon a stall, not ben verelie knowlige that they werr the keis of the barre, toke theme in his handes and John Metcalf merchaunt toke thame apon hyme and openyd the barre and left the same keis stekyng in the lok, that oon John Sponer resavyd the same keis and broght thame unto the maire, **[f.139v]** and ther the same Thomas Wandesford shewing that he remembred that the taking of the keis was doon of a oversight, for the which oversight he offerd hym to abide the correccion of the maiour, aldermen and the common counsell, the which maiour and counsell determyned that lesse couth not be (noon) doon for his oversight bot tobe punysshed by way of inprisonament, and apon that he was commyt to prison, and ther to abide unto the tyme the maiour and counsell be otherwise advised and at his commyng furth to lay (suffica) sufficiant suretie of his gude beryng.

Item the same day Thomas Knollez drapour, one of the chaumberleyns ⟨elect⟩ for this yere insuyng, was sent for, cam before the said presence and ther and then it ⟨was⟩ laid unto hym to tak his oth apon the chamberleynship, he curtaslie answerd and said that he trusted that he had a lauful discharge under the common seall of occupyng that office and all othre within this cite, and for that he content and paid to the behufe of the communaltie x marces, the which if so evere that he must nedes notwithstanding that discharge to be compellid to occupie the said office, he trusted to be repaid the said x marces, that doon he wold indevour hym to accomplish ther myndes and els to pardon hym ⟨of⟩ his oth he wold abide the content of the writyng under the said common seall etc., and apon ⟨that⟩ it was thoght that (the) his sayng was to reason and conscience grauntyd unto hym is said oth takyn tobe repaid of his said x marces tobe takyn and alowed this yere in his owen handes apon his accompt, and apon that he tuke his oth.

**[f.140]   Election of Mayor and Other Officers, King's Proclamation to Keep the Peace During Elections
3 February 1489**

Die Martis in ffesto Sancti Blasii episcopi

12: Thomas Wrangwish, John Fereby, Nicholas Lancastre, William Chymney, William White. Sheriff: Thomas Gra. 24: Thomas Allan, Henry Williamson, William Spence, Richard Clerk, William Tayte, (John) Michael White, William Barker, Miles Grenebank, Richard Herdsang, Thomas Fynch, John Shawe, Roger Appilby, Robert Johnson.

Ad quem diem in Guihald civitatis Ebor' multi concives eiusdem civitatis congregati fuerunt ibidem et unanimi assensu et concensu eligerunt venerabilem virem Johannem Harper mercatorem maiorem civitatis predicte ad occupandum officium illud (ad) ⟨a⟩ dicto ffesto Sancti Blasii episcopi anno iiij^to regni regis Henrici septimi usque idem festum anno eiusdem regis quinto videlicet per unum annum integrum secundum antiquam ordinacionem civitatis predicte.

Item eodem die omnes prescripti eligerunt Johannem Ellys et Henricum Alleyn custodes pontis Use, et ulterius Johannem White et Johannem Robynson bocher custodes pontis Fosse, ad occupandum officia illa a dicto ffesto Sancti Blasii anno regis predicti usque idem festum anno quinto eiusdem regis etc.

Et eodem die quandem proclamatio ⟨pro⟩ rege in tribus locis infra civitatem, videlicet primus locus eiusdem ad stallago, secundus locus ad ostium Guihald, tercius (adr) infra Guihald in forma sequenti facta fuit:

[On this day in the Guildhall of the city, many citizens were gathered and with unanimous assent and consent elected the venerable John Harper, merchant, mayor of the city, to occupy the office from the feast of Saint Blaise in the fourth year of Henry VII's reign to the same feast in the fifth year, namely for one whole year according to ancient ordinance of this city.

On the same day, all the abovewritten elected John Ellys and Henry Alleyn keepers of Ouse bridge, and finally John White and John Robynson, butcher, [to be] keepers of Foss bridge, occupying the office from the said feast of Saint Blaise in the year of the king's reign as above, to the same feast a year later.

And on the same day, a proclamation on behalf of the king was made in three places in the city, namely [at first at] the place of the stalls, the second place at the door of the Guildhall, and the third place inside the Guildhall, in the form following:]

Oiez, oiez, oiez. We charge and comaund in the kynges name our most redoubted sovereyn lige lorde the maiour and shireffes of this cite, that no man of what estate or degre he be of tak apon hym to go defensable arraied this day within this same cite, be it estraunger or ffraunchest man, contrarie the keping of the kinges peax, bot that every estraunger leve his wapyn at his innes and not to entermeit hym ne thame of the eleccion of the maiour of this cite this day tobe had, according to the kynges grauntes and the auncient custome of the said cite; and that every fraunchest man go in peseable wise withoute harnesse or defensable wapyn unto the common hall and ther to determyn hym according to theffect of the same grauntes and conservacion of the kinges peace; and that noon unfraunchest man presume ne tak apon hym to enter the common hall ne entermeit hym of the said eleccion apon payn of inprisonament and forfating of his goodes and his body at the kinges will.

[f.140v]   Preparations for Election
23 and 27 January 1489

On Friday, that is to say the xxiij^{ti} day of Januar' the iiijth yere of the reign of our sovereyn lige lorde King Henry the vijth in the Guyhall of this cite according unto the auncient custom of the same, the right wirshupful sir Robert Hancok maiour of the said cite comaundet his vj seriantes to the maise to yif warnyng to every sercheour to appere afore hym ther the same day; the sercheour roule was callid and the sercheours appering the said maiour laing to thame that the day of ⟨ther⟩ eleccion aproched nere, willing thame that they and every of thame to common with his craft in lovyng wise to thentent that such a wirshupful ⟨man⟩ the which by the grace of God apon Saynt Blaise day they shold determyn tobe ther maiour for the yere ensuyng, myght be had and doon in peseable and lovyng wise withoute noise or cry, first to the pleasour of God, the king and the content of the mynd of that said wirshupful ⟨man⟩ at that day of Saynt Blaise shalbe elect and chosyn maiour, and according to the kinges gracious lettres ⟨patentes⟩ in that behalf to the cocitesyns of this cite graunted, laying unto thame over that that if eny person ⟨or personez⟩ be disposed to the contrarie, thay sholdbe put in suretie to the kinges grace understode ther demenaunce and to knowe forther his high pleasour and apon ⟨that⟩ charged thame the premissez to be fermelie kept in the kinges name our sovereyn lorde.

And the Tuysday the said Friday next ensuyng eftsonez the said Robert Hancok maiour in his propre person for certan causez and for the conservacion the kinges peax in the said Guyhall being, and ther and then the said seircheours appering afor hym to thame shewid and declared howe that it was doon hym to understand that ther was som private personez which intendit to the disturbaunce of goode ⟨and⟩ peseable reull, for the tranquilite and peace he willid thame to common togydder ther and then or they departed in lovyng and peseable wise, and such communicacion as they at that tyme ⟨had⟩ emonges thame myght be writen and sealed and the counsaill of ther communicacion myght be kept so writen and and [sic] sealed to the said Saynt Blaise day, and then tobe openyd and shewid to thentent that he that shold that ⟨day⟩ ⟨to be and⟩ ⟨be⟩ elect **[f.141]** maiour myght have it with a hole and peseable mynde, first to the pleasour of the king and conservacion of his peace, and also to the content of hym that shalbe so chosen and elect that day ⟨tobe ther maiour⟩ that ⟨⟨ther maiour⟩⟩ tobe observed and first fulfilled the said maiour comaundet two of his chaumberleyns, that is to say Peris Cooke and John Petty, and also Thomas Davyson to giff ther attendaunce apon the said seircheours, which according to the same (de) they did.

Bond to Accept Arbitration
8 April 1489

Memorandum quod viij° die Aprilis anno iiij^{to} regni regis Henrici vij^{mi} in camera consilii civitatis Ebor' Corandus Gossep (et), Robertus Burnet cord[wainer] et Willelmus Robynson (ffo) ffullour comparentes coram Johanne Harper maiore civitatis Ebor', assumpserunt et eorum cuiuslibet assumpsit pro seipso in x libris legalis monete Anglie ⟨de⟩ bonis et catallis ipsorum et eorum cuiuslibet levandis ad opus domini regis quod ipsi et eorum quilibet stabunt et perimplebunt ordinacioni, arbitrio et iudicio Johannis Huton potter, (Willelmi Barker mercatoris) ⟨et⟩ Petri Cooke (et Joh') arbitratorum ex parte dicti Corandi electorum, (J) Willelmi Barker mercatoris et Johannis Robynson arbitratorum pro parte dictorum Roberti et Willelmi Robynson electorum ⟨ad arbitrandum⟩ de et super omnibus et singulis querelis, transgressionibus, contraversiis, debitis, debatis et demandis inter predictas partes habitis, motis sive pendentibus, a principio mundi usque in diem confeccionis presencium, ita quod eadem ordinacio, arbitrium et judicium dictorum arbitratorum in forma predicta electorum fiant et reddantur inter partes predictas citra festum Pasche proximum futurum post datam prescriptam, et si predicti arbitratores inter se citra eundem festum concordare non poterint nec dicte partes ad pacem (trx) traxerunt tunc predicti Corandus, Robertus et Willelmus Robynson stabunt et perimplebunt et quilibet eorum stabit et perimplebit ordinacioni, arbitrio et judicio Henrici Williamson imparis in hac parte indiferenter per maiorem electi, ita quod ordinacio, arbitrium et judicium dicti Henrici imparis fiat et reddatur ⟨inter partes predictas⟩ citra festum Sancte Elene extunc proximo sequentem etc.

[On 8 April 1489, in the council chamber of York, Corand Gossep, cordwainer Robert Burnet, and fuller William Robynson appeared before mayor John

Harper and each bound himself for £10 levied of his goods and chattels that they would adhere to and carry out the ordinance, arbitration and judgement of potter John Huton and Peter Cooke, arbiters elected on Corand's side, and [arbiters] merchant William Barker and John Robynson on the side of the said Robert and William, over all complaints, trespasses and controversies had, moved, or pending between them from the beginning of the world to the day these presents [bonds] were made, the said judgement to be made and rendered by Easter next coming, and if the arbiters are unable to agree and lead the parties to peace, then Corand, Robert and William will adhere to and carry out the judgement of Henry Williamson, umpire, impartially elected by the mayor, whose judgement is to be made and rendered by the next coming feast of Saint Helen.]

[f.141v]   Thomas Wandesford Leaves Sheriff's Custody, Offers Bond for Own Good Behavior
13 February 1489

xiij° (xij) die Februarii

Mayor: Robert Hancok. Mayor elect: John Harper. 12: Thomas Wrangwish, William Chymney, William White. 24: Thomas Catour, Thomas Allan, William Spence, John Hagg, Richard Clerk, Richard Hardesang, Michael White, Miles Grenebank, William Barker, Thomas Fynch.

At the which day it was laid by the right wirshupful sir Robert Hancok maiour that it wasnot oute of ther remembraunce how the iiij^t day of this present moneth Thomas Wandesford gent[leman] was sent for, apperid within this counsell chaumber, and ther and then shewid unto hym how that it was complenyd that he shold contrarie the maiour comaundment toke the keis of Bouthom barr and openyd the same barr, as in the act (of the) aforsaid doeth appere; he for the same his oversigh[t] in that put hym to the correccion of the maiour and his brethern, and (theie) the same Thomas for that offence was thoght ther couth no les be than to commyt hym to prison, and yit notwithstonding for his lowlie submission it was avodet the prison and put towarde of Thomas Gray oon of the shireffes and with hym remayned by the space of thre days, and efter that thre days he fond suretie to appere tofore the counsell this day; at this same day he apperid and forther answerd that for his said oversight he hath ben sufficientlie punysshed, trusting forther they wilbe his goode maisters and to that he humblie besechith thame; and so for his curtas saing it was thoght that he sholdbe bound in a hundreth pound of laufull money of England tobe redy at all tymez within xiiij days of this present day to appere, to the which he agreith tobe bound in maner felowing:

(Thomas Wandesford gent' venit in propria persona coram presentibus et manucepit pro seipso quod ipse de die in diem paratus pro seipso in centum marcis legalis monete Anglie.)

Thomas Wandesford gent[leman] Thomas Wandesford gent' coram Roberto Hancok maiore et aliis prescriptis in camera concilii ⟨civitatis⟩ predicte xiij° die Februarii anno iiij^{to} regni regis Henrici septimi comparens assumpsit pro seipso in C libris legalis monete Anglie solvendis et levandis de bonis et catallis, terris et tenementis suis ad usum et proficium dicti domini nostri regis quod ipse aliquo tempore infuturum a dicto xiij° die mensis **[f.142]** Februarii usque vicesimum septimum diem eiusdem mensis extunc proximi sequentis super premunicionem littera sibi facta sigandeat viribus suis personaliter comparebit et in omnibus paratus erit ad respondendum quibuscumque rebus seu materiis que sibi et adversus eum quovismodo obicientur, ex parte dicti domini regis seu alterius cuiuscumque, et quod decetero habebit se magis paciface tam in verbis quam in factis etc.

[*Thomas Wandesford, gentleman* Thomas Wandesford, gentleman, appeared before mayor Robert Hancok and all the abovewritten in the city's council chamber on 13 February 1489 and bound himself for £100, paid and levied of his goods and chattels, lands and tenements to the use and profit of our lord king, that at any time between the thirteenth day of **[f.142]** February and the twentieth-seventh day of that month, Wandesford will be prepared to respond to any and all things brought against him on behalf of the lord king and any others, and that henceforth he behave peacefully in words and deeds.]

Sheriff of Yorkshire Ignores City's Rights and Privileges
8 and 13 March 1489

The restoring of the body of William Thweyng Memorandum the viij day of March the iiij^t yere of the reign of Kyng Henry the vij^t ⟨that⟩ it was shewed to the right wirshupful sir John Harper maiour that by the comaundment of Sir Marmaduc Constable knyght and shireff of Yorkeshire, contrarie the libertiez and ffraunchesse of this cite, comaundet by force of his office of ⟨the⟩ said shirefwyk oon sir William Thweyng gentilman beyng present tofore the said shireff in his loging, than being loged in the prior place of Bridlington ⟨with⟩ in Aldwerk within the cite of Yorke, to the castell thare surelie tobe kept for such matters at that tyme hym ⟨movyg⟩ movyng for the arrest and comaundment of the shireff aforsaid; the said right wirshupful sir John Harper maiour sent ⟨Marmaduc⟩ ⟨Humfrey⟩ Maners the berer of the gylt maise unto the said shireff, shewing hym that contrarie the said libertiez and grauntes etc., that it hath ben ⟨shewing⟩ shewid to the maiour that he hath comaundet the said William Thweyng to the castell etc., shewing hym over that withoute that be refourmyd and he restoryd to the officers of the cite of York, it wolbe complenyd unto the kinges juges being at the assise and ⟨gale⟩ gaole delyvere ⟨hol⟩ next assigned at Yorke of Monday in the secund weke of Lent. The said shireff understonding the said message and that he had overseen hym self in his said comaundment contrarie the said grauntes and libertiez, graunted withoute eny forther compleynt to deliver the said William Thweyng to the officerez of the said cite and over that to shewe hym self to the said maiour at his pleasour to amend the said his oversight and defalt etc., and apon that the xiij day of this present moneth of March the said Sir Marmaduc Constable shireff delyverd the body of the said William Thweing ⟨owte of the said castell⟩ to John Sponer and Roland Robson seriantes to the maise, and they at that tyme so being charged with the body of the said William Thweyng delyverd hym to the keping of the shireffes of York in conservation of the said grauntes and libertiez.

[f.142v]   **Selection of Moremasters, Bridgemasters, and Chamberlain, and Deputation Sent to Earl of Northumberland 16 February 1489**

Die Lune in festo Sancte Juliane

Mayor: Robert Hancok. Mayor elect: John Herper. 12: Thomas Wrangwish, Nicholas Lancaster, William Chymney, William White. Counsellor: Thomas Asper. Sheriff: Thomas Gra. 24: Thomas Allan, Henry Williamson, William Tayte, William Spence, Richard Clerk, John Hagg, Miles Grenebank, Richard Hardesang, Thomas Fynch, Roger Appilby, John Shawe, Robert Johnson.

At the which day the said presence of oon assent and consent elect and chose for this yere ensuyng to be the moremaisters of this cite Master Thomas Wharf and John Tirrell, or els to pay and content withoute pardon the penylte therof maid.

Item the same day it is agreid that Henry Albeyn elect and chosyn tobe oon of the brigmaisters of Ouse brig forsomuch as he have ⟨ben⟩ required according to the auncient custom of this cite to tak his oth, and he that denyed and refused, that the said Henry so abiding contrarie the said his eleccion to content and pay C s. withoute pardon, and the same Henry to stond at his iuperdie at all tymez herafter to be elect and chosyn in the same office.

Item the same day it is agreid according to a peticion ⟨the⟩ this same day presentid ⟨by⟩ bill that immediatelie efter the commyng home of the right noble lorde therle of Northumbreland, that two or thre with othre accompenyd shall ryde unto his said lordship shewing hym the myndes of the communaltie of this cite laid and shewid in the said bill, and to thentent his lordship if ther be eny mysreporte maid unto hym may be acertanyd of the treuth.

Item the same day James Lounesdale newe elect to be oon of the chaumberleyns for this yere ensuyng was sent for tofore the said presence, and ther and then his oth of the chaumberlanship to tak ⟨was laid upon hym⟩; he that denyed and refused, saing that he had a discharge for that office and all othre under the common seall etc., apon ⟨that forther⟩ it ⟨b⟩ was laid unto ⟨hym⟩ he for to tak that office apon hym shodbe recontent and paid of the x marcs which he paid to the behufe of the commonaltie in maner and ⟨forme⟩ fourme as Thomas Knollez is graunted withoute delay, and apon that he tuke his othe etc.

[f.143]   **Discharge of Bridgemaster**
                20 February 1489

xx^{mo} die Februarii

Mayor: John Harper. 12: William Chymney, Robert Hancok. Sheriff: Thomas Gra. 24: Thomas Catour, William Spence, William Tayte, Richard Clerk, John Hag, Miles Grenebank, Richard Hardesang, Michael White, Thomas Fynch, John Shawe, Robert Johnson.

Assembled in the counsaill chambre determyned that the act tofore past toching Henry Albeyn elect tobe brigmaister of Ousebrig, which penaltie to stand in strenthe and vertu, and tobe paid withoute eny pardon therof, that doon he tobe for that occupation of forther occupying tobe utterlie discharged.

Bond to Keep the Peace
9 April 1489

ix° die Aprilis anno iiij^{to} regni regis Henrici vij^{mi} [R] *Georgius Kirke mercator, Jacobus Kirke goldsmyth* Manucapcio Ricardi Smalez capellani et rectoris ecclesie parochie Omnium Sanctorum in Northstrete in Ebor' quod ipse dampnum vel malum aliquod corporale Johanni Rayner capellano vel alicui de populo domini regis non faciet nec fieri procurabit quovismodo quilibet manucaptorum sub pena x librarum, et predictus Ricardus Smalez sub pena xx librarum de bonis et catallis suis ad opus regis levandarum.

[9 April 1489, merchant George Kirke, goldsmith James Kirke Mainprise of Richard Smalez, chaplain and rector of the parish church of All Saints in North Street, York, that he do neither damage nor bodily harm to chaplain John Rayner nor to any other of the king's subjects, nor cause any harm to be done whatsoever, under penalty of £20 levied of his goods and chattels, his sureties bound for £10.]

[f.143v]   **New Sheriff's Oath Delayed**
                23 February 1489

xxiij^{cio} die Februarii

Mayor: John Harper. 12: Nicholas Lancastre, William Chymney, Robert Hancok, William White. Sheriffs: Thomas Foulneby, Thomas Graa. 24: Thomas Catour–jur[ator?], Henry Williamson, (Richard) ⟨William⟩ Spence, William Tayte, Richard Clerk, Richard Hardesang, John Hagg, Michael White–jur[atores?], Miles Grenebank, Thomas Fynch, John Shaw, Robert Johnson.

Wer assembled in the counsaill chaumbre and ther and then determyned and concludet that Thomas Foulneby, oon of the shireffes of this wirshupful cite, forsomuch as ⟨he⟩ was required to tak his othe pertenyng to the counsaill according to the auncient custom of this said cite and as other both alderman, the other the shireff his brothre, and the xxiiij^ti above present hath takyn the which, he desired of of [sic] a respect in that behalf unto the tyme that Master York and Master Todd knyghtes be common home etc., at the which tyme he wilbe redy to accomplissh all and every thing to that belonging etc., the said maiour and all othre above writen understanding his desire yaf the said Thomas Folneby his peremptore day to yif answer upon Thursday next etc.

Bond to Keep the Peace
28 March 1489

xxviij° die Marcii anno iiij^to regni regis Henrici vij^mi Manucaptio Johannis Chelorer de Acom' iuxta Ebor' in comitatu civitatis Ebor' wever quod ipse dampnum vel malum aliquod corporale Ricardo Bentley (et de morte et mutulatis membrorum suorum) vel alicui de populo domini regis non faciet nec fieri procurabit quovismodo videlicet quilibet manucaptorum sub pena x librarum, et predictus Johannes Chalorer sub pena xx librarum de bonis et catallis suis ad opus dicti domini regis levandarum, videlicet Willelmus Moreson couper, Thomas Roger milner, Thomas Robynson glover, et Thomas Watson couper.

[*28 March 1489* Mainprise of weaver John Chelorer of Acomb next to York in the county of the city of York, that he do no damage nor bodily harm to Richard Bentley nor to any other of the king's subjects, nor cause any harm to be done whatsoever; his sureties, namely cooper William Moreson, miller Thomas Roger, glover Thomas Robynson, and cooper Thomas Watson under penalty of £10, and the said Chelorer under penalty of £20 levied of his goods and chattels to the work of the said lord king.]

[f.144]   King's Letter Read, Sheriff Takes Oath
24 February 1489

xxiiij^to die Februarii

Mayor: John Harper. 12: Nicholas Lancastre, Robert Hancok, William White, John Gylliot–juratores. Counsellor: Thomas Asper. Sheriffs: Thomas Foulneby–jurator, Thomas Graa. 24: Thomas Allan, Henry Williamson, William Spence, John Hagg, William Tayte, Richard Clerk, (John Hag) Richard Clerk, Michael White, Richard Hardesang, William Barker–juratores, Thomas Fynch, John Shawe, Roger Appilby, George Kirke–juratores, Robert Johnson.

At the which day wer assembled in the Guidhall and in the counsaill chambre ther the said presence, and ther and (du) then the kinges gracious lettres missyves was shewed closed to hym, his brethern aldermen and the commonaltie direct, which (shewed) shortlie efter the same day was disclosed and openlie red in the said hall tofore the hole communaltie. And also the same day Thomas Foulneby shireff toke his (the) oth in the said counsaill chaumbre.

Bond to Keep the Peace
28 March 1489

xxviij° die Marcii anno iiij^{*to*} *regni regis Henrici vij*^{*mi*} Manucapcio Ricardi Ivenson de Scardeburgh in comitatu Ebor' mercator alias ffissher quod ipse dampnum vel malum aliquod corporale Willelmo Bailley vel alicui de populo domini regis non faciet nec fieri procurabit quovismodo videlicet quilibet manucaptorum subscriptorum sub pena x librarum, et predictus Ricardus sub [pena] xx librarum de bonis et catallis ad (app) opus domini regis levandarum si etc.; Willelmus Freston de Ebor' wever, Willelmus Wodd de Ebor' et (Es) Eustaquis Hunter de Ebor' belman.

[*28 March 1489* Mainprise of merchant Richard Ivenson of Scarborough, Yorkshire, that he do no damage nor bodily harm to William Bailley nor to any other of the king's subjects under penalty of £20 levied of his goods and chattels to the work of the lord king; his sureties, namely weaver William Freston, William Wodd, and bellman Eustace Hunter, each bound themselves under penalty of £10.]

[f.144v]   Mayor Forgives Miller's Slander
**   3 March 1489**

Memorandum the third day of March the iiij^t yere of the reign of King Henry the vijth in the counsaill chaumbre of Ousebrig oon Robert Slater milner commit to prison for certan sediciouse language by hym uttered and said under the fourme felowing: the said Robert confessed that or ever he sawe the right wirshupful sir John Harpour maiour that he emonges feliship where he sat shold shew and say emonges thame that he was ffraunchest, and the day of his fraunchissing the said maiour shold question hym where he dwelt and he answerd and said, 'without Boutham', the maiour shold answer and say, 'thou art oon of thame that was ayanest me; well, I shall bring ⟨you⟩ in this by oon and oon'; and this same day eftsonez the maiour sent for the said Robert [who] was broght in by Robert Wallez the gaoler, and ther and then the said maiour being in the counsaill chaumbre and with hym present the chaumberleyns, the maister (T) of the taillours, and other, the said [Robert] humble besoght the said maiour tobe his good and tender lorde and to forgyve hym of his greit defalt; and at the request of the (maiour) said maister of the tailours and othre the said Robert was dismissed of prison unto the tyme that the said maiour wer otherwise advised by his counsaill and under the condicion that he shold be redy to appere in his propre person at such tyme as he wer sent for, and apon that the said maister of the taillours be cam suretie at all tymez to inlawe the said Robert at the comaundment of the mairour etc.

[f.145]   Disturbances at Mayoral Election
**   5 March 1489**

v^{to} die Marcii

Mayor: John Harper. 12: Richard York, Thomas Wrangwich, William Chymney, William Todd–juratores, Robert Hancok, William Whit, John Giliot. Recorder: John Vavasour.

Sheriffs: Thomas Fulnatby, Thomas Grey. 24: Alan Baxster, Thomas Catour, Henry Williamson, William Spense, William Tayte, John Hagg, Richard Clerc, Miles Grenebaunk, Richard Hardsang, Thomas Fynche, William Barker, George Kyrk.

At this day John Vavasour, Sir Richard York ⟨and⟩ Sir William Todd by force of the credence yeven unto theme by the king as touchyng (y) his noble mynde deliverd and his letters direct lately unto the maier, aldermen and communaltie of this citie shewed the kinges mynde was to have dew examinacion made of the demeanaunce had at thellection (of) of the sade maier etc., such riotes as shallbe funden to be (punyshed founden) punyshed accordyng to his lawes, and for an ordour in the partie the sade recordour on the kinges behalf willed and requird the sheriffes to ⟨make⟩ indifferent pannell at same tyme as the sade examinacion shalbe had.

Bond to Accept Arbitration
11 June 1489

Memorandum quod xj° die Junii anno regni regis Henrici vij^mi [*year omitted*] (vener') ⟨venit⟩ personaliter (tam) Thomas Appelby porter coram Johanne Harper maiore et recognovit se debere domino regi xx libras de bonis et catallis suis levandas ad opus domini regis quod ipse stabit et perimplebit ordinacioni, arbitrio et judicio Johannis Thomson, Edwardi Forster, Johannis Hopkynson et Dionisii Brokden arbitratorum indiferenter electorum de et super omnibus et omnimodis accionibus, transgressionibus, contraversiis, debatis et demandis inter predictum Thomam Appelby et Willelmum Symson porter; et predictus Thomas Appilby ex parte sua bene et fideliter perimplebit (ex) ordinacioni et judicio predictorum arbitratorum, ita quod eadem ordinacio, arbitrium et judicium dictorum arbitratorum inter partes predictas fiant et reddantur citra Dominicam proximam post festum natalis Sancti Johannis Baptisti proximum etc.

[On 11 June, porter Thomas Appelby came personally before mayor John Harper and bound himself to owe the lord king £20 levied of his goods and chattels that he will adhere to and carry out the ordinance, arbitration and judgement of John Thomson, Edward Forster, John Hopkynson and Dennis Brokden, arbiters impartially elected over all actions, trespasses and debates between Thomas Appelby and porter William Symson; Thomas Appilby on his part will well and faithfully carry out the judgement of the arbiters, which is to be made and rendered by the Sunday after the feast of the Nativity of Saint John the Baptist next coming.]

[f.145v]   Delegation Sent to Earl of Northumberland
**   6 March 1489**

vj^to die Marcii

Mayor: John Harper. Recorder: John Vavesour. 12: Richard York knight, Thomas

Wrangwissh, Nicholas Lancastre, William Todd knight, Robert Hancok, William White. Sheriff: Thomas Gra. 24: Thomas Allan, Richard Clerk, John Hagg, Richard Hardesang, Thomas Fynch, John Shawe, George Kirke.

At the which day wer assembled in the counsaill chaumbre of Ousebrig the said presens, and ther and then determyned that the right wirshupfull sirs Master Nicholas Lancastre and William White aldermen, Thomas Fynch, (George Kirke) ⟨John Shawe⟩ [of the] xxiiij^{ti}, Master John Haryngton common clerk, and William Neleson oon of the chaumberleyns shall ryde unto the right noble lorde therle of Northumberland aswele shewing hym the myndes of the cocetysyns by thame put in (by) to the maior, aldermen and the common counsaill by bill of Saynt Julian day last past as othre concernyng the publique wele of the said cite etc., and also shewing unto his said lordship the reule and guyding of the eleccion of the maiour apon Saynt Blaise day last.

Bond to Accept Arbitration
4 April 1489

Memorandum quod quarto die Aprilis anno iiij^{to} regni regis Henrici septimi Robertus Grene sissor et Johannes Custance junior mercator personaliter comparentes coram Johanne Harper maiore civitatis Ebor' assumpserunt et eorum alter assumpsit pro seipso in xx libris legalis monete Anglie solvendis et levandis de bonis et catallis ipsorum Roberti et Johannis Custance quod ipsi et eorum alter stabunt et perimplebunt ordinacioni, arbitrio et judicio (Georum) Georgii Essex, Willelmi Stubbes, Roberti Goldsmyth et Willelmi Barton taillour arbitratorum tam ex parte dicti Roberti quam ex parte dicti Johannis indiferenter per dictum maiorem (ad) electorum de et super omnibus querelis, transgressionibus, contraversiis et aliis offensiis inter predictos Robertum et Johannem a principio mundi usque in diem confeccionis presencium motis, habitis et factis, et eadem ordinacio, arbitrium et judicium fiant et reddantur citra Dominicam in Ramispalmarum proximam futuram et quod dicte partes gerent pacem dicti domini in medio tempore etc.

[On 4 April 1489, tailor Robert Grene and merchant John Custance junior personally appeared before mayor John Harper and bound themselves for £20 paid and levied of their goods and chattels that they will adhere to and carry out the ordinance, arbitration and judgement of George Essex, William Stubbes, Robert Goldsmyth and tailor William Barton, arbiters impartially elected by the mayor on the side of both Robert and of John, and over all complaints and trespasses moved, had or made between Robert and John from the beginning of the world to the day these presents [bonds] were made, this judgement to be made and rendered by Palm Sunday next coming, the said parties to keep the peace in the meantime.]

**[f.146]   Earl of Northumberland's Letter Read
10 March 1489**

x^{mo} die Marcii

Mayor: John Harper. Recorder: John Vavesour. 12: Richard York knight, Thomas Wrangwish, Master Nicholas Lancastre, William Chymney, William Todd, Robert Hancok, William White, John Gylliot. Sheriffs: Thomas Foulneby, Thomas Graa. 24: Thomas Catour, Thomas Allan, Henry Williamson, William Spence, William Tayte, John Hag, Richard Clerk, Miles Grenebank, Richard Herdesang, Thomas Fynch, Roger Appilby, John Shawe, George Kirke.

Assembled in the counsaill chambre and ther and then a lettre missive direct from the right prepotent lord therl of Northumberland to the maiour, aldermen, and common counsaill of the cite of York, which lettre was opynlie redd and understond his noble mynde conteigned in the same, which lettre remaneth in keping in the hondes of the said maiour and the tenour therof ensueth [*sic, contents not copied into record*].

**[f.146v]   Attendance List
17 March 1489**

The xvijth day of March

Mayor: John Harper. 12: Richard Yorke knight, Thomas Wrangwish, Master Nicholas Lancastre, William Chymney, William Todd knight, Robert Hancok, William White, John Gylliot. Sheriffs: Thomas Folneby, Thomas Graa.

**Bond to Accept Arbitration
20 March 1489**

recognitio inter Grene et Flesshewer Memorandum quod xx^{mo} die mensis Marcii anno iiij^{to} regni regis Henrici septimi Robertus Grene taillour et Johannes Flesshewer fissher coram Johanne Harper maiore civitatis Ebor' personaliter comparentes assumpserunt et alter eorum per se assumpsit pro seipso in viginti libris bone et legalis monete Anglie levandis de bonis et catallis eorundem et alterius eorum ad opus domini nostri regis, quod ipsi Robertus et Johannes et eorum alter stabunt et obedient ac stabit et obediet laudo, ordinacioni et judicio Willelmi Tayte, Georgii Kirke, Johannis Huton coci et Willelmi Barker mercatoris arbitratorum tam ex parte dicti Roberti quam ex parte dicti Johannis Flesshewer indiferenter electorum et nominatorum, in, de et super omnibus et omnimodis accionibus, transgressionibus, querelis, debitis, debatis et demandis inter partes predictas motis, exortis et pendentibus, a principio mundi usque in diem confeccionis presencium, et eadem ordinacio, arbitrium et judicium dictorum quatuor arbitratorum inter partes predictas fiant et reddantur citra Dominicam in Ramispalmarum proximam futuram, et quod dicte partes inter se (de) gerent ⟨pacem⟩ dicti domini regis in medio tempore sub pena predicta.

[*bond between Grene and Flesshewer* On 20 March 1489, tailor Robert Grene and fisherman John Flesshewer personally appeared before mayor John Harper and bound themselves for £20 levied of their goods and chattels, that they would adhere to and carry out the advice, ordinance and judgement of William Tayte, George Kirke, cook John Huton and merchant William Barker, arbiters impartially elected and named by the mayor between Robert and John, over all actions, trespasses and complaints moved, arisen and pending between the said parties, from the beginning of the world to the day these presents [bonds] are made, this judgement to be made and rendered by Palm Sunday next coming, and the said parties to keep the peace of the lord king in the meantime under the aforementioned penalty.]

[f.147]   Investigation of Election Disturbance
19 March 1489

xix° die Marcii

Mayor: John Harper. Recorder: John Vavesour. 12: Richard Yorke knight, Thomas Wrangwissh, Nicholas Lancastre, William Todd knight, William White, John Gylliot. Sheriff: Thomas Graa. 24: Thomas Allan, Henry Williamson, John Hagg, Thomas Fynch, George Kirk. From the council of the earl of Northumberland: the knights William Eure, Gerevall Clyfton, John Pikering. Legal Counsellors: Edward Redeman, William Babthorp, William Chaumberleyn, (R) Brian Palmer.

Assembled in the counsaill chambre within the Guydhall of the cite of Yorke, and ther and then it was shewid by the right wirshupful Sir Richerd York knyght ⟨and Sir William Todd knyght⟩ the credence the which was comaunded (hym) ⟨thayme⟩ to shewe by the kinges grace unto the maiour and (commalit) the communaltie of this ⟨cite⟩ as toching the unkyndlie deling of the cocitesyns at ther eleccion apon Saynt Blaise day last, as in the kynges gracious lettres missives more planelie doeth appere, which (he) ⟨they⟩ shewid in nowise the kinges grace woldnot bot that tobe ponysshed, and apon that for the correccion of ⟨the same⟩ the kinges grace shewid forther unto (hym) ⟨theym⟩ he wold have a commission tobe direct unto the moost reverend ffadder in God tharchiebisshop of York, therl of Northumberland and othre to inquir etc., to thentent his highnes may be acertanyd apon the said dealing; and apon ⟨that⟩ the said counsaill of this cite every man by hym self was examyned as toching the said commission; they and every of thame determyned it warr necessarie according to the kinges mynde and pleasour to have the same not tobe labored at the request ne pursuyte of the said maiour and counsaill in eny wise, bot at it myght be at the request of the said moost reverend fadder in God, and that tobe doon the said Sir Gervax Clyfton and Sir John [Pikering] knyghtes afferd thame self to mak labour to the said moost reverend fadder in God so that the right wirshupful Sir Richerd York and Sir William Todd knyghtes wold do the labour to go with thaim, etc., to the which they agreid, the said maiour and counsaill shewing and sayng that the same labour ne suyt not to be in ther namez etc.

**[f.147v]   Collection of King's Tax, Replacement of Absent Chamberlain
                March 1489**

[*blank*] die Marcii

Mayor: John Harper. Recorder: John Vavesour. 12: Richard Yorke knight, Thomas
Wrangwish, John Newton, Nicholas Lancastre, William Chymney, Robert Hancok. Sheriffs:
Thomas Foulneby, Thomas Gra. 24: Thomas Catour, Thomas Allan, Henry Williamson,
William Tayte, Richard Clerk, John Hagg, Miles Grenebank, Richard Hardesang, William
Barker, Thomas Fynch, Roger Appilby, George Kirke.

This day assembled in the counsaill chaumbre it was shewid by the mouth ⟨of⟩
the recorder that he had commoned with Thomas Wandesford gent[leman], oon of
the collectours of the kinges tax, and the same Thomas shewed unto hym so that he
myght have a reward etc., and also that he may have sufficiant suretie for his
discharge he wolbe of goode will to ⟨al⟩ delyver all such money as he hath in his
hondes of the secund half tax.

Item the same day it is agreid that forsomuch as Thomas Derby which was elect
tobe oon of the chaumberleyns apon Saynt Blaise day last (is no) was not at home
at the day of (this) ⟨his⟩ eleccion and ne yit is, and also no certantie of his
commyng home, that forsomuch as the place (myght) ⟨must⟩ be kept and suche
chargez as belongeth unto the same must be content and paid, have elect and
chosyn tobe chaumberleyn in the rowme of the said Thomas Darby, Robert Tutbag
merchaunt.

**[f.148]   Attack in City Streets
                28 March 1489**

Be it in mynde the xxviij day of Marche the iiij[t] yere of the reign of King Henry the
seventh, cam personalie tofore John Harper maiour within his mancion place oon
Brian Dereson dier, and shewyd unto ⟨the⟩ said maiour howe he being in
Goddes peax and the kinges as he was walking in a strete callid (Ousebrig)
Ousegate, John (Martyndale) Barrowdale cordwener met hym and shewid shortlie
unto hym saing, 'I owe the a stripe'; the said Brian (said) answerd and said unto
hym, 'I ow the noon', and sodanlie stroke hym with his fyst apon the eire, and efter
that cast hym under his fete saing that he shold strike hym throgh with his dagger
and than left hym at that tyme withoute more hurt, saying unto hym that at thare
next metyng he shold pay hym better; the said Brian fering his sayng desired the
said maiour that ⟨he⟩ myght be and stond in rest, (and) and apon that the
maiour sent Roland Armorer, oon of the yoman seriantes to the maise, for the said
Burowdale, ⟨he being in John Sponer house⟩, saing unto hym 'ye must com
unto the maiour'; he answerd and said he woldnot, and so the same John
Barrowdale departed from thense and went to Mitford taverne; the said Roland
understode that and fillod hym to the same tavern, and ther oon Thomas Smyth
cordwener becam suretie for the same John Barrowdale to bring unto the maiour at
what tyme he wold send for hym, and in the mean ⟨season⟩ cam diverse

cocitesyns unto the maiour shewing unto hym thai wold not suffre such reule at ther neghbours so to be bet, and for inconvenients that myght fall by reason of the same, the said maiour went unto the said tavern with his ffelliship for the same John Barrowdale and ther sent the said Roland unto hym to bid hym com to hym, and the same Roland fulfilled the maiours commaundment and cam to the same Barrowdale, he being in a chaumbre, saing unto hym, 'my lord maiour is at the tavern dore and woll that ye shal com to speke with hym', and he shortlie answerd and said he woldnot, and apon ⟨that⟩ drugh his dagger and wold aben apon the said officer, he seing that stirt bak and for his suretie drugh his knyfe and so arrestid the same John Barrowdale, and broght hym to the said maiour, and for his disabeing the said maiour commyt hym unto the prison ther to abide unto the tyme he fynd suretie of his goode bering.

[f.148v]   Selection of New Chamberlain
1 April 1489

Primo die Aprilis

Mayor: John Harper. 12: Richard Yorke knight, Thomas Wrangwish, Master Nicholas Lancastre, William Chymney, William Todd knight, Robert Hancok, William White, John Gylliot. Counsellor: Thomas Asper. 24: Thomas Catour, William Tayt, Thomas Fynch, Richard Clerke, Roger [sic] Kirke, Miles Grenebank.

Robert Tutbagge Assembled in the counsaill chaumbre of Ousebrig, and ther and [then] it was fully determyned and concludet fforsomuch as Thomas Darby merchaunt the which with othre was chosen apon Saynt Blaise day last to be oon of the chaumberleyns of this cite for this yere ensuyng, which Thomas the said day of eleccion as is knowen wasnot at home ne yit is and no certantie of his commyng home, and greit chargez liez apon the chaumberleyns to be paid shortelie, the which chargez (the) William Neleson and othre his felowez chaumberleyns grogeth and shewid they in nowise wold bere ne content ⟨the same⟩ with⟨owte⟩ thai myght have the sext chaumberleyn named and chosen (therunto) to thame, for the which causez was elect and chosyn Robert Tutbag merchaunt to be chaumberleyn in the place and rowme of the said Thomas Darby; and incontinentlie that doon the said Robert Tutbag was sent for, cam personalie tofore the said presence and ther and then the premissez (⟨laid⟩) be hym shewid ⟨and laid⟩, he curtaslie shewing unto thame saing that he doubtnot bot (as) ⟨at⟩ they wele knewe that he under the common seale of this cite had a discharge in bering that office or eny othre within this said cite for term of his naturall lieff (natwithstanding that he offerd), and for that in the tyme of the right wirshupful sir John Newton maiour [1483–84] he content and paid x marcs of lauful money of England to the behufe of the commonaltie of this said ⟨cite⟩ as in the countes of the chaumberleyns at that tyme more planelie doeth appere. Natwithstanding that he desired that he myght be recontent the said x marcs, and he wold fulfill ther myndes or els to be forborn for the term and tyme (of x yeres) ⟨of x yeres next felowing⟩ from the first day of Aprile (unto the end) aforsaid the iiij^t yere of the reign of our sovereyn

lige lorde King Henry the sevent, of bering of thoffice of shirefwyk within the said
cite, to the which desire the said maiour and all other abovewriten graunted so that
he wold releax the said x marcs they wold graunt unto hym and graunted to forbere
hym so that he wold curtaslie tak the oth **[f.149]** of (of) the chaumberleynship apon
hym and to fulfill all and every [*c.3 words cropped during conservation*] to the same
belonging, he sholdbe forborn and wold forbere hym of the said office of shirefwyk
or eny othre above that to be elect or chosen for the term of viij yeris next ensuyng
the said first day of Aprile [*one word cropped*], except that it be thoght within the
said viij yeris the said Robert be so growen in goodes that he be able to take the
same office apon hym provided alwey that he within the said tyme and term of viij
yeres be not compellid to the same office, and he at eny tyme within the same wolbe
sworn that he is not in substance of goodes etc., to the which he curtaslie submit
hym self to ther desirez, and furthwith toke his oth of chaumberleynship and to
execute and fulfill all and every thing to thame belonging.

Bond to Keep the Peace
6 August 1489

recognitio R. Busby Robertus Busby de Ebor' bocher personaliter comparens in
camera consilii civitatis coram Johanne Harper vj^{to} die Augusti anno iiij^{to} regni
regis Henrici septimi assumpsit pro seipso in xx libris necnon Johannes Gylmon
bocher, Thomas Knaton bocher, Johannes Clerk bocher et Willelmus Smyth
comparentes personaliter loco predicto et coram prefato maiore et alii assumpserunt et eorum quilibet assumpsit pro dicto Roberto Busby in xl libris legalis monete
Anglie solvendis et levandis tam de bonis et catallis dicti Roberti Busby quam
manucaptorum suorum superius nominatorum ad usum et proficium domini nostri
regis quod ipse Robertus Busby aliquo tempore in futuro super premunicionem
legitimam sibi factam si gaudeat viribus suis personaliter comparebit et in omnibus
paratus erit ad respondendum quibuscumque rebus seu materiis que sibi et
adversus eum quovismodo obicientur ex parte dicti domini regis seu alterius
cuiuscumque, et quod decetero habebit se magis pacifice tam in verbis quam in
factis etc., et ulterius dictus Robertus in forma predicta deliberata fuit a prisona ex
assensu et consensu Ricardi Tunstall militis etc.

[*bond of R[obert] Busby* Butcher Robert Busby of York personally appeared in
the council chamber before John Harper on 6 August 1489 and bound himself for
£20, and also butchers John Gylmon, Thomas Knaton, John Clerk and William
Smyth appeared in the same place before the mayor and others and each bound
himself for £40 on Robert's behalf [as sureties], that Robert Busby at any time in
the future will be prepared to respond to whatever things and materials brought
against him by the lord king or others, and that henceforth he act peacefully in
words and deeds, and finally the said Robert was delivered from prison by the
assent and consent of Sir Richard Tunstall.]

[f.149v]   **Earl of Northumberland Attacked and Killed**
                  28 April 1489

xxviij die Aprilis

Mayor: John Harpour. 12: Thomas Wrangwish, John Fereby, Nicholas Lancastre, ⟨William Chymney⟩, Richard Hancok, William White, John Gylliot. Sheriff: Thomas Foulneby. 24: Thomas Catour, ⟨Henry Williamson⟩, William Tayt, Richard Clerk, Richard Hardesang, Thomas Fynch, John Shawe, George Kirk, Robert Johnson.

At the which day assembled oon Thomas Fissher taillour commyng as he said in all gudelie hast from Thriske, and ther and then shewing that affray was this same day in a place beside Thriske (b), and ther and then as he said my lord of Northumberland takyn and hurt by certan commons of the cuntrie ther aboutes. For the suretie of this cite, it is determyned that proclamacions shalbe maid for the king in diverse parties within the same.

Bond to Accept Arbitration
18 November 1489

Memorandum quod xviij° die Novembris anno quinto regni regis Henrici septimi venerunt personaliter coram Johanne Harper maiore civitatis Ebor' Robertus Waryn de Knaresburgh in comitatu Ebor' gent' et Laurencius Cotom de parochia de Garton' in Lancashire yoman, et recognoverunt se debere et eorum alter recognovit se debere domino regi xl libras levandas de bonis et catallis suis ad opus dicti domini regis quod stabunt et eorum alter ⟨per se⟩ stabit ordinacioni, arbitrio et iudicio Johannis ⟨Bankh'⟩ Tenaunt et Thome Bankhouse arbitratorum pro parte dicti ⟨Laurencii Cotom⟩ ⟨Roberti Waryn⟩ nominatorum et electorum, ac Ricardi Thorneton et Christofori Thomlynson arbitratorum pro parte dicti Laurencii Cotom nominatorum et electorum ad arbitrandum inter partes predictas de et super omnibus et omnimodis transgressionibus, contraversiis, debitis, debatis et demandis inter partes predictas aliqualiter motis, habitis sive pendentibus a principio mundi usque in diem confeccionis presencium, ita quod eadem ordinacio, arbitrium et iudicium dictorum iiij⁰ʳ arbitratorum fiant et reddantur inter partes predictas citra diem Martis proximo ⟨post⟩ ⟨ante⟩ festum Conceptionis Beate Marie Virginis proximum futurum, et si dicti arbitratores inter se non concordent per dictum diem Martis quod tunc tam dictus Robertus Waryn quam suprascriptus Laurencius Cotom stabunt et alter eorum ⟨per se⟩ stabit ordinacioni, arbitrio et (jur') judicio dicti Johannis Harper maioris imparis per partes predictas nominati et (lec') electi de et super premissis, ita quod arbitrium alius imparum fiant et reddantur inter partes predictas citra diem Martis proximo post festum Conceptionis Beate Marie Virginis extunc proximum futurum.

[On 18 November 1489, Robert Waryn of Knaresborough, Yorkshire, gentleman, and yeoman Laurence Cotom of the parish of Garton, Lancashire, came personally before mayor John Harper and bound themselves to owe the lord king £40 levied of their goods and chattels that they will adhere to the ordinance, arbitration and judgement of John Tenaunt and Thomas Bankhouse, named and elected arbiters on behalf of Robert Waryn, and also Richard Thorneton and Christopher Thomlynson, arbiters on behalf of Laurence Cotom, over all trespasses and debates moved, had or pending between the said parties from the beginning of the world to the day these presents [bonds] were made, the judgement of the four arbiters to be made and rendered by the Tuesday before the feast of the Conception of the Blessed Virgin Mary next coming; and if the said arbiters are unable to agree by the said Tuesday, then Waryn and Cotom will adhere to the judgement of mayor John Harper, named and elected umpire over all disputes, his judgement to be made and rendered by the Tuesday after the same feast.]

[f.150]   Civic Officers to Stay in York and Guard Against Rising of the Commons
29 April 1489

xxix° die Aprilis

Mayor: John Harper. Recorder: John Vavesour. 12: Richard Yorke knight, John Fereby, John Newton, Nicholas Lancastre, William Todd knight, ⟨William Chymney⟩, Robert Hancok, William White, John Gylliot. Sheriffs: Thomas Foulneby, ⟨Thomas Graa⟩. 24: John [*sic*] Catour, Thomas Allan, Henry Williamson, William Tayte, Miles Grenebank, Michael White, ⟨Richard Clerk⟩, William Barker, Richard Herdesang, Thomas Fynch, John Shawe, Roger [*sic*] Kirke, Robert Johnson.

At the which day the said presence wer assembled in the counsaill chaumbre and ther and then for suretie, tuicion and keping of the kinges cite the maiour commaundet every alderman and othre of the xxiiij^ti in the kinges name our sovereyn lige lorde that noon of thame depart oute of this cite unto the tyme the kinges mynde be forthre understond, and that as they woll answer to the king at thare perell and the imprisonment of ther bodys.

Item the same day it is agreid and determyned that incontinent ther shall thre sharp men ryde in ⟨to the cuntries in⟩ thre parties aboutes this cite to understand the demeanance of the commons and in all goodlie hast to certefie the maiour and the counsaill (to t) to thentent the kinges highnes may be adcertayned of ther demeanance, and this perfitelie and ripelie understondet it is determyned that Richerd Burgh esquire shall ryde and shew that to the kinges grace etc., in all hast possible.

Item the same day it is agreid that the maiour shall send unto ⟨thabbot of⟩ Saynt Mary, the Mynster, Saynt Leonardes [and] the foure ordres of freris that they be redy with such felliship as they ⟨may⟩ mak redy in defensable arrey for keping of this cite as they woll answer to the king.

**[f.150v]   Richard Burgh Rides to King Henry
3 May 1489**

iij die Aprilis [*sic, the sequence of the preceding and following folios dictates a May date*]

Mayor: [John Harper.] 12: Richard Yorke knight, Thomas Wrangwish, William Snawsell, John Fereby, John Newton, Nicholas Lancastre, William Chymney, William Todd knyght, Robert Hancok, John Gylliot. 24: George Kirke, Robert Johnson.

At the which day by the said presence it is concluded and determyned that where tofore this it was agreid that Richerd Burgh esquire and servaunt to the kynges grace shold ride unto his highnes for certain matters etc., and to have attending apon two personez to thentent that oon of thaym may at his commyng to the kinges grace have one of thaym to resorte unto the maiour and the counsaill shewing the kinges mynde etc., and forsomuch as the chambre is gretelie indetted therfore it is determyned and concludet that the said Richerd Burgh shall have and persave apon the chaumberlayns (apon) ⟨of⟩ the city to ⟨his full⟩ cost and charge vj marcs, and the same Richerd no forther to charge ne clame any more money tarie he long tyme or short, and for the said vj marcs he tobere all maner chargez of his horse and othre, the said chaumberleyns and the commones forthre to be discharged.

**[f.151]   Sheriff and Force Allowed to Enter City
3 May 1489**

Et eodem die Aprilis [*sic*] post nonam

Mayor: [John Harper.] 12: Thomas Wrangwish, John ⟨Harper⟩ Fereby, John Newton, William Chymney, William Todd knight, Robert Hancok, John Gylliot. Sheriffs: Thomas Foulneby, ⟨Thomas Gray⟩. 24: Thomas Catour, ⟨Thomas Allan⟩, Henry Williamson, Richard Clerk, Miles Grenebank, William Tayte, Richard Hardesang, Michael White, William Barker, Thomas Fynch, Roger [*sic*] Kirke, Robert Johnson.

At the which tyme the said presence was determyned forsomuch at tofore this it was concluded that what estate commyng with people to the nombre of iij^C or undre ⟨in the kinges name⟩ shall apon the light of the day that he may have tyme and laser convenient to passe furth of this cite to othre placez for loging and relevyng of his people and no longer to terry except he com with such nombre or othre ayanest nyght and of the morowe at a convenient tyme to depart etc. It was so that the right wirshupful Sir Marmaduc Constable knyght and shireff of Yorkshire for certan consideracions hym movyng and for that at he is the kinges officer within the countie of Yorkshire and that he wold have concourse unto the kinges castell of York to execute things con-sernyng his office etc., desired ⟨by his message⟩ that he myght of my lorde maiour ⟨have licence⟩, aldermen and other the common counsaill have licence to com and loge within this cite havyng resorting to the said castell; it was by the said presence that he shold be accept and takyn to the nombre of lx personez or under and at his commyng forthre to have communicacion with hym etc.

[f.151v] **Letters from King Henry and Lord Clifford Read, Latter Refused Entry into City**
4 May 1489

iiij^{to} die Maii

Mayor: John Harper. 12: Richard York knight, John Fereby, John Newton, William Chymney, William Todd knight, Robert Hancok, John Gylliot. Counsellor: Edmund Thwaytes. Sheriffs: Thomas Foulneby, Thomas Graa. 24: Thomas Allan, William Tayte, Michael White, Richard Clerk, Miles Grenebank, Richard Hardesang, Thomas Fynch, John Shawe, George Kirke, Robert Johnson.

At the which day the kinges gracious lettres missives was direct to the maiour and his brethern aldermen bering date at his castel of Hertford the third day of May, which lettre was opynlie red in the counsail chaumbre (t) tofore the said presence, the content wherof with othre was for the tuicion, (so) savegard and keping of this his cite, as in the same more planelie doeth appere.

Item a othre lettre was delyverd to the said maiour and his brethern from Henry Lord Clifford bering date at Skipton the third day of May, the content wherof was to resorte to this cite with such othre lordes, knyghtes and esquirez of the cuntrie the iiij^t day of this same moneth, and here by the advise of the said maiour and the counsail and thame such a ⟨sad⟩ direccion may be takyn as may stand to the pleasour of God, the king and the suretie of this ⟨cite and the⟩ cuntre.

Item efterward the same day the said lettres was red openlie tofore the commones in the comon hall by the advise of the said presence.

Item the same day in the counsail chaumbre it ⟨is⟩ agreid that where the said Lord Clyfford desireth to resorte and be within this cite as is above rehersed, that he shalbe resavyd within the same with a hundreth personez and to have a sad communicacion here with the maiour, his brethern and the common counsail, and to rest here for the space of a day and a nyght (and) ⟨or more etc. if⟩ the commones woll assent and agre unto the same, the which in every braunch was incontinentlie both the lettrez openlie red tofore the commonez in the said hall with also shewed by the mouthez of the maiour, Sir Richerd York and othre, exhorting and movyng thame to the same, to the which thai in nowise wold agre thame to resave the said Lord Clifford ne noon othre, bot at the maiour, aldermen, shireffes and the commonaltie to kepe this same cite to the kinges most roiall person.

[f.152] **Commons Also Refuse Sheriff Entry**
8 May 1489

viij^o die Maii

Mayor: John Harper. 12: Richard York knight, Thomas Wrangwish, John Fereby, John Newton, Nicholas Lancastre, William Chymney, William Todd knight, Robert Hancok,

William White, John Gylliot. Sheriff: Thomas Foulneby. 24: Thomas Catour, Henry Williamson, William Tayt, Richard Clerk, Miles Grenebank, Thomas Fynch, Richard Hardesang, John Shawe, George Kirke, Robert Johnson.

At the which day by the said maiour it was shewed that he had in message from Sir Marmaduduc [*sic*] Constable knyght, sheriff of Yorkshire, that he in the kinges name had warned diverse knyghtes, esquirez and othre gentilmen of the body of Yorkshire to attend apon hym and them within the cite of York apon Monday next (what entent) to thentent that he for the kynges pleasour and in subduyng of the kynges rebelles nowe commotyd and assembled within the northparties etc.; to the which it was answerd ⟨aswel⟩ by the said presence ⟨as the comones⟩ that forsomuch as the kynges grace hath sent is (l) gracious lettres missives to the maiour, shewing and comaunding in the same that this his chaumbre surelie to be kept to the behufe of his ⟨most⟩ roiall person, and forsomuch as they had denyed the entre of the Lord Clifford and othre, that in nowise noon othre gentilman of what (decr) degre or condicion he be of be suffred to enter this the kynges chaumbre, and so all to be excludet etc., and noon to have reule bot the maiour, aldermen and the shireffes.

**[f.152v]   Payment to Chamberlain Confirmed
                14 May 1489**

xiiij° die Maii

Mayor: John Harper. 12: Richard York knight, Thomas Wrangwissh, John Newton, Nicholas Lancastre, William Chymney, ⟨William Todd knight⟩, Robert Hancok, William White, John Gylliot. Sheriffs: Thomas Foulneby, Thomas Graa. 24: Thomas Allan, Richard Clerk, Miles Grenebank, Michael White, Richard Hardesang, William Barker, Thomas Fynch, Robert Johnson.

At the said day the said presence concludet and determyned that the act past in the xv leif [*recte: xi; see above, [f.138v]*] tofore preceding as toching (xx)xxiij li. the which Peris Coke and othre his ffelowez content and paid to John Stokdale, as in the same more largelie doeth appere, shall stand in his strengthe according to the same etc., and not to be chaunged in nowise.

**[f.153]   City Provides Soldiers to Rebel Leader
               17 May 1489**

xvij° (xvj) die Maii

Mayor: John Harpour. 12: Thomas Wrangwish, John Fereby, (John Newton) Nicholas Lancastre, William Chymney, Robert Hancok, William White, John Gylliot. Sheriff: (Thomas Foulneby) Thomas Graa. 24: Henry Williamson, William Tayt, Richard Hardesang, Michael White, William Barker, Thomas Fynch, George Kirk, Robert Johnson.

At the which day ther cam a prest from Sir John Egremond unto the maiour in All Holowez church apon the Payment, shewing unto hym that the said Sir John willed and comaundet hym and his brethren that ther myght be prepared shortlie xx^{ti} pratie men well horsed to attend and go with certain felliship of his into Richemond shire, and that not tobe failled as thai wold answer to hym at ther iuperdie; apon the which message the said maiour sent for the said presence into the said church, shewing unto thame the said message, desiryng thame of ther advise and counsaill in that, apon the which they and every of thame shewed that forsomuch as he had reule and his people here (for), that to denye hym (that) they thoght he and his people wold rob the cite, and if he wold pay ther costes in avoding such iuperdies unto the tyme thai myght be better providet that to graunt hym.

[f.153v] King's Tax and Archbishop of York to Be Kept Safe
17 May 1489

xvij die (May) Maii

Mayor: John Harper. 12: Thomas Wrangwish, John Fereby, John Newton, Nicholas Lancastre, William Chymney, Robert Hancok, William White, John Gylliot. Sheriff: Thomas Gray. 24: Thomas Allan, Henry Williamson, William Tayt, Michael White, Richard Clerk, Thomas Fynch, John Shawe.

At the which day aswele the maiour and aldermen as the common counsail hath of oon assent and consent promised and by this writing bound thame to Peris Coke and othre his felowez late chaumberleyns to save and kepe tham and every of thame harmeles ⟨and withoute hurt⟩ enenst our sovereyn lord the king and all othre in and for the sowme of xvj li. parcell of xxx li., the which they resavyd of Thomas Wandesford gent[leman] and othre his felowez collectours of the kinges tax etc., the which said xvj li. the said Peris Coke and othre his felowez hath content and paid to (Joh) the handes of the said John Harper maiour.

Item the same day it is agreid of oon assent and consent that if thise commonez woll in eny wise of ther malice do hurt bodelie to the most reverend fadder in God that they shall with the hole body of the cocitesyns and inhabitantes of this cite put thame endevour to the resisting of thame.

[f.154] Deputation to Archbishop of York
21 May 1489

xxj (xviij) die Maii

Mayor: John Harpour. 12: Richard York knight, Thomas Wrangwish, John Fereby, Nicholas Lancastre, William Chymney, William Todd knight, Robert Hancok, William White, John Gylliot. Counsellor: Thomas Asper. Sheriff: Thomas Graa. 24: Thomas Catour, Henry Williamson, William Tayt, Richard Clerk, Michael White, Richard Hardesang, William Barker, Miles Grenebank, Thomas Fynch, John Shawe, Robert Johnson.

At the which day assembled for the publique wele of this cite, determyned that Sir Richerd York knyght, John Fereby, (Willelmus) William (Ta) Chymney and William Todd knyght shal go and common with the most reverend ffadder in [God] tharchiebisshop of York, desiring his lordship to be goode lord and mean for this cite unto the kynges g[race].

This byll mayd [*incomplete*]

[f.154v]   City Knights to Ride to King Henry
21 May 1489

xxj die Maii

Mayor: John Harper. 12: Richard York knight, Thomas Wrangwish, John Fereby, John Newton, Nicholas Lancastre, William Todd knight, Robert Hancok, William White, John Gylliot. 24: Michael White, George Kirk, Robert Johnson.

At the which assembled in the counsail chaumbre determyned and concluded that Sir Richerd York and Sir William Todd knyghtes shall ride to mete the kynges grace, shewing to the same the (humb) humblynes of the maiour, his brethren and the hole body of this cite with othre thinges consernyng the publique wele of the same; and also it is determyned that the said [Richard and William] shalhave two jakkettes of the kynges lyvera of sattan, white and grene, contenyng both in the hole (v) ⟨iiij⟩ yerdes ⟨and dimidium⟩, and ethre havyng vj servauntes attending apon hym and every man havyng a jaket of white and grene cloth which shalbe boght by the chaumbreleyns of the common cost.

Bond to Keep the Peace
2 January 1490

[*marginalia faded*] Henricus Blakehay sissor venit coram Johanne Gylliot maiore civitatis, Ricardo Yorke milite aldermanno eiusdem civitatis, custodibus et justiciis domini de pace conservandum infra libertatem civitatis predicte, die Sabbati proximo post festum Sancti Thome Cantuar' anno v^{to} regni regis Henrici septimi et recognovit se debere eidem domino regi xx libras legalis monete Anglie in camera consilii eiusdem civitatis (s) solvendas et levandas de omnibus bonis et catallis suis si Henricus predictus erga ⟨dominum regem⟩ et populum (domini regis) suum amodo transgrediatur aut pacem perturbaverit per se vel suos seu per insur-recciones, confideraciones aut congregaciones illicitas aut per minas, insidias seu aliquo modo que in lesionem seu perturbacionem pacis cedere valeant, et super hoc Magistri Willelmi Burton devenit plegium pro dicto Henrico quod perimpleverit omnibus premissis sub pena forisfactura dicta xx librarum et hoc in propria persona sua concessit solvere etc.

[On the Saturday after the feast of Saint Thomas of Canterbury, tailor Henry Blakehay came before mayor John Gylliot and alderman Sir Richard Yorke, keepers and justices of the peace within the liberty of the city, and bound himself to owe the lord king £20 paid and levied of his goods and chattels if he committed any trespasses or disturbed the peace by himself or others by way of insurrections, confederations or illegal gatherings, or through threats or plots, and over this Master William Burton became a surety for Henry and will carry out all the premisses under penalty of forfeiture of £20 and in his own person agreed to pay etc.]

[f.155] Gift to Archbishop of Canterbury
24 May 1489

xx(ij)⟨iiij⟩ die Maii

Mayor: John Harpour. 12: Richard York knight, (Thomas Wrangwish) John Fereby, John Newton, William Chymney, Robert Hancok, William White, John Gylliot. Counsellor: Thomas Asper. Sheriffs: Thomas Foulneby, Thomas Graa. 24: Thomas Catour, Henry Williamson, William Tayt, Michael White, Thomas Fynch, John Shaw, George Kirk, Robert Johnson.

At the which ⟨day⟩ assembled determyned and concludet that the most reverend fadder in God tharchiebisshop of Canterbury and chaunceller of England shalhave a hogges of clarret wyne and othre of white of the common cost and charge of this cite, to thentent he tobe gode and tender lord to this cite and to be mean to the ⟨kinges⟩ grace for the same. And the chaumberleyns furthwith to mak purviance for the same and to mak it ⟨to be⟩ had unto the said sel of the said lord.

[f.155v] Changes Suggested in Mayoral Elections
25 May 1489

xxv^to die Maii

Mayor: John Harpour. 12: Richard York knight, John Fereby, John Newton, Nicholas Lancastre, William Chymney, William Tod knight, Robert Hancok, William White, John Gylliot. 24: Thomas Catour, William Spence, Henry Williamson, William Tayt, Richard Clerk, ⟨Michael White⟩, Miles Grenebank, William Barker, John Shawe, George Kirk.

At the which day assembled matters laid and shewed etc., for the publique wele of this cite, forsomuch as greit and unkyndlie dealing hath tofor this ben emonges the cocitesyns of this cite in the eleccion of ther maiour, for the pacifying of the same a humble supplicacion to be had unto the kynges grace, shewing unto the same by thassent of the commonaltie of this said cite that the chartour myght be chaunged, and to thentent thre eslites of thame that ben aldermen and have not ben of thre yeres tofore maiour by the commones myght be put (in by) ⟨in⟩, and one of thame by the (advise of the counsaill to be) ⟨eleccion of the maiour, aldermen and the common counsail myght be⟩ takyn as thame shall seme most best for the honour and the common wele of this cite.

[f.156]   More Citizens Deny Lord Clifford Entry
**   26 May 1489**

xxvj^{to} die Maii

Mayor: John (Fereby) Harper. 12: Richard York knight, John Fereby, John Newton, Nicholas Lancastre, William Chymney, William Todd knight, Robert Hancok, William White, John Gylliot. Counsellor: Thomas Asper. Sheriffs: Thomas Folneby, Thomas Gra. 24: William Spence, Henry Williamson, Richard Clerk, Michael White, Thomas Fynch, John Shawe, George Kirk, Robert Johnson.

[*entry torn on right side, with loss of two to three words per line, as noted*] At the which day assembled in the counsail [chamber], and ther and then William Moreson couper which . . . complenyd apon that he shold be oon of thayme [to] denye the commyng in of the Lord Clifford . . . the said William Moreson being in prison . . . was sent for and cam tofore the said pre[sence and] ther and then he denyed the same, shewing how . . . willing (that) the said Lord Clifford to com . . . and (that) at that was true, Sir Richerd York knyght shewed the same etc., and notwithstonding . . . was committed to prison etc.

Item in like case John . . . committed to prison for the same etc.

Item Robert Symson walker examyned in the premissez shewing that day he was not in the hall and so delyverd etc.

Item John Orde[ux was] sent for, examyned in the premissez said in like wise he was not in the common hall that day, and apon . . . Richerd Jeanson which shewid the same efter was sent for, and laid that Robert Symson and John Ordeux was not (ap) at home that day, the said Robert (and John) was dimissed and departed.

Item Thomas Topshawe examyned in the premissez shewid . . . his mynd ⟨⟨(was)⟩⟩ the maiour and aldermen to have reule and no lord ne othre to his . . . entres or reule etc.

Item John Williamson taillour etc., denyed said that he yaf noon such language.

[f.156v]   Incomplete Entry
**   3 June 1489**

iij die Junii anno iiij^{to} regni regis Henrici vij

This same day the kynges high comaundment [*incomplete*]

Payment of King's Tax Kept Safe
23 September 1489

Memorandum the xxiij day of September the fyfte yere of the reyn of our soferan lyghe lord Kyng Herre the vij yn the consell chamber of Owys bryge withyn the cite of Yorke tofor the ryght wyrschipfull sir John Herper then beyng mayre of the sayd cite and chamberlans of the same then and ther beyn present, I Thomas Daynell grantes to sayf and kyepe hermles ⟨from thys day forward⟩ Robert Hankock layt mayre of the sayd cite, Pers Cuk and oder hys chamberlans of xxx pownd by me resayfed of tham a parcel of the fyrst halff qwydecim, that ys to say only for the payment of the same yn the kynges exchequer yn Mykelmes time next commyng, and that then thei trewly payd the same ⟨Thomas⟩ no ferrer to stond of the sayd xxx li. nor oder wyes charged.

[f.157]   **King Orders Defence of City, His Secretary To Receive Profits of Tangfield Common**
5 June 1489

v^{to} die Junii

Mayor: John Harper. 12: Richard York knight, John Fereby, William Snawsell, John Newton, Nicholas Lancastre, William Chymney, Robert Hancok, William White, John Gylliot. Counsellor: Thomas Asper. Sheriff: Thomas Foulneby. 24: William Spence, Richard Clerk, William Barkere, Thomas Fynch, John Shawe, Robert Johnson.

At the which day assembled in the counsaill chaumbre the kinges comaundment was shewid by the mouthez of the said maiour and Sir Richerd York, the content wherof (wh) was that [in] all gudelie hast provision to be maid for the preparing [of this] cite, that is to say in makyng sufficiantlie ther gates and othre necessarie in implementes of wer for the tuicion and savegarde of the same, wherapon it was ordeigned that ther sholdbe a generall request and labour maid throughout this cite for the benevolence of evere man according to his havour to the same, and at the utter gates of every barre and the gates of the posternez to be maid of iren with certan drawe brigges as shalbe thoght necessarie, and also the dikes and walles of this cite to be clensid by thenhabitantes of every warde begynnyng wher it shalbe thoght most nedeful.

Master Oliver Kyng, Tangfeyld Item the same day it is agreid in consideracion of that ⟨at⟩ Maister Oliver Kyng the kynges secretery (prep) prebendarie of Fridathorp and by reason of the same auner of the Tangfeld, the usage of common (therin) wherin from the ffest of Saynt Michel unto our Lady day in Lent yerelie the cocitesyns of this cite hath occupied as ther right, and yit aswell the said maiour, aldermen and counsaill of the said cite as the forsaid cocitesyns clamez as ther right and dewtie of the cite in that behalf, hath promised in all causes and sutes of this cite to be maid unto the kynges highnes for the tyme to be speciall selistour and lovyng frende, that if the said cocitesyns during the pleasour of the maiour, aldermen and counsail shall forbere the (usage) ⟨etage⟩ of the said common, suffring the aforsaid Maister Oliver and his assignez in name of a ffee in the mean tyme to have and persave the profettes of the same, providet alwey that (by) the said abstinence and forbering of usage of common aforsaid shalnot be preiudiciall to the right of the said cite and the cocitesyns of the same, bot at they may enioy the same as far as ther right shall require at such tyme as it shalbe please the said maiour, aldermen and counsaill, that the said ⟨cot⟩ cocitesyns shall reinioy the same common.

Item the same ⟨day all⟩ gates and posternez every day be shet and opyned ayane by the officers of ⟨ther⟩ every gate and posterne according to ⟨the⟩ auncient ordynauncez maid therof.

[f.157v]   Banishment of Two Citizens, Bond to Keep the Peace
5 June 1489

avoidaunce of the cytie Item it is agreid that ⟨Agnes Lister, the wife of Will'⟩ William Lister and Agnes his wife within viij days of this present date shall avoid this cite and suburbes of the same, and the ⟨said⟩ Agnes not to enter this same at eny tyme herefter apon pay[n] of inprisonament xl days, and efter that she to be burned of both hir chekes with a hote iren in tokenyng of a woman of mysreule and unthriftie guyding.

recognitio Manucaptio Ricardi Jeon sissor quod decetero sit fidelis ligens domini regis et quod imposterum ⟨sit honestus⟩ ⟨se bene gerat⟩ maiori, aldermannis et toto consilio civitatis tam in verbis quam aliis condicionibus etc., videlicet Willelmus Robynson wever et Willelmus Robynson walker ⟨quilibet⟩ ⟨uterque⟩ eorum sub pena xx librarum, et predictus Ricardus sub pena xl librarum de bonis et catallis suis levandarum etc., ad ⟨apud⟩ opus domini regis etc.

> [*bond* Mainprise of tailor Richard Jeon that henceforth he be a faithful liege subject of the lord king and that hereafter he behave well towards the mayor, aldermen, and all the city council in words as under other conditions, under penalty of £40 levied of his goods and chattels, and [sureties] namely weaver William Robynson and walker William Robynson each under penalty of £20.]

Delivery of Royal Commission
12 June 1489

Memorandum quod Robertus Jakes serviens domini regis deliberavit maiori civitatis Ebor' commissionem dicti domini regis xij^{mo} die Junii anno regni ⟨eiusdem⟩ sui iiij^{to}.

> [On 12 June 1489, servant of the lord king Robert Jakes delivered a commission of the said king to the mayor of the city of York.]

Problem with Wine Sale in Kingston upon Hull
5 November 1489

certificate Universis et singulis Christi fidelibus ad quorum noticiam presens scriptum pervenerit, Laurencius Swatok maior ville de Kingeston super Hull salutem in Domino sempiternam. Cum nuper datum est michi intellegi quod nuper mota est quedam contraversia et variacionis materia inter venerabilem virum Johannem Harper maiorem civitatis Ebor' parte ex una, et Johannem Metcalf de civitate Ebor' mercatorem parte ex altera pro una pipa rubii vini Gasconie, igitur vobis certifico per presentes quod quidem Robertus Prott de Kingeston predicta mercator die Jovis quinto die Novembris anno quinto regni regis Henrici septimi sua spontanea voluntate apud Kingeston predicta venit coram me prefato Laurencio Swattok maiore ville de Kingeston predicta, Radulpho Langton, Johanne Dalton et Thoma Dalton aldermannis ville de Kingeston predicta et coram me cum predictis aldermannis adtunc et ibidem presentibus per sacramentum Dei evaungelia per ipsum corporaliter tacta, predictus Robertus Prott affirmavit, asseruit et juravit quod ipse erat Ebor' et videbat dictam pipam rubii vini Gasconie et quod dicta pipa rubii vini Gasconie est proprium bonum dicti Johannis Metcalf et quod (quidem) proprietas inde restat prefato Johanni Metcalf et non prenominato Johanni Harper nec Willelmo Carter nec eorum alter. In cuius rei testimonium ego memoratus Laurencius Swattok maior ville de Kingeston predicte ad instanciam et specialem supplicacionem predicti Johannis Metcalf sigillum officii ville de Kingeston predicta presentibus apponi. Data apud Kingeston predicta quinto die mensis Novembris anno regni regis Henrici septimi post conquestum Anglie quinto.

[*certificate* To each and every one of the faithful in Christ to whose notice this present letter reaches, Laurence Swatok mayor of the town of Kingston upon Hull, greetings in the Lord everlasting. Whereas recently I was given to understand that lately a certain dispute and discrepancy in material was moved between the venerable John Harper, mayor of the city of York, on the one side, and John Metcalf of York, merchant, on the other side, for a pipe of red Gascon wine, therefore I certify to you by these presents [letters] that whereas merchant Robert Prott of Kingston on Thursday 5 November 1489 of his free will came before me, the aforesaid Laurence Swatok mayor of Kingston, at Kingston, and before Ralph Langton, John Dalton and Thomas Dalton, aldermen of the aforesaid town, and under sacred oath by touching the gospels declared, asserted and swore that he was at York and saw the said pipe of red Gascon wine which is the property of the said John Metcalf and which should be restored to him and not to the aforenamed John Harper nor to William Carter nor to either of them. In testimony of this, I, the aforesaid Laurence Swattok, mayor of the town of Kingston, at the request and special entreaty of the aforesaid John Metcalf, affix to these presents [letters] the seal of the office of mayor of the town. Given at Kingston 5 November 1489.]

[f.158]   Collection Taken to Build Iron Gates
11 June 1489

xj die Junii

Mayor: [John Harper]. 12: John Fereby, John Newton, Nicholas Lancastre, William (C)
Chymney, Robert Hancok. Counsellor: Thomas Asper. Sheriff: Thomas Foulneby. 24:
William Spence, William Tayte, Richard Clerk, Richard Hardesang, Miles Grenebank,
Thomas Fynch, Robert Johnson.

[*right margin torn, passage transcribed with help from similar entry in YCA E.35,
page 1242*] This same day assembled in the counsail chaumbre [forsomuch] as the
kynges comaundment is that for tuicion and save[guard] of this cite, the utter gates
of every barre and the [posterns be] maid of iren for the perfourmyng of the same in
[all] hast, it is determyned and concluded that the war[dens] of every warde shall
name and chese within ther [ward] vj wele disposed personez, which vj personez
shall [go within] ther warde to move the cocitesyns and inhabitantes [of the same]
what they of ther benivolence woll yiff to the [making] of the said gates and
posterns of iren.

[f.158v]   Bonds to Accept Arbitration and Keep the Peace, Pledges Found for
Husbandman
13 June and 3 November 1489

Memorandum quod xiij° die Junii anno iiij^{to} regni regis Henrici septimi Laurencius
Chaumbre and Christoforus servientes Seth' Snawsell armigeri coram Johanne
Harper maiore civitatis Ebor' comparentes assumpserunt et eorum alter assumpsit
pro seipso in xx libris et (predid) predictus Seth Snawsell assumpsit pro predictis
Laurencio et Christoforo in xx libris; necnon Willelmus Pigod tanner assumpsit pro
seipso in xx libris de bonis et catallis, terris ⟨et⟩ tenementis levandis ad (apud)
opus domini regis eorum et cuiuslibet quod ipsi Laurencius et Christoforus ac
Willelmus Pygod et cuiuslibet eorum stabunt et perimplebunt ac stabit et perimplebit ordinacioni, arbitrio et iudicio Roberti Tubbag, Willelmi Barker, Johannis
Stokdale et Johannis Petty arbitratorum indiferenter electorum de et super
omnibus et omnimodis accionibus tam realibus quam personalibus inter prescriptos
Laurencium et Christoforum ex una parte et Willelmum Pygod indiferenter elect'
[*sic*]; ita quod eadem ordinacio, arbitrium et iudicium inter partes predictas (ft)
fiant et reddantur per dictos arbitratores inter partes predictas citra Dominicam
proximam post festum nativitatis Sancti Johannis Baptiste proximum futurum, et
⟨quod⟩ dicte partes gerent pacem domini regis inter se in medio tempore sub
pena predicta.

iij^{cio} die Novembris Robertus Wedeld de Whorlton yoman et Johannes Burton de
eadem yoman devenerunt plegios pro Thoma Middelton de Est Roukton h[us-
bandman?] ad intrandum corpus ipsius ⟨Thome⟩ hic in camera consilii civitatis
ad omne tempus super racionabilem premunicionem eis factam sub [pena] xx
librarum de bonis et catallis (sua sas) suis etc., ad opus domini regis levandarum.

Manucapcio Roberti Ragget de Carltan Husthwayt yoman quod ipse dampnum vel malum aliquod corporale Willelmo Martyn glasyer vel alicui de populo domini regis non faciet nec fieri procurabit quovismodo videlicet quilibet manucaptorum sub pena x librarum, et predictus Robertus Ragget sub pena xx librarum de bonis et catallis, terris et tenementis suis ad opus dicti domini regis levandarum etc.; Johannes Tenaunt yoman, Robertus Dowe armorer, Robertus Hopkyn dyer.

[On 13 June 1489, Laurence Chaumbre and Christopher, servants of Seth Snawsell, esquire, appeared before mayor John Harper and each bound himself for £20, and the aforesaid Seth Snawsell bound himself for £20 on behalf of Laurence and Christopher; and also tanner William Pigod bound himself for £20 levied of his goods and chattels, lands and tenements, that Laurence, Christopher, and William Pygod will adhere to and carry out the ordinance, arbitration and judgement of Robert Tubbag, William Barker, John Stokdale and John Petty, arbiters impartially elected over all actions both real and personal between Laurence and Christopher on the one side and William Pygod [on the other side], this judgement to be made and rendered by the Sunday after the next coming feast of the Nativity of Saint John the Baptist, and that in the meantime the parties are to keep the peace between themselves.

On 3 November, yeomen Robert Wedeld and John Burton of Whorlton became pledges for Thomas Middleton of East Roukton, to bring the said Thomas in personally to the council chamber at all reasonable times demanded of him, under [penalty] of £20 levied of his goods and chattels etc., to the work of the lord king.

Mainprise of yeoman Robert Ragget of Carlton Husthwaite that he do no damage nor bodily harm to glasier William Martyn nor to any other of the king's subjects nor cause any harm to be done under penalty of £20 levied of his goods and chattels, lands and tenements, and sureties yeoman John Tenaunt, armorer Robert Dowe, and dyer Robert Hopkyn each under penalty of £10.]

[f.159] Reading of King's Letters, Return of Unused Bows and Arrows
14 June 1489

xiiij die Junii

Mayor: John Harper. Counsellor: Richard Tunstall knight. 12: Richard Yorke knight, John Fereby, John Newton, Nicholas Lancastre, William Chymney, William Todd knight, Robert Hancok, John Gylliot. Sheriff: Thomas Graa. 24: Thomas Catour, William Spence, Richard Clerk, William Tayt, Michael White, Miles Grenebank, Thomas Fynch, John Shawe, George Kirke.

At the which day assembled in the common hall of of [sic] this cite, and ther and then the kinges comaundment was shewed by [the] mouth of the said Sir Richerd Tunstall etc.; and also the kynges gracius lettres under his private seall was direct to [the] maiour, aldermen and the common counsaill, which ther and then was openlie red tofore the said presence etc. And over [that] where certan bowez and arrowez was (bough) ⟨takyn by price⟩ of certain bowers and ffletchers within this cite for the defence of the same, immediatelie after the departour of Sir John Egremond and othre at his retenue, forsomuch as it was at that tyme shewid and said that the said Sir John and othre wold shortlie retourne efter the same ⟨departour⟩ to the cite ayane and mak a new salt therunto, which they did not, and so the said bowez and arrowez was unocupied, the said maiour, Sir Richerd Tunstall and all othre above rehersed, remembring the greit det the which the chaumbre was in, determyned and concludet that every bower and ffletcher shold tak ther bowez and arrowez ayane, and that every man (th) of this cite that had eythre bowe or arrowez delyverd by the chaumberleyns or othre at that tyme to bring thame in ayane to the said chaumberleyn without contradiccion apon payn of inprisonament ther to remayn to thai and every of thame delyver all such bowez and arrowez or els to content for the same efter the price etc.

[f.159v]   Moremaster Refuses to Pay, List of Subscribers to Iron Gates 3 July 1489

iij^{cio} die Julii

Mayor: John Harper. Counsellor: Richard Tunstall knight. 12: John Fereby, John Newton, Master Nicholas Lancastre, William Chymney, Robert Hancok, William White, John Gylliot. Sheriffs: Thomas Foulneby, Thomas Gray. 24: Thomas Catour, Thomas Allan, William Tayt, William Spence, John Hagg, ⟨Miles Grenebank⟩, Richard Clerk, Thomas Fynch, John Shawe, Robert Johnson.

At the which day it was shewid by the said maiour that where John Tirrell elect to be one of the moremasters in nowise woldbe agreable to content ne pay x li. in like fourme as othre moremasters have done tofore hym etc., for the which cause the maiour comaundet hym to prison etc., and efter the same John Tirrell was sent for cam into the counsail chaumbre tofore the said presence and eftsonez the premissez laid unto hym he ther and then shewid that he was not of power of his own propre goodes to (contend) ⟨content⟩ ne pay the same sowme, and over that at he be noon meinez couth of credence mak no chevisance of the same, and apon that was laid unto ⟨hym⟩ by the right wirshupful Sir Richerd Tunstall knyght that he wold remembring his [c]leym of povertie and that he wasnot able to content and pay the same, (v) afferd hym to tak hym x li. for the tyme that he shold by the ordynaunce of the chaumbre forbere it so that he (was) wald be bound unto hym by obligacion to content hym at a certain day apoynted (to repay him) ⟨comprehendit in the same⟩, and for his curtas (office) offer the said maiour and all othre above rehersed yaf unto hym a laudable thank (for his said offer) and apon that offerd aswele the said maiour and all othre above writen to be bound to content (hym) ⟨the said John Tirrell⟩ according to his paying with delay, he still standing and lodging in his said openyon, the said maiour by the advise of the said presence ⟨yaff forthre day⟩ that he shold remembre hym betwix that and the morowe at x of the clok and to yif a answer to the maiour of his mynde in that behalf, and efter that the said maiour and all othre above writen determyned and concludet he refusing that according to the ordynaunce therof to be committed to prison ther to abide unto the tyme he mak ful contentacion of the said x li.

iron yatez Item the same day to the making of the iren yates of ther benevolence and fre will aswele the said maiour as all othre above writen every man by thame self graunted aswele in iren as in money, as doeth appere particulare in a bill of every man, which bill is delyverd to William Tayt, John Shawe and othre to rere and gadder the same etc., as is above graunted etc.

[f.160]   Moremasters Pay Fee
                31 July 1489

Memorandum that the last day of July the iiij^t yere of the reign of Kyng Henry the sevent cam personalie tofore the right wirshupful sir John Harpour maiour and the chaumberleyns of the cite in the counsaill chaumbre of Ousebrig of the same ⟨Maister Thomas Wharf⟩, and ther and then promised to content and pay x li. within xiiij dais of this present day by reason of the moremasters, to the which he is by the advise of the maiour and the hole counsaill cald for this yere, he protesting alwey to be content ayane apon the same as othre ben chosyn in like case etc. And efter that cam Maister Rauf Fasset and Maister William Wright in ther propre personez tofore the said maiour, John Fereby, Magister Nicolas Lancaster, Robert Hancok and William White aldermen in the same chaumbre, bringing with thame the said x li. so promysed by the said Maister Thomas Wharff, and ther and then content the said sowme to the handes of the said William White, shewing the said Master Thomas to be recontent of the same as othre tofore this have ben chosen in the moremastership, to the which the said John Harper maiour in the name of the hole counsaill and commonaltie of this cite graunted to the said Master Rauf Fasset and Maister William Wright that to be observed and fulfilled withoute delay.

Bond to Accept Arbitration
7 August 1490

Memorandum quod vij° die Augusti anno quinto regni regis Henrici septimi venerunt personaliter coram Johanne Gylliot maiore civitatis Ebor' Johannes Laverok janitor castri domini regis Ebor' et Robertus Herryson et recognoverunt se debere domino regi x libras legalis monete Anglie quod ipsi et eorum alter stabunt et perimplebunt ordinacioni, arbitrio et judicio Elie Cure et Johannis Hogeson arbitratorum per dictum maiorem indiferenter electorum de et super omnibus transgressionibus, querelis, debatis et demandis inter partes predictas habitis, motis sive pendentibus a principio mundi usque in diem confeccionis presencium, ita etc., citra festum Sancti Bartholomei proximum futurum.

[On 7 August 1490, John Laverok, keeper of the lord king's castle in York, and Robert Herryson came personally before mayor John Gylliot and bound themselves to owe the lord king £10 of legal English money that they and each of them would adhere to and carry out the ordinance, arbitration and judgement of Elias Cure and John Hogeson, arbiters impartially elected by the said mayor over all trespasses, complaints and demands had, moved, or pending between them from the beginning of the world to the day these presents [bonds] were made, [the judgement to be made] by the next coming feast of Saint Bartholomew.]

**[f.160v]   Defence of City, Collection of Tax
                    7 August 1489**

vij die Augusti

Mayor: John Harper. Recorder: John Vavesour. 12: Richard York knight, William Snawsell, John Newton, William Chymney, Robert Hancok, William White, John Gylliot. Sheriff: Thomas Foulneby. 24: Thomas Catour, Thomas Allan, William Tayt, Richard Clerk, William Barker, John Shawe.

At the which ⟨day⟩ assembled determyned and concludet that every warden in his warde in all hast gudelie shall se for the preparing of (his) the same aswell in gonnez as other implementes of werr, and also to charge that every man within the same wardes able to have jak, salet, bowe, arrowez and othre defensable wapyns for the tuicion, savegard and keping of this cite to the kinges (he) behufe, if eny case of nede herafter (shalf) shal com.

Item the same day it is agreid that Thomas Wandesford and othre his felowez collectourz of the kynges tax shall apon Tuesday or Wethenesday next efter this present date com into the maiour and the chaumberleyns within this counsaill chaumbre bringing with thaym such writing as they have of the maiour and chaumberleyns and they to delyver that writing have all such money as is in ther handes belonging to the said tax.

**Bond to Keep the Peace
17 August 1489**

Brettan recognitio Willelmus Brettan venit coram Johanne Harpour maiore civitatis Ebor', Johanne Fereby, Magistro Nicholao Lancastre et Roberto Hancok aldermannis eiusdem civitatis custodibus pacis et justiciis domini regis de pace conservandis in libertatem civitatis predicte die (Lu) Martis proximo post festum Sancti Laurencii anno regni regis Henrici septimi post conquestum quarto in camera consilii eiusdem civitatis et recognovit se debere dicto domino regi xx libras; necnon Johannes Borowdale cord[wainer] et Johannes Lond shirman manucaptores pro dicto Willelmo in (viginti m) xl libris legalis monete Anglie solvendis et levandis de omnibus bonis et catallis suis terris et tenementis si predictus Willelmus erga populum domini regis amodo transgrediatur aut pacem perturbaverit per se (w) vel per suos seu per insurrecciones, confidiraciones aut congregaciones illicitas aut per omnes (insida) insidias (sel) seu aliquo alio modo que in lesionem seu perturbacionem pacis cedere valeant quovismodo et precipue versus communitatem civitatis predicte et quamlibet per sociam singularem dicte civitatis etc.

[*Brettan bond* William Brettan came before mayor John Harpour, John Fereby, Master Nicholas Lancastre and Robert Hancok, aldermen and keepers of the peace and justices of the lord king in the liberty of the city on the Tuesday after the feast of Saint Laurence in the fourth year of Henry VII's reign in the council chamber and bound himself to owe the lord king £20; and also cordwainer John Borowdale and shearman John Lond [became] sureties on behalf of William for £40 levied of their goods and chattels, lands and tenements, if William trespassed against or disturbed the peace of any of the king's subjects by way of insurrections, confederations or illegal gatherings, or by all threats of any kind that disturbed the peace of the commonalty or any member of the said city.]

**[f.161]   Attendance List
                10 September 1489**

x^mo die Sempembris

Mayor: John Harper. Recorder: John Vavesour. 12: John Fereby, Master Nicholas Lancastre, William Chymney, ⟨William Todd knight⟩, Robert Hancok, William White, John Gylliot. Sheriffs: Thomas Folneby, Thomas Graa. 24: Thomas Catour, Thomas Allan, George Kirke.

At the which day assembled in the counsaill [*incomplete*]

**Debate Over Common Field
11 October 1489**

xj die Octobris

Mayor: John Harper. Counsellor: Richard Tunstall knight. 12: Richard Yorke knight, Nicholas Lancastre, William Chymney, William Todd knight, Robert Hancok.

Halfeyld Assembled in the Frere Austens ⟨within the cite of York⟩ and ther and then it was determyned that the contraversie and debate depending betwix Sir Jamez Danby knyght and the commonaltie of the cite of York toching the ⟨commonaltie⟩ common in the Halfeld shalbe contynue ⟨and⟩ in all thinges to the next assise in hagh and lawe tobe at that tyme determyned by the lerned counsaill aswele of the said Sir Jamez as of the cite of York.

**[f.161v]   Common Lands and the Vicars Choral
                 28 September 1489**

xxviij° die ⟨Octobris⟩ Septembris

Mayor: John Harper. Recorder: John Vavesour. 12: Richard Yorke knight, Master Nicholas Lancaster, John Gylliot, William White. 24: William Barker, Miles Grenebank, John Hagg.

vicars leez At the which day assembled determyned and concludet that where such writinges ⟨unsealed⟩ as the vicars of the Bedern belonging to the Mynster shewid, clamyng by the same all tymes of the yere to have (a closyng ⟨it closed⟩) ⟨closing⟩ to thame belonging ⟨closed⟩, callid the vicars leis severall to ther behufe, which writinges seen and understondet by the recorder, the said recorder by his lernyng ⟨said that it⟩ is not in the same writinges shewid to exclude the cocitesyns of entries of ther common in the same; albeit for a peace and a lovyng dealing to be had in the premissez, the said presence sent the forsaid recorder to the said vicars to have a communicacion with thame with that ⟨at⟩ all thinges in variance toching the premissez betwix thame and the cocitesyns, at a convenient tyme ther counsaill and the counsaill of the cite to meit and common apon the premissez, the said presence protesting the right of ⟨the⟩ cocitesyns in using of ther common in (ther) the said vicars leis in the mean seasyn to use and occupie; and over that at the vicars by ther comaundment shold comand ther officer keping the same vicar leis ⟨at Michaelmes day at noon⟩ in conservyng of the right of the said cocitesyns in usyng ther common in the same to opyn the ⟨yate⟩ or (the) yates ther, and if thai that refuse and wilnot, that thame twan common officers to the maise shal go aswel to the yate of the said vicar leis as othre closyns within the fraunches of this cite, ⟨being in travax⟩ for the conservacion of the kinges peax and savyng of the whikfall (to), and opyn the yate or yates.

[f.162]   **Purchase of New Charter, Discharges from Office, Entry Tolls, Closing of City Gates**
     7 October 1489

vij die Octobris

Mayor: John Harper. Counsellor: Richard Tunstall knight. 12: Richard Yorke knight, John Newton, Master Nicholas Lancaster, William Chymney, William Todd knight, Richard Hancok, William White, John Gylliot. Counsellor: Thomas Asper. 24: Thomas Allan, William Tayt, Richard Clerk, Richard Hardesang, George Kirke, Robert Johnson.

[*right side of folio torn, with one to two words missing per line, as indicated*] At the which day assembled in the counsaill chaumbre [determined] and concludet that Maister Haryngton shal ryde up to London [as] selistour for the cite in purchessing of the chartour of . . . of the maiour havyng (in) ⟨part of his⟩ reward to his costwerd . . . the chaumberleyn at his ryding up; and over that certain . . . to be maid unto certan lordes for ther benevolence toching [the] same chartour to the kinges grace; and on the same day at the said Master Haryngton ⟨at his⟩ commyng home for ⟨his⟩ greit labour and cost over that to be curtaslie entretied.

Master Latoner Item the same day it is agreid, determyned and concludet that where as Master Richerd Lataner hath in lesnyng of the greit det of this cite and specialie to the eisse of such money belonging to the moremastership yeven tofore the said presence for cause abovesaid xx s., shall from this day ⟨forwerd⟩ to be discharged of all and every inordinate chargez within this cite duryng his naturall lief.

littere alie de diversis super waynes Item the same day it is agreid that (the) every bound wayn commyng to this cite with eny cariage gere to pay iiij d. to the reparacion of the brigges of Ouse and Fosse and the pavage of the toun (beid) ⟨beit⟩ specified in the chartour or nay.

Item the said lettres to be maid to the chanceller, the privey seall, master secretary, the dean of York, Master Lovell, Master Bra, the erle of Oxford, my lorde of Elie, erle of Derby.

Item the same day it is agreid that the chaumberleyns shall content and pay to John Northeby late moremaster all such ⟨money⟩ that restes besides yiftes yeven to the eisse of the same, and if they refuse that, that than the xx li. yeven by the king and his noble progenitours to the wallez by taken and the said John to be paid ⟨of the same⟩ the residue forthre to be expendit according to the graunt.

Item the same ⟨day⟩ by all abovesaid it is graunted fermelie to be kept to Robert Appilby barker that he for xx s. by hym content and paid to the eisse and lesnyng of the soume of the moremastership shall in nowise from this day forwerd shalbe put in eny maner office or otherwise charged by eny inordinate chargez within this said cite duryng his naturall lieff.

[f.162v] Item the vij day of Octobre within writen it is graunted to John Tirrell that he in like wise (that he) for xx s. by hym content and paid shalbe duryng his naturall lieff be disharged in maner and fourme as Maister Latoner and Robert Appilby is.

Item it is agreid that the shireffes last being shal content and pay the xxx li. parcell of the lx li. to the cocitesyns by the kynges grace ⟨graunted⟩ etc., they ⟨to⟩ have under the common ⟨seall⟩ (writrn) writing as othre ther (noble p) predicessours have had for the same soum.

Item the same day it is determyned and concludet that from this present forwerd for the tuicion and savegarde of this cite the barres of the same nyghtly at ix of the clok to be shet and lokkid and (p) openyd every day ⟨ayane⟩ at v of the clok in the mornyng.

Bond to Accept Arbitration
3 November 1489

Memorandum quod tercio die Novembris anno quinto regni regis Henrici septimi venerunt personaliter coram Johanne Harper maiore civitatis Ebor' in camera consilii super pontem Use tam Johannes Brounberd baker quam Jacobus Symson parisshe clerk et recognoverunt se debere domino regi x libras libras [sic] legalis monete Anglie solvendas in festo Sancti Martini episcopi proximo futuro post

datam istius recognitionis ad opus maioris et communitatis civitatis predicte quod
ipsi et eorum alter stabunt seu stabit ordinacioni, arbitrio et judicio Petri Cooke,
Thome Chapman, Johannis Robynson et Roberti Tubbac arbitratorum indiferenter
electorum inter partes predictas ad arbitrandum inter eos de et super omnibus et
omnimodis accionibus tam realibus quam personalibus inter eos motis, habitis sive
pendentibus a principio mundi usque in diem confeccionis presencium, ita quod
eadem ordinacio etc., fiant et reddantur inter partes predictas citra dictum festum
Sancti Martini proximum futurum etc.

[On 3 November 1489, baker John Brounberd and parish clerk James Symson
came personally before mayor John Harper in the council chamber on Ouse
bridge and bound themselves for £10 payable in the feast of Saint Martin next
coming after the date of this bond that they would adhere to the ordinance,
arbitration and judgement of Peter Cooke, Thomas Chapman, John Robynson
and Robert Tubbac, arbiters impartially elected between the two parties over all
actions both real and personal moved, had or pending between them from the
beginning of the world to the day these presents [bonds] were made, the
ordinance etc. to be made and rendered by the said feast of Saint Martin next
coming.]

[f.163]   Payment of Part of Fee Farm
25 October 1489

xxv^to die Octobris

Mayor: John Harper. 12: John Fereby, John Newton, William Chymney, William White,
John Gylliot. 24: Thomas Catour, Thomas Allan, William Tayt, Richard Clerk, John Hagg,
Richard Hardesang, Robert Johnson. Sheriffs: Thomas Folneby, Thomas Gray.

[*right margin torn, with loss of one to two words per line, as noted*] At the which day
it was determyned and concludet that where an (acter) act late past as toching the
parcell of the lx li. graunted to the cocitesyns by [the king's] grace of the ⟨fee⟩
ferm of this cite shall stond in his . . . and at the shireffes without delay pay the
same as othre shireffes have doon tofore, thai havyng . . . under the common seall
as othre ther predecessours . . . have had of the maiour and chaumberleyns apon
the said Thomas Folneby and Thomas Graa (hath) ⟨is agreid and⟩ promised to
content and pay the said xxx li. within xxviij dais next ensuyng this present day etc.

Bond to Accept Arbitration
3 August 1490

recognitio inter Rayner et Martyn Memorandum quod tercio die Augusti anno
quinto regni regis Henrici septimi venerunt personaliter coram Johanne Gylliot
maiore civitatis Johannes Rayner capellanus et Johannes Martyn peuterer de
civitate predicta et recognoverunt se debere domino regi xx libras legalis monete

quod ipse et eorum alter stabit et perimplebit ordinacioni, arbitrio et judicio ⟨Thome Graa⟩ (Milonis Harper), ⟨Petri Cooke⟩, Johannis Petty et Johannis Elwold arbitratorum (di) per dictum maiorem indiferenter electorum de et super omnibus et omnimodis transgressionibus, querelis, contraversiis, debitis, debatis et demandis inter predictas partes habitis, motis sive pendentibus a principio mundi usque in diem confeccionis presencium, ita quod eadem ordinacio, arbitrium et (jo) judicium fiant et reddantur per dictos arbitratores inter partes predictas citra festum (assumpcionis) Sancti Bartholomei proximum (fututur') futurum, et si dicti arbitratores inter partes predictas concordare non poterint [*incomplete*]

[*bond between Rayner and Martyn* On 3 August 1490, chaplain John Rayner and pewterer John Martyn came personally before mayor John Gylliot and bound themselves for £20 that they would adhere to and carry out the ordinance, arbitration and judgement of Thomas Graa, Peter Cooke, John Petty and John Elwold, arbiters impartially elected by the said mayor over all trespasses, complaints and demands had, moved or pending between the two parties from the beginning of the world to the day these presents [bonds] were made, the judgement to be made and rendered by the next coming feast of Saint Bartholomew, and if the said arbiters are unable to agree [*incomplete*]]

[f.163v]   **Payment of Parliamentary Members, Dispute with Vicars Choral, Charter for Mayoral Election**
5 January 1490

v^to die Januarii

Mayor: John Harper. 12: Richard Yorke knight, John Fereby, Master Nicholas Lancastre, Robert Hancok. Counsellor: Thomas Asper. Sheriffs: William (Har') Barker, Thomas [*sic*] Dauson. 24: Thomas Catour, Thomas Allan, Richard Clerk, John Hagg, Michael White, Miles Grenebank, Richard Herdesang, (Robert) ⟨Roger⟩ Appilby, George Kirke, Robert Johnson, Thomas Folnetby.

Assembled in the counsaill chaumbre of Ousebrig and ther and then it was determyned and concludet that Sir Richerd York and Sir William Todd knyghtes for the parliament shall have and persave of the chaumberleyns all such expenses as belongeth unto thame and ethre of thame by the day for tyme of ther nowe last being furth at London at the last said parliament over the x li. yeven unto ther expenses maid at ther going up unto the same.

leez Item the same day it is agreid that ⟨the⟩ variaunce betwix the commons of the cite and the vicars of the Bedern toching the common in the vicars leis shall the right aswell in evidence as othrewise (wise) apon the both parties byde apon lerned counsaill at the (said) next assise to be determyned without forthre delay and the writtes by the said vicars takyn they (shall) ⟨to⟩ contynue thame unto the same ⟨tyme⟩.

[On 5 July 1490, Henry Mettiller of Stockton and sub-bailiff of Howdenshire, and also fuller John Williamson of York came before mayor John Gylliot and bound themselves for £10 that they would adhere to and carry out the ordinance, arbitration and judgement of Miles Harom, John Petty, John Robynson and John Hogeson, arbiters impartially elected over all complaints and debates had, moved or pending between the parties from the beginning of the world to the day these presents [bonds] are made, [the said judgement to be made] by the feast of [blank] next coming.]

[f.165v]   Commons' Petition, Return of Writ
January 1490

[blank] die Januarii

Mayor: John Harper. 12: Richard York knight, William Chymney, ⟨William Todd knight⟩, Robert Hancok, John Gylliot. Sheriffs: William Barker, Alexander Dauson. 24: Thomas Catour, Thomas Allan, Richard Clerk, William Tayte, William Barker baker, Thomas Fynch, John Shawe, Roger Appilby, George Kirk, Robert Johnson.

At the which day assembled in the counsaill chaumbre and ther and then a bill of certain peticions delyverd by the commones for a common well was openly redd (for) and apon that forthre to be contynued to theleccion be doon and than forthre to procede etc.

Item the same day it is agreid that the shireffes to be savyd harmeles toching the retourn of a writ taken ayanest certain cocitesyns by the (w) vicars of the Bederne, which retourne is thoght most convenient and most eisse (to) ⟨quod⟩ non sunt inventi etc.

Bond to Accept Arbitration
29 January 1490

recognitio [entry struck through] (Memorandum quod xxix° die Januarii anno quinto regni regis Henrici septimi venerabilis vir dompnus Robertus Haulowez prior domus sive prioratus Sancte Trinitatis Ebor' venit personaliter in camera consilii eiusdem civitatis coram Johanne Harper maiore civitatis predicte et recognovit se debere domino regi xl libras (lib') bone et legalis monete Anglie solvendas ad opus domini regis quod ipse stabit et perimplebit ordinacioni, arbitrio et judicio Johannis Fereby [et] Johannis Newton aldermannorum, Georgii Kirk et Thome Gra arbitratorum indiferenter electorum inter predictum venerabilem priorem ⟨et suos⟩ ex una parte et Willelmum Barker et Alexandrum ⟨Dauson⟩ vicecomites civitatis predicte et suos ex altera parte, de et super omnibus et omnimodis accionibus realibus et personalibus inter eos ⟨partes⟩ motis, habitis sive pendentibus a principio mundi usque in (de) diem confeccionis presencium, ita etc., (v) citra vij diem Februarii proximum futurum etc., et hoc scriptum etc.)

concordate sunt, vacat

[*bond* (On 29 January 1490, the venerable lord Robert Haulowez, prior of the house or priory of Holy Trinity, York, came personally into the council chamber before mayor John Harper and bound himself to owe the lord king £40 of good and legal English money paid to the work of the lord king, that he will adhere to and carry out the ordinance, arbitration and judgement of John Fereby [and] John Newton, aldermen, and of George Kirk and Thomas Gra, arbiters impartially elected between the venerable prior and his [party] on the one side and William Barker and Alexander Dauson, sheriffs of the city, and their [party] on the other side, over all actions both real and personal moved, had, or pending between them from the beginning of the world to the day these presents [bonds] are made, [the judgement to be made] by 7 February 1490, and this writing etc.)

they are agreed, void]

[f.166]   **New Rules for Mayoral Election, Discharge from Bearing Office of Sheriff**
                  15 January X 3 February 1490

[*blank*] die Januarii

Mayor: John Harper. Counsellor: Richard Tunstall knight. 12: John Fereby, John Newton, William Chymney, William Todd knight, Robert Hancok, John Gylliot. Counsellor: Thomas Asper. Sheriffs: William Barker, Alexander Dauson. 24: Thomas Catour, Thomas Allan, William Tayt, John Hagg, Richard Clerk, Michael White, William Barker, Thomas Fynch, Roger Appilby, John Shawe, Robert Johnson, Thomas Folneby.

Chartre of Eleccion

[*right margin torn, with loss of one to two words per line, as noted*] At the which day assembled in the counsaill c[hamber] apon Ousebrig and ther and then the kinges [grace his] lettres patentes under the greit seall of . . . by his grace ⟨to⟩ the cocitesyns of this cite . . . the peseable eleccion of the maiour yerelie . . . apon Saynt Maures day [*15 January*] and to tak his oth [upon] Saynt Blaise day [*3 February*], and forsomuch as the said [Saint] Maures day is past tofore the receyt of the same lettres, therfor it is determyned and concludet that the maiour, aldermen and the commones of this cite shall apon Saynt Blaise next assemble in the Yeldhall, and ther and then such a alderman as at that tyme shalbe namyd and chosen according to theffect of the said lettres, shall tak his oth the same day t[ofore] all the commones ther assembled and so furthwith . . . occupie the same office for this yere ensuyng etc.

William Nelson Item the same day it is agreid fermelie to be observed and kept for diverse consideracions the s[aid] presence movyng that William Neilson naw oon of the chaumberleyns shalnot from this present day be charged ne put into the office of the shirefwyk of this cite within the space of vj yeres ⟨than next felowing⟩, bot he to be forbourn for the same space and the ⟨same⟩ vj yeris fully expendit to be lefull to thame at eny tyme ⟨efter⟩ to charge and tak hym to the same office or eny othre at ther pleasours etc.

[f.166v]   Petition from the Commons
**   3 February 1490**

Tercio die Februarii

Mayor: John Harper. Counsellor: Richard Tunstall knight. 12: William Snawsell, John Fereby, John Newton, Nicholas Lancastre, William Chymney, William Todd knight, Robert Hancok, John Gylliot. [Counsellor:] Thomas Asper. Sheriffs: William Barker, Alexander Dauson. 24: Thomas Catour, Thomas Allan, Henry Williamson, Richard Clerk, William Tayt, Miles Grenebank, John Hagg, Richard Herdesang, William Barker baker, Thomas Fynch, Roger Appilby, John Shawe, George Kirk, Robert Johnson, Thomas Fulneby, Thomas Gra.

At the which day assembled in the counsaill chaumbre within the Yeldhall determyned and (concle) concludet that a bill of peticion yeven in by the commones which is thoght for a common wele etc., and is openlie red, which the said commones desireth of a answer hastelie for the sure and stablenesse of the same, which day of answer the said presence withoute forthre delay to be answerd apon Saynt Gelian day next etc. [*St. Juliana's day, 16 February?*]

(Item eodem die eligerunt in officio camerariorum Willelmum Marshall mercatorem, Thomam Derby mercatorem, Robertum Dauson mercatorem, (Ricardum Symson) ⟨Edwardum Forster⟩, (Edwardum Forster) ⟨Ricardum Symson⟩ hosyer et Thomam Watson (b) tanner.) [*Elected as chamberlains:*] Willelmus Marshall, mercator; Thomas Darby, mercator; Robertus Dauson, mercator; Edwardus Forster; Ricardus Symson; Thomas Watson, tanner.

  [(On the same day they elected to the office of chamberlain merchants William Marshall, Thomas Derby, Robert Dauson, and Edward Forster, hosier Richard Symson, and tanner Thomas Watson.)]

[f.167]   Arbitration Award
**   Undated**

[*right margin torn, with loss of one to two words as indicated*] This is the award yeldet and yeven by Peris Cooke, Thomas Saddler, [John] Robynson and Robert Tubbac a[r]bitrours indiferently chosen betwix John [Brounberd] (bakers) baker and Jamez Symson parisheclerk, that is to say ffirst . . . award that the said Jamez shall bere all the costes and . . . of the court maid by hym and the fyne to the shireffs . . . to agre with hym that hight the saddill that was left with John Brounberd to stand with his costes and charges.

Bond to Accept Arbitration
17 February 1490

vacat [*entry struck through*] (Memorandum quod xvij die Februarii anno v^to regni regis Henrici septimi venerunt coram Johanne Gylliot maiore civitatis Ebor' Rogerus Brokholez [et] Thomas Glover, bowers civitatis Ebor' predicta ⟨ex una parte⟩ predicta [et] Henricus Monkton, Willelmus Hertford, Willelmus Shirburn et alii bowers ex altera parte, et recognoverunt se debere domino regi xx libras de bonis etc., quod ipsi et eorum quilibet stabunt ordinacioni et judicio Johannis Elwald, Johannis Stokdale, Johannis Norman et Roberti Tubbac arbitratorum indiferenter electorum ad arbitrandum inter partes predictas de et super omnibus et singulis querelis, debitis, debatis et demandis inter eos motis, habitis sive pendentibus a principio mundi usque in diem confeccionis presencium, ita etc., citra Dominicam proximam post dictum ⟨xvij⟩ diem Februarii etc., et quod gerent pacem domini regis in medio tempore inter se, sub pena forisfaciendarum xx librarum etc.)

Vacat ista recognitio quia partes concordate sunt et perimpleverunt iudicium.

[*void* (On 17 February 1490, Roger Brokholez [and] Thomas Glover, bowers of York, on the one side, [and] Henry Monkton, William Hertford, William Shirburn and other bowers on the other side, came before mayor John Gylliot and bound themselves for £20 that they would adhere to the ordinance and judgement of John Elwald, John Stokdale, John Norman and Robert Tubbac, arbiters impartially elected to arbitrate between the said parties over all complaints, debates and demands moved, had, or pending between them from the beginning of the world to the day these presents [bonds] are made, [the judgement to be made] by the Sunday following 17 February, and that in the meantime they are to keep the king's peace towards one another, under penalty to be forfeited of £20.)

This bond is void because the parties are agreed and the judgement was carried out.]

[f.167v] **Fees of Civic Officers, Attendance at Council Meetings, Fees and Expenses**
5 February 1490

v^to die Februarii

Mayor: John Gylliot. Counsellor: Richard Tunstall knight. 12: John Fereby, John Newton, Nicholas Lancastre, William Chymney, William Todd knight, Robert Hancok. Counsellor: Thomas Asper. Sheriffs: William Barker, Alexander Dauson. 24: Thomas Catour, Thomas Allan, William Spence, William Tayt, William Spence [*sic*], John Hagg, Michael White, Miles Grenebank, Richard Herdesang, William Barker, Thomas Fynch, Roger Appilby, George Kirk, Robert Johnson, Thomas Folneby, Thomas Gra.

At the which day assembled in the counsaill chaumbre within the Yeldhall of the cite of York, and there and ⟨then⟩ the articles comprehendit in a bill of peticion by the commones was openlie red tofore all the presence; and to the first article as in mitigacion of the maiour ffee, where it is thoght that the maire to have bot xx li. for keping of his officiours, it is shewid that as for lesnyng of the maires ffe not to be don bot to stand ⟨in⟩ ease for the wirshup of this cite as it hath doon tofore tymes past; and forthre it is determyned and finally concludet that ther shalbe an audict set apon every maires compt from the (j) ⟨first (yere of the)⟩ tyme of the (right wirshupful sir William Holbek late maier) maioraltie of Sir Richerd York [*1469–70*] unto this present ⟨day⟩ to thentent that such inordynate costes and charges don and maid within ther days may be understondet and the same expens so maid to be eased and casten apon thame that hath ayanest conscience so doon etc.

Item (ther) it is (aswele) concludet the recorder to have xx s. by yere of the commones and no more. Item it is forthre determyned that ther shall no lernyd men from nowforth have fe of the chaumbre bot (Thomas Asper, Leonard Knyght, Thomas Aspar, Herryson, and John Bradford) ⟨all to be discharged according to the peticion in that⟩ and this to be shewid to the commones.

Item the same day it is agreid that where Herry Barbour shewid a writing under the seall of office etc., toching a pencion of xx s., that forsomuch as the cite is in greit det he to have and occupie his office ayane of sergiantship and the commones (ng) noght to be forthre charget, and so furwith he resavyd his office ayane and sworn, [**f.168**] and forthre it is determyned for the ease of the greit det of this cite th[e said] Herry not to be discharged of that office herefter for tyme that he may be [*right margin torn, with loss of one to two words*] to do service in the same office to the wirshup and profet of (this) ⟨the⟩ cite.

Item the same day it is agreid fermlie to be observed and kept that all . . . alderman and the common counsaill shall at all tymes herefter com . . . thay and every of thame laufully warned, that is to ⟨say⟩ the aldermen by . . . and the xxiiij[ti] by the vj common (servantes) seriantes to the maise, and who that defalt and commys not at all [to] such counsails be (i)x of the clok smytten [by the] cathiderall church of the Mynster (or within the quarter of the same hour) [without] a resonable excuse, to pay at every tyme so makyng defalt iiij d. And if thai be not laufully warned by the gentilmen and the common sex seriantes, than they to pay the said payn of iiij d.

Item in like case every (man) alderman and the xxiiij[ti] shall kepe every procession and sermones within the cathedral church of Mynster, and he that makes defalt to pay without pardon the said payn of iiij d. And forthre it is finallie concludet that this ordre fermelie herafter in every counsaill to be observed and kept, that is to say every man to speke in his own ⟨royme⟩ when he is demaundet by the maiour for tyme being and he that interupes in speking to that man have said his reason to forfet at every tyme ij d.

feez del officers Item by all the said presence it is thoght as toching the variance in common within certan groundes in divers tyme the lordes of all such grondes to be commoned with to thentent that ther may be acurtas and a lovyng end, and if thay woll reserve a yerelie ferm to the commones for keping severall those grondes, and this to be commoned and laid by ⟨to all such⟩ the right wirshupful and our especial and singuler gude maister Sir Richerd Tunstall knyght.

Item it is agreid that the (the) common clerk for tyme being shall attend apon the maiour in his own propre person and not by his depute ⟨jurator⟩, and he to have in wages yerelie of the commones C s. and all othre casualties.

Item it is agreid that the ⟨two⟩ gentilmen to have yerelie doring the tyme of the pencion yeven by thame to John Strangwish, they paing the pencion to the same John etc.

Item it is agreid the vj seriantes every of thame to have xxvj s. viij d. and twise (clos) clothing **[f.168v]** by yere.

Item it is agreid that therbe no rewardes yeven by yere from this day forwerd to eny minstralles bot to the kinges, and also that therbe no forthre expens maid apon Corpus Christi day bot xl s., and if ⟨it⟩ over go that the chaumberleyns to pay it of ther own charges.

Item it is agreid that as toching (a bill) unto two men to be deputed and ordegned to have oversight of the common rent belonging to Ouse and Fosbrig, that apon Saynt Gelian day that to be (pit) put to the commones to this entent if they can fynd of ther myndes two able men, they to name thame and els the counsaill that day to go to thelleccion of brigmasters etc.

Item the same day it is agreid fermlie to be observed and kept that William Marshall elect to be chaumberleyn, he takyng that office curtaslie apon hym etc., to be forborn for the space of vij yeres immediatle after this present day ensuyng to be el[e]ct shireff of this cite or eny othre office within this same space.

Selection of Bridgemasters
16 February 1490

in festo Sancte Juliane The same day was chosen to be brigmasters of Ousbrig: Robert Dale shipman, Thomas Kendale smyth.

Item the same day was chosen for Fosse brig to be brigmasters ther: Thomas Lewlyn tanner, John Ordeux tanner.

[f.169] **Selection of New Recorder, Merchant Refuses to Be Made Alderman**
24 February 1490

xxiiij^{to} die Februarii

Mayor: John Gylliot. 12: William Snawsell, John Fereby, John Newton, Nicholas Lancastre, William Chymney, Robert Hancok, John Harper. Sheriffs: William Barker, Alexander Dauson. 24: Thomas Catour, William Spence, William Tayt, Richard Clerk, John Hagg, Michael White, Miles Grenebank, Richard Herdesang, Thomas Fynch, William Barker, Roger Appilby, George Kirk, Robert Johnson, Thomas Folneby, Thomas Gray.

[*right margin torn, with loss of one to two words per line, as indicated*] At the which day forsomuch as the re[corder the] wirshupful sir John Vavesour late rec[order] of this wirshupful ⟨cite⟩ now being one of [the king's] juges and the place of the same [now being] voide, it is by the said presence fully [determined] and concludet that the right wirshup[ful sir] William Farefax, for certain consideracions is able and beneficiall for that rowme, and so by the hole assent ⟨and⟩ consent of the said presence, the said William Farefax is elect and chosen to be recorder of this cite.

Item the same day Thomas Scotton elect to be a alderman was sent fore to tak his othe of the same, cam presentlie the said day tofore the said maire and aldermen, and ther and then laid unto hym to tak his oth he desired to be eased apon the same (which), and apon that ⟨it was⟩ laid unto hym he that refusing to content and pay the penaltie belonging to the same, he the said Thomas forthre desiring of respect of his answer which day was yeven unto hym of his penitorie answer within xiiij days of this present day.

[f.169v] **Bond to Keep the Peace, Arbiters Chosen**
25 February 1490

Memorandum quod xxv^{to} die Februarii anno quinto regni regis Henrici septimi Henricus Barbour unus servientis maioris ad clavem, Georgius Barbour et Johannes Barbour filii eiusdem Henrici venerunt personaliter coram Johanne Gylliot mercatore maiore civitatis Ebor' in camera consilii eiusdem civitatis.

[Manucapcio] Henrici Barbour unius servientis ad clavem maioris, Georgii Barbour et Johannis Barbour filiorum eiusdem Henrici quod ipsi nec eorum (aliquod) aliquis dampnum vel malum aliquod corporale Johanni Barrowdale cordwener (vel alicui de populo domini regis non faciet nec aliquis eorum faciet) ⟨non faciet nec fieri procurabit⟩ videlicet quilibet eorum sub pena xx librarum. Et predicti manucaptores ⟨utrique⟩ (quilibet) eorum sub pena x librarum domino regi forisfaciendarum, et super hoc Willelmus Sawer et Nicholaus Garnet cives civitatis predicte devenerunt plegios pro predictis Henrico, Georgio et Johanne Barbour videlicet uterque eorum sub pena x librarum dicto domino regi forisfaciendarum si etc.

Manucapcio Johannis Barrowdale cord[wainer] quod ipse dampnum vel malum aliquod corporale Henrico Barbour uni servientis maioris ad clavem, Georgio

Barbour et Johanni Barbour filiis eiusdem (quod ipse dampnum vel malum aliquod co' vel alicui de populo domini regis) ⟨⟨quod ipse dampnum vel malum aliquod corporale ut supra⟩⟩ non faciet nec fieri procurabit quovismodo videlicet uterque eorum sub pena x librarum; Thomas Johnson yoman et Thomas Smyth cord-[wainer].

Milo Harom, Robertus Preston, Willelmus Skipton, Willelmus Sawer–arbitratores indiferenter electos [*sic*] inter partes predictas.

Thomas Johnson yoman, Thomas Smyth cord[wainer]

[On 25 February 1490, Henry Barbour, one of the macebearers of the mayor, George Barbour, and John Barbour, sons of the same Henry, came personally before merchant and mayor John Gylliot in the council chamber.

Mainprise of Henry Barbour, one of the macebearers of the mayor, of George Barbour and John Barbour his sons, that they all would do no damage nor bodily harm to cordwainer John Barrowdale, nor cause any harm to be done to him, under penalty of £20. The sureties were each under penalty of £10 to be forfeited to the lord king, and over this William Sawer and Nicholas Garnet, citizens of York, became pledges on behalf of Henry, George and John Barbour, each under penalty of £10 to be forfeited to the lord king.

Mainprise of cordwainer John Barrowdale, that he do no damage nor bodily harm to Henry Barbour, a macebearer of the mayor, to George Barbour and to John Barbour his sons, nor cause any harm to be done to them, sureties Thomas Johnson and Thomas Smyth each under penalty of £10.

Miles Harom, Robert Preston, William Skipton, William Sawer: arbiters impartially elected between the aforesaid parties.

Thomas Johnson, yeoman; Thomas Smyth, cordwainer]

[f.170]   Bonds to Accept Arbitration
26 February and 3 March 1490

[*right margin torn, with loss of one to two words per line, as noted*] Memorandum quod xxvj^{to} die mensis Februarii anno quinto regni regis Henrici septimi [venerunt personaliter] coram Johanne Gylliot maiore civitatis Ebor' in camera consilii eiusdem tam Mi' . . . Rogerus Brere et Ricardus Scott cives Ebor' quam Ricardus Biscam, T' . . . recognoverunt et eorum quilibet recognovit se debere domino regi xx libras legalis [monete] Anglie quod ipsi et eorum quilibet (recognovit se) stabit et perimplebit ordin[acioni, arbitrio] et iudicio Petri Coke, Johannis Elwald, Corandi Gossep et Johannis . . . arbitratorum inter partes predictas indiferenter electorum, de et super omnibus et [omnimodis] accionibus tam realibus quam personalibus inter partes predictas motis, habitis sive pendentibus a principio mundi usque in diem confeccionis presencium, ita quod ordinacio, arbitrium et iudicium dictorum quatuor arbitratorum inter partes predictas fiant et reddantur citra festum Annunciacionis Beate [Marie] Virginis proximum futurum etc.

Memorandum quod tercio die Marcii anno quinto regni regis Henrici vij^{mi} coram Johanne Gylliot maiore civitatis Ebor' in camera consilii Robertus Derby prikendyne-maker et Michael Lyth coppersmyth comparentes et recognoverunt se debere domino regi x libras legalis monete Anglie quod ipsi et uterque eorum stabunt et perimplebunt ordinacioni, arbitrio et judicio Rogeri Brere et (h) Roberti Goll arbitratorum inter partes predictas indiferenter electorum ad arbitrandum tam ex parte Thome Derby et Roberti Derby ex una parte quam ex parte dicti Michaelis, de et super omnibus et omnimodis accionibus tam realibus quam personalibus inter partes predictas habitis, motis sive pendentibus, a principio mundi usque in diem confeccionis presencium, ita etc., citra secundam Dominicam in xlme proximam futuram, et super hoc coram dicto maiore Willelmus Inskip yoman devenit plegium pro predicto Michaele quod stabit ordinacioni, arbitrio et judicio iiij^{or} arbitratorum etc.

[On 26 February 1490, Mi . . . , Roger Brere and Richard Scott, citizens of York, and also Richard Biscam, T . . . came personally before mayor John Gylliot in the council chamber, and bound themselves for £20 that they would adhere to and carry out the ordinance, arbitration and judgement of Peter Coke, John Elwald, Corand Gossep and John . . . , arbiters impartially elected between the said parties over all actions both real and personal moved, had, or pending between them from the beginning of the world to the day these presents [bonds] are made, the judgement of the four arbiters to be made and rendered by the next coming feast of the Annunciation of the Blessed Virgin Mary.

On 3 March 1490, locksmith Robert Derby and coppersmith Michael Lyth appeared before mayor John Gylliot and bound themselves for £10 that they would adhere to and carry out the ordinance, arbitration and judgement of Roger Brere and Robert Goll, arbiters impartially elected to arbitrate between the said parties, both that of Thomas and Robert Derby and that of Michael Lyth, over all actions both real and personal had, moved or pending between them from the beginning of the world to the day these presents [bonds] are made, [the judgement to be made] by the second Sunday in Lent next coming, and over this in the presence of the said mayor yeoman William Inskip became a surety on Michael's behalf, that he will adhere to the ordinance, arbitration and judgement of the four arbiters etc.]

[f.170v]   Chamberlain to Pay Fine and Be Replaced, Payments to Common Crane, Visit of Earl of Surrey
11 March 1490

xj° die Marcii

Mayor: John Gylliot. 12: William Snawsell, John Fereby, John Newton, William Chymney, Robert Hancok, John Harper, William White. Counsellor: Thomas Asper. Sheriffs: William

Barker, Thomas [*sic*] Dauson. 24: Thomas Catour, ⟨William Spence⟩, William Tayt, ⟨Richard Clerk⟩, John Hagg, ⟨Miles Grenebank⟩, Richard Herdesang, William Barker, John Shawe, George Kirk, Robert Johnson, Thomas Folneby, Thomas Graa.

At the which day assembled in the counsaill chaumbre of Ousebrig, and ther and then forsomuch as Robert Dauson merchaunt apon Saynt Blase ⟨day⟩ last elect with othre to be one of the chaumberleyns for this yere ensuyng, and he absenting (the same) hym self for the same office, and also hath occupied within this cite as a ffraunchestman in bying and selling by certain yeris for that at he have so occupied, to forfet and pay (withoute pardon) to the behufe of the communaltie x li., to be rased of his gudes herafter commyng within this cite and ffraunches of the same.

nota, ordenaciones de commune crane, crane ware [illegible] Item the same day it is agreid fermelie herafter to be observed and kept that every forent herafter commyng to this cite with leid, wyne and all maner other merchandise callid crane ware, pay in maner and fourme folowing: in primus, of every pece leid for wynding and striking, vj d., that is to say ij d. to the crane man and iiij d. to the chaumbre. Item, xij d. a pak lyne–iiij d. ⟨cranage⟩, viij d. camere, and so tun and tun lyk to be paid withoute pardon, that is to say of every tun, xij d.

Item the same day it is agreid forsomuch as (Thomas) Robert Dauson merchaunt late chosen to be oon of the chaumberleyns for this yere and have absent hym self and also unfraunchest, that John Dogeson merchaunt to be and occupie as chaumberleyn in the roume of the said Robert, he that refusing to content and pay withoute pardon xl li. according to the ordynaunce therof maid.

[f.171] Item the same day it is agreid that my lorde the maiour, [aldermen and] the common counsaill shal in murrey or ⟨violet⟩ meit the right wor[shipful] lord therl of Surr' at Boutham Barr and with . . . his commyng to this cite at this assise and welcom hym . . . same with reverence according.

Award of Arbitration Made to Carmelite Friars
12 May 1490

Memorandum the xij day of May the fift yere of the reign of King Henry [the seventh] tofore the right wirshupful sir John Gillyot maier of the cite of [York], ⟨William Tayte⟩, Robert Johnson grocer, Peris Coke and John Stokesley arbitrours betwix ⟨H. Thwayet⟩ prior of the White Freris of the cite of York of the one partie, and the (⟨Sir Thomas Davell⟩) parson of Saynt Saveour within the same cite ⟨of that othre partie⟩, awardes that for such receiting of freris of the same and certan gudes by the same freris to hym (brg) broght, the said parson to content and pay to the ⟨said⟩ prior (of the said prior) and behufe of the co[n]vent of the said white freris xl s. be [*incomplete*]

Bond to Accept Arbitration
5 July 1490

recognitio inter Christoforum Edmunson et alios de Dringhouse Memorandum quod quinto die Julii anno quinto regni regis Henrici vij^{mi} venerunt personaliter coram Johanne Gylliot maiore civitatis Ebor' tam Christoforus Edmunson yoman quam Johannes (Colman) Coupland, Willelmus Staynton et Ricardus Corbrig de Dringhouse, et recognoverunt se debere domino regi (centum) ⟨x⟩ marcas quod ipsi et eorum quilibet (recog') stabunt et perimplebunt ordinacioni, arbitrio et judicio Johannis Ellys, Johannis Brokholez, Ricardi Raby et Johannis Patyner arbitratorum indiferenter inter partes predictas (ind) electorum, de et super omnibus et omnimodis accionibus tam realibus quam personalibus inter partes predictas motis, habitis sive pendentibus a principio mundi usque in diem confeccionis presencium, ita quod etc., citra festum Sancte Marie Magdalene proximum futurum etc.

[*bond between Christopher Edmunson and others of Dringhouses* On 5 July 1490, yeoman Christopher Edmunson and also John Coupland, William Staynton and Richard Corbrig of Dringhouses came personally before mayor John Gylliot and bound themselves for ten marks that they would adhere to and carry out the ordinance, arbitration and judgement of John Ellys, John Brokholez, Richard Raby and John Patyner, arbiters impartially elected between the said parties over all actions both real and personal moved, had or pending between them from the beginning of the world to the day these presents [bonds] are made, [the said judgement to be made] by the feast of Saint Mary Magdalene next coming.]

[f.171v]   Problems with Common Fields, Arbitration Set, Payments Due
15 March 1490

xv^{mo} die Marcii

Mayor: John Gylliot. 12: Richard York knight, John Newton, Nicholas Lancastre, William Todd knight, John Harper, William White. Sheriffs: William Barker, Thomas [*sic*] Dauson. 24: Thomas Catour, Thomas Allan, William Spence, William Tayt, Miles Grenebank, Richard Clerk, John Hagg, William Barker, John Shawe, George Kirk, Robert Johnson, Thomas Folneby.

At the which day assembled in the counsail chaumbre and ther and then it was shewid by the mouth of the maiour how that Sir James (day) Danby knyght brak with hym as toching the variances betwix hym and the commones of this cite toching common in the Hall Feld, that as this assise according to the promise maid unto hym by the right wirshupful John Harper late maier.

Arbitrours betwix Herry Pannall bower and John Cure walker by the right wirshupful John Gillyot maire namyd and chosen, that is to say William Payntour plommer and Elis Cure tapitour.

William Pygod This is the day that William Pygod shall pay xxxiij s. to Sir John Garnet parson of Saynt Mary church (by the plege of) and Sir Thomas Hausman prest, that is to say Whitsonday next by the plege of John Hardewyk and John Nicolson, and forthre lx s. to be paid to the said Sir John and Sir Thomas at the ferm days withoute forthre delay, pleges the said John Hardewyk and John Nicolson.

[f.172]　　　Payments Made, Bonds to Accept Arbitration
　　　　　　29 April and 5 July 1490

Thur'

[right folio top torn, with loss of three to four words per line as noted] Item Sir Christofferre Mychylle chantre preste off Cruxe . . . hasse geffyne Harry Wylliamsone marschande . . . to paye att Mechelmies and att Martynmes . . . comynge be evyen porschens sum ys . . . .

recognitio Memorandum quod penultimo die mensis Aprilis anno quinto regni regis Henrici sep[timi] . . . personaliter coram venerabile Johanne Gylliot maiore civitatis Ebor' in camera [consilii] eiusdem et recognoverunt se debere domino regi x libras legalis monete Anglie quod [ipsi] et eorum uterque stabunt et perimplebunt ordinacioni, arbitrio et judicio Johannis Hopkyn, Willelmi Shirburn, Ricardi Raby et Johannis Pecher arbitratorum inter Johannem Liddale glover et Isabelle Avner vidue indiferenter electorum, de et super omnibus et omnimodis accionibus personalibus, calumpniis, transgressionibus, querelis, debatis et demandis inter eos motis, habitis sive pendentibus a principio mundi usque in diem confeccionis presencium, ita etc., citra festum Sancte Trinitatis proximum futurum.

recognitio Memorandum quod v^{to} die Julii anno v^{to} regni regis Henrici vij venerunt personaliter coram Johanne Gylliot maiore civitatis Ebor' tam Thomas Rypon alderman textorum eiusdem civitatis et scrutator eiusdem artis in nomine tocius artis etc., quam Johannes Taillour ffissher, et recognoverunt se debere domino regi decem libras legalis monete Anglie, quod ipsi et eorum obligavit [et] stabit ordinacioni, arbitrio et judicio Johannis Ordeux, (Robertus) Roberti Symson, Johannis Stokez, Thome Kendall litster arbitratorum inter partes predictas electorum ad arbitrandum . . . se, de et super omnibus et singulis contraversiis, querelis, debitis, debatis et demandis inter partes predictas motis, habitis sive (pedend) pendentibus a principio mundi usque in diem confeccionis presencium, ita quod etc., citra festum Sancte Marie Magdalene proximum.

[*bond* On 29 April 1490, [they came] personally before mayor John Gylliot in the [council] chamber and bound themselves to owe the lord king £10 that each of them would adhere to and carry out the ordinance, arbitration and judgement of John Hopkyn, William Shirburn, Richard Raby and John Pecher, arbiters impartially elected between glover John Liddale and widow Isabel Avner, over all personal actions, accusations, trespasses, complaints, disputes and demands moved, had or pending between them from the beginning of the world to the day these presents [bonds] are made, so that [the said judgement to be made] by the feast of Holy Trinity next coming.

bond On 5 July 1490, Thomas Rypon, alderman of the weavers of York and searcher of the same craft in the name of the whole craft, and also fisherman John Taillour came personally before mayor John Gylliot and bound themselves for £10 that they will bind themselves to [and] adhere to the ordinance, arbitration and judgement of John Ordeux, Robert Synson, John Stokez, and dyer Thomas Kendall, arbiters elected to arbitrate between the said parties . . . over all disputes, complaints, demands and debts moved, had or pending between them from the beginning of the world to the day these presents [bonds] are made, [the said judgement to be made] by the next coming feast of Saint Mary Magdalene.]

[f.172v]   Bonds to Keep the Peace
          10 and 26 January 1490

[Manucapcio] Johanne Guy de Harwod in comitatu Ebor' vidue quod ipsa dampnum vel [malum] aliquod corporale Willelmo Mankha' vel alicui de populo domini regis (regis) non [faciet nec] fieri procurabit quovismodo etc., videlicet quilibet manucaptorum (sub) x librarum et [predicta] Johanna sub pena xx librarum. [Manucaptores:] Thomas Spicer merchaunt, Johannes Coke wexchaun-deller, Ricardus Bistam [et] Christoforus Payntour taillours.

[Manucapcio] Christiane Guy de Harwod in comitatu Ebor' singlewoman etc. (quod) quod ipsa dampnum etc., Willelmo Mankha' etc., videlicet quilibet manucaptorum sub pena x librarum et predicta Christiana sub pena xx librarum. [Manucaptores:] Thomas Spicer merchaunt, Johannes Coke wexchaundeller, Ricardus Bistam [et] Christoforus Payntour taillours.

x^{mo} die Januarii anno v^{to} regni regis Henrici vij^{mi} Manucapcio Hugonis Robynson taillour quod ipse dampnum vel malum aliquod corporale Thome Wright alias Grayson husbondman vel alicui de populo domini regis non faciet nec fieri procurabit quovismodo, videlicet quilibet manucaptorum sub pena x librarum et predictus Hugo sub pena xx librarum de bonis et catallis terris et tenementis levandarum ad opus domini regis si etc. [Manucaptores:] Johannes Payntour generosus, Johannes Halme yoman.

xxvj^{to} die Januarii anno [quinto] regni regis Henrici vij^{mi} Manucaptio Jacobi Bolling de Bradford in comitatu Ebor' gent[leman] quod ipse dampnum vel malum aliquod corporale Ricardo Bakhouse vel alicui de populo domini regis non faciet nec fieri procurabit quovismodo videlicet quilibet manucaptorum sub pena xx librarum et predictus Jacobus sub pena (xx li.) ⟨xl librarum⟩ ad opus domini regis levandarum de terris et tenementis suis etc., si etc. [Manucaptores:] Willelmus Norton (gent') et Henricus Kent mercator.

[Mainprise of widow Joan Guy of Harewood, Yorkshire, that she do no damage nor bodily harm to William Mankha' nor to any other of the king's subjects, nor cause any harm to be done, under penalty of £20; sureties each under penalty of £10, namely merchant Thomas Spicer, waxchandeler John Coke, and tailors Richard Bistam and Christopher Payntour.

Mainprise of singlewoman Christiana Guy of Harewood, Yorkshire, that she do no damage etc. to William Mankha' etc., under penalty of £20; sureties [listed above] each under penalty of £10.

10 January 1490 Mainprise of tailor Hugh Robynson that he do no damage nor bodily harm to husbandman Thomas Wright alias Grayson nor to any other of the king's subjects, nor cause any harm to be done, under penalty of £20 levied of his goods and chattels to the work of the lord king; sureties each under penalty of £10, namely John Payntour, gentleman, and yeoman John Halme.

26 January 1490 Mainprise of James Bolling of Bradford, Yorkshire, gentleman, that he do no damage nor bodily harm to Richard Bakhouse nor to any other of the king's subjects, nor cause any harm to be done, under penalty of £40 levied of his lands and tenements to the work of the lord king; sureties each under penalty of £20, namely William Norton and merchant Henry Kent.]

**[f.173]   Successful Bond to Accept Arbitration
                  13 March 1490**

vacat [entry struck through and torn on right margin with loss of two to three words per line, as noted] (Memorandum quod xiij° die Marcii anno v^{to} Henrici vij^{mi} venerunt personaliter in camera cons[ilii coram] Johanne Gylliot maiore eiusdem tam Johannes Elwald mercator quam Thomas [Herryson] et recognoverunt se debere domino regi xl libras legalis monete Anglie quod [ipsi et eorum] stabunt et perimplebunt ⟨seu stabit et perimplebit⟩ ordinacioni, arbitrio et judicio Johannis Norm . . . arbitratorum per dictum maiorem indiferenter electorum, de et super omnibus et om[nimodis accionibus] ac aliis (assens) materiis tam realibus quam personalibus inter partes pr[edictas motis, habitis] sive pendentibus a principio mundi usque in diem confeccionis [presentium], quod eadem ordinacio, arbitrium et judicium fiant et reddantur [inter partes] predictas citra Dominicam in tercia septimana xlme proximam futuram, et super hoc . . . Carter devenit plegium per predictum Thomam Herryson quod stabit vel . . . sub pena forisfaciendarum summe xl librarum suprascripte.)

cancellatum quia partes concordate sunt

[*void* (On 13 March 1490, merchant John Elwald and Thomas [Herryson] came personally into the council chamber before mayor John Gylliot and bound themselves to owe the lord king £40 that they would adhere to and carry out the ordinance, arbitration and judgement of John Norm . . . arbiters impartially

elected by the mayor over all matters both real and personal moved, had or
pending between the parties from the beginning of the world to the day these
presents [bonds] are made, the judgement to be made and rendered by the
Sunday in the third week of Lent, and moreover . . . Carter became a surety for
Thomas Herryson that he would adhere to [the said judgement] under penalty to
be forfeited of the abovewritten £40.)

cancelled because parties are agreed]

Examination of an Apprentice
16 April 1490

Memorandum the xvj day of April the vth yere of the reign of King Henry the vij^{th}
in the counsail chaumbre of Ousbrig tofore the right wirshupful sir John Gylliot
maiour of the cite of York personalie appering William Hertford, William Shirburn
(jo) swern and examyned said (that) that John Brounberd bower was apprentice to
William Shirburn bower and served hym as apprentice by the space of iiij yeres and
no more; John Warde bower affirmed the same by his oth. Item John Gegges and
Thomas Aclyff bowers sworn shewed that Roger Brokholez in the tyme he being
seircheour ⟨charget⟩ that noman s   shold tak (hym to service) the said John
Brounberd (of) ⟨to⟩ wark bot as ⟨a⟩ straunger according to ther ordynaunce
apon payn the contempt comprehendit in the same.

[f.173v]   Arrests Made During Mayoralty of John Harper
3 February 1489 X 3 February 1490

Tempore Johannis Harper maioris civitatis Ebor'

[*left margin of entry torn, with loss of one to two words per line as noted*] [Preceptum
capias] (Alexandrum Lawson) ⟨Johannem Sanderson⟩ ffissher et Laurencium
Effotte laborer ad sectam . . . ington.

[Preceptum capias] Ricardum Ivenson de Scardeburgh in comitatu Ebor' mercatorem [et] ffissher ad sectam Willelmi Bailley.

[Preceptum] capias Johannem Robynson de Ebor' parissheclerk ad sectam Alicie
Note uxoris Gilberti Note baker.

Preceptum capias Johannem Cundall de civitate Ebor' ffullour ad sectam Johannis
Thomson lister.

Preceptum capias Jacobum Speght de Ebor' mercatorem ad sectam Johanne
Armorer singlewoman.

Preceptum capias Johannem Caulton alias Johannem Cokson nuper de Ebor'
escrevyner ad sectam Johanne Huchon vidue.

Preceptum capias Willelmum Wilberfosse de Wilberfosse yoman ad sectam Roberti Williamson carpenter.

Preceptum capias Bartholomeum Thorp de parochia de Helmesley smyth ad sectam Johanne Whitecroft singlewoman.

Preceptum capias Johannam Guy de Harwod in comitatu Ebor' ⟨viduam⟩ et Christianam Guy ⟨filiam eiusdem Johanne⟩ de eadem in eodem comitatu singlewoman.

Preceptum capias Jacobum Bolling de Bradford in comitatu Ebor' gent[leman] ad sectam Ricardi (Bakhas) Bakhouse etc.

[In the time of John Harper, mayor of the city of York

Order for the arrest of fisherman John Sanderson and laborer Laurence Effotte, at the suit of. . . .

Order for the arrest of merchant [and] fisherman Richard Ivenson of Scarborough, Yorkshire, at the suit of William Bailley.

Order for the arrest of parish clerk John Robynson of York at the suit of Alice Note, wife of baker Gilbert Note.

Order for the arrest of fuller John Cundall of York, at the suit of dyer John Thomson.

Order for the arrest of merchant James Speght of York, at the suit of singlewoman Joan Armorer.

Order for the arrest of John Caulton, alias John Cokson, formerly of York, scribe, at the suit of widow Joan Huchon.

Order for the arrest of yeoman William Wilberfosse of Wilberfoss, at the suit of carpenter Robert Williamson.

Order for the arrest of smith Bartholomew Thorp of the parish of Helmsley, at the suit of singlewoman Joan Whitecroft.

Order for the arrest of widow Joan Guy of Harewood, Yorkshire, and of singlewoman Christiana Guy, her daughter, of the same place.

Order for the arrest of James Bolling of Bradford, Yorkshire, gentleman, at the suit of Richard Bakhouse.]

[f.174]   Collectors in the Wards
Undated

Mikellith: Johannes Kyng, Ricardus Blakburn, collectores.

Northstrete: Thomas Watson, Henricus Bettes, collectores.

Castelgate: Willelmus Watson, Thomas Wright, collectores.

Bouthom: Willelmus Middelton, Thomas Inglishe, collectores.

Monkbarre: Thomas Barbour, Robertus Parke, collectores.

Walmegate: Georgius Essex, Willelmus Wynter, collectores.

[f.174v]   Various Jottings, Lists of Collectors in Wards, Bond to Keep the
Peace
Undated

[*left side of folio badly torn, entire surface worn and faded*]

. . . Robertus Tyndale

. . . liber homo et non admissus

. . . quid loksmyth ante alte Scole ⟨est⟩ commun' forstall' cas' iab' victuall'
veniend' ad . . . contra . . . .

Collectores wardarum civitatis:

. . . Brokden, . . . Kyng

. . . Robertus Denton, Thomas Glover bower.

Warda de Monkbarre: Robertus (Rede) ⟨Park⟩, Thomas Barbour, (Robertus
Shirley).

Warda postern de Northstrete: (Thomas Watson dyer) (Thomas Bankhouse)
Henricus Bettes.

Warda de Walmegate: Johannes Clerk cord[wainer]–b, Willelmus Broune dyer–a.

Warda de Bouthom: Johannes Chapell, Rogerus Brere.

Memorandum quod Thomas Herryson cord[wainer], Thomas Saddeller, Thomas Smyth manuceperunt et quilibet eorum manucepit pro Laurencio Scoreby clerico parochie Sancti Martini de Mikelgate ad intrandum corpus dicti Laurencii coram maiore super racionabilem premunicionem etc., sub pena cuiuslibet eorum x librarum etc., ad respondendum etc.

[Be it remembered that cordwainer Thomas Herryson, Thomas Saddeller [and] Thomas Smyth became sureties and each bound himself on behalf of Laurence Scoreby, parish clerk of Saint Martin's, Micklegate, under penalty of £10, to bring Laurence bodily before the mayor upon reasonable warning to answer etc.]

[*various jottings, single letters formed and practiced*]

Collectores in Boutham: Robertus Banes, Johannes Fiddeller, Rolandus Falowfeld, Thomas Lewlyn.

Serchours of milners: Willelmus Seller, Johannes Barker.

[*marginalia faded and damaged*] Thomas Wharf, Johannes Tirell.

Memorandum my most rev[erend?]

Memorandum ther is delyverd (vij) ⟨viij⟩ chartours more and les to the most reverend fader in God tharchiebisshop of Caunterbury and chaunceller of England [*incomplete*]

Richard Trent porter porter payment [*incomplete*]

NOTE TO APPENDICES

There are five appendices. With one exception, each appendix contains an edition of a manuscript in the York City Archives and is described more fully at the head of each entry. The fifth appendix is a transcription of a passage from an important but scarce printed work. Although not physically bound with the House Books themselves, this material supplements the evidence found within the volumes, and in some cases may have been separated from the bound books. Editorial procedure for these appended materials follows that used for the preceding volumes.

APPENDIX I
Y.C.A. MS. E.35

Source: Y.C.A. E.35, Liber Miscellanea Volume 4 (Ouse Bridge precedents Volume 3, edited by Darcy Preston in 1699). This source contains the so-called missing House Book One, recording material dated 1461 to 1465, and only briefly and incompletely calendared by antiquary Darcy Preston. Pagination refers to E.35, foliation to the missing House Book. Dating of many of these entries is problematical. William Stockton and John Thirsk receive special mention by Preston in his calendars, as though they headed an attendance list whose other members he did not bother to copy. However, Stockton was mayor during the 1446–47 and 1461–62 terms, and Thirsk held office 1442–43 and 1462–63; these dates do not conform to some of the dates Preston provides or the order in which he has calendared the entries. Three entries apparently were duplicated in the lost original, and one entry bears no foliation.

[p.1276]:

[f.16]   **Disobedience of Summons**
                 20 April, no year

John Thirsk major stapul'

⟨to be⟩ *comitted for not appearing according to sumons* For asmuch as Richard Ryland was sumoned to have been afore the mayor and counsel of the chamber at this same day and came not, therefore it was agreed and consented by all the whole counsel that he shall be putt in prison and kept unto the next comeing together of the counsel again etc., and what officer as shall be comanded to take him and he be remiss and see him and will not take him, he shall loose his service and office therein.

[f.8]   **Wardens' Duties in Wards**
                 4 November 1461

William Stokton mayor

wardens to punish rebells and tresspassors in their wards Item ordinatum de communi assensu quod quilibet aldermannus et custos cujuslibet warde habeat potestatem capiendi et puniendi quoscumque rebellos et transgressores contra dominum regem et legem suam infra wardam suam hujus civitatis. Et si quis aldermannorum et custodum neglexerit execucionem hujus ordinationis sit punitus per majorem et eius consilium eadem forma qua huiusmodi transgressor punitus fuisset.

[ff.17v,38]   Defence of the City
                 29 April 1463

William Stokton, penultimo die Aprilis, 3 Edwardi 4

two tall watchmen at each barr and their duty It is agreed that from henceforth every barr shall be dayly kept with two tall men unarrayed to the intent that if any suspected person comes in at any of the said barrs they may have knowledge of them and be ascertained of the cause of their comeing and whence they come and whither that they purpose.

4 men of the ward to watch each night Item that 4 men of every ward shall nightly watch within the ward from 9 of the clock at even unto 4 a clock at morn.

barrs to be shutt at 9 at night and opened at 4 in the morning Item that the barrs of this city shall be nightly sparred at 9 of the clock at even and so kept untill 4 of the clock at morn and the keys nightly brought into the mayor's keeping.

[f.25]   Guns and Walls Repaired
                 18 July, no year

William Stokton mayor

barr walls repaired The gunns of the city to be reparelled, gunpowder bought and that the walls of this city shall be overseen and the defaults of them amended by the oversight of the wardens of the walls.

[f.26v]   Discharge from Office
                 17 August, no year

John Thirsk

an ald[erman] laid down his gown and paid a fine for it John Ince for his discharge from that office to pay 50 marks, videlicet £20 in hand and 5 marks yearly for 4 years.

[ff.2,32v]   **Gowns for City Officers**
                   c.25 December, no year

In super vigilia Natalis Domini, William Stokton

aldermen skarlett and 24 violet gowns Agreed every alderman shall provide him
against the comeing of the king and parliament unam togam decentem de scarlett et
quod quilibet de numero 24 habebit togam decentem et honestam violett ad tempus
supradictum.

[f.37v]   **Gowns in Summer**
                   22 March, no year

crimson vesture for all the counsel in sumer Quod omnes de consilio camere
habebunt vesturam suam estivalem hoc anno de uno [*sic*] secta de crimson sub pena
6 s. 8 d. cujuslibet deficientis levanda ad fabricam Guihald' et sub pena 20 s.
levanda de majore si ipse negligent fuerit in levacione dicte 6 s. 8 d. de illis qui non
proficerit hanc ordinacionem.

[f.39]   **Toll and Murage Payments**
                   11 April, no year

tenants and inhabitants of Thurne and Hatfield to pay toll and murage respectuatur
Concesserunt unanimiter quod ab hoc die in futurum omnes et singuli tenentes et
habitantes in Thurne et Hatfield solvent theoloneum et muragium quotiescumque
et quandocumque venerint seu eorum aliquis venit ad civitatem cum rebus et
mercandisis suis venalibus ad vendendos prout solvere consueverunt a tempore
cujus contraria memoria hominum non existit.

[p.1277]:

[not foliated] Officers to Attend Processions
                   1 December 1462

1 December 2 Edward IV, William Stokton

councel to attend major at processions on pain of 4 d. Item it is agreed that every
man of the counsel chamber shall from hense forth in every general procession
come personally and walk with the mayor in the said procession without any
sumons or warning to be made unto him without that they have a reasonable excuse
upon pain of loosing of 4 d. of every person that shall make default.

*[An entry labelled Liber 3, 1475 to 1479, fo.1, hereafter follows, dated 28 February
[blank] Edward IV, Thomas Wrangwish mayor [1476–77], duplicating the entry*

transcribed above in Book One, f.1, concerning attendance of civic officials in Minster processions.]

[p.1301]:

**[f.6v]   Committee Appointed, Aldermen as Members of Parliament
                  30 September 1462**

William Stokton mayor, ultimo [die] Septembris 2 Ed[wardi] 4

courts, issues and amerciaments; committee for them A comittee appointed to sett a certain rule and form how the courts, issues and amerciaments shall be governed and received in time comeing, and then it to be shewed to the counsel and after to the comons.

burgesses wages if they keep house, 4 s. a day; if they board, 2 s. Agreed that for asmuch as now late some aldermen being at the parliament in time past have gone to board, where as they have at all times tofore holden house for the worship of the city, that from henseforth what alderman so ever shall go to the parliament and will hold house shall have for his costs dayly 4 s. and if he goes to board he shall have but 2 s. upon the day and no more from now forth.

**[f.17]   Marginalia without Entries
                  Undated**

two aldermen electi sunt custodes clavorum communis sigillii [no entry]

an al[derman] fined 5 marks for laying down office, fo. 26b [no entry]

**[f.16]   Instructions for Receipt of Estreats
                  16 April, no year**

(William Stockton) ⟨John Thirsk⟩ mayor

estreats before the justices of peace, how to be levied Agreed that all amerciaments and issues lost afore the justices of the peace of this city shall be received by the mayor's sarjeants as follows: videlicet, the clerk of the sessions of peace shall write out the estreats within 8 days after the sessions and then the sargeants to make levy thereof within other 8 days, and if they do it not, then the sums thereof unraised by the said sargeants to be sett in their fees, and if any comoners will resist or take part to lett the payment thereof, that then all the 12 and the 24 shall take part with the mayor and support him in the said act, etc.

[f.6v]   **Marginalia without Entry**
                    Undated

Guy Fairfax recorder [*no entry*]

[ff.7v,17v]   **Marginalia without Entry**
                    Undated

watch [*no entry*]

[f.16v]   **Marginalia without Entry**
                    Undated

one being summoned to appear before mayor and council came not, is therefore order[ed] to be comitt till next court [*no entry*]

[f.8v]   **Marginalia without Entry**
                    Undated

wardens and aldermen within their wards to arreast and punish trespassers against the king and his laws [*no entry*]

APPENDIX II
Y.C.A. E.32

Source: Y.C.A. E.32 Liber Miscellanea Volume I, pp. 1–2, 49, 487–95. This source contains 557 pages consisting mainly of lists of citizens in arrears, bonds for good behaviour, and acts of local interest such as arrests of bales of wood. Scattered throughout the source are the following entries which deal mainly with Edward IV's Scottish campaigns 1480–82. City elections and the reputation of the duke of Gloucester are also discussed. For the most part, the entries consist of copies of letters to the city from the king, Gloucester, and Henry Percy earl of Northumberland. Many are dated by day and month but not by year, and the determination of the date of each letter is not without its problems, as discussed at the heads of the following entries. All but the last two letters, dated 14 May and 14 July 1482, are copied by the same hand.

[p.1]   **King Edward Orders Preparations for War with Scotland**
              3 February X 3 March 1481

[Robert Amyas was elected 3 February 1481; Edward IV completed his twentieth year on the throne on 3 March 1481; hence the letter's composition falls between the two dates.]

Tempore Roberti Amyas maioris civitatis Ebor' anno regni regis Edwardi quarti post conquestum vicesimo

Tharticles of credence by the kynges commaundement to be delyverede to the duc of Gloucestr' and therle of Northumberland by Thomas Lynom and Rauff Hothom:

(Ri R Right honorabill)

First, uppon delyvere of the kynges lettres unto aither of theme, it is to be shewed that the kynges mynde, will and and [sic] desire is that thei in all godely hast uppon the same shulde comme to gidder in a conveniant place for thexecusion of theffect of the seid lettres.

Item, that aither of theim incontinent theruppon shall addres theim severally to their parties calling unto theim theire servauntes and inhabitauntes of the same, shewing the kynges mynde and entent compresed in the seid lettres, and theruppon aither of theim shall desire to undrestaunde the gude will and ascistance of every gentylman or touneships in that behalve so that the kyng may therby be assertanede of such nombre as will asciste and serve him in those contres accordyng the kynges desire in his seid letters.

Item, that aither of the(im) seid lordes in all goodly haste upon the foresaid shewyng the kynges mynde unto the seid countres, addresse thaim to come personally un[to] the kynges highnes and to depute in the meane seasone of the wisest ande moste discret and best willing persones to the kyng of those countres to avaunce the kynges entent in that behalve, and to understande as breefly as thei can every mannys mynde therin, so that the kyng may may [sic] be withoute delay acertaynede therof to thentent that he may furnysshe the remenauntes of his armes to the well, suerty and honour of him and of his land.

Item, that provisicion be maide for vitall in every place frome Trent furthwarde as the armee shall come, and that every good towne be entreted in those parties to appoynt and ordeyne vitalers to serve the king and his host by lande and also by water, aswell within his realme of England as within Scotland, for every vitalere shalbe well entreted and well and truely paid for his seid vitaillers.

Item, that every mane that shall go with the kyng in his seid viage to have uppon him a white jaket with a crosse of Seynt Georgie sweed theruppon, and if ony mane woll have beside that his particurer bagge of him list he may have it so that it be upon a jaket of armes of Seint Georgie withoute chaunge of coloure.

Item, that besides the kinges cariage and provisicions, provisicion be made for carige of cartes aboute Newcastell as shall nowe serve such of the kynges host as will by them, and also other cartes to the nombre of v^c ever goyng after the host with vitaill.

Item, that gode espies be contenually (maide) and daly within the realme of Scotland, so that the king may be daly assertaned therof as the case will require.

[p.2] Item, it shalbe shewd that the king settes to the see an armee roiall to the nombre of iij^{ml}v^c sowldiours with the Lord Haward and Cobham viged, vitaled and furnesshed for xx wekes.

Item, it is to be shewed what provisicion the king maketh aswell of vitaill as of artillare and his harmee in the south parties so that he highnes trusteth with the mercy of Gode it shalbe to the honour of him, the suerte of his subiettes and invincible to his enemys for ever.

Item, if ther be brought frome the south parties to Newcastell x^{ml} quarters of whete maide in maynde floure, whether the baker of Newcastell will do bake it and ordeyne cariage for it daly to serve the host, and to sell it ther and to content the marchaundes that bryught the seid floure at a resonable prise, as shalbe set by the clerk of the markett.

Item, that the bakers of Yorke, Doram and Newcastell, and other in the countre be spoken with, that if the kynges grace sendith ther floure to Newcastell thei to tak it at vij s. a quarters floure by indenture of the merchaundes, and to mak paiment to the seid merchauntes therfore when they have uttred it or els that thei woll mak purverance of whet after the same rate thameself, they shall have a prise of the kyng toward the performaunce of the same, and to repay the kyng ayien uppon the uttraunce therof.

Item, shewe to the vitelers that if any of theim be robbed or spoled by the kynges enemys, or by any other that sufficiently provide, the kyng shall se him restored to the valowe.

[p.49]   Slander of the Duke of Gloucester
24 June 1482

Memorandum that in the vigell of Saynt John Baptest in the xxij^{ti} yere of our sovereyn lige lorde Kyng Edward the iiij^t, John Davyson taillour was sent fore tofore Richerd Yorke, than being maiour, for a variaunce betwix the said John and one Roger Brere saddiller, the which John Davyson (emg) emonges other shewed howe that he hard Master William Melrig say in a place where he and other was, that he hard Master Roger Brere say that as toching my lorde of Gloucestr', 'What myght he do for the cite? Nothing bot gryn of us'. The said William Melrig the same day was sent fore, cam personalie tofore the said maiour, and ther and then demanded by the same maiour what sedicious wordes he hard at eny tyme Roger Brere say of my lorde of Gloucestre; he answerd and said noon; and then it(s) was forther shewed whether he hard ever (v) the said Roger say, 'What (my) ⟨may my⟩ lorde of Gloucestre do for (you) us of the cite? No thing bot gryn of us'. The said William Melrig answerd and said that he hard never the said Roger say noon such wordes ne other wordes, the which shold sound eny thing to my said lord of Gloucestre dishonour ne displesour and that he answerd and said that he is and wilbe at all tymez redy ⟨that⟩ to approve etc. This was shewed tofore the said maiour, shireffes, chamberleyns and other diverse cocicesyns of this said cite of Yorke etc.

[p.487]   King Edward Tries to Ease City's Military Burden
12 April 1482

[This letter bears no year, but it must be dated to 1482. Not only did the 1482 campaign prompt serious concerns about food and equipment, but it is confirmed from privy seal documentation that Edward IV spent much of the winter and spring of that year at the Tower of London, from whence this letter is dated: Cora Scofield, *The Life and Reign of Edward the Fourth*, 2 vols. (London, 1923), II.333.]

By the kyng

Trusty and welbelovyd we grete you wele, and where as oure right trusty and right entierlie belovyd brother the duc of Gloucestre for the gude lordship and favour he bereth unto you hath sued unto us, that in consideracion ye be not of such richesse as ye have been in tyme past, we wold be content to have a capitan and six score archers at your costes and charges tattend uppon us in this our voyage, that with

Goddes grace we think to make against (or) our enymies and rebelles the Scottes; we lat you wite that for the prayer and at instance of our said brother we be pleasid with the said capitan and vj^{xx} archers, willyng you in every wise to se that the said costes and charges be not laid uppon eny pour (cocitesyn) comoner bot uppon such citezins within our said citie as may easelie bere the same. And over this, we wol that ye pourvey for us asmany cartes for cariages of vitailles, and asmuch vitaille as ye by your gude pollesies and diligence can arredie for the vitaillyng of oure hoost, wherynne and in all the premissez we have shewyd our mynde to oure said entierlie belovyd brother, to whome (see) see that ye yeve ful feith and credence. Yeven undre oure signet at oure Toure of London the xijth day of Aprile.

To our trustie and wellbelovyd the maiour and his brethern of our cite of Yorke

[p.488]   **Prince of Wales Orders City to Investigate Servant's Delivery of Harness**
26 June, year uncertain

[The dating of this letter and the one following is problematical. Edward IV planned to lead his army north himself in both 1481 and 1482. It is likely, but not certain, that the letter dates to the latter year, during which preparations for war were more complex. It would also allow the young prince, born 1470, to have matured enough for him and his council to participate in such preparations. It should be noted that William Spence, a member of the council of twenty-four, was mayor in neither of those years.]

By the prince

Right trustie and welbelovyd we grete you wel, and where as it is shewed unto us on the behalve of our welbelovyd servaunt Thomas Fisshe howe that he delyvered unto William Spence, inhabited within your office of marialtie of the cite of Yorke, certayn harneysse to thentent to have had the same kepte to his use and behove, and although he to his greit cost and charge hath oft tymes demaund and required (delyverd) deliverance of his said harneyse, yit in noo wise he can have it; wherfore, and for asmuche as we have assigned hym to yeve his personall attendaunce uppon my most drad lorde and fadre in his roial voiage into Scotland, we desire and hertelie pray you at our instaunce and contemplacion of thees our lettres in all gudelie hast to doo call before you the said William Spence and examyn hym of the premissez and to take such direccon therin as shalbe thought by your wisdome most according, wherin ye shall doo unto us thyng of right acceptable pleasir. Yeven undre our signet at the castell of Ludlowe the xxvjth day of June.

To our ryght trustie and welbelovyd the maire of the cite of Yorke

Right trustie and welbelovyd we grete you wel [*incomplete, and in a hand different from the entry above*]

[p.489]   **Earl of Northumberland Asks for Troops**
                     2 July, year uncertain

[Because of the scale of preparations during the 1482 campaign season, the following letter could belong to that year. On the other hand, in June 1481 the city officials were in touch with Percy about mustering troops and this letter could be part of correspondence from that summer. However, the following could also be the letter referred to in House Book 2–4, f.9, an entry dated 13 August 1480 which mentions receipt of a letter from the earl but does not include a copy in the register.]

Your (lover) lovyng ffrend, H. Northumberland

Right wirshupful and right hartelie belovyd frend and right trusty and welbelovyd frendes, I commaund me unto you and desire and pray you within viij days efter the sight herof to certefie me of howe meny able persones defensible arraied ye kan purvey within the cite of Yorke and the fraunches of the same, to take the kynges wages bisid such persones as the said cite hath grauntid at this tyme to fynd into Scotland; this I pray you be perfourmed as ye entend the subduyng of the kynges our sovereyn lordes greite rebell and auncient enemyes the Scottes and the suretie of this his reame; and the blissed Ternite preserve you. Writen in my castel of Wresill the secund daie of July.

To the right wirshipful and my right hertelie belovyd frende and right trusty and welbelovyd ffrendes the maiour and shireffes of the cite of Yorke

Earl of Northumberland Asks York Troops to Join Him
7 September, year uncertain

[P. M. Kendall provides good reasons for dating this letter to 1481 when he observes that on the following day the city, perhaps prompted by this letter, made hasty preparations for the campaign, and on 9 September changed the date of departure from Monday (as stipulated below by Percy) to Tuesday: P. M. Kendall, *Richard the Third* (New York: W. W. Norton and Co., Inc., 1955), p.535 n.6. However, one may object that too much haste was required. 7 September 1481 fell on a Friday, and the city had to receive this letter from Wressle, 18 miles away, prepare its forces, and march them the 32 miles to Northallerton before 8 a.m. the following Monday, a task stretching the capacities of an urban amateur army.]

Your hertelie lover H. Northumberland

Right worshipful frend and right hartelie bilovyd frendes I commaund me unto you, and for asmuch as the Scottes in greit nombre ar entred into Northumberland, whos malice God helpyng I entend to resist, therfor on the kyng our soveraine lordes behalve I charge you, and on myn behalve as warden desire and praye you that all suche persones as ye goodly may make in thair beste and most defensible array on horsse, be with me upon Monday next cumyng by viij of the clok to fore none apon Northallerton more; this I pray you be applyed as my speciall trust is in you, and as ye entend the welle and (sure) suerty of thos parties, and I beseche God send you all good ffortunet [*sic*] and us gud spede. Writtyn in my castell of Wresyll in hast the vij^th daie of Septembre.

To the right worshypfull and my ryght hartely belovyd frende and frendes the maiour and his bretheryn of the citee of York and the comons of the same and every of them

[p.490]   Duke of Gloucester Asks for Troops at Durham
                    8 September, year uncertain

[Kendall argues that the letters of 7 and 8 September, from Percy and Gloucester respectively, both date from 1481 and thus explain why the city postponed its troops' departure from Monday to Tuesday in order to join Richard's forces at Durham: Kendall, *Richard the Third*, pp.164–65. More recent research by A. J. Pollard, as yet unpublished, points out the incongruity of Gloucester and Northumberland calling independently but simultaneously on the city of York, with the earl reporting that the Scots had already crossed the border, and the duke knowing a day later only that the enemy was about to descend on Saturday night. Pollard prefers a 1481 date for the Northumberland letter and relates the Gloucester letter to a raid by the earl of Angus on Bamburgh in September 1480. Indeed, on 30 August 1480, the city council received a letter from Gloucester advising them of his intention to attack the Scots: see above, Book 2–4, f.10.]

The duc of Gloucestre

Right trusty and welbeloved we grete you wele, and let you wyt that it is shewyd unto us that the Scottes in grete multitude entende this Saterday nyght in thre hoostes to entre into the thre marches of these north partyes, and by suche knowlage as our cosin of Northumbirland hath that they entende to entre into hys marches, we trustyng to God to be mete to resiste their malice whatsoever marches that they do entre, on the kyng our soverayn lordes behalve we desire and require you therfore and on our owne hertely praye you that for the defence of this his realme and resistence of their said malices, ye do send unto us to Duresme on Thursday next comyng a servaunt of yours accompanyd with suche certen nombre of your citee defensibly araied, as that ye entende and may deserve right speciall thankes of the kynges hyghnes and us, and that this be not failled as our faithfull trust is in you. Yeven under our signet the viij[th] day of September.

To our right trusty and welbelovyd the maiour, schereffes and aldermen of the cetie of Yorke

Earl of Northumberland Writes of Raid and Need for Additional Soldiers
13 October, year uncertain

[This letter does not fit easily into any year. Kendall dates it to 1480 in order to explain a delegation the city sent the next day to the duke of Gloucester (Kendall, p.535 n.2). However, the House Book record of the delegation does not specify the day on which it occurred (Book 2–4, f.11v). In 1481, the activity of mustering had already taken place in York, so Percy's letter would have been old news unless he was writing of a second–and perhaps only threatened–Scottish raid, or a second offensive. In October 1481, Gloucester was still fighting in Scotland, and the siege of Berwick lasted all winter, so continued activity is not unlikely.]

aboutes thelleccion of the maire for this yere, to the grete trouble of the same, whiche sowneth to oure right displeasir, we entending in all goodly haste to have the causes and matier thrughly to be examind and undirstanden, wol therfor and desir you that for the mean season ye wol take upon you and contynue furth the saide mairaltie to suche tyme as that schall have from us knowlache of oure pleasure to the contrary withoute faylyng, as oure truste is in you, lattyng you witt that we have commaunded both Richard York and Thomas Wraungwysh for the meane season to successe of any dealyng or clayme unto the same, and that ye ne fayle herof as ye desire to do us singulier pleasir. Yeven undre oure signet at our Towr of London the xij day of February.

To oure trusty and welbeloved Robert Amyas late mairer of our citie of York

King Edward Disturbed by Election Problems
14 February 1482

By the kyng

We grete you wele, and where it is soo that for the variaunce of theleccion of thoffice of mairaltee of our cite of York for this yer bitwene Richard of York and Thomas Wrangwysh, citezyns of our saide cite, we late wrote unto you and theme undre our signet and schewid our wille and pleaser for the peas and restfulnesse of our saide citee, whiche our writing not withstonding our said peax ys ther gretely troubled as we be credibly enformyd, we therfor yit eftsonys by the advise of the lordes of our counsail write unto you charging you that ye conforme you to that that maye best serve for the wele and quiete of our said citee according to suche advertisementes and instruccions as we have (writtyn) yeven to our trusty and welbeloved Sir Edmond Hastinges knyght and Mylys Medcalf berers herof, to whom we wol ye gif feith and credence as to our self in alle that on our behalf they schall schewe unto you touchyng the premissez, not failing herof upon the feith and liegaunce that ye owe unto us. Yeven undre our pryve seal at our palays of Westm' the xiiij day of February.

To Robert Amyas late maire of our citee of York

[p.494]   City Sends Good Wishes to Duke of Gloucester
c.14 May 1482

[John Tong is first listed as mayor *locum tenens* on 2 May 1482 (Book 2–4, f.57v). The House Book entry dated 14 May 1482 (f.58) discusses the duke of Gloucester's military needs and musters the men promised to him in the following letter.]

To the ryght hygh and myghti prince and our ful gude and gracius lorde the duc of Gloucestre, gret chamberleyn, constable, admirall of England, and warden of the west marchis ⟨of Yngland⟩ ayanst Skotland

Ryght hygh and myghti prince and our ful gude and gracius lorde, we your humble servauntes recommandes us un to your gude grace, and where of late it is don us to undyrstand that ye in your nobile person entendith by the grace of God apon Wedynsday next commyng to entre the ground of Scotland in subdewyng our most dred sovereyn lordes auncient enemys Scottes, in the wich viage we besek God and Saynt George to be your gude gyde and send your gracius lorde victorie of the said Scottes and ther adherantes; have at our pore powers at thys tyme sent by our gentilman ⟨servant⟩ to the maisez John Brakebury unto your said grace, to whom we besech to gyf credence, a certeyn people defensable arraid, not chargyng the pour commonaltie with the costes and charges uppon thame, to attend and be at your gracius commandment, besechyng your gude grace to be un to us and to the cite of Yorke as ye have (bene) ben at al tymis gude and gracius lorde, and we shalbe redy to accomplish that at may be to your gracius pleasour, that knoweth the immortale God who have your gracius lord and all odyr attendyng of your said grace in hys kepyng.

Redy to your gracius pleasour, your homble servantes John Tonge leutenaunt, the shyryffes, (ad) aldermen and odir of the chambyr of the cite of Yorke

[p.495]   City Thanks Duke of Gloucester for Reducing Number of Soldiers Required
14 July 1482

[On 13 July 1482, the council discussed the mustering of soldiers, their wages, and the selection of captains John Brakenbury and Thomas Davyson (Book 2–4, f.63). The following letter, undoubtedly, reports those findings to the duke of Gloucester.]

Ryght hygh and myghti prince and our full gude and gracius lord, we your humble servantes humbly recommandes us to your gude grace with all our servicez and thankes you of your gude and gracius lordship to us shewyd her afore, and in especiall of that at wher we here afore promittid to our most drad suffreyn legh lord the kyng the nombyr of vj^{xx} archers to this viage now to be had in to Skotland, that it lyst your gude grace of your benevolens to concedyr the povert of thys pure cite to pardon us to the nombyr of v skor archers and a capiten, the wich nombyr we have sent at thys tym with our gentilman servant John Brakynbery and Thomas Davyson to atend apon your nobill person, to whom and to us we besek you to be as ye have beyn at all tyms gude and gracius lord and to doo your gracius commandment, both we and tha at all tymis shalbe ⟨⟨rydy⟩⟩ (ridde) ⟨redy⟩ to our powers be the grace of God, whom we besek to preserve your full nobill person in thys your nobill yorney and all odyr. At York the xiiijth day of July.

To the ryght hygh and myghti prince and our full gude and gracius lord the (ducere) duce of Gloucestre, grete chamberleyn, constabill, admirall of Yngland and wardeyn of the west marches of Yngland ayanst Skotland

By your homble servantes the maire and hys bredir, sheryffes and all the hole counsell of the cite of York

APPENDIX III
Y.C.A. MS. A/Y APPENDIX

Source: Y.C.A. A/Y appendix, ff.1–2, 23–37v (ff.3–22v contain an index to the main body of the manuscript). This is a paper manuscript bound at the end of a major source for York history published by the Surtees Society as *York Memorandum Book* Volumes 1 and 2. The paper appendix has its own foliation separate from the 381 parchment folios preceding it. The folios of the appendix contain entries referring to Richard duke of Gloucester's usurpation of the throne and his first months as king. This information may have been considered too dangerous to retain in House Book 2–4 after 1485, but the appendix also refers to the ordinary business and transactions overseen by the city council. That this material always constituted a separate volume apart from the House Books is indicated by the continuity of original foliation in Book 2–4, and by the references on folio 27v, below, to the separate 'pawpir boke of the counsell chambir of the cite'.

[f.1]   **Attack Outside Bootham Bar**
                   18 and 22 June 1482

[R] *examinacion of an variance* Memorandum that the xviij day of June the xxij yere of Kyng Edward the iiij^th come ⟨in to the chambyr⟩ a for Richard Yorke the maire, Thomas Cok, Lowrans [Wyldman], John Davyson, and the said Thomas Cok as a indeferent man (chos) sworn than and thar showyd whow that he and ⟨the said⟩ Lowrans Wyldman ⟨went arm in arm the xvij^th day of the said moneth⟩ and war walkyng out of Bowthhom ⟨barr⟩ to the (abbet) abbey of Saint Mare and thar (that) met with ⟨the said⟩ John Davison tayllyour and the said John Davyson gave the said Lowrans a pon the show⟨d⟩ir and strake both the said Lowrans and the (T) said Thomas Cok to the guttyr, and thar apon the said John Davyson drewe hys dager and wold a bene apon the said Lourans, and the said Thomas Cok seyng that gat the said John Davyson in hys armys and held hym, and thar apon the said Lowrans drewe hys dager and the said Thomas Cok seyng that the dager of the said Lowrens was owt that the said John Davison not gretly preisid, the said Thomas Cok left the said John Davyson and went to hold the said Lowrans and when the said John Davyson was lows thys wys, 'wele Lowrens thow and I shall meit here [*one word illegible*],' and ther apon the said John Davyson put upp hys dagyr and went hys wa, wher apon for as ⟨moch as⟩ the said John Davyson was a fore thys boundyn to kepe the peas and comys to the said bond demend hym as is above wrytyn, the said mair committid ⟨and comaundid the⟩ (to) said John Davison to prison etc.

Item upon the said variaunce the said John Davyson ⟨the⟩ xxij^ti day the yere abovesaide of our sovereyn lige lorde the kyng tofore the said Richerd Yorke maiour shewed howe that he was sory that he shold offend to eny person of this cite and desired the said maiour that ony person that coude fynd or shewe ayanest hym eny mater or maters that he wold abide by the sight (of the sight) of the maiour or of whome the said maiour wold assigne.

[f.1v] Pledges Found, Bond to Accept Arbitration
22 and 25 June 1482

Eshden xxij° die mensis Junii anno regni regis Edwardi iiij xxij° Johannes Custans pistor et Ricardus Symson wa[l]ker devenerunt plegios pro Rogero Eshden quod idem Rogerus erit coram Ricardo York maiore civitatis Ebor' quandocumque ad hoc congrue requisitus fuerit.

recognisaunce Johanne Gilfeld [two words illegible] Memorandum quod ars de wakers civitatis Ebor' ⟨et ars de wakers de Beverl' videlicet Johannes Nutall et alii⟩ et Johannes Gylfeld de civitate predicta xxv° die mensis Junii anno regni regis Edwardi iiij^ti xxij° coram Ricardo York maiore civitatis predicte posuerunt se stare arbitrio, ordinacioni et judicio Johannis Williamson, Johannis Gurnard, (Roberti Stay Symson) ⟨Willelmi Thomson⟩, (et) Thome Muse, Roberti Atkynson et Henrici Topham ad arbitrandum inter partes predictas de et super omnimodis sectis, querelis, debatis et controversiis in (d) eos habitis a principio mundi usque in diem confeccionis presencium, ita quod dicta arbitrium, (a) ordinacio et judicium ⟨dictorum arbitratorum⟩ fia[n]t et reddantur inter partes predictas citra festum Sancti Petri Advincula proximum etc., (sub pena [2 words torn] et obligerunt) ⟨quolibet eorum⟩ obligavit se (stro) stare arbitrio dictorum arbitratorum sub pena xl solidorum solvendorum parta etc.

[On 22 July 1482, fisherman John Custans and walker Richard Symson became sureties for Roger Eshden to assure Roger's presence before the mayor when required.

bond for John Gilfeld On 25 July 1482, the craft of the walkers of York and the same craft of Beverley, namely John Nutall, John Gylfeld, and others, came before the mayor and agreed to abide by the judgement of John Williamson, John Gurnard, William Thomson, Thomas Muse, Robert Atkynson, and Henry Topham, arbiters between the said parties and judging all suits and complaints they have had, before the feast of Saint Peter's Chains. Each of the parties agrees to abide by the judgement under penalty of 40 s.]

Ingre' Johnson, Robert' Spofford [*bottom line damaged and illegible*]

[f.2] Bond to Keep the Peace
22 June 1482

Supersedeas pro Johanne Davyson sissore

Vicesimo secundo die mensis Junii anno regni regis Edwardi quarti xxij° venit Johannes Davyson de civitate Ebor' tayliour coram Ricardo York maiore civitatis predicte in camera civitatis predicte super (Us) Ousam et ostendit breve domini regis de supersedeas et petit breve illud de recordo irrotulari inter recorda civitatis predicte cuius tenor sequitur in hec verba et est talis:

Edwardus Dei gracia rex Anglie et Francie et dominus Hibernie, custodibus pacis sue infra civitatem Ebor' ac vicecomitibus eiusdem civitatis et eorum cuilibet salutem. Quia Ricardus Goldyng de parochia Sancti Martini in Campis in comitatu Midd' glover, Johannes Asterley de eadem parochia sherman, Johannes Gunter de eadem parochia yoman et Willelmus Blekynsop de parochia Sancti Dacorum extra barram Novi Templi London' in comitatu Midd' patenmaker, coram nobis in cancellaria nostra personaliter constituti manuceperunt, videlicet quilibet eorum sub pena xx^{ti} librarum pro Johanne Davyson taillour ac idem Johannes Davyson assumpsit pro se ipso sub pena quadraginta marcarum quod ipse dampnum vel malum aliquod alicui de populo nostro de corpore suo aut de incendio domorum suarum non faciet nec fieri procurabit quovismodo quam quidem summam xx librarum quilibet manucaptorum predictorum ac dictam summam quadraginta marcarum prefatus Johannes Davyson concesserunt de terris et catallis suis ad opus nostrum levari si dampnum vel malum aliquod alicui de populo nostro predicto de corpore suo aut de domibus suis predictis per huiusmodi incendium per prefatum Johannem Davyson seu procurationem suam eveniat ullo modo vobis mandamus quod cuicumque securitati pacis de prefato Johanne Davyson ad prosecucionem alicuius de populo nostro predicto coram vobis ulterius capiende quocumque nomine idem Johannes Davyson censeatur supersedeates omnino. Et si ipsum Johannem Davyson ea occasione ceperitis tunc ipsum a prisona qua ac detinetur si ea occasione et non alia detineatur in eadem sine dilatione deliberare faciet per manucapcionem et assumpcionem supradictas. Teste me ipso apud Westm' xxvj die Octobris anno regni nostri sextodecimo.

Wodward

[[Writ of] *supersedeas* for tailor John Davyson

On 22 June 1482, John Davyson came before the mayor and showed a royal writ of *supersedeas* and asked that it be enrolled in the city records. Its form is as follows:

Edward by the grace of God, etc., to the keepers of his peace in the city of York and to the sheriffs of the same, greetings. Glover Richard Goldyng of the parish of Saint Martin in the Fields, shearman John Asterley, yeoman John Gunter, and patenmaker William Blekynsop of the parish of Saint Clement Danes outside the gate of New Temple, London, came before us in our chancery and each bound himself for £20 on behalf of tailor John Davyson. Davyson bound himself for forty marks that he would do no harm to the bodies or properties of any of our subjects. Therefore we command a stay of execution of all other writs that might be sued out against him, and if he is imprisoned for any other reason he should be

released without delay. Witnessed by me at Westminster 26 October 1476.
[Subscribed] Wodward]

[f.2v blank]

[ff.3–22v, index to main body of A/Y]

[f.23]   **Reported Slander of Duke of Gloucester**
                  14 and 15 February 1483

Memorandum that the xiiij[th] day of February in the xxij[ti] yere of Kyng Edward the
iiij[th] come afore (t) John Marshall leutenaunt Robert Rede gyrdeler in to the
counsell chamber with odir persons with hym, and than and thar shewyd whow that
William Welles ⟨cowper⟩ shold report that the last day of Januari last past sityng
at the ale at Eden Berys in Gothyrngate (the) that one askyd and said emong the
felliship sittyn at ale, 'Syrs, whom shall we have to owr mair thys yere?' Wher unto
awnswerd and said Stevyn Hoghson, (sirs) 'Syrs, me thyng and it plees the
communs I wold we had Maister Wrangwysh, for he is the man that my lord of
Gloucestre will doo for'; and the said Rede says that the said William Welles
reportes of hym that he shold awnswer and say thar to na, and said that if my lord
Gloucestir wold have hym mair the communs woldnot have hym mare; and her
apon the said Welles sent for afore the said leutenaunt the xv[th] day of the said
moneth, examend be the said leutenaunt of the premissis, said na, he said not so,
bot he (said) says that the said Rede said and awnswerd the said Hoghson and said
that myght not be, for the mair must be chosyn be the commonalte and not be no
lord. Wher apon the said Stevyn, Robert Jackson gyrdler, Thomas Pollow, Robert
Shyrley, John Holme, John Kyng gyrdler, Thomas Nelson smyth, Hubard Brygges
pynner, Thomas Wryght bocher, beyng at the said all hows in whose presens the
langage that was said was said, be the said leutenaunt examynd, said that the
langage of the said Rede was that (the said) my lord of Gloucestir woldnot be
displesid whomsomewyr it pleasid to communs to chos for thar mare, and that that
was the sayngs of the said Rede and no nodyr. **[f.23v]** Wherapon John Awnwyk
examynd afor the said leutenaunt, said (the) that he hard the said Welles say that
the said Rede said that yf my lord of Gloucestir wold have Maister Wrangwysh mair
that than ⟨he⟩ (it) shol not be, for he hard hym (sha) say that the mair shalnot
be chosyn be no mare [sic].

[f.24]   **Minstrel Pays Fine to Capmakers**
                  3 March 1483

De tempore Johannis Newton maioris anno xxij° Edwardi iiij[ti]

Memorandum quod tercio die mensis Marcii anno regni regis Edwardi iiij[ti] preceptum fuit (per predictum maiorem) Johanni Swynburn minstrell alias capmaker per predictum maiorem quod se begerit et amorosi ⟨decetero⟩ omnibus et singulis de arte de capmakers de civitate Ebor' sub pena xl solidorum communitati huius civitatis solvendorum.

[During the mayoralty of John Newton in the twenty-second year of Edward IV:

On 3 March 1483, John Swynburn, minstrel and also capmaker, was ordered to make peace with all members of the craft of capmakers, under penalty of 40 s.]

Weaver Imprisoned for Disobedience
22 April 1483

Copeland Memorandum that the xxij*ti* day of Aprill in the yere of our lord God M*l*CCCClxxxiij, Jamys Copeland wever was committit to prison by my lord the mare (for the disobesaunce of ⟨thar to abyd⟩) for that at he disabeid the alderman of thar occupacion in soch thynges as concernyd thar occupacion at the will of my said lord the mair, thar to abyd for all the offensisis and trespasses that he has done to the said alderman and the said occupacion.

Delivery of Gunpowder
30 April 1483

gunpowdyr, quietus quia postea [illegible] [entry struck through] (Memorandum that the last day of Aprill in the yer of our lord God M*l*CCCClxxxiij° the chamberlayns deliwyrd to John Cravyn gentillman a barell with gunpowdyr weyng xlviij lb., the (berer) barrell and all.)

Complaint Against Misgoverned Woman
12 May 1483

Chyrylipps Memorandum that the xij*th* day May in the yere of our lord God (l) M*l*CCCClxxxiij°, the hole parishon of Saint Martyns in Mykillgate come afore my lord the mair and compleynyd apon Margery Gray, odirwys callyd Cherylipps, that she was a woman ill disposed of hyr body to whom ill dispossid men resortys, to the newsaunce of the neghbburs.

Keeper of the Staith Appointed
26 February 1483

custos de la stayth Memorandum quod xxvj*to* die mensis Februarii anno regni regis Edwardi quarti xxij° coram prefato maiore, Johannes Grayson porter juratus est ad custodiendum le staythe.

[*keeper of the staith* On 26 February 1483, porter John Grayson was made keeper of the staith.]

[f.24v]   Indenture Between Workmen
14 May 1483

Willelmus Wylton indentura Memorandum quod Willelmus Wilton camsmyth monstrabat quamdam indenturam inter ipsum et Willelmum Huchonson, xiiij° die mensis Maii anno domini millesimo CCCClxxxiij° coram Johanne Newton tunc maiore civitatis E[bor'] que quedam indentura sequitur in hec verba:

[*the William Wylton indenture* On 14 May 1483, combmaker William Wilton showed the mayor an indented document drawn up between himself and William Huchonson, which reads as follows:]

This indentur maid betwix William Wilton of York camsmyth on the to [*sic*] pairtie, and William Hochonson of York loksmyth on the odir pairtie, wittnessith that the said William Hochonson byndes hym fast by this presens to make wele and warkmanly xxij^ti dosan of awmery tyers with all ther pertinentz wele and warkmanly callyd gude merchand weir of the stuff and yern of the said William Wilton to the same ⟨William⟩ Wilton; and the forsaid William Wilton byndes hym fast by this presens to pay to the said William Hochonson for every dosan awmry tyers wele and war⟨k⟩manly maid iij s. of gude ⟨and⟩ lawfull money of Ynglond at eny tym when he brynges tham to hym, providyd allway that the said William Hochonson sall not wirk no odyr wark to hym self ne to none odyr man till the forsaid xxij^ti dosan awmere tyers be maid and fenychid and delyverid to the said William Wilton, to the which comandes and (ordinaunc') ⟨condicions⟩ to be weile (willyd) ⟨and⟩ trewly fullfillyd and keppid as is above said, adyr pairty to odir sunderly byndes tham fast by this presentz and all their gudes in the payn of forfatour of xl s. sterlyng to be paid by the pairty that is (forfait) ⟨founydyn⟩ defectyfe in brekyng of the premyssez to the odir party, kepyng and fullfyllyng the premissez in the furm abovesaid by the ovyr syght of ij indeferent men by the said pairtes to be elect to fynd and examyn the trewith of such defaltes fundyn in the forsaid pairtes. In wittnesse herof adir parti to odir sunderly haith sette thair seals to the pairtes of this indentur, writtyn the xxiiij^ti day of December in the xxij yer of Kyng Edward the iiij^ti.

[f.25]   Arrest of Husbandman Ordered
Undated

Capias pro securitate pacis

capias Johannem Marshall de Copmanthorp husbandman ad sectam Rogeri Hyrd.

  [Arrest for the keeping of the peace

arrest [Order for the arrest of] John Marshall of Copmanthorp, husbandman, at the suit of Roger Hyrd.]

Release of Writ
28 May 1483

relaxatio facta Thome Neilson Memorandum quod xxviij° die mensis Maii anno regni regis Edwardi quinti post conquestum Anglie primo, Johannes Shor⟨e⟩swod et Willelmus Shoreswod filii Thome Shoreswod et Margarete uxoris sue (et) venerunt coram Johanne Newton tunc maiore civitatis Ebor' et Milone Grenbank tunc uno vicecomitum eiusdem civitatis in camera consilii civitatis ⟨predicte⟩, Thoma Asper legisperito et Thoma Mynskip generoso tunc clerico communi civitatis predicte, presentibus et liberaverunt ⟨ad tunc et ibidem⟩ (quodam) unum scriptum (relac') ⟨relaxacionis⟩ per ipsos factum Thome Neleson ut scriptum ⟨et factum⟩ suum prefato Thome Neleson quod quidam scriptum ad specialem rogationem (T) prefatorum Johannis Shorswod et Willelmi Shor⟨e⟩swod de verbo in verbum irrotulatur de recorda in registerio dicte civitatis cum (cum) le crucifix desuper quasi in fine eiusdem registerii.

[*release made for Thomas Neilson* On 28 May 1483, John Shoreswod, William Shoreswod the son of Thomas Shoreswod, and Margaret his wife came before the mayor, one of the sheriffs, man-at-law Thomas Asper, and common clerk Thomas Mynskip and showed a letter of release made by them for Thomas Neleson, to be recorded at the end of the city register with the crucifix on it.]

Investigation of Sale
31 May 1483

Memorandum quod ultimo die Maii anno regni regis Edwardi quinti ⟨primo⟩ Johannes Brown horner coram maiore (fatebaba') concessit quod ipse quolibet tempore vendere voluerit salem minore precio quam alii vendent seu vendere voluerint (perie) in foro per obolum in quolibet bushell.

[On 31 May 1483, horner John Brown came before the mayor and agreed that he undersold goods in the market.]

[f.25v]   Lease of City Land, Mayor Records Receipt of Payment
**   2 June 1483**

(dimissio) dimissio Memorandum quod secundo die mensis Junii anno regni regis Edwardi (iiij^ti) ⟨⟨primo⟩ quinti⟩ post conquestum Anglie primo, Johannes Kyng de Ebor' wever venit coram Johanne Newton tunc maiore et camerariis eiusdem civitatis et ⟨cepit⟩ (ceperit) de dictis maiore et camerariis unum mesuagium ⟨iacentem inter quandam venellam ex parte australi semiterii ecclesie Beate

Marie episcopi super Bishophill ante et cimiterium monasterii Sancti Trinitatis retro⟩ et unum gardinum ⟨(iacentem inter quandam venellam ex (parte) parte communitatis huius civitatis)⟩ iacentem in Bagargate inter terram dicte communitatis ex parte una et terram Martini del See militis nuper Johannes Askham ex parte altera, habenda et tenenda dicta mesuagium et gardinum cum suis pertinentiis prefatis Johanni Kyng et assignatis suis (a) de festo Pentecostes ultimo preterito usque ad finem et terminum xx annorum extunc proximum sequentium, reddendo inde annuatim custodibus pontis Use pro (temporibus) tempore existente ad usum communitatis huius civitatis quolibet anno durante termino predicto duos solidos ad terminos Pentecostes et Sancti Martini in yeme per equales porciones primo termino solucionis incepiente in festo Sancti Martini proximo futuro, durante quo termino idem Johannes Kyng bene et compitenter dicta mesuagium ⟨et gardinum⟩ reparabit et sustentabit de suo proprio exspensis et eundem messuagium sufficienter reparatum toto tempore termini predictis custodiet et in fine eiusdem termini in sufficienter reparacionem dimittet et dat communitati pro suo ingresso iiij denarios.

[*lease* On 2 June 1483, weaver John Kyng came before the mayor and chamberlains and leased a messuage lying between the street on the south side of the cemetary of the church of Saint Mary Bishophill in the front and the cemetary of the monastery of Holy Trinity behind, and also leased a garden lying in Baggergate between land of the commonalty on one side and land of Sir Martin del See (formerly held by John Askham) on the other. He and his assignees are to have and to hold the messuage and garden with their appurtenances for a term of twenty years, rendering each year 2 s. at the terms of Whitsuntide and Martinmas, beginning next Martinmas, during which term John Kyng is to repair and maintain the messuage and garden at his own expense, to keep them in good order, and pay the commonalty 4 d. for his entry.]

Gilbert Greyn Memorandum that the secund day of Jun in the furst yere of the reyng of Kyng Edward the fyfth (co) Gilbert Greyn esquier com afoe John Newton then mair of the cite of York in to the counsell chambyr of the said cite, and than and thar confessid that he has rescevyd of Richard Blakburn of the said cite merchaunt, to the use and behove and in the name of Christofor Hawe of the cite of London groser, xxviij s. viij d., the wich payment the said Gylbert and Richard than and thar desiryd the said mair to record and testefy.

[f.26]   **Bond to Accept Arbitration**
                  9 June 1483

[R] *Sellar* Memorandum quod ix die Junii anno predicto Milo Greynbank (de v vic') civitatis Ebor' et Milo Harn de civitate predicta vestmentmaker (vest') venerunt coram Johanne Newton maiore civitatis E[bor'] et obligaverunt se et eorum (quemlibet) utrumque in xl libris legalis monete Anglie quod (ipse d) ipsi obedierunt ordinacionem, arbitrium etc., Willelmi Potman (d) in legibus doctoris, Thome Peirson in legibus doctoris, Thome Wrangwyssh et Johannis Fereby aldermannorum civitatis predicte, de et super omnibus accionibus, causis, querelis (et) debitis, debatis et demandis inter ipsos motis, habitis, motis seu pendentibus a principio mundi usque in diem confeccionis presencium, ita quod ordinacio etc., dictorum arbitratorum f⟨i⟩ant et reddantur inter partes predictas citra xv diem mensis predicti etc.

[*Sellar* On 9 June 1483, Miles Greynbank [sheriff] of York and vestmentmaker Miles Harn came before the mayor and bound themselves for £40 to abide by the judgement and arbitration of doctors at law William Potman and Thomas Peirson, and aldermen Thomas Wrangwyssh and John Fereby, concerning all actions and complaints moved, had, or pending between them, the judgement to be made by the fifteenth day of this month.]

Duke of Gloucester Promises to Ease City's Financial Burden
14 June 1483

Memorandum that the xiiij[th] day of the moneth of Jun in the ffurst yer of the reing of Kyng Edward the ffyfth, John Brakynbery, gentilman of the mairs at the mais, broght a lettyr from the gude grace of my lord of Gloucestre, protectour and defensour of thys realme, to the mair, aldermen, shereffes and the commonalte of the cite of York, the tenour of the wich insuyth in the furm ffollwyng:

The duc of Gloucestre, brother and uncle of kinges, protectour and defensoure, gret chamberleyn, constable and admirall of of [*sic*] Englond

Right trusty and welbelovyd we gretys you well, and wher by your lettres of supplicacion to us delyveryd by your servaunt John Brakenbery, we understand that by reason of your gret chargez that ye have had and sustenyd asweile in the defence of this realme ayanst the Scottes as other wyse, your worshipfull citie remanyth gretly in poverte, for the which ye desir us to be gud mean unto the kynges grace for ane ese of such chargez as ye yerly bere and pay unto his (grace) highnesse, we lat you wit that for such gret materes and bysynessez as we now have to do for the wele and usefullnes of this realme, we as yit ne can have convenient leyser to accomplysh this your besnes, but be assured that for your kynd and luffyng disposicions to us at all tymez shewid which we ne can forget, we in gudly hast schall so indevour us for your ease in this behalve as that ye shall varaly understond we be your especiall gude and lovyng lord, as your said servaunte shall shew you, to whom it wull like you herin to gyf forther credence, and for his diligent service which he haith done to our synguler pleasour unto us at thys tyme, we pray you to (gy) geve ⟨unto⟩ (to) hym laude and thankis, and God kepe you. Yeven under our (syngnet) signet at the towr of London the (ff) v[th] day of Juyn.

To our right trusty and welebelovyd the mair, aldermen, (shirrefes) shereffes and communalte of the citie of York

The credence of wich lettre is [*incomplete*]

[f.26v]   **King Richard's Secretary Advises City About Royal Visit**
                23 August 1483

To my gud maisterz the mair, recorder, aldermen and sherreffs of the cite of York:

Ryght worshipfull sirs, I recommaunde me unto you as hertly as I can, and thanked be Jeshu the kinges grace is in good helth, and in lyke wyse the quenys grace, and in all their progresse have beyn worshipfully ressayved with pageantes and other etc., and hys lordes and juges in every place sittyng, determynyng the compleyntes of pore folkes with due punycion of offenders [against] hys lawes. The cause I writt to you now is for somoch as I veraly knawe the kinges mynde and entier affeccion that hys grace bereth towardes you and your worshipfull cite, for manyfold your kynde and lovyng deservynges to hys grace shewed hertofore, wich is grace will never forgete, and entendeth therfor so to do un to you that all the kynges that ever reigned upon you did never so moche, doubte not herof, ne make no maner peticion of desire of ony thing by hys hignes to you to be graunted, but this I advyse you, as honorably as your wisdomes can imagyne, to ressayve hym and the quene at their (cum) commyng, dispose you to do aswell pageantes with soch good speches as can goodly, thys short warnyng considered, be devised, and under suche forme as Master Lancastre of the kynges counsell, this brynger, shall sumwhet advertise you of my (my) mynd in that behalve, as in hangyng the streites thorough wiche the king grace shall come with clothes of arras, tapistre werk and other, for ther commen many sothern lordes and men of worship with them, wich woll marke gretly your ressayving their graces. Me nedeth not thus to advise you, for I doubte not ye have provided therfore better than I can advyse you (howe) how be it on my (fath) ffeith I shewe you thus of good hert, and for the singuler zele and love that I bere to you and your cite, afore all other, ye shall (well) well knowe that I shall not forbere calling on hys grace for your weales ne unremembre it, as Master Lancastre shall shewe you, wich in part hard the kinges grace speke heryn, to whom touching the premisses it may like you geve credence. Scribled in hast the xxiij day of August at Not[tingham] with the hande of your servaunt and hertly lover, John Kendale secretory.

[f.27]   **Duke of Gloucester Asks for Military Help**
                15 June 1483

Memorandum the xv[th] day of Juyn in the furst yer of Kyng Edward the vth, Richard Ratclyff knyght delyvered to John Newton mair of the citie of York a lettre from my lord of Gloucestre, the tenour of which insueth:

The duce of Glocestre, broder and uncle of kynges, protectour, defender, gret(e) chamberleyn, constabill and admirall of England

Right trusty and welbelovyd we grete you well, and as ye love the wele of us and the wele and surtie of your own selff, we hertely pray you to come unto us to London in all the diligence ye can possible, aftir the sight herof, with as mony as ye can make defensibly arraied, thair to eide and assiste us ayanst the quene, hir blode adherenttes and affinitie, which have (endendi) entended and daly doith intend to murder and utterly distroy us and our cousyn the duc of Bukkyngham and the old royall blode of this realme, and as it is now openly knowen by their subtile and dampnabill wais forcasted the same, and also the finall distruccion and disheryson of you and all odir thenheritourz and men of haner, as weile of the north parties as odir contrees that belongen us, as our trusty servaunt this berer shall mor at large shew you, to whom we pray you (gyf) ⟨geve⟩ credence, and as evyr we may do for you in tym commyng faille not but hast you to us hidir. Yovyn under our signet at London the xth day of Juyn.

To our right trusty and welbelovyd John Newton mair of York and his bredir and the communs of the same and every of thame

The credence of the which lettre is that such felichip as the citie may make defensably arraid as wele of hors as of ffute, be one Wendynsday at evyn next cummyng at Powmfret, their attendyng apon my lord of Northumberland and so ⟨with hym⟩ to go up to London thar to attend apon my said lordes gud grace.

[f.27v]   Duke of Gloucester Orders Soldiers Join Him
19 June 1483

Forma proclamacionis facte in civitate xix° die mensis Junii anno regni regis Edwardi quinti primo sequitur in hec verba et est talis:

[Form of a proclamation made in the city 19 June 1483, in the following words:]

proclamacio Richard, brodyr and unkill of kynges, duce of Glocestre, protectour, defendour, gret chamberleyn, constabill and admirall of Englond, streitly charges and commandes that all maner of men in their best defensabill araie incontenent aftir this proclamacion maid, do rise and cum up to London to his highnes in the compeny of his cosyn the erle of Northumberland, the lord Nevill and odir men of wirship by his highnes appontyd, ther to aide and assist hym to the subdewyng, correctyng and punysshyng (and pu) of the whene, here blode, and othir hyr adherentes, which haith intendyd and dayly doith entend to murther and utterly distroi his roiall person, his cosyn the duke of Bukkyngham, and other of old roiall blode of this realme, and also the nobill men of their companyes, and as it is noterby knawn by mony subtile and dampnabill ways fforcastyd the same, and also the speciall distruccion and disheryson of theynd and of all other thenheritourz and men of haneour, as weill of their north parties as of other contrees that belongen tham, and therfor in all deligence prepar yourself and come up as ye love their honourz, weles and surties, and the surties of yourself and the common weile of this said realme.

Discharges from Office
21 March and 13 September 1483

Knowlls Memorandum that Thomas Knowlls draper haith a sufficient discharge undir the commun seal to be discharged of all maner of officez within thys cite acordyng to the graunt and agremend of the mair and all the counsell of the cite the xxj^ti day of March in the xxiij^ti yere of the reing of King Edward the iiij^ti as it aperith in the boke of the counsell chambir of the cite in the tym of John Newton mair.

[Thur]land Memorandum that Thomas Thurland draper haith a sufficient discharge undir the common seall beryng date the xiij^th day of Septembyr in the furst yere of the reing of King Richard the thyrd, to be dischargid of all maner of officez within the said cite acordyng to the graunt and agreemend of the mair and all the hole counsell of the cite, the said xiij^th day of Septembyr made and had as it aperith in the pawpir boke of the counsell chambir of the said cite the said day (in the tym) John Newton then beyng mair.

[f.28]   **Arrests and Bonds to Keep the Peace**
                    3 February 1483 X 3 February 1484

Precepta pro securitate pacis et supersedeas facta tempore Johannis Newton maioris

capias Preceptum quod capias Johannem Burton yoman alias dictum Johannem Burton bucher ad sectam Willelmi Towthorp capellani.

capias Preceptum quod capias Johannem Nappet de E[bor'] mercatorem ad sectam Willelmi Gyllyng capellani.

manucapcio Manucapcio Johannis Nappet de civitate Ebor' mercatoris quod ipse dampnum corporale non faciet nec fieri procurabit quovismodo in Willelmum Gyllyng capellanum; Johannes Hagg de civitate predicta mercator, Patricus Hall de eadem wever, Johannes Andyrson de eadem mylner et Johannes Nicholson de eadem yoman, videlicet quilibet manucaptorum predictorum sub pena x librarum et predictus Johannes Nappet sub pena xx librarum.

capias Preceptum quod capias Robertum Wallys de Ebor' taillour ad sectam (Johannis) Johanne Rymyngton.

capias Preceptum quod capias Ricardum Cotys de Newark mercatorem ad sectam (Johannis) Johanne Cuke uxoris Roberti Cuke de eadem.

memorandum iiij^to die Junii anno primo Edwardi quinti, Willelmus Burges capellanus, Johannes Strynger de eadem yoman, Johannes Esyngwold capellanus et Johannes Fery yoman manuceperunt pro Ricardo Coytes de Newark mercatore quod ipse dampnum vel malum corporale in (Johannem) Johannam Cuke de Newark aut aliquem alium de populo dicti domini regis, sub pena quilibet manucaptorum predictorum x librarum et dictus Ricardus Coytes sub pena xx librarum.

capias Preceptum quod capias Johannem Marshall de Copmanthorp husbandman ad sectam Rogeri Hyrd.

capias Preceptum quod capias Thomam Teverd de E[bor'] baker et Johannem Taillour de eadem ffysher ad sectam Rogeri Eshdale baker.

[Orders for the keeping of the peace and [writs of] *supersedeas* made in the mayoralty of John Newton

arrest Order for the arrest of yeoman John Burton, also known as a butcher, at the suit of chaplain William Towthorp.

arrest Order for the arrest of merchant John Nappet at the suit of chaplain William Gyllyng.

mainprise Mainprise of merchant John Nappet that he do no harm to chaplain William Gyllyng under penalty of £20. John Hagg, Patrick Hall, John Anderson, and John Nicholson were each bound for £10 as sureties.

arrest Order for the arrest of tailor Robert Wallys at the suit of Joan Rymyngton.

arrest Order for the arrest of merchant Richard Cotys of Newark at the suit of Joan Cuke, wife of Robert Cuke.

mainprise On 4 June 1483, chaplain William Burges, yeoman John Strynger, chaplain John Esyngwold, and yeoman John Fery each bound himself for £10 on behalf of Richard Coytes of Newark, who himself was bound for £20.

arrest Order for the arrest of husbandman John Marshall of Copmanthorp at the suit of Roger Hyrd.

arrest Order for the arrest of baker Thomas Teverd and fisherman John Taillour, at the suit of baker Roger Eshdale.]

[f.28v]   Orders for Arrests
Undated, 1483–84

capias Preceptum quod capias Johannem Turnour de Acastir Selby in Aynste (infra comitatu) ⟨in⟩ comitatu civitatis Ebor' laborer ad sectam Thome Peryn de eadem.

capias Preceptum quod capias Willelmum (Coll) Cole servientem Hans' Hatmaker, Garet servientem Nicholai Regient ⟨et⟩ Lokyn servientem dicti Hans' ad sectam Johannis de Serise.

capias Preceptum quod capias Thomam Hancok ffissher ad sectam Katerine Bailley.

capias Preceptum quod capias Johannam Fressell viduam Willelmi Walsh alias dicti Willelmi Bailly et Katerinam uxorem eius ad sectam Margarete Hancok uxoris Thome Hancok ffyssher.

[*arrest* Order for the arrest of laborer John Turnour of Acaster Selby in the Ainsty, at the suit of Thomas Peryn.

arrest Order for the arrest of William Cole, servant of Hans Hatmaker, of Garet, servant of Nicholas Regient, and of Lokyn, servant of the said Hans, at the suit of John de Serise.

arrest Order for the arrest of fisherman Thomas Hancok at the suit of Katherine Bailley.

arrest Order for the arrest of Joan Fressell, widow of William Walsh, also known as William Bailly, and Katherine his wife, at the suit of Margaret Hancok, wife of fisherman Thomas Hancok.]

Bonds to Keep the Peace
20 July 1483

xx^mo die mensis Julii anno regni regis Ricardi tercii primo Manucapcio Johanne Fryssell vidue quod ipsa dampnum corporale non faciet nec fieri procurabit quovismodo in (t) Margaretam Hancok etc.; Johannes Robynson taillour, Ricardus Symson dier, Ricardus Garnet tyxtwriter, Alexander Lameman, videlicet dicta Johanna sub pena xx librarum et quilibet manucaptorum predictorum sub pena x librarum etc.

xx^mo die Julii anno regni regis Ricardi tercii primo Manucapcio Thome Hancok ffyssher quod ipse dampnum etc., non faciet nec fieri procurabit etc., in Katerinam Baillyey etc.; Johannes Robynson taillour, Johannes Smyth ffyssher, Robertus Wyld, Alexander Lameman, videlicet dictus Thomas sub pena xx librarum et quilibet manucaptorum predictorum sub pena x librarum domino regi forisfaciendarum.

xx^mo die Julii anno regni regis Ricardi tercii primo Manucapcio Radulphi Verney ⟨nuper⟩ de London' mercatoris quod ipse dampnum (etc.) ⟨corporale⟩ non faciet nec fieri procurabit quovismodo alicui de populo domini regis; (Johannes) Ricardus Marston de civitate Ebor' cardmaker, Johannes Hagg de eadem mercator, Michell White de eadem lytster et Thomas Watson de eadem dyer, videlicet dictus Radulphus Verney sub pena xl librarum et quilibet manucaptorum predictorum sub pena xx librarum domino regi forisfaciendarum.

[f.29] *xx^mo die Julii anno regni regis Ricardi tercii primo* Manucapcio Roberti Sley nuper de London' mercatoris quod ipse dampnum corporale non faciet nec fieri procurabit quovismodo alicui de (populio) populo domini regis; Ricardus Marston de civitate Ebor' cardmaker, Johannes Hagg de eadem mercator, Michell White de eadem dyer et Thomas Watson de eadem dyer, videlicet dictus Robertus sub pena xl librarum et quilibet manucaptorum predictorum sub pena xx librarum domino regi forisfaciendarum etc.

[*20 July 1483* Mainprise of widow Joan Fryssell that she do no harm to Margaret Hancok etc., under penalty of £20. John Robynson, Richard Symson, Richard Garnet, and Alexander Lameman were each bound for £10 as sureties.

20 July 1483 Mainprise of fisherman Thomas Hancok, that he do no harm to Katherine Baillyey, under penalty of £20. John Robynson, John Smyth, Robert Wyld, and Alexander Lameman were each bound for £10 as sureties.

20 July 1483 Mainprise of merchant Ralph Verney, formerly of London, that he do no harm to any of the king's subjects, under penalty of £40. Richard Marston, John Hagg, Michael White, and Thomas Watson were each bound for £20 as sureties.

[f.29] *20 July 1483* Mainprise of merchant Robert Sley, formerly of London, that he do no harm to any of the king's subjects, under penalty of £40. Richard Marston, John Hagg, Michael White, and Thomas Watson were each bound for £20 as sureties.]

Bond to Keep the Peace, Arrests Ordered
2 August 1483

ij° Augusti anno regni regis Ricardi tercii primo Manucapcio Radulphi Johnson ⟨de Ebor'⟩ shipman quod ipse dampnum corporale non faciet nec fieri procurabit quovismodo in Willelmum Watson de ⟨Kyngeston super Hull⟩ seu alicui ⟨alio⟩ de populo domini regis; ⟨Ricardus Byrswod⟩, Henricus Munkton de civitate Ebor' bower, Edwardus Patynson de eadem bower, Johannes Rusell ⟨paynter⟩ et Nicholaus Rawlyn de civitate predicta ffyshmonger, videlicet dictus Radulphus sub pena xx librarum et quilibet manucaptorum predictorum sub pena x librarum domino regi forisfaciendarum etc.

capias Preceptum quod capias Thomam Welles nuper de Bolton Percy laborer et Margaretam uxorem eius ad sectam Johannis Hartley de Bolton Percy predicta.

capias Preceptum quod capias Isabellam Bolton ⟨viduam⟩ nuper de Newall in parochia de Otley ad sectam Johannis Brown de Farnley in parochia de Otley predicta.

capias Preceptum quod capias Johannem Brown de Farnley in parochia de Otley (yoman hus') husbandman ad sectam Roberti Bolton de Newall in parochia de Otley predicta.

capias Preceptum quod capias Johannem Richardson de Thorp super Teyse in comitatu Ebor' laborer ad sectam (R) Rollandi Meburn clerici.

manucapcio capias Preceptum quod capias Robertum Levysam de civitate Ebor' mercer ad sectam Thome [Beyn] de eadem capmaker.

[*2 August 1483* Mainprise of shipman Ralph Johnson, that he do no harm to William Watson of Kingston-upon-Hull or to any of the king's subjects, under penalty of £20. Richard Byrswod, Henry Munkton, Edward Patynson, John Rusell, and Nicholas Rawlyn were each bound for £10 as sureties.

arrest Order for the arrest of laborer Thomas Welles, formerly of Bolton Percy, and Margaret his wife, at the suit of John Hartley of Bolton Percy.

arrest Order for the arrest of widow Isabella Bolton of Newall in the parish of Otley, at the suit of John Brown of Farnley in the same parish.

arrest Order for the arrest of husbandman John Brown of Farnley in the parish of Otley, at the suit of Robert Bolton in the same parish.

arrest Order for the arrest of laborer John Richardson of Thorp on Tees, Yorks., at the suit of clerk Rolland Meburn.

mainprise for arrest Order for the arrest of mercer Robert Levysam at the suit of capmaker Thomas [Beyn].]

[f.29v]   Bonds to Keep the Peace
October–November 1483

ix° die Octobris anno primo regni regis Ricardi tercii Manucapcio Roberti Levysam de civitate Ebor' mercer quod ipse dampnum corporale non faciet seu fieri procurabit quovismodo in Thomam Beyn de eadem capmaker; Alexandrus Dawtre de civitate predicta generosus, Georgius Kyrk de eadem mercer, Thomas Welles de eadem goldsmyth et Henricus Fawsett de eadem shyrman, videlicet dictus Robertus Levysam sub pena xx librarum et quilibet manucaptorum predictorum sub pena x librarum domino regi forisfaciendarum.

xxiij° die Octobris anno primo regni regis Ricardi tercii Manucapcio Rogeri Esshdale de E[bor'] baker quod ipse dampnum corporale non faciet nec fieri procurabit quovismodo in Thomam Tebard de E[bor'] baker et Johannem Taillour de eadem ffyssher ⟨seu eorum alterum⟩; Alexander Lamyman, Rogerus Sawer, Robertus Pety, Robertus Priket, videlicet dictus Rogerus sub pena xx librarum et quilibet manucaptorum predictorum sub pena x librarum regi forisfaciendarum.

vj° die Novembris Preceptum quod capias Henricum Dressour de Bolton Percy et Elezebetham uxorem eius ad sectam Cecilie Dressour vidue.

(Willelmus Paynter pl')

preceptum pacis, xxiiij° die Novembris anno primo regni regis Ricardi tercii Preceptum quod capias Ricardum Yon de (civid) civitate Ebor' vintener et dompnum Simonem Senews ⟨canonem ecclesie parochie⟩ [et] vicarium de Heley ad sectam Willelmi Paynter de civitate predicta plumer.

xxiiij° die Novembris anno primo Ricardi tercii Manucapcio Ricardi Yon de civitate Ebor' vintener quod ipse dampnum corporale non faciet nec fieri procurabit quovismodo in Willelmum Paynter de civitate predicta plumer; Alexandrus Dautre de civitate predicta generosus, Thomas Tubbac, Christoforus Thomli[n]son de eadem shomaker et Ricardus Thornton de eadem groser, quilibet manucaptorum predictorum sub pena x librarum et predictus Willelmus sub pena xx librarum.

[*one word torn*] *die Novembris anno primo Ricardi tercii* Manucapcio dompni Simonis Senews canonici ac vicarii de Helay quod ipse dampnum (corperall') corporale non faciet seu fieri procurabit quovismodo in Willelmum Paynter plumer; Alexandrus Dautre generosus, Thomas Tubbac, Christoforus Thomlynson sho-maker et Ricardus Thornton groser, quilibet manucaptorum predictorum sub pena x librarum et predictus Simon sub pena xx librarum.

vide plus in predicti

[*9 October 1483* Mainprise of Robert Levysam, mercer of York, that he do no harm to capmaker Thomas Beyn, under penalty of £20. Alexander Dawtre, George Kyrk, Thomas Welles, and Henry Fawsett were each bound for £10 as sureties.

23 October 1483 Mainprise of baker Roger Esshdale, that he do no harm either to baker Thomas Tebard or to fisherman John Taillour, under penalty of £20. Alexander Lamyman, Roger Sawer, Robert Pety, and Robert Priket were each bound for £10 as sureties.

6 November Order for the arrest of Henry Dressour of Bolton Percy and Elizabeth his wife at the suit of widow Cecilia Dressour.

order to keep the peace, 24 November 1483 Order for the arrest of vintner Richard Yon and Simon Senews, canon of the parish church and vicar of Healey, at the suit of plumber William Paynter.

24 November 1483 Mainprise of Richard Yon, vintner of York, that he do no harm to William Paynter, under penalty of £20. Alexander Dautre, Thomas Tubbac, Christopher Thomlinson, and Richard Thornton were each bound for £10 as sureties.

[*blank*] *November 1483* Mainprise of Master Simon Senews, canon and vicar of Healaugh, that he do no harm to William Paynter, under the penalty of £20. Alexander Dautre, Thomas Tubbac, Christopher Thomlynson, and Richard Thornton were each bound for £10 as sureties.

for further, see above]

**[f.30]   Delivery of Release to Mayor
               12 July 1483**

Rysworth Memorandum that the xij^{th} day of July in the ffurst yer of the reign of Kyng (E) Richard the thyrd, (R) Nicholes Ryshworth citizen of the cite of York deliwyrd ⟨to the kepyng of my lord the mair⟩ a reles by hym made ⟨to John Ryshworth of Coldley gentilman⟩ of all the right and titill that the said Nicholes haith in (l) and of all and every of the messis, landes and tentamentes, rentes and services with thar appurtensez ⟨lying⟩ in Mikilgate in the parish of Saint John the Evangelest in the cite of York of and apon thys condicion, yf the said (Nichis) Nicholes Rissworth afor the fest of Saint Michell the archangell next cumyng and fylluyng the above wryttyn day of the said [de]livere of the said reles to my said lord the mair ⟨made to⟩ (th) pay or mak to be paid to the said John Ryssworth all soch money as the said Nicholes aws to the same John with all soch costes as the same John Ryssworth has made and lade down for the matyrs of the said Nicholes (that then the said mair to reliwyr the said releas to the said Nicholes and if not the said Nicholes pay to) and also (disch) lawfully discharge and get the said John Rysshworth a sufficient discharg and sufficient discharges (of of all soch) afor the said fest of Saint Michell next (f) cumyng of (all) all soch bondes as the saide John is bondyn in for the said Nicholes, that then my said lord the mair to (deliwyr the said relea') reliwer the said releas to the said Nicholes, and if yf [*sic*] the said Nicholes perform not the said condicion in every poynt that then my said lord the mair to deliwyr the said releas to [the] said John Ryssworth as the deid and relas of the said Nicholes, and over thys wher as (to) the said John (Rysh) Ryssworth and John Cravyn deliwyr in to the kepyng of my said lord the mair a pair of indentourz made be the wich the said John Cravyn gaff and grant to the said John (Rysshew) Ryssworth all hys mesys, landes and tenements, rentes and services with thar appurtensez in Mykilgate in the parish of Saint John at Ows bryg end, and as be the said indentur more playnly it aperys, it is agred betwyx the said John [and Nicholas] that yf the said Nicholes perform every of the condicions ⟨of hys pairte⟩ above wrytyn **[f.30v]** (that) that then my said lord the (mar) mair shall deliwyr the said indentourz to the said Nicholes, and yf not that then (the said ma') my said lord the mair shall re⟨de⟩liwyr one pairt of the said indentourz to the said John Ryssworth and the odyr pairte of the said indentourz to the said John Cravyn, and that then the said John Cravyn shall make livere session to the said John Ryssworth of all the messis, landes and tenements contenyd in the said indentourz acordyng to the same indentourz.

Testimony Before Mayor
20 July 1483

Nelson and Gybbys Memorandum that the xx^{ti} day of July in the ⟨ffurst⟩ yere of the reing of King Richard the thyrd (the ffurst) Michell ⟨White⟩ of the cite of York dyer come afor my lord the mair ⟨in to the counsell chambyr of the cite of York⟩ and then and thar afore my said lord the mair testefied for trewth that wher as John Gybbis citizin and shyrman of London left with Thomas Neilson the older merchaunt vj long pypys of tuly wad, that the said Michell haith wroght a quarter of the said wad and that he ⟨cowdnot⟩ (cannot) make ne rays of the said quartir owr the som of (xxvij) xxvj s. viij d. to the cost, and all and thys is trew as the said Michell will awnswer afore God at the dreidfull day of dome.

Receipt of Silver Goods Acknowledged
28 July 1483

acquitancia facta per dompnam Johannam Nevill Ricardo York Memorandum quod xxviij° die mensis Julii anno regni regis Ricardi tercii post conquestum Anglie primo, dompna Johanna Nevill nuper uxor Johannis (Nevyll) Glasyn nuper de Ebor' mercatoris venit coram Johanne Newton tunc maiore civitatis Ebor' et ostendit quandam acquitanciam per ipsam factam Ricardo York de Ebor' predicto mercatori quam quedam acquitancia ut facta (suum) dicta dompna Johanna eadem dompna Johanna in presencia dicti maioris prefato Ricardo deliberavit die et anno predicto et ut facta dicte dompne [f.31] Johanne petit irrotolari de recordis coram prefato maiore cuius quidam tenor sequitur in hec verba et est talis:

Noverint universi per presentes me dompnam Johannam Nevill nuper uxorem Johannis Glasyn nuper de Ebor' mercatoris ac executricem testamenti eiusdem Johannis recepisse et habuisse die confeccionis presencium de Ricardo York de Ebor' mercatore unum salsarum argenti per dimedium de aurato, unam murram cum pede argenti et de aurato et ligato cum argento et de aurato, unam stantem peciam argenti et de aurato cum coopertoro cum aquila argenti et de aurato, unam aliam murram ligati cum argento et deaurato, et sex cocliaria argenti cum knoppys deaurato ut patet in una cedula inter predictum Ricardum et prefatum Johannem inde confecta de quibus vero predictis murris cum argento, ligato et deaurato, uno salsario argenti per dimedium deaurato, una pecia argenti stante et deaurato cum coopertoro cum aquila deaurato et sex cocliaribus argenti cum knoppes deaurato fateor me fore bene solutum et contentum et predictum Ricardum York et executores suos inde acquietant per presentes. In cuius rei testimonium presentibus sigillum meum apposui. Data xxvj^{to} die Julii anno regni regis Ricardi tercii post conquestum Anglie primo. Et adtunc et ibidem predictus Ricardus Yorke (deliver') deliberat prefate dompne Johanne omnes predictas parcellas in dicta acquitancia specificatas in presencia dicti maioris.

[*quittance made by Lady Joan Nevill for Richard York* On 28 July 1483, Joan Nevill, wife of the late John Glasyn, merchant of York, came before the mayor and showed a quittance made by her for merchant Richard York, which quittance **[f.31]** she asked to be enrolled in the city records. Its form is as follows:

Know all men by these presents [documents] that I, Joan Nevill, wife of the late John Glasyn merchant of York and executrix of his will, received and had this day from merchant Richard York of York a gilded silver salt-cellar, a maple-wood bowl [mazer] with a gold and silver foot and chain of gold and silver, a standing piece of plate in gold and silver with a cover of gold and silver, another mazer chain of silver and gold, and six silver spoons with golden knobs, as is clearly stated in a schedule made between Richard and Joan, and that Richard is well paid and contented. In testimony of which I affix my seal. Given 26 July 1483. And also the aforesaid Richard York delivered to Joan all the items specified in this quittance in the presence of the mayor.]

[f.31v]   **Neighbours Complain About Local Prostitute**
            28 July 1483

Mariorie Gray alias Cherilippis meritrix Memorandum quod xxviij° die mensis Julii anno regni regis Ricardi ⟨tercii⟩ (secundi) primo plurima pars tocius parochie Sancti Gregorii in Mykilgate venerunt in camera concilii civitatis Ebor' coram Johanne Newton tunc maiore eiusdem civitatis et conquesterunt quod Marioria Gray alias dicta Cherilippis fuit male disposicionis et gubernacionis de corpore sua et una skald inter vicinos suos ad ⟨grave⟩ nocumentum vicinorum ibidem comorantium non primum est eidem Mariorie per predictum maiorem quod amoveat extra barras civitatis predicte citra crastino ad noctem et quod amodo non inhabitet infra ea[n]dem civitatem sub pena tumelarie et imprisonamenti ad voluntatem maioris pro tempore existente etc.

[*Marjorie Gray, alias 'Cherrylips', prostitute* On 28 July 1483, a great many people from the parish of Saint Gregory in Micklegate came into the council chamber before the mayor and complained that Marjorie Gray, also known as 'Cherrylips', was of bad disposition and governance of her body, and also a scold with her neighbours, not for the first time causing serious harm to the neighbourhood. She was ordered by the aforesaid mayor to remove herself beyond the boundaries of the city by evening of the following day and not to live in the same city again, under penalty of imprisonment at the will of the mayor.]

Servant Not Present at Killing of Merchant
5 August 1483

record for Robert Slay that he wasnot at the kyllyng of John Brown late merchant of York Memorandum that the vth day of August in the ffurst yere of the reing of Kyng Richerd the thyrd, Richard Marston of the cite of York cardmaker, Michell Wite of the same dyer, William White of the same dyer, Rawf Nevyll gentilman and William Brown of the said cite dyer, com afore John Newton then beyng mair of the said cite in to the counsell chambyr of the said cite and then and thar of thar awn ffre will (will) withowt ony compoulcion apon the holy evangelestz by tham bodely touchid swor ⟨and showid⟩ that wer by divers personz evill disposid it hath beyn said that one Robert Slay servaunt un to John Jakes citizin and draper of the (said) cite of London shold be one of tham that was at the deith and slaying of John Brown late of the said cite of York merchaunt, that (unto) at the tym of the kyllyng of the said John Brown the forsaid Robert Slay was sytyng in the hows of the forsaid [f.32] Richard Marston apon (Owes) Ows bryg in the company of the forsaid Richard Marston, Michell White, William White, Rawf Newyll and William [Brown], and not knawyng of the kyllyng of the said John Brown to aftirward that it was done, and this ⟨is⟩ trew as tha will awswer afore God at the dreidffull day of dome. And her uppon a testimoniall was sent upp to London acordyng to the premissis undir the seals of the said mair, Richard Marston, Michell White and William White etc.

Delivery of Slings
8 August 1483

slynges (sh) Memorandum that the viijth day of (July) August, Makblyth had deliwyrd to hym a pair of slynges for the crane.

Bonds to Accept Arbitration
25 August and 20 September 1483

Johannes Wyndrys et Thomas Robynson Memorandum quod Johannes Wyndrys ⟨ex parte una⟩ et Thomas Robynson taillour ⟨ex parte altera⟩ xxv° die (Augst) Augusti anno primo regni regis Ricardi tercii coram Johanne Newton maiore ⟨civitatis Ebor'⟩ et posuerunt se stare arbitrio, ordinacioni et judicio Christofori Mason magistri artis (T) sissoris in civitate Ebor', Johannis Stokysley, Nicholai Greynhode et Johannis Robynson (se) de et super omnimodis accionibus, sectis, querelis, debatis, contraversiis, transgressionibus (et) debitis et demandis in eos habitis a principio mundi usque in diem presencium; et arbitrium, ordinacio et judicium dictorum arbitratorum ⟨fiend inter partes predictas⟩ ad implere obligerant se et uterque eorum (obligat') obligavit se in x libris domino regi solvendis, ita quod dicti arbitratores ordinacionem, arbitrium et judicium sua fiant et reddantur de premissis inter partes predictas citra festum Exaltacionis Sancte Crucis proximum futurum etc.

Johannes Wyndris et Thomas Robynson Memorandum quod xx^mo die Septembris anno primo regni regis Ricardi tercii Johannes Wyndris ex parte una et Thomas Robynson ex parte altera obligerunt se et uterque obligavit se domino regi, coram Johanne Newton tunc maiore ⟨civitatis Ebor'⟩ in x libris stare et obedire arbitrio, ordinacioni et judicio Willelmi Pykard, Christofori Thomlynson, Elis (of) Cure et Henrici Wattson de et super [omnibus] accionibus, sectis, querelis, transgressionibus, contraversiis et demandis inter partes predictas habitis sive movendis a principio mundi usque in diem confeccionis presencium, ita quod [arbitrium,] ordinacio et judicium (int') dictorum arbitratorum fiant et reddantur inter partes predictas citra festum [*folio torn*] proximum etc.

[*John Wyndrys and Thomas Robynson* On 25 August 1483, John Wyndrys and tailor Thomas Robynson came before the mayor and promised to abide by the judgement of Christopher Mason, master of the tailors' craft in York, of John Stokysley, Nicholas Greynhode, and John Robynson concerning all actions and complaints they have had between them. Wyndrys and Robynson are each bound for £10 to obey the arbitration, which should be given by the feast of the Exaltation of the Holy Cross.

John Wyndrys and Thomas Robynson On 20 September 1483, Wyndrys and Robynson bound themselves before the mayor for £10 to abide by the judgement of William Pykard, Christopher Thomlynson, Elis Cure, and Henry Wattson over all actions and complaints had or moved between them, the judgement to be made by the feast of [*folio torn*].]

[f.32v]   **New Craftsmen Made Free of City**
                 3 February 1483 X 3 February 1484

Thes ffylluyng ar the namys of the capers that wer abyld to wyrk in the said occupacion in the tym of the ryght worshipfull John Newton mair: Jacobus Stace capper, Rogerus Hall capper.

upsetes of the craftes in the tym of John Newton mair Thomas Essay tapiter.

[f.33]   **Bond to Accept Arbitration**
                 18 June 1483

Memorandum that the ⟨x⟩viij^th day of June in the yer of (the reing of) our lord God M^lCCCClxxxiij, [*blank*] Gybson of Pomfret of the one pairte and Henry Barbour of the cite of York [*blank*] and [*blank*] his sunne ⟨of the odyr pairte⟩ come in to the counsell chambyr of the said cite apon Ows bryg afore John Newton then beyng mair of the said cite and then and (thar) ther a fore the said ⟨maid [*sic*]⟩ adir of the said partes bond tham in the some of x li. ⟨to⟩ our sufferayn lord the kyng to be forfait and paid of and apon thys condicion, that yf tha stand, obeye and fullfyll the award, ordinance and jugment of Thomas Asper gentilman and (Th) [*blank*] Fullbayrn gentilman of and apon all maner of matyrs, warauntez, dettes, (terre) trespassez and grughys betwyx the said pairtes had afore the said viij day of June so that (to at) the said arbitourz make thar award, ⟨ordinaunce and jugment⟩ betwyx the said pairtz of ⟨and in⟩ the premissis within [*blank*] wekes then next ffylluyng, and yf the said arbitourz make not ther award, ordinaunce and iugment betwyx the said pairtes of ⟨and⟩ in ⟨the⟩ premissis and yf within the said pairtes that then yf the said pairtes stand, obeye and full[fill] ⟨the⟩ award, ordinaunce and iugment of and apon the said mair oumper by the (the) said pairtz indifferently chosyn to award, (and) ordeyn and deme bytwyx the said pairtz of and apon the premissis, that then (then) the said bond of x li. (as) be voide, and els it to be in stre[n]ght and vertew. And for as moch as the saide Thomas Asper and [*blank*] Fullbarne made not ther award bytwyx the said pairtz of ⟨and⟩ in the premissis ⟨with in the said [*blank*] wekys⟩, the said mair as oumper indifferently chosyn by the said pairtes the [*incomplete*]

[f.33v]   **Exoneration from Tolls**
                12 September 1483

Ricardus Robert Memorandum quod xij° die mensis Septembris anno primo regni regis (E) Ricardi tercii quidam Ricardus Robert venit coram Johanne Newton tunc maiore civitatis et ostendit quandam litteram quam debet exhonerari ab omni theoloniis cuius tenor sequitur in hec verba:

Universis et singulis presentes litteras inspecturis Radulphus Amyas senescallus decani et collegii libere capelle Sancti Stephani infra palaciam domini regis iuxta Westm' salutem in Domino sempiternam. Cum dominus rex per litteras suas patentes inter ceteras libertates prefatis decano et collegio concesserit quod ipsi et tenentes sui quieti forent de omnimodis theoloniis per totum regnum Anglie notum sit universitati breve per presentes (quod) Ricardus Robert est tenens predictorum decani et collegii et diu fuit ante datam huius scripti et fidelitatem fecit prout plenius apparet in rotulis curie predictorum decani et collegii; quare vobis omnibus et singulis prefatis tenentibus dictorum decani et collegii placeat admittere benigne et favorabiliter ipsum quia Ricardum ab omnibus theoloniis quietos esse in omnibus mercandisis suis emendis et vendendis et aliis libertatibus huiusmodo tenentibus per predictum dominum regem et progenitores suos concessis et confirmatis uti et gaudere permittatur ipsum secundum formam et tenorem cartarum regiarum in hac parte non (molestetes) molestantem in aliquo seu gravantem. In cuius rei testimonium presentibus sigillum meum apposui. Data secundo die Octobris anno regni regis Edwardi quarti vicesimo primo, quamquam litteram idem maior allocavit et ipsum Ricardum a solucione theolonii infra ⟨civitatem⟩ (catem) predictam exhonoravit imperpetuum.

[*Richard Robert* On 12 September 1483, Richard Robert came before the mayor and showed a certain letter by which he ought to be exonerated from all tolls, in the following words:

To each and every person who inspects these letters, greetings in the Lord everlasting from Ralph Amyas, steward of the dean and college of the free chapel of Saint Stephen in the palace of the lord king at Westminster. Whereas the lord king by his letters patent granted that the dean and college and their tenants ought to be quit of all tolls throughout the realm of England, let it be noted that Richard Robert holds from the dean and college and did so before the date of that writing, as is fully detailed in the records of the court of the dean and college. Therefore the dean and college ask that Richard be quit of all tolls on his purchases and sales of merchandise according to the liberties granted by the king and his ancestors. In testimony of which I affix my seal; given 2 October 1481, which letter the mayor gave allowance to and discharged Richard from payment of tolls in the city in perpetuity.]

[f.34]   **Confession of Theft of Horses**
                    15 September 1483

[*left margin torn, one word missing from start of each line, as noted; both marginalia and entry struck through*] (Stephanus . . . taillour . . . confession) . . . *quia falsum . . . ut probat . . . fuit (per)* ⟨*coram*⟩ *maiore*) (Memorandum that the xv[th] day of Septembir in the furst yere of the reing of King Richard the thyrd, Stephanus ⟨Newly of Rypon⟩ taillour come afore my lord the mair and confessid that ⟨he and [*blank*]⟩ Seill of Doncastir ⟨and one Richard Milner late of Topclyff⟩ ([*illegible*]) a lityll beyond from Wentbryg ⟨stale⟩ ij hors, one blake anodir dun, yisterday at (⟨viij⟩) eght of clok at night and come with tham to Tadcastir and la therin the yhiges to day bryght.)

Freedom from Toll Claimed
16 September 1483

Memorandum ⟨quod⟩ (that the) xvj[th] (day of) ⟨die⟩ Septembris anno primo regni regis Ricardi tercii quidem Johannes Crosier venit coram (maiore) Johanne Newton tunc maiore civitatis Ebor' et ostendit quod fuit tenens decani et collegii libere capelle Sancti Stephani ⟨domini⟩ regis apud Westm', ita quod de omni theolonio per totum et regnum Anglie dishonerari debeat et in probacione quod fuit tenens dictorum decani et collegii ostendit quandam ⟨litteram senescalli⟩ (copiam curia) dictorum decani et capituli cuius tenor sequitur in hec verba et est talis:

Universis et singulis presentes inspecturis Radulphus Amyas senescallus decani et collegii libere capelle regis Sancti Stephani infra palaciam domini regis iuxta Westm' salutem in Domino sempiternam. Cum dominus rex per litteras suas patentes inter ceteras libertates predictis decano et colegio concesserit et confirmaverit quod ipsi et tenentes sui quieti forent de omnimodis theoloniis per totum regnum Anglie notum sit (unii) universitati vestre per presentes quod Johannes Crosier litster est tenens predictorum (ca) decani et collegii et diu fuit ante datam huius scripti prout plenius patet in rotulis curie predictorum decani et collegii;

quare vobis omnibus et singulis prefatum Johannem tenentem dictorum decani et
collegii placerat admittere benigne et favorabiliter ipsum quia in omnibus et
omnimodis theoloniis quietum esse in omnibus mercandisis suis emendis et
vendendis et aliis libertatibus huiusmodo tenentibus per predictum dominum
regem et progenitores suos concessis et confirmatis uti et gaudere permittatur
ipsum secundum formam et tenorem cartarum regiarum in hac parte non molestantem in aliquo seu gravantem. In cuius rei testimonium presentibus sigillum meum
apposui. Data xvº die Septembris anno regni regis Ricardo tercii primo.

[On 16 September 1483, John Crosier came before the mayor and showed that he
held from the dean and college of the free chapel of Saint Stephen, Westminster,
and thus he ought to be free of all tolls throughout the realm. He showed a letter
from the steward of the dean and college, the form of which follows [*letter given
15 September 1483, form same as preceding, [f.33v]*].]

[f.34v]   **Question of Nationality Settled**
            17 September 1483

testimoniall testimoniall Meldrom Memorandum quod xvijº die mensis Septembris
anno primo regni regis Ricardi tercii Johannes Meldrom watirleder venit coram
Johanne Newton tunc maiore civitatis civitatis [*sic*] Ebor' et ostentid [*sic*] quandam
litteram testimonialem per quam manifeste patet quod predictus Johannes Meldrom est verus Anglicannus natus infra regnum Anglie quam litteram petit
irrotolari de recordis inter recorda dicte civitatis remanere. Et predictus maior
videns dictam litteram fore veram (ad instanciam) et non fictam intuitu caritatis
fecit eandem litteram inter recorda dicte civitatis irrotolari cuius tenor sequitur in
hec verba et est talis:

[*Meldrom's testimonial* On 17 September 1483, waterleader John Meldrom came
before the mayor and showed a testimonial letter stating that Meldrom is a true
Englishman born within the realm of England, and he asked that the letter be
enrolled in the city records. The mayor examined the letter and saw that it was
truth, not fiction, and thus ordered it be enrolled in the city records. Its form is as
follows:]

For as mikill as it [is] meritable to bere wittnes and suthfast record in any causes
whilk myght bene trubill, losyng of goodes or good fame today trewe Cristen man
in defaute of soothfast knawlege, therfor it is that we, Sir Henry Percy lieutenaunt
of thest marches of England affornemptes partes Scotland, Sir Thomas (Gray)
Grey of (Hir) Heton, Sir Roger Heron of Forde, Sir Thomas Grey of Horton
knyght and William of Fowery of the same, berth wittnes and suthfast record that
John Meldrom duellyng in York is Englishman gottyn by hys ffadir and born of hys
modir with in the reyme of England, hys ffadir duellyng in Fowery a pon the wattir
of Tyll clyse callid William Meldrom, the said John Meldrom born in Northame
apon Twede and cristned within the fount of the paroch kirk of the same; hys two
god ffadyrs, one callid John Roothirford constabill of the castell of Northame on

lyfe at the makyng of thys writtyng, one othir callit Robert of Maxwall duellyng in the castell of Morpeth; hys godmodir callit Annes Jacson, the wife of Adam Jacson, duellyng in Dudo both on lyfe; wherfor we the aforsaid knyghtes and swyer willith and preith every goode Englishman not to presom nor sey ony thyng contrary thys our wryttyng in so mikill; if any man wold presome the contrery this our record and witnessyng we shall make good afor the king and werdeyne if it shuld nede. In wittnes of the wilkes to thys our writtyng we have sett to our signettes havyng the strynegh of our selys, the ix day of Septembir the xxjth yere of the reyne of Kyng Edward the iiij^{ti}.

[f.35]   King Richard Relieves City of Tolls, Mayor Made King's Sergeant at Arms
17 September 1483

Dona regis Ricardi tercii facta civitati Ebor' ac maiori eiusdem, anno domini M°CCCClxxxiij°

[Gift that King Richard gave to the city of York and to its mayor, in the year 1483]

Memorandum that the (thyr) xvijth day of the moneth of Septembir in the ffurst yere of the reing of (the reing) King Richard the thyrd, John Newton (ma) then beying mair of the cite of York, our said sufferayn lord the kyng of hys ⟨most⟩ speciall good grace remembryng the good service that the said cite haith done to hys good grace, ffurst in the yorney made to Dunffreys and (seth then) ⟨in⟩ the yorney made the same yere to Edynburgh, and also ⟨in⟩ the yorney late made to London to the coronacion of hys good grace, callid afore hys good grace the said day in ⟨to⟩ the (chaby) chapitour howse of the cathederall chyrch of Saint Petir at York the said mair, hys bredyr the aldermen, and many odir of the communs of the said cite, and then and ther our said suffereyn lord opynly rehercid the said service to hys good grace done, and also the (deky) dekey and the grete povert of the said cite, of hys most speciall good grace, withowt ony petecion or askyng of any ⟨thyng by the said mair or of ony odyr, our said sovereyn lord of onely of hys most aboundaunt grace⟩ (of the said) most graciusly and haboundauntly grauntid and gave in releve of the said cite in esyng of the tolles (and), murage, ⟨bucher penys and sk⟨a⟩itgyld⟩ of the said cite yerly (l li.) ⟨lviij li. xj s. ij d.⟩ for ewyr, ⟨that is to say, for the murage xx li. and the resedew to the sheryffes⟩, so that from then forwerd it shold be lefull to every person ⟨frely⟩ to cum to the said cite with thar goodes and catell and tham frely to sell in the same withowt onythyng gyffing or paying for toll or murage of ony of ther said goodes; and owyr that (of hys) ⟨hys grace⟩ most graciusly grauntyd to the mair and commonaltie of the said cite yerly (C) xl li. for ewyr to the behove of the communalte and chambyr of the said cite, and yerly to the (in s) mair ⟨for the tym beyng⟩ as hys cheffe seriaunt of ayrms xij d. of the day, that is to say by the yere xviij li. v s.

[f.35v]   **Bond to Keep the Peace**
                    26 June 1482

Vicesimo sexto ⟨die⟩ mensis Junii anno regni regis Edwardi iiij^{ti} post conquestum Anglie xxij°, venerunt coram Ricardo York tunc maiore civitatis Ebor' in
camera civitatis predicte Willelmus Burges capellanus, Ricardus Estwod pistor et
Jacobus Ranald, et manuceperunt pro Johanne Davyson sissore quod ipse
dampnum ⟨vel malum⟩ aliquod corporale alicui de canonibus civitatis predicte
non faciet (infra libertatem eiusdem civitatis vel extra) ⟨ac de se bene gerendum
erga eosdem canonicos⟩, quilibet manucaptorum supradictorum sub pena x
librarum et predictus Johannes Davyson sub pena xx librarum dicto domino regi
forisfaciendarum.

[On 26 June 1482, chaplain William Burges, fisherman Richard Estwod, and
James Ranald came before the mayor and bound themselves for £20 each on
behalf of tailor John Davyson, that he do no harm to any of the canons of the city
and that he conduct himself well towards them, under penalty of £20.]

Bond to Accept Arbitration
7 October 1483

ad hoc tempore Johannis Newton Memorandum quod vij° die mensis Octobris anno
primo regni regis Ricardi (re) tercii Johannes ⟨Smyth⟩ de civitate Ebor'
cordwener et Thomas Cok de eadem wynter venerunt coram Johanne Newton tunc
maiore civitatis predicte et obligerunt se et uterque eorum obligavit se domino regi
in xx marcis, quod ipsi (et eorum uter') steterint ⟨et obedierint⟩ et eorum
uterque steterit ⟨et obedierit⟩ arbitrio, ordinacioni et judicio Elis de Cure,
Thome Hawslyn, Willelmi Ayrton et Ricardi Jakson (de) arbitratorum inter dictos
Johannem Smyth et Thomam Cok indifferenter electorum ad arbitrandum, ordinandum et judicandum inter dictos Johannem et Thomam de et super omnimodis
accionibus, sectis, querelis, demandis, contraversiis inter eos habitis a principio
mundi usque in diem confeccionis presencium, ita quod arbitrium, ordinacio et
judicium dictorum arbitratorum fiat et reddatur citra festum Sanctorum Simonis et
Jude proximum futurum, et si dicti arbitratores judicium et arbitrium se non
reddunt citra dictum festum quod dicti Johannes Smyth et ⟨Thomas⟩ Cok
steterint et obedierint arbitrio, ordinacioni et judicio imperatoris per dictos
arbitratores [electos?], ita quod dictus imperator judicium suis reddat inter dictos
Johannem et Thomam [*folio torn with loss of c.4 words*] dies ex proximo sequenti
dictum festum.

[*in the mayoralty of John Newton* On 7 October 1483, cordwainer John Smyth
and vintner Thomas Cok came before the mayor and bound themselves each for
twenty marks that they would abide by the judgement of Elis de Cure, Thomas
Hawslyn, William Ayrton, and Richard Jakson, impartially chosen as arbiters to
determine all actions and complaints John and Thomas had between them. The
judgement is to be made by the feast of Saints Simon and Jude, and if the arbiters

are unable to render a decision by that time then they will elect an umpire to make a judgement within [*folio torn*] days, and Thomas and John agree to abide by that judgement as well.]

[f.36]   **Bond to Accept Arbitration**
                 11 October 1483

[Thomas Beyn] et Robertus Levysham [right margin faded, with loss of 4–6 words per line, as noted] Memorandum quod xj° die mensis Octobris anno primo regni regis [Ricardi tercii Thomas Beyn] de civitate Ebor' capmaker et Robertus Levysam [de eadem mercer] coram Johanne Newton tunc maiore civitatis predicte et . . . se alteri in x libris legalis monete Anglie stare et obedire arbitrio, ordinacioni et judicio Willelmi Deykyn, Rogeri Apilby, Johannis . . . Wyndill arbitratorum ad arbitrandum, ordinandum et judicandum inter dictos Thomam Beyn ex parte (et) una et Robertum Levysam ex parte altera . . . omnibus sectis, querelis, demandis, contraversiis et debatis inter eos habitis, motis sive movendis a principio mundi usque in diem confeccionis presencium . . . dicti arbitratores perimplere, ita quod predicti arbitratores arbitrium, ordinacio et judicium (dict') suum inter partes predictas [*last five lines faded*]

   [*[Thomas Beyn] and Robert Levysham* On 11 October 1483, capmaker [Thomas Beyn] and mercer Robert Levysam came before the mayor and each [bound] himself for £10 to abide by the judgement of William Deykyn, Roger Apilby, John [*folio torn*] Wyndill, concerning all disputes between Beyn and Levysam. The judgement is to be made by [*folio torn*].]

[f.36v]   **Illegal Sale of Fish, Searches for Deed and Lease, Various Jottings**
                 Undated

Scrutatores artis pistorum aque recentis presentant super Johannem Wastell quod vendidit apud pontem Fosse pistes aque dulcis contra ordinacionem eiusdem artis etc. Item presentant super Thomam Hardesang quod ipsum est socium cum dicto Johanne in venditionem dictos pisces etc., aqque dulcis.

   [The searchers of the craft of fishers of fresh fish show that John Wastell sold fresh-water fish on Foss bridge against the ordinance of the craft. They also show that Thomas Hardesang sold such fish as well with his friend John.]

In domino confido – to trest in God, it is the best

Notum sit omnibus his hoc

John Hemyngburgh or John Burn walker anno iiij^{to} H. iiij^{ti}

Memorandum to serch for a deid maide (for) be William Wryght to Sir John

Knapton and to Sir William Awn. Also yf Sir John Knapton or the said Awn made one graunt of xiij s. iiij d. rent to (ama) anawtyr of Saint Stephan out of a hows in Colyergate.

Memorandum to serch for a leis made (b t) by Thomas Holme to John Brals roper.

Henry delay the sum of lower deley

xvº die Maii anno tercio Henrici octavi Johannes Pye clericus cepit unam cameram infra capellam Sancti Willelmi super pontem [Ouse] incepiente post punctum proximum post datam presentem soli eidem custodi [*c.3 words torn*] pro tempore existente ad tempus usuale.

> [On 15 May 1488, clerk John Pye leased a room inside the chapel of Saint William on [Ouse] bridge beginning after the present date in his own custody for the time being at the usual terms [*?*].]

[*c.6 words faded*] gonnes with the chambres belongyng unto them was delivered.

[*c.8 words faded*] tyme of the right wirschepfull Sir Bertram Dawson

[*final entry, c.5 lines, faded*]

APPENDIX IV
Y.C.A. MS. E.58A4

Source: Y.C.A. E.58A4. Parchment, 260 m.m. x 186 m.m., seal missing. This royal precept was given by Richard III to the sheriffs of York 19 September 1483, while the king was visiting the city on his royal progress. The letter acted upon complaints made by city weavers concerning weavers in the Ainsty who did not contribute to the annual rent of one hundred shillings due the Exchequer. Because of damage to the right side of the letter, phrases in brackets have been supplied from a version of the letter dated 23 September 1483 printed in Rosemary Horrox and P. W. Hammond, eds., *British Library Harleian Manuscript 433*, 4 vols. (Upminster and London, 1979–83), II:22–23.

RR

Richard by the grace of God king of England and of Fraunce and lord of Irland, to the shrieffes of this oure cite of Yorke and to their deputies at Ansty that nowe been and that herafter shalbe and to every of them greting. Where as it hath been shewed unto us on the behalve of the wevers of oure said cite that almaner of weavers using that occupacion within the suburbes precincte of the frasuncheses and liberties of the same [have been accustomed] to be contributories of the annuell rent of C s. that they yerely doo yeld unto us in oure Eschequer [and] that the wevers dwelling within the said Ansty being within the precincte and libertie of our said cite refuse to bere their porcion of the said annuel rent contrary to the privilege of the same our cite as it is said, we willing the good constitucions, custumes and ordenaunces used within our said cite to be observed and kept, desir you and nathelesse wol and charge you that in due exercising of the same and in leveing the said annuell rent ye geve unto them your lawful favor and assistences at alle tymes as the caas shall require, not fayling herof as our trust is in you and as ye wol doo us pleaser. Yeven undre oure signet at oure cite of Yorke forsaid the xix[th] day of Septembre the ffirst yere of our reigne.

APPENDIX V
FRANCIS DRAKE, EBORACUM
AUGUST–SEPTEMBER 1485

Source: Francis Drake, *Eboracum, or the History and Antiquities of the City of York* (London, 1736), pp. 121–23. The following selections from Drake are missing from Book 2–4. The eighteenth-century antiquary apparently copied the entries before the disappearance of the folios. The entries provide insight into the turbulent weeks following the death of Richard III.

[p.121]   **Meetings with Sir Henry Percy and Henry VII's Messenger, Wages of Bosworth Soldiers**
24 August 1485

Mercurii festum Sancti Bartholomei, videlicet xxiiii° die Augusti, anno etc., vacat regalis potestas

Mayor: Nicholaus Lancastre, etc., N° 13.

Wer assembled in the counsail chambre wher and when it was determined that the maire with his brethre shuld attend and mete Sir Henry Percey at ii. o' the clok at afternone, at the miln in the strete without Walmgate-bar, ther to understand how they shall be disposed enent the king's grace Henry the sevent, so proclamed and crowned at the feld of Redemore.

Also it was determined that oon Sir Roger Cotam knight unto the said kings grace, now comen to this citie to proclame the said king Henry, shuld be presented with ii. [*blank*] and ii. gallons of wyne at the chambre cost.

Also John Nicholson which was sent to Wressell to the erle of Northumberland with writing, appered in the counsail chambre, and shewed how it was shewed unto hym by Sir Henry Percy being ther, that the said erle was with the king at Leicestre for the well of himself and this citie, and that the said Sir Henry wold be at the milne without the bar as above. Wherfore it was determined to meet with hyme ther.

Also the same day forsomuch as the forsaid Sir Roger Cotam durst not for fere of deth come thrugh the citie to speake with the maire and his brethre, it was thought that they shuld goo unto him, wherupon the maire and his brethre went unto the sign of the boore and ther they speak with the said knight, which shewed unto them that the king named and proclamed Henry the vii. grete them well, and wold be unto them and this citie as good and gratiouse soveraign lord as any of his noble progenitors was before. With othyr words of comforth. Wherof the maire and his brethre thankes him moch and soo departed.

Also it was determined that such sogiers as went furth of this citie having wages for x. dayes, xii d. by the day, and was furth but iiii dayes and a half, shuld have wages for vi. dayes and no more, and the residue of the money to be repaid to the chamberlaynes to pay to such parishes as paid the same.

City Officials Ride to King Henry, Royal Proclamation Read in City
25 August 1485

Jovis post festum Sancti Bartholomei, videlicet xxv° die Augusti anno domini M.CCCC.LXXXV.

Mayor: Nicholaus Lancastre, etc., N° 11.

Wer assembled in the counsail chambre, wher and when it was determined that William Wells, William Chimney, Robert Hawk aldermen, [and] William Tayte and John Hay of the xxiv, shall ride unto the kings grace Henry the vii. in the name of th'ole bodie of this citie, beseching his grace to be good and gracious lord unto this citie as othyr his noble progenitours hath ben tofore, and to confirme of his most habundant grace all such franchises, liberties, fees and freedoms as hath ben granted to the said citie hertofore by his said noble progenitours; and that ther be several letters made as well to the erle of Northumberland as the lord Stanelay for the good speed of the premises. Also that the said aldermen and ii. of the xxiiii. be accompanyed with xv. yomen and horses, and have gownes of must[er]deviles, and ther [blank] gownes of othyr color convenient for them. And that Alexander Dauson chamberlayn, ride with the same personnes and bere all costs provided of the chambre.

Also, that ther shal be a proclamacion mad thrugh out this citie, which procla-.macion was delivered unto the mayre and his brethre by one of the kings herolds called Wyndsore in the counsail chambre, having upon hym a cote armor of the armes of England and Fraunce; which herold shewed unto the mayre by mouthe, that the kings grace grete hym and his bredre wele, and would be as good and gracious lord unto this citie as any of his progenitours were before him, with othyr moch wordes of comforth, wherfore he desired hym on the kings behalve to make a proclamacion after the tenor that foloweth:

[p.122] Copia proclamationis Henrici regis Anglie VII.

Henry by the grace of God, king of England, and of Fraunce, prince of Wales, and lord of Irland strictly charges and commaundeth upon peyne of deth, that no manner of man robbe nor spoyle na manner of commons comyng from the feld; but suffre theme to passe home to ther cuntrees and dwelling places with their horses and harnesse. And morover that noo manner of man take upon hym to goe to noo gentilmanz place neither in the cuntree nor within cities nor borows, nor pike no quarells for old or for new matters, but kepe the kings peace upon payne of hanging, etc. And morover if ther be any man affered to be robbed and spoyled of his goods, let hym come to master Richard Borow, the king's sergeant here, and he shall have a warrant for his bodie and his goods, unto the tyme the kings pleasure be knowne. And morover the king assertayneth you, that Richard duc of Gloucestre, late callid king Richard, was slayne at a place called Sandeford, within the shyre of Leicestre, and brought dede of the feld unto the towne of Leicestre, and ther was laide oppenly that every man might se and luke upon him. And also ther was slayne uppon the same feld John late duc of Northfolk, John late erle of Lincoln, Thomas late erle of Surrey, Fraunceys vicount Lovell, Sir Walter Deveres, Lord Ferreres, Richard Ratcliff knight, Robert Brachenbury knight, with many othyr knights, squires and gentilmen, of whose soules God have mercy.

After which proclamation made, the said mayre and his brethre comyng to the chambre agayn, determined that the said harold for his message and comforthable words shuld have in reward of the chambre vi. marks iiii. aungells.

Letter to Earl of Northumberland
26 August 1485

Copie of a letter directed to the erle of Northumberland for the good spede forsaid:

Right potent and right noble our moost especial and singular good lord in our moost humble wise we recommend us unto your good lordship, loving almighty God of your prosprouse lif the which Jesu continue in felicity both ghostly and bodily, thanking your good lordship of your tendre luff and favor which your lordship ever hath borne towards us and this citie, whom we beseeche you continue and in especial at this season, in the which we know right wele your lordship unto us is moost necessarye. And wheras we send up unto the kings grace iii. of our aldermen and othyr of our counsail chambre to besche his grace to accept us benignely unto his grace, graunting unto us and this citie all such fraunchises, liberties, freedoms, and annual fees, with all othyr commodities and prouffitts unto the same belonging and graciously graunted by all othyr his moost noble proge-nitours; we besche your good lordship in the good furtherance and spede herof to shew unto our said brethre your noble advise how to labor to the said kings grace for the same; and we shall ever pray for the staite of you right potent and right noble our moost especial and singular good lord in felicitie ever to endure.

From York the xxvith day of August

Your orators and servants, the mayre, aldermen and sheruffs, and xxiv of the counsail of the citie of York, with th'ole communalitie of the same

King Henry Sends Warrant for Arrests
27 August 1485

Sabbati, videlicet xxvii° die Augusti anno regni regis Henrici septimi primo incipiens

Mayor: Nicholaus Lancastre, etc., N° 5.

Wer assembled in the counsail chambre, when and wher oon Robert Rawdon gentilman, sergeant unto the kings grace personally appered and gave unto the maire and the counsail a commandement and warrant under the kings signet and signe manual to him direct to attache Robert [Stillington] bishop of Bath, and Sir Richard Ratcliff knight, and to bring them personaly unto his highnesse and to sease into his hands all their goods, moveable, and immoveable, as it appereth more at large in the warrant, wherof the tenor wherof followeth herafter. Wherupon the said Rawdon instantly desired the said maire and sheriffs on the kings behalve as his true liege men and subgetts that in thexecution of his said warrant they wold geve ther attendaunce, aid and assistence. Wherin after som consultation upon the same, for so moch as the said bishop was attached tofore by oon herald Wyndsore and Robert Borow gentilman, the kings servants, and broght unto the citie and lay within the franchesse and liberty of the same, and was sore crased by reason of his trouble and carying, the maire taking with hym the above written of the counsail of the chambre the said Rawdon and Rob[ert] Borow, instantly prepared to go to the said bishop to master Neleson place, to speke with him; being come unto hym unto the said place, **[p.123]** wher and when it was appointed of the consent of the said Rawdon, that the said bishop shuld continue still within the said citie for iv. or v. days for his ease and rest. The tenor of the warrant foloweth:

Henry by the grace of God, king of England, and of Fraunce, and lord of Irland, to our trusty and wel-beloved Robert Rawdon gentleman, greting. For as moch as Robert bishop of Bath and Sir Richard Ratcliff knight, adherents and assistents to our grete enemy Richard late duc of Gloucestre, to his aide and assistance, have by deverse ways offended agenst the crowne to us of right appurteyneyng, we will and charge you and by this our warrant commit and geve you power to attache the said bishop and knight, and them personaly bring unto us, and to sease into our hands all such goods, moveables and immoveables as the xxii^d day of August the first year of our reigne appurteyned and belonged unto them whersoever they be found, as well in places privileged as elleswhere, and the same soo seased to put into such suerte and savegard as ye will answer to us for them at all tymes. Chargyng morover, and strictly commaundyng all our true subgettes and legemen that to thexecution herof they geve you attendaunce, aide, and assistence, without doeing of any thyng that shall be prejudicial to the premisses, as they will avoyde our grievious displeasure and answer unto us at their peril.

Geven undre our signet at our towne of Leicestre the xxiii^d day of August, the first yere of our reign.

Per signetem et sigillum manuale

Fox

Defence of the City, King Asks Officials to Receive His Servant
30 August 1485

Lune, videlicet penultimo die Augusti, anno regni regis Henrici primo

Mayor: Nicholaus Lancaster, etc., N° 9.

Wer assembled in the counsail chambre, where and when it was determined, that
the gates and posturnes of the citie shuld be shut evere night at ix of the clock, and
opened at morowning at iiii. And that iiii men of every warde be warned to watch at
evere gate evere night for the safegard of the citie, and the inhabitants of the same.
Also ther was a lettre direct from the kings grace unto the maire and his brethre
charging them by the same to geve ther assistence and aide in such matters as
appereth in the said letters, wherof the tenor followeth:

By the king

Trusty and welbeloved we grete you wele, and late you wit that for diverse causes
us touching, we send unto your partes our trusty and welbeloved servant Sir John
Halewell knight, wherfore we woll and pray you, and upon that on your liegeance
instantly charge and command you, that in all such matters as the said Sir John shall
shew unto you on our behalve yee geve your assistence and aide, and that yee ne
faile therof as yee will deserve of us our especial thankes.

Geven undre our signet at our towne of Leycestre, the xxiii day of August.

Superscribed, to our trusty and welbeloved the maire, aldermen and sherriffs of our
citie of York

King Henry Confirms City's Privileges
4 September 1485

Sabbati, videlicet iiii° die Septembris regni regis Henrici VII. primo

Mayor: Nicholaus Lancastre, etc., N° 16.

Wer assembled in the counsail chambre within the Guildhall, when and where it
was shewed by Thomas Wrangwishe, William Welles, William Chymney,
aldermen, William Tate and John Hay of the xxiv late sent unto the king for the
well of this citie, that the said kings grace accept them in the name of tholl bodie of
this citie, graciously unto his highnesse graunting that the said citie shuld be holdein

of the same, and that the inhabitants and citizens of the said citie shall have and enjoy all and all manner of fraunchisses, liberties, freedoms, graunts, issues and prouffits unto them belonging in as large and ample manner and forme, with better, as any of his noble progenitours had graunted to the said citie at any tyme hertofore. The which premisses was shewed by the mouth of the said Thomas Wrangwishe, not only unto the mayre and the counsail, but also incontinently to the commons assembled the said day in the Guild hall forsaid. After which the maire taking with hym all above written entered the chambre agayn, where after due thanks geven unto the said Thomas Wrangwishe and his felows for ther grete labor and comfortable tidings, it was determined that William Welles and William Chymney shuld towards ther horsehyre have in reward xx s. and either of the xxiv. v s. And on this [blank] desunt caetera.

GLOSSARY

Included in this glossary are English and Latin words and phrases which may present some difficulty to the modern reader, as well as locations and place names in and around the city of York no longer extant and often difficult to determine. The spelling of the initial entry follows that which is found in the House Book passage of origin; the most frequent variant spellings follow thereafter, but not all of the variants are included. I have restricted the definitions to the context of the word or phrase used in the House Books. Works consulted include:

Dobson, R. B., ed., *York City Chamberlains' Account Rolls 1396–1500,* Surtees Society, vol. 192 (1978–1979).

Halliwell, J. O., *A Dictionary of Archaic and Provincial Words,* 2 vols., London 1889.

Latham, R. E., *Revised Medieval Latin Word-List,* London, 1965.

Middle English Dictionary, edited Hans Kurath and Sherman M. Kuhn, University of Michigan Press, 1956 continuing.

Oxford English Dictionary, Corrected Re-Issue, edited J. A. H. Murray and others, 12 vols., and supplement, Oxford 1933.

Raine, Angelo, *Mediaeval York: A Topographical Survey Based on Original Sources,* London, 1955.

Spelman, Henry, *Glossarium Archaiologicum,* London, 1687.

Stone, G. C., *A Glossary of the Construction, Decoration and Use of Arms and Armor,* New York, 1934.

Wright, J., ed., *The English Dialect Dictionary,* 6 vols., New York, 1898–1905.

Zupko, R.E., *A Dictionary of Weights and Measures for the British Isles: The Middle Ages to the Twentieth Century,* American Philosophical Society, vol. 168 (1985).

Affere, to assess, to affix the price or market value.

Alien, a stranger, usually of another country; see *Forent.*

Almyfluent, beneficent, bounteous.

Ambry, or *aumery,* a chest or cupboard, often for keeping food.

Appurtenances, a minor property, right or privilege belonging to another; an appendage or subordinate.

Averes, see *Haver.*

Aungel, or *angel-noble,* a gold coin first issued in 1465 by Edward IV, worth 6 s. 8 d. as was the earlier coin the noble, and bearing as its device the archangel Michael standing upon and piercing the dragon.

Austen Friars, the Augustinian friary located next to the Guildhall.

Awmery, see *Ambry.*

Bailiwick, originally the district of jurisdiction of a bailiff, but used generally to include the jurisdiction of a sheriff and other civic officers.

Barker, tanner, one who dresses and prepares leather.

Barker Hill, area outside the city walls, northeast of Monk Bar.

Barrel ferres, container for holding liquids while travelling.

Baselard, a kind of dagger, worn at the belt.

Baxter, a baker, usually applied to women.

Bean Hills, the area outside of the city walls, southeast of Fishergate Bar.

Bilburgh Cross, probably the cross or five-mile stone at Bilbrough, North Yorkshire, a meeting place at which the civic officers waited to meet important visitors.

Bill, broad blade mounted on a long pole, often with spikes and hooks projecting from the back and end, used as a weapon though with agricultural origins.

Black Monday, the Monday following Easter, considered to be unlucky because calamity was thought to be the natural consequence of rejoicings such as those of Easter Sunday.

Bloodwite, penalty for assault if blood is drawn.

Botham, bottom.

Bottell, or *bottle*, a bundle of hay or straw weighing seven pounds.

Brekles Mills, not identified, probably located on the road from Tadcaster to York, closer to the former and a favourite welcoming place at which the civic officials waited to greet important visitors to the city.

Brembys, bream, a fresh and sea-water fish.

Buckstall, fine to maintain hunting nets.

Bumbard, ancient armament or cannon, that which bombards.

Camsmith, combmaker.

Cardmaker, one who makes cards for combing wool.

Chape, metal mounting of a scabard, covering the point.

Chapman, one who buys and sells, often an itinerant traveller to markets and fairs.

Chevage, arbitrary payment, originally made in recognition of personal bondage.

Cocitizens, or *concitizens*, fellow citizens.

Cognizance, or *connysance*, a device, badge or emblem by which one is known.

Compromit, to enter into a compromise, to refer a matter to arbitration.

Connysanc, see *Cognizance*.

Cooper, or *cowper*, one who makes and repairs casks, tubs or barrels.

Cordwainer, a worker in leather, usually a shoemaker.

Corpus cum causa, a writ ordering the removal to the court of king's bench of both the body and the record explaining the cause of any person waiting upon a judgement, usually for debt.

Corpus pro corpore, the personal responsibility, 'body for body', of mainpernors.

Council chamber, located on the north side of Ouse bridge near Saint William's chapel. Regular meetings of the city council were held in the upper rooms of the building, and the ancient records of the city were kept there.

Couriour, see *Currier*.

Curialitie, gifts, presents, or fees given in addition to a salary, out of courtesy.

Currier, or *couureour*, one who dresses and tans leather.

Diem clausit extremum, a writ directed to the king's escheators to ascertain the lands of which a tenant was seised in chief on the day he died or 'closed his last day'.

Disaveing, misbehaviour, disorder; see *Havour*.

Discure, discover, uncover or reveal secrets.

Disports, sports or diversions.

Dissave, to deceive.

Distress, to levy a distress upon, to distrain, to seize or detain property to force a person to perform an obligation such as payment of a debt or appearance in court; also, the property so seized.

Easterling, a citizen and merchant of the Hanse towns of eastern Germany and the Baltic coasts.

Engrayned, or *engrained*, fast dyed in grain, using the Kermes insect to produce an intense scarlet or crimson colour for cloth.

Escheator, officer in each county responsible to the king for looking after the escheats or royal possessions which have reverted back to the Crown. In York, the mayor was also the royal escheator during the term of his office.

Eslite, elite, in the sense of those to be elected or chosen.

Farm, a fixed payment; to take the fees or profits of an office or tax upon payment of such a sum; to let to another for such a payment.

Fishgarth, an enclosure, often a trap made of wicker, set in the river to catch fish.

Fletcher, one who makes arrows.

Flymenafirmth, right to proceed against those who harbour outlaws.

Forent, foreign, a person not of one's own town, but usually English; see *Alien*.

Forestal, fine for obstruction or assault on the highway.

Forum Jovis, see *Thursday Market*.

Frankalmoign, tenure without performance of secular duties.

Frankpledge, pledge or surety guaranteeing corporate responsibility for the good behaviour of all adult members of a tithing.

Friar Tower, tower on the riverbank near Skeldergate bridge, it formed part of the wall that enclosed the Franciscan friary.

Friars Toft, the Dominican friary occupying the King's Tofts on the west side of the city, adjacent to Pageant or Toft Green.

Fuller, one who treats and treads upon cloth to cleanse and thicken it.

Galtres Forest, forest to the north of the city, beginning outside of Bootham Bar.

Gardewyan, or *gardeviance*, a trunk for travelling.

Garth, small enclosed area.

Girdle, belt. *Girdler*: one who makes belts and girdles, and often metal hoops as well.

Girse, grass, to put out to grazing.

Glaive, a broad-bladed pole arm or thrusting weapon on a long handle, the edge curving backwards near the point.

Gorget, armor covering the throat.

Grithbrech, criminal jurisdiction over a breach of the peace.

Gyrse, see *Girse*.

Hairster, or *haster*, a manufacturer of hair cloth or horsehair.

Halberd, a weapon combining spear and battle-axe, formed of a sharp-edged blade and a spear-head mounted on a long pole.

Halfendell, or *halfendeal*, the half part, moity.

Hallyngs, tapestries or hangings for the wall.

Hamsoke, assault on a person within his/her house.

Harness, the defensive armor of a footsoldier; all his equipment for both himself and his horse.

Haver, oats. *Havermeal*: oatmeal. *Havertime*: harvest.

Havour, *haviour* or *haver*, substance, wealth.

Hayster, see *Hairster*.

Heavy, sad or serious.

Hengwite, fine for hanging a thief.

Herberger, or *harbinger*, one who goes on ahead to announce the arrival of another and to procure lodging.

Holy Trinity, Benedictine priory of Holy Trinity inside Micklegate Bar on the southwest side of the city.

Horngeld, tax within a forest, paid for horned beasts, or exemption from having to blow horn upon enemy's approach.

Horsebread, *horseloaves* loaves for horses made of peas and beans.

Horsefair, large open space beyond Gillygate on the northwest side of York.

Hosteler, innkeeper.

Huckster, a retailer of small goods in a shop or stall, or a pedler or hawker of wares.

Hynglave, see *Glaive*.

Iakette, jacket, uniform for municipal militia.

In, to gather in or harvest crops.

Inlaw, to receive, or to bring under the protection of the law; opposite of outlaw.

Infangtheof, *outfangtheof*, rights to judge and punish a thief from, or caught inside, or outside, a liberty.

Kidcotes, or *Kytton*, the civic prisons on Ouse bridge, one pertaining to the mayor and the other to the sheriff. Each had two divisions, for men and women, and the former was often known as the Gentlemen's Kidcote.

Kiddle, a weir or barrier in a river, with an opening fitted with nets for catching fish.

Kiln hares, or *kiln cloth*, a cloth on which grain was laid in a kiln or furnace used for drying grain and hops or making malt.

Knopys, knobs or decorative protuberances.

Lairwite, fine for sexual promiscuity, usually paid to the lord of the manor.

Lastage, toll paid by traders attending fairs; payment for the right to load a ship.

Latten, a mixed metal, brass or a metal closely resembling it, often hammered into thin sheets.

Less register, see *Register*.

Litster, or *lister*, a dyer.

Livelode, livelihood, way of making a living.

Longedebefe, or *langue de boeuf*, a spike or halbert, a weapon with a head shaped like an ox tongue.

Lorimer, one who makes bits and mountings for horse bridles.
Lyvelode, see *Livelode*.

Mainpernor, one who acts as bail or surety for another, assuring that the accused
  will appear in court on any day commanded and to answer any charge
  whatsoever.
Mainprize, delivery of a person into the custody of mainpernors; also the name of a
  writ commanding the sheriff to take the surety of the mainpernor and deliver the
  prisoner into his keeping.
Mark, a money of account, valued at 13 s. 4 d.
Maudlandes Chapel, the chapel of the hospital of Saint Mary Magdalene, on the
  high road outside of Bootham Bar.
Maysis, or *maisis*, mease; a measurement of quantity for herrings, usually 500 to
  630.
Messuage, the portion of land occupied by a house and its appurtenances; also, a
  dwelling-house, its outbuildings, and the adjacent land designated for its use.
Met, a measure for grain and other dry products, often containing two bushels.
Milner, miller.
Miskenning, fine paid for incorrect pleading in court.
Moorage, or *moriage*, toll paid for the privilege of mooring a vessel.
Moremaster, or *muremaster*, officer elected to repair and maintain the city walls.
Murage, tax or toll levied for building and repair of town walls.
Murrey, mulberry or purple-red in colour; also, cloth of this colour.
Musterdevillers, a grey woollen cloth, named after the town of Montivilliers in
  Normandy.
Mystery, trade guild or company.

Nun Ings, the meadow or swampland near Ouse River in the area of the
  Clementhorpe nunnery, south of the city.

Ordell, right to adjudge trials by ordeal in a liberty.
Osteler, see *Hosteler*.

Pageant House, a storehouse for accessories and props used for the Corpus Christi
  plays, located on the southwest side of York's Dominican friary on Toft Green.
Pane dominico, pane demaine, 'lord's bread', or a fine white bread or cake, given to
  nobles and royalty as gifts.
Parchemener, one who makes and sells parchment.
Pariching, parish.
Passage, ferry toll, or toll paid to cross river.
Patenmaker, one who makes pattens or overshoes to raise shoes out of mud and
  water.
Pedagium, toll paid by travellers.
Perceve, to receive or obtain.
Pertencie, pertinacity, stubbornness, a perverse obstinacy.
Petiegrew, pedigree.
Pickage, toll paid for breaking the ground in setting up stalls or tents at fairs and markets.

Pinner, one who makes and sells pins and other metal wire goods.

Pipe, a measure for wine and other liquids, usually containing 126 gallons and therefore one-half of a tun. Generally synonymous with butt. Can also be used for dry measure such as peas, holding twelve bushels.

Pontage, toll paid for use of a bridge.

Porrect, to direct or present.

Porter, a bearer or carrier of goods.

Potter, one who makes and sells earthenware.

Powter, poulterer, seller of poultry.

Pratie, or *pretty*, in the sense of clever, skilful, crafty.

Prest, a loan of money.

Pryket, or *pricket*, a candle or taper stuck on a pricket candlestick.

Purve, to purvey or provide.

Queen Bow, with King's Bow, two of the central arches on Ouse bridge.

Raton Raw, row of buildings erected on Toft Green, probably gaining its name from being infested with rats.

Recreaunt, resident.

Register, Y.C.A. A/Y Memorandum Book, published in two parts by Maud Sellers as *York Memorandum Book*. The 'less register' refers to that part of the manuscript known as the *novum registrum*.

Renay, to deny, disown, renounce.

Respect, or *respite*, to postpone.

Rightings, that which restores, redresses or makes right; in this sense, confession and communion.

Ryall, or *royal*, a gold coin worth ten shillings.

Saint James's church, located on the highest point of The Mount, the road approaching York from the southwest.

Saint Leonard's Tower, tower marking the termination of the city walls on the banks of the Ouse, south of Saint Leonard's Hospital. Also called Lendal Tower.

Saint Nicholas's hospital, largest of the four leper hospitals, outside of the city beyond Walmgate Bar.

Saint William's chapel, located at the northwest end of Ouse bridge, near the council chamber.

Salthole, dry arch at east end of Ouse bridge, used for storing salt and herrings.

Sawyer, sawer of timber.

Scabell, or *Scayt-bell*, the bell that opened the fishmarket on Foss Bridge, York.

Searcher, one appointed by the guild to examine its members and enforce its regulations.

Skaitgeld, or *scaytgeld*, a toll on fish for sale.

Sledman, one who transports goods by land, usually in a sledge.

Spurrier, one who makes and sells spurs.

Stainer, one who ornaments cloth with painted pictures and designs.

Staithe, wharf or landing stage, the land bordering on water.

Stallage, fee paid to erect stall in market.

Stander, a device on a coin, an image or superscription.

Stethy, or *stithy*, an anvil or forge.

Streyt, or *strait*, to oppress or subject to hardship.

Supersedeas, a writ ordering a stay of proceedings, commanding the officer to whom the writ is addressed to desist from enforcing the execution of another writ already in his possession or about to come into his hands.

Surety, see *Mainpernor*.

Sye, material used for caulking, often cow hair or rope fibre.

Talkandtoure, Talkan Tower, identified with Fishergate postern tower, probably named after Robert de Talkan, mayor of York 1399–1400.

Tapiter, weaver, usually of tapestries and carpets.

Teildes, tent ropes?

Tenement, a building or dwelling-house for single occupancy; land or real property held of another at tenure; freehold interest in immovable property.

Ten-men-tale geld, form of frankpledge.

Testie, the witness clause of a writ, often the final clause naming the person or persons who have witnessed the document and who affix their seal in testimony thereof.

Thursday Market, the main food market of medieval York, now called Saint Sampson's Square.

Tithing, originally, a group of ten householders in the system of frankpledge; later, a rural division, generally one-tenth of a hundred.

Toft Green, an open space inside the city walls on the southwest side of York, adjacent to the Dominican friary and containing the Pageant House and other buildings such as Rattan Row.

Tollbooth, office on Ouse bridge at the south end of the roadway, opposite the Kidcotes.

Tristtrist, fine to avoid attending lord during the chase.

Trussell, the piercing tool for making the impress on the upper side of a coin.

Trussing coffers, tied chests for packing goods.

Tuly, or *Tulle*, chief town of the department of Correze, giving its name to a fine net cloth. Also, the rich red colour of silk or tapestries.

Tun, a measure for wine and other liquids, usually containing 252 gallons.

Tyre, metal trim or ornamental edging used by cabinet makers.

Tyre wine, sweet wine usually imported from Sicily, referring to the Syrian vintage.

Uncoact, of one's own free will, not compelled or constrained.

Unsitting, unfitting or unbecoming.

Upset, to set up in business as a master or freeman in a trade; the sum paid to the guild of the craft on this occasion.

Venelle, or *vennel*, little street or lane.

Venire facias, a judicial writ addressed to the sheriff commanding that he 'cause to come' before the court on a certain day twelve good and lawful men of his jurisdiction to investigate the truth of the matter of a case.

Viace, device or machine.

Vintener, taverner, seller of wines.
Viteller, supplier of food, victuals.

Wad, or *wode*, woad, a blue dye-stuff.
Waffrons, wafers.
Wait, musician.
Walker, see *Fuller*.
Wap, to wrap or enfold.
Wapentake, from the Danish, the subdivision of shires corresponding to the hundred.
Waterleaders, carters of water for sale.
Wax chandeler, makers and sellers of wax candles.
Weir, see *Fishgarth*.
Wekid, or *wicket*, a small gate within a larger one, used to let people in and out when the large gate is closed.
Wonning, a dwelling.
Wotsave, to vouchsafe.
Wreck, the right to goods or cargo cast on the shore from a wrecked or foundered vessel.

INDEX

Place names in this index have been cross-referenced to their modern spelling; unidentified place names are printed in italics. The British counties cited are those existing prior to the 1974 governmental reorganization. Alternate spellings of surnames have been included in parentheses; the leading entry is the form used first (when the references are limited in number) or most frequently. Members of the nobility are cross-referenced to their family names. The dates of office supplied for civic officials pertain to references in the text and do not pretend to summarise the person's entire career. Translations have not been separately indexed, and second references on one page have not been noted. Subject matter of cancelled entries is indexed; details of their contents and participants are not noted. References to frequently-mentioned items, such as the Guildhall or the council chamber on Ouse bridge, are made only in unusual circumstances. Square brackets enclose editorial comment and material not derived from the text itself.

Baxter, John, mealmaker, 17, 19, 98, 151, 180
Baxter, John, shearman, 49, 157
Baxter, William, 597
Baxters, *see* Bakers
Baylye, John, 44–5
Baynes, Robert, 574
Bayok, *see* Baok
Bean Hills (Benhilles), York, 78
Beane, Henry, 151, 156, 185
Beane, Richard, 164
Bedern, York, 611
    vicars of, 664, 667, 670
Bedford, John duke of, 396, 397
Beene (Beyn), Thomas, 349, 719, 731
Beene, William, 540
Beerbrewers and brewers, 16, 23, 97, 99, 100, 101,
    101, 107, 145, 148, 154, 177, 183
    Flemish, 6, 22
Beggers, *see* Vagrants and beggers
Beilbe, Beilby, *see* Bileby
Beisby (Beseby, Beysby), John, 275
    chamberlain (1484–5), 300, 318, 320, 438
    sheriff (1486–7), 525, 527, 530, 533, 537, 553,
        558, 560, 563, 566, 567, 568, 573, 584, 589,
        591
    councillor (from 1488), 623
Bek, Thomas, 148, 156, 576
Belamy, Thomas, 126
Beleby, Richard, 77, 552
Bell, Christopher, 49, 59, 196, 206
Bell, Ellis, 399, 455, 534, 617, 619
Bell, John, 17, 70, 99, 105, 154, 158, 183, 187,
    191, 201, 375, 398, 489, 500, 617
    wife of, 398
Bell, Richard, 66, 134, 161, 451
Bell, Thomas, 17, 26, 105, 158, 187
Bellmen, 638
Belton, Thomas, 296
Bene, Thomas, capper, 74, 139, 355
Benet, Christiana, 204
Benhilles, *see* Bean Hills
Benson, John, 102, 106, 108, 147, 155, 170, 175
Benson, Richard, 98, 151
Benson, Thomas, 20, 25, 96, 150, 179
Bentley, Christopher, 87, 166, 218, 235, 375, 417,
    430, 431, 451, 499
Bentley, Richard, 637
Bentley, Thomas, 95, 148, 152, 154, 176, 177, 182,
    500
Benton, Robert, 62
Benyt, Thomas, 152, 180
Berham, *see* Barham
Berley, *see* Birley lordship
Berley, John, 311
Bernard, William, 95, 101
Berrey, Christopher, 148
Berwick upon Tweed, Northumberland, 699
    siege of, 699
Berwik, Hugh, 393
Berwik, John, bower, 11, 12, 13, 91, 198
Berwik, John, fuller, 12, 13, 23, 91, 92, 97
Berwyk, John, draper, 101, 106
Berwyk, John, walker, 434

Berwyk, John, occupation unspecified, 183
Beskwood, 368
Betham, William, 148, 156, 184
Bettes, Henry, 155, 184, 686
Beverley, John, chamberlain (1483–4), 414, 438
    city sheriff (1485–6), 379, 385, 388, 391, 393,
        395, 397, 398, 399, 465, 466, 467, 469, 470,
        473, 474, 475, 476, 478, 479, 480, 485, 486,
        496, 509
Beverley, William, 527, 546
Beverley, Yorks ER, 71, 86, 171, 205, 276
    walkers of, 705
Bewly, *see* Bowlye
Bewyk, Richard, 151, 156, 184
Beyn, *see* Beene
Bighton, Robert, 203
Bigod, Ralph, 555
Bilbrough (Bilburgh), Yorks WR, Bilburgh
    Cross, 478
Bilburgh, Thomas, 319
Bileby (Beilbe, Beilby), John, 18, 96, 100, 150, 153
Bileby (Beilby), Richard, 415, 419–20
Bille (Billy, Bylly), Nicholas, 13, 24, 91, 93, 103,
    144, 145, 146, 173, 174
Biller (Byller), Master William, 432, 599–600, 620
Bilton, John, 493
Bilton, Yorks ER, church of, 237
Birdsall (Byrdsall), John, 4, 57, 592
Birkhede, John, 365, 450, 576, 600, 604–6, 616
Birley lordship, 311, 319
Birswod, Richard, 22
Birtebek, Robert, 11, 12, 91, 143, 173
Biscam, Richard, 677
Bishop, William, 433
Bishopthorpe, Yorks WR, 378, 422
Bisshop, John, 319
Bistam, Richard, 682
Bladesmiths, 13, 18, 19, 26, 81, 91, 92, 105, 144,
    158, 187, 410
Blakamore, *see* Scaling
Blakbourne (Blakburn), John, 17, 26, 95, 104,
    149, 158
Blakbourne (Blakburn), Richard, 348, 356, 365,
    375, 431, 432, 433, 449, 499, 598, 607, 612,
    686, 711
Blakbourne (Blakburn), Thomas, 148, 156, 184
Blakburne, Robert, 320
Blakehay, Henry, 652
Blakehay (Blakey), John, 201, 532
Blakelok, Richard, 43
Blakman, John, 319
Blakwell, William, 24, 103
Bland, John, barker, 219
Bland, John, senior, walker, 218
Blawfrount, Robert, 326
Blenkhoo (Blenkoo), John, 364, 499
Blenkynsop, Thomas, 194–5
Blenkynsop, William, 118, 706
Blessing, *see* Blissyng
Blevet, George, 540, 600
Blinkehowe, John, 406
Blissyng (Blessing, Blyssyng), John, 12, 15, 91,
    143, 201–2, 579